# Federal Anti-Indian Law

# Federal Anti-Indian Law

## The Legal Entrapment of Indigenous Peoples

Peter P. d'Errico

BLOOMSBURY ACADEMIC
NEW YORK • LONDON • OXFORD • NEW DELHI • SYDNEY

BLOOMSBURY ACADEMIC
Bloomsbury Publishing Inc
1385 Broadway, New York, NY 10018, USA
50 Bedford Square, London, WC1B 3DP, UK
29 Earlsfort Terrace, Dublin 2, Ireland

BLOOMSBURY, BLOOMSBURY ACADEMIC and the Diana logo
are trademarks of Bloomsbury Publishing Plc

First published in the United States of America by ABC-CLIO 2022
Paperback edition published by Bloomsbury Academic 2024

Library of Congress Cataloging-in-Publication Data
Names: D'Errico, Peter P., author.
Title: Federal anti-Indian law: the legal entrapment of indigenous peoples /
Peter P. D'Errico.
Description: 1st edition. | Santa Barbara, California: Praeger, an Imprint
of ABC-CLIO, LLC, [2022] | Includes index.
Identifiers: LCCN 2022018930 (print) | LCCN 2022018931 (ebook) |
ISBN 9781440879210 (cloth) | ISBN 9781440879227 (ebook)
Subjects: LCSH: Indigenous peoples—Legal status, laws, etc.—United States. |
Indians of North America—Legal status, laws, etc. | Indians
of North America—Government relations. | Indians of North America—Land
tenure—Law and legislation. | Navajo Indians—Legal status, laws, etc. |
Self-determination, National—United States. | Indigenous peoples (International law)
Classification: LCC KF8205.D47 2022 (print) | LCC KF8205 (ebook) |
DDC 342.7308/72—dc23/eng/20220617
LC record available at https://lccn.loc.gov/2022018930
LC ebook record available at https://lccn.loc.gov/2022018931

ISBN: HB: 978-1-4408-7921-0
PB: 979-8-7651-2373-7
ePDF: 978-1-4408-7922-7
eBook: 979-8-2161-8416-4

To find out more about our authors and books visit www.bloomsbury.com
and sign up for our newsletters.

He got up and went to the refrigerator and . . . pulled something from deep on the back shelf. He brought it over to the table. It was one of Clemence's uneaten casseroles, there so long the noodles had turned black, but stashed near enough to the cold refrigeration coils that it had frozen and so didn't stink, yet. . . .

With a savage thump he turned the casserole over onto the table. He lifted off the pan. The thing was shot through with white fuzz but held its oblong shape. My father rose again and pulled the box of cutlery from the cabinet counter. I thought he'd gone crazy at last and watching him I could hardly speak.

. . . I'm going to illustrate this for you, son.

He sat down and waved a couple of forks at me. Then with cool absorption he laid a large carving knife carefully on top of the frozen casserole and all around it proceeded to stack one fork, another fork, one on the next adding a spoon here, a butter knife, a ladle, a spatula, until he had a jumble somehow organized into a weird sculpture. He carried over the other four butcher knives my mother always kept keen. They were good knives, steel all the way through the wooden shank. These he balanced precariously on top of the other silverware. Then sat back, stroking his chin.

That's it, he said.

. . . That's Indian Law. . . .

He pointed to the bottom of the composition and lifted his eyebrows at me.

Uh, rotten decisions?

You've been into my dad's old Cohen *Handbook*. . . . He poked at the fuzzy black noodles. Take *Johnson v. McIntosh*. It's 1823. The United States is forty-seven years old and the entire country is based on grabbing Indian land as quickly as possible in as many ways as can be humanly devised. Land speculation is the stock market of the times. Everybody's in on it. George Washington, Thomas Jefferson. As well as Chief Justice John Marshall, who wrote the decision for this case and made his family's fortune. . . . Justice Marshall went out of his way to strip away all Indian title to all lands viewed—i.e., "discovered"—by Europeans. . . . What particularly galls the intelligent person now is that the language he used survives in the law. . . .

—Louise Erdrich, *The Round House* (New York: Harper, 2012)

When I finished law school, I quite often described the feeling at graduating as the same feeling of relief combined with fear I had after leaving an abusive man. It felt like I had been just so battered for so long. Finishing law school is an accomplishment, yet I did not feel proud of myself—I just felt empty. This feeling forced me to begin considering why I felt the way I did. It was through this process that the ways in which law is fully oppressive of Aboriginal people began to be revealed. . . .

I went to law school believing that it was the access route to justice and fairness. I went to law school believing that it was an answer not only for First Nations people but for the many people that I grew up with on the streets. . . . I thought law was the answer. I was naïve. Law was not (and is not) the answer. Law was, and remains, a significant obstacle for Aboriginal people and Aboriginal nations. . . .

Think about everything that First Nations people have survived in this country—the taking of our land, the taking of our children; residential schools, the current criminal justice system; the outlawing of potlatches, sundances and other ceremonies; as well as the stripping of Indian women of their status. Everything that we survived as individuals or as "Indian" peoples, how was it delivered? The answer is simple, through law. Every single one of the oppressions I named, I can take you to the law library and I can show you where they wrote it down in the statutes and in the regulations.

—Patricia Monture-Angus, "Considering Colonialism and Oppression: Aboriginal Women, Justice and the 'Theory' of Decolonization," *Native Studies Review*, 63 (1999) 12(1)


Law reflects, but in no sense determines the moral worth of a society. . . . The better the society, the less law there will be. In Heaven, there will be no law, and the lion will lie down with the lamb. . . . The worse the society, the more law there will be. In Hell, there will be nothing but law, and due process will be meticulously observed.

—Grant Gilmore, *The Ages of American Law*
(New Haven, CT: Yale University Press, 1977)

# Contents

# Preface

## *Seeing between Worlds*

This book tells the story of Christian discovery, the legal doctrine underpinning U.S. dispossession and domination of Indigenous peoples—it says that the United States owns all Native lands. The doctrine haunts U.S. law to this day in what is known as "federal Indian law." In fact, federal Indian law is a matrix for domination, which is why I call it "federal anti-Indian law."

Logically and historically, federal anti-Indian law carries a significance far beyond the relations between the United States and Native peoples. Indeed, challenging Christian discovery and the U.S. claim to own Native lands and to have "plenary power" over Native peoples produces a metaphysical crisis for America. As one scholar said, "If the federal government . . . exercises unrestrained power over Indian nations, then . . . we have a different kind of government than we think we have."[1]

Before we dive into all this, I want to tell you how I got here.

My Yakama colleague and friend, JoDe Goudy, asked me what in my life laid the foundation for my deeply personal response to Indigenous peoples underlying this book. He said that I should explain that up front.

I think the answer to JoDe's question begins with my childhood. When I was just over a year old, my father, impatient to escape his World War II draft-protected job as a petroleum engineer in West Virginia and do something more directly in the war, joined the U.S. Navy. The war would end before he finished training; but at the time he departed, my mother was pregnant with a second child, and they decided that I should go to Massachusetts to live among my father's extended family—my grandparents, aunts, and uncles. The train trip there with my aunt Angela is beyond conscious memory, but I sense that I saw between worlds. That sense grew as I learned about my Italian heritage (my father was born in Italy) and the pain of emigration and immigration. It grew more when I learned about my mother's Appalachian heritage and the class divide within American society. I experienced difference intimately—culture, skin tone, language, class. My grandfather's anti-Catholicism enhanced the awareness of difference; it was unusual for an Italian. He taught me his views through history, from Giordano Bruno—burned at the stake by the Inquisition in 1600 for saying that the universe is in motion—to Nicola Sacco and Bartolomeo Vanzetti, executed in the electric chair in 1927 by Massachusetts for first-degree murder amid an outpouring of anti-Italian, anti-immigrant, and anti-anarchist sentiment.

The sense of difference, of seeing between worlds, was triggered again for me in Navajoland, first simply by living among Navajo neighbors, and second by working as a lawyer at the border between the Navajo people and the American state. The sense of difference resonated at a great depth in me.

In 2014, Professor Angelique Townsend EagleWoman movingly described the "two worlds" of Native life and U.S. law. She wrote, "I often feel that I am a long-term visitor balancing in a foreign political and historical system, serving as a translator from the tribal traditional and historical world."[2] In an odd way, though I was an outsider to the Navajo, I could also suddenly see the United States from the outside, as a foreign system. As Steven Newcomb, a Shawnee Lenape colleague and friend puts it, I could sense the original free existence of the Navajo. This perspective illuminated life questions for me, questions beyond law: What are we here for? What does it mean to be human? What is my relation to everything and everyone else?

When I began teaching about U.S. law and Native peoples, this perspective was crucial to developing a critical understanding. I was not a true believer in law, and the broad liberal arts legal studies curriculum meant that I was not bound to teach students to professionally practice the law that colonized Native lands and dominated Native peoples.

In litigation, I discovered seeing between worlds was a strong place from which to argue a case. I found that, when given a sense of Native realities, judges were startled out of their sense of the inevitability of the dominating laws. Like Professor Rennard Strickland, I found Native cases are "in many ways . . . like the potato chip . . . jurisprudentially so tasty that once people who are very bright have seen what is there, they find it hard to go back"[3] to ordinary cases.

The point I'm making here in my response to JoDe's question is that my engagement with Indigenous peoples' legal issues is not the result of an altruistic impulse. Rather, it arises from and serves my own life. I learn from seeing the United States from outside—seeing between worlds.

I was 10 years old when seeing between worlds extended beyond my family. The year was 1954, and the U.S. Supreme Court had just decided *Brown v. Board of Education*,[4] overturning the racist legal doctrine of "separate but equal" and ending the legalized segregation of Blacks from Whites in public schools. In the fall of that year, I would enroll in a school in Ruston, Louisiana, where my father had a job teaching civil engineering at the polytechnic college. I recall the atmosphere of racial tension in Ruston; skin color lines were clearly drawn. Literally. For example, there was a refrigerated drinking fountain in the department store with a sign, "Whites only." Next to it was a small bubbler on a pipe coming out of the wall; it had a sign, "Colored." At the grocery store one day, my mother arrived at the checkout counter just as a Black woman was unloading her cart. The White clerk told the Black woman to put her things back and said to my mother, "Let me help you." My mother declined, saying, "No, she was here first. I'll wait my turn." The clerk flared up in anger, the Black woman moved back, and my mother reluctantly moved ahead, saying it wasn't right. More instances of racism, subtle and blatant, occurred over the three years we were in Ruston. We weren't church-goers, but my parents joined an Episcopal church in an effort to find a community interested in progressive change. In 1957, we left Ruston before my sisters and I got any further into the still-segregated school system.

We moved to Fargo, North Dakota, where the schools were of very high quality and overt racism seemed far removed. We reconnected with the Episcopal church, where I met Anna Standing Elk, Turtle Mountain Chippewa, the first person whom I specifically recall being "American Indian." I recall nothing that seemed problematic about Native peoples and Christianity. I am sure that no one around us had heard about *Tee-Hit-Ton v. United States*,[5] a case decided by the Supreme Court in March 1955, less than a year after *Brown*. The *Tee-Hit-Ton* decision upheld the U.S. Department of Justice argument that said the U.S. legal doctrine of "Christian discovery" meant that the United States could do as it pleased with Native lands. We will look at that argument and the case itself in detail in Chapter 5.

By 1963, the midpoint of my college years at Bates, war and poverty had joined race as major issues in American politics; many students became activists. In the spring semester of 1964, my junior year, a group of students and faculty organized a weeklong visit to Florida Memorial College, then an all-black school in St. Augustine (it would move to south Florida in 1968). For me, this return to the South 10 years after living in Ruston was a chance to take part in the ongoing ramifications of the *Brown* decision, which had not even come close to eliminating racism in American society.

My memory of the visit is still sharp, from the wonderful botanical aroma in the air as we stepped off the plane fresh from a Maine winter to the sharp feelings of sadness as we left. Some experiences were special lessons. When the owner of the car rental agency told us that no cars were available despite the lineup in the lot, our professor went into the office and emerged smiling while the proprietor handed over a set of keys; later, he told us a Masonic handshake had reached across the racist divide. One evening later in the week, as I walked along a back road arm in arm with fellow students singing "We Shall Overcome," a Florida Memorial College girl and I kissed. Soon after, we were sharply scolded; our youthful energies endangered the college because the local White response to racial mingling could be violent. So I learned about myself and society, about how social differences might be bridged by intimacy or secret association, and about how bridging such differences may ignite controversy.

As college graduation neared, my roommate and student newspaper coeditor, Peter Reich, and I were offered jobs running a small weekly paper in Rangeley, Maine. But Sam Withers, another good friend, warned me to prepare for other possibilities; he suggested that I apply to law school, and I did. Before the semester ended, Peter got a draft notice; his journalist's job was not to be. For whatever reasons, my draft board decided that going to law school was in the national interest and deferred me; I worked in Rangeley for the summer. Years later, I learned that General Lewis Hershey, director of the Selective Service System, had said, "The deferment is the carrot that we have used to try to get individuals into occupations and professions that are said by those in charge of Government to [sic] the necessary ones."[6] Peter Reich spent his tour of duty in an office at Fort Hamilton Army Base in Brooklyn, New York, a training base for the Vietnam War, and afterward went to graduate school in public health. I went to Yale Law School. Three years later, I was a lawyer working in Navajoland. As the small world would have it, so was Sam Withers.

But law school was not what I wanted. Halfway through the first semester, I decided to quit. Friends persuaded me to finish the semester so it would be a clean break and I would have the possibility of picking it up later. I told Associate Dean Jack Tate I was leaving. "Why?" he asked. "I'm bored," I said. "Class discussions are superficial." I complained that the cases we studied all boiled down to money. I said that we rarely discussed basic concepts that permeated judges' opinions, sometimes incoherently. I wanted to explore existential questions, but these were irrelevant to "thinking like a lawyer." Years later, I encountered Professor James Gordley's description of philosophical confusion in contract law; what he wrote captured the scene as I remembered it: "The truly fundamental philosophical problems of the age were sidestepped. Concepts and principles were stated in elegant language, but so imprecisely that often one cannot be sure of their meaning. The links between philosophical principles and the legal doctrines supposedly founded on them were left obscure."[7] Dean Tate said that he regretted my decision and added, "You're welcome back if you change your mind."

What I recall is that what passed for philosophical inquiry in law school were abstract questions like, "What principles should govern the relationship between the individual and society, and how far did our obligations to others extend?" I take that question from former president Barack Obama's book,

*A Promised Land*, where he said, "I couldn't get enough of this stuff."[8] To my mind, questions like that are superficial, asked from an imaginary perspective removed from lived experience; they have no existential grounding. There is no such thing as "the individual" not embedded in society, there is no "our" not already entangled with "others." Before I went to Dean Tate, I was so frustrated that I visited a Yale philosophy professor, who told me that I had to make up my own mind whether to stay in law school.

When the semester ended, I said goodbye to my friends and flew to Edinburgh, where a college friend was in art school. I quickly realized that I didn't want to live in exile, which meant prison and law school were my only remaining alternatives to the war against Vietnam. I decided to return to Yale after the winter break, in time for the second semester. Dean Tate welcomed me back. I learned a lesson about being a member of an elite group: Once you're in, it doesn't matter if you criticize it.

I continued to be frustrated in class. Professor James William Moore, one of the original drafters of the Federal Rules of Civil Procedure, was the only teacher in my entire three years who, on his own, broached the question of whether a particular decision was unjust. (It was a rule against retroactive application of constitutional rights changes in criminal law.) Most teachers left such naive questions to students. Ronald Dworkin was an exception; I recall writing a paper for him about "the public law definition of 'private.'" Charles Reich had already written "The New Property," a 1964 law review article that influenced the U.S. Supreme Court to expand due process rights for welfare beneficiaries in a 1970 case; but his course on property law was fairly conventional. The book that he would publish in 1970, *The Greening of America*, presented a counterculture view that he kept out of his teaching. As it turned out, the class of 1968 was at the threshold of a tumultuous time for Yale Law School, with faculty and students increasingly at odds on philosophical issues.[9]

Starting in my fourth semester, I interned at the New Haven Legal Assistance Association, funded by the Ford Foundation as a prototype for what President Lyndon Johnson's War on Poverty would later do. I was encouraged by a friend who said that it was a chance to use law in a humane way, for people in need (rather than for people in greed, as it seemed to me were the primary participants in cases we studied). After several months, during which I worked with a Black Panther organizer and saw daily urban life for poor Black and White people, the managing attorney spoke to me about what he called my penchant for direct action.

He singled out two cases: one involved a woman with a baby, whose landlord had turned off the heat to force her to abandon an apartment in the middle of winter; the other involved the Connecticut welfare bureaucracy that repeatedly destabilized families by cutting monthly stipends to make up for midmonth emergency payments that were needed because the current monthly stipend had been cut to make up for an emergency payment in the previous month that had been necessary because . . . well, you get the picture.

The director scolded me for my handling of both cases: he said that I had gotten too involved and needed to learn to rely on legal process instead of direct action. In the case of the woman with the baby, he said that I should not have gone into the apartment building to turn the heat back on, let alone do it three times (the third time, after which the landlord gave up, I negotiated with a German shepherd chained to the furnace). He said that I should have filed pleadings with the court to get an order to the landlord to turn the heat back on. When I asked what the woman and baby were supposed to do in the meantime, starting with the night they came to the office for help, and why the landlord should be expected to obey a court order when he was already violating the law, the director said those were not a lawyer's proper concerns.

In the case of the welfare bureaucracy and the recurring disruptions of support, he criticized my solution, which was to work with the central payments office to create a shortcut so the records of people caught in the endless loop could be corrected prior to the issuance of the next check, thereby eliminating the need for another cycle of stipend and deduction. He said I should have let these individual cases accumulate, perhaps over a period longer than my internship, to a point when there might be a sufficiently large problem statewide that a judge could be persuaded to certify a class-action lawsuit against the state, setting the stage for litigation and perhaps negotiations that might lead to a change in the bureaucratic processing of payments. He was unimpressed with my response that my efforts constituted negotiations in the context of the possibility of a lawsuit. He said that I wasn't acting like a lawyer.

Luckily, he didn't know about another of my direct actions: I physically blockaded our office door when New Haven police tried to enter "to use the toilet" during the so-called New Haven riots in August 1967. We represented many of the people who were arrested for curfew violations during that time, and our office staff included a neighborhood organizer who worked with the Black Panthers. The fact that the police wanted to use the toilet immediately after they arrived in their van was too suspicious. He also didn't know how I resolved the illegal effort to close down a day camp that brought Black children to a suburban park outside New Haven. I arrived at the park office with a few Black Panthers, who explained that they would be back with a larger group to accompany the children if the park insisted on its illegal actions. The office reread the rules I brought with me and realized their "mistake."

In spring 1968, my final semester in law school, I still hadn't heard of the *Tee-Hit-Ton* case and had had no exposure to federal anti-Indian law (Yale had no course at the time, which was probably lucky for me—better to have learned by doing), but I was intrigued when recruiters arrived from Dinébe'iiná Náhiiłna be Agha'diit'ahii (DNA), a new Navajo legal services program funded through the War on Poverty that President Johnson hoped would somehow balance out the war on Vietnam. I was not a true believer in poverty law after my experience at New Haven Legal Assistance, but I wasn't interested in a New York law firm, a Washington bureaucratic job, or a judicial clerkship. I knew that the Navajo program would be different.

In the days before my interview with DNA, I was also thinking about my other options—exile, draft, or prison. Sometimes I thought that the simplest path would be to follow my interest in journalism, accept the publisher's offer to edit the weekly paper in Maine, and take my chances with the draft. This bewilderment circulated in me even as I walked through the wood-paneled corridors in the upper reaches of the law school, past portraits of the rich and powerful ancestors of my graduating class, to a small, wood-paneled room where the DNA interviewers waited.

I can still see the faces of Peterson Zah, DNA's Navajo executive director, and Ted Mitchell, the White (or as I would learn to say, Anglo) lawyer who headed the staff, sitting at a desk in that little room. Our eyes met and held for a moment; they greeted me and invited me to sit down. I had a sudden intuition that this was going to be memorable. We talked about Navajoland and history and politics and law. They invited me to Navajoland to make up my mind. I visited Window Rock, Shiprock, and Crownpoint, riding with Charley John, Raymond Benally, and other Navajo advocates—lay attorneys who handled cases in the Tribal Courts. Their sense of excitement about the work was palpable. And the land was breathtaking: long vistas punctuated with broad mesas, startling pinnacles, and surprising rock outcroppings.

The journey triggered chords in me deeper than a job search. I understood the "Indian wars" had not ended. Rangeland was now less important than the minerals beneath it; cowboys had been supplanted by giant energy corporations in a quest for ever-greater accumulation of material wealth. The corporate money cases that had bored me in class took on new meaning as I saw whose resources they were fighting over. I accepted a job as staff attorney in the Shiprock office.

What I learned in Navajoland became the foundation of my career. At the University of Massachusetts Amherst, I developed a legal studies curriculum not to train lawyers, but to critique law, with a special focus on Indigenous peoples.[10] My teaching position also provided a platform to do legal work. In 1976, I helped Lew Gurwitz, a National Lawyers Guild attorney specializing in Native cases, successfully defend the "Mashpee Nine," a group of Mashpee Wampanoag ceremonial drummers arrested in a midnight raid by a multitown SWAT team on a charge of excessive noisemaking. The drummers were part of a camp for Wampanoag children at the site of a re-created

Tsé Bit'a'í (Rock with Wings), at a distance of approximately 7 miles. Known as "Shiprock" in English. (author photo)

seventeenth-century Wampanoag village on Wampanoag land. The trial judge dismissed all the charges after a strong defense and vivid testimony.[11]

In 1978, I worked with Slow Turtle, Wampanoag medicine man and director of the Massachusetts Commission on Indian Affairs, to negotiate the recovery and reburial of human remains uncovered during the construction of a septic system at the University of Massachusetts Field Station on Nantucket and taken to the Peabody Museum in Boston.[12] Our negotiations with the museum, the state archeologist, and the university accomplished the reburial and established a procedure for repatriation of Native remains that prioritized the Commission on Indian Affairs. In 1990, the passage of the federal Native American Graves Protection and Repatriation Act[13] would mandate a similar process.

In 1995, Slow Turtle asked if I would represent a Native American Spiritual Awareness Council in a Massachusetts prison, to defend and expand inmate access to ceremonial items (such as headbands and pipes), purification (aka "sweat") lodges, and a weekly talking circle. I met with the men, was impressed by their sincerity, and agreed to represent them. A local lawyer, Bob Doyle, agreed to assist me as local counsel so I could appear *pro hac vice* (i.e., as a lawyer admitted in another jurisdiction). After 10 years of litigation in state courts, the Department of Corrections finally settled, under an order of the Appeals Court.[14]

In 1996, I represented two Mashpee Wampanoag men, Michael Maxim and David Greene, who were charged with shellfishing without a Massachusetts town permit. We won unanimous decisions from the Massachusetts Appeals Court and Supreme Judicial Court upholding Wampanoag aboriginal fishing rights.[15] Bob Doyle worked with me on this case too.

During this period, I worked in a variety of ways with Western Shoshone chief Raymond Yowell and the Western Shoshone National Council, including assisting them to represent themselves in federal and state courts and on petitions to the United Nations and the Organization of American States. This work brought mixed results for protecting their land rights.

I continue to collaborate on Indigenous cases, sometimes out front, sometimes behind the scenes, but always mindful of the Muskogee-Creek elder and medicine man Phillip Deere's comment that federal anti-Indian law is a U.S. game, and the United States changes the rules as we litigate.[16]

# Acknowledgments

This book started as an exposé of a single case—the 1955 *Tee-Hit-Ton* decision. As I parsed Stanley Reed's disingenuous opinion and excavated the papers filed by the Tee-Hit-Ton and the United States, I realized the focus would broaden and deepen. As I wrote, I reached out to other writers for advice.

Friends and colleagues in the Five College Native American and Indigenous Studies program helped me. Barry O'Connell, a partner in founding the program years ago, encouraged me to hone my writing to keep nonlawyer, nonacademic readers in mind; his critiques of early drafts and our ongoing conversations were a major help. Lisa Brooks reviewed a separate essay on an early version of the theoretical critique of sovereignty and exception. Manuela Picq offered the opportunity to publish that essay with the Max Planck Institute for the Study of Religious and Ethnic Diversity; she became a close reader of my writing. Alice Nash provided me with opportunities to present my thinking to Native Studies teachers from across the country at National Endowment for the Humanities Summer Institutes, organized in conjunction with Linda Coombs, an Aquinnah Wampanoag author and filmmaker. The teachers' lively responses greatly encouraged me.

Beyond the Five Colleges, Ali Watson, professor of international relations, and her research partner, Bennett Collins at the University of St. Andrews, Scotland, provided a forum for me to present my thoughts at a workshop held at the Carnegie Endowment for International Peace in Washington, D.C., and encouraged me to keep writing. Peter Reich, a friend since college, helped me move past legalese; he also told me that a writer's discipline is to "apply the seat of the pants to the seat of the chair." T. R. Rosenberg, who testified as an expert witness in the case to protect access to Native spiritual practices in Massachusetts prisons, also helped me write clearly. Robert Maxim II, Mashpee Wampanoag (the nephew of Michael Maxim, one of the defendants in the fishing rights case) and a researcher at the Brookings

Institution, gave me detailed suggestions on a late stage of the manuscript. Historian Steve Schwartzberg gave me insights about early American political thinking.

Steve Newcomb, a Shawnee/Lenape author and activist, has been an intellectual partner and friend for decades. Our earliest conversations deconstructing *Johnson v. McIntosh* set the agenda for research that led to this book.

I have been fortunate to know and work with many other Native activists and colleagues who have helped me understand the survival and resistance of Native peoples. I especially give thanks to Slow Turtle (Mashpee Wampanoag), Phillip Deere (Muskogee-Creek), Corbin Harney (Western Shoshone), Raymond Yowell (Western Shoshone), John Mohawk (Seneca), Wamsutta Frank James (Aquinnah Wampanoag), Ramona Peters (Mashpee Wampanoag), Frank Begay (Navajo), Charley John (Navajo), Wilma Redhorse Charley (Navajo), Robert Allan Maxim (Mashpee Wampanoag), Michael Maxim (Mashpee Wampanoag), David Greene (Mashpee Wampanoag), Mikki Aganstata (Cherokee), Sherman Paul (Maliseet), gkisedtanamoogk (Mashpee Wampanoag), Dennis Banks (Anishinaabe), John Trudell (Santee Dakota), Birgil Kills Straight (Oglala Lakota), Winona LaDuke (Anishinaabe), Vernon Lopez (Mashpee Wampanoag), Floyd Westerman (Dakota), Vine Deloria, Jr. (Standing Rock), Roberta Blackgoat (Navajo), Danny Blackgoat (Navajo), David Monongye (Hopi), Vernon Bellecourt (White Earth Ojibwe), Arvol Looking Horse (Cheyenne River), Earl Mills, Jr. (Mashpee Wampanoag), Shirley Mills (Mashpee Wampanoag), Mary Dann (Western Shoshone), Carrie Dann (Western Shoshone), Tim Dann (Western Shoshone), Leonard Crow Dog (Lakota), John Kane (Mohawk), JoDe Goudy (Yakama), and Tupac Enrique Acosta (Izkaloteka).

Angela Taylor has a place in my work rooted in our life together. She nourishes me physically and emotionally. Her life perspective, rooted in childhood living in the mountains with her Cherokee grandmother, among other descendants of those who evaded "Indian removal," provides a special context for her reading and suggestions. My children, Julian Kee (born in Shiprock, now deceased), Adrian, and Hannah, have been wellsprings of love. Likewise, my sisters Nancy and Lisa.

Beyond all these is a large group of people with whom I have discussed ideas that inhabit this book. Their questions were a continuing stimulus.

Finally, the Praeger editorial and production team were marvelous to work with. Their enthusiasm and the careful and skillful work they devoted to the book were of enormous value.

I give my deepest thanks to you all.

# Introduction

## *The Plan of the Book*

This chapter provides a guide to the structure and purpose of this book and a hint about its destination.

Stories of dispossession and domination of Indigenous peoples are often told (and often elided) when talking about American history. A crucial part of this genocidal history—one that is rarely discussed—is the story of the legal doctrines underpinning this dispossession and domination. This book tells that story and examines doctrines that haunt U.S. law to this day in what is known as "federal Indian law."

The first thing to understand is, as Professor Elizabeth Reese succinctly put it, "Federal Indian law is not really *Indian* law." She quoted Vine Deloria, Jr.'s famous remark, "What is missing in federal Indian law are the Indians." She added, "Indians and their tribes are the objects of federal Indian law, not its architects," and "federal Indian law's domination" consists of "laws the United States has come up with to legitimize or shape Indians' conquest."[1] As I said already, this is federal *anti-Indian* law.

However, as we will see when we examine *Johnson v. McIntosh* (1823), the foundation case in the field, federal anti-Indian law does not actually legitimize *conquest*, but a *pretense* of conquest. Chief Justice John Marshall expressly stated that in his adoption of the fifteenth-century doctrine of "Christian discovery." He described the doctrine as the "extravagant . . . *pretension* of converting the discovery of an inhabited country into conquest."[2] We will see why this distinction between "discovery" and "conquest" is juris-prudentially significant.

Chief Justice Marshall constructed federal anti-Indian law domination in three early nineteenth-century cases. First came *Johnson v. McIntosh* (1823), a property law decision declaring that Native peoples did not own their lands after they had been "discovered" by Christian colonists; the second was

*Cherokee Nation v. State of Georgia* (1831), which said that Native nations were not independent of the United States and Native peoples were subject to U.S. "guardianship"; and the third, *Worcester v. State of Georgia* (1832), declared "U.S. ultimate dominion" over all Native peoples and lands.

As the legal historian Paul Finkelman explained, "Marshall's years on the court . . . coincided with a relentless push to remove Indians from the eastern part of the United States. Thomas Jefferson developed the idea of Indian removal. Under James Madison and James Monroe, the nation's policy of war and removal devastated the southeastern Indians. President Andrew Jackson continued these policies. Marshall's decisions in *Johnson and Graham's Lessee v. M'Intosh*, . . . *Cherokee Nation v. Georgia*, . . . and *Worcester v. Georgia* . . . provided the legal basis for taking all land from Indians."[3]

Steven T. Newcomb said in his 1992 law review article "The Evidence of Christian Nationalism in Federal Indian Law: The Doctrine of Discovery, *Johnson v. McIntosh*, and Plenary Power" that U.S. law related to Indigenous peoples is "premised on the ancient principle of Christian dominion and a distinction between paramount rights of 'Christian people' and subordinate rights of 'heathens' or non-Christians." He described the Christian/heathen distinction as "the tacit, underlying basis of all subsequent determinations of Indian right[s]."[4]

In 1986, Professor Robert A. Williams, Jr., described the field as a "jurisprudence distilled from the heritage of Christian medieval legal mythology." The foundations of U.S. legal doctrines related to Indigenous peoples, he said, "once revealed, would shame those who cite them."[5] That moment of shame has not yet arrived.

The United States has not yet repudiated the doctrine that it holds title to Native lands by "Christian discovery," nor its claims of "ultimate dominion" and "guardianship"; twenty-first-century courts at all levels cite the Marshall trilogy frequently, although the root word "Christian" is now usually redacted, as in Justice Ruth Bader Ginsburg's opinion in *City of Sherrill v. Oneida Nation* (2005), where she referred simply to "discovery." She wrote, "Under the 'doctrine of discovery,' . . . fee title to the lands occupied by Indians when the colonists arrived became vested in the sovereign—first the discovering European nation and later the original States and the United States."[6]

In 2020, in *McGirt v. Oklahoma*, the Supreme Court relied on the "Christian discovery" doctrine without even using the word "discovery"; instead, it referred to the claim of domination only obliquely, calling it the "significant authority" of the United States "when it comes to tribal relations."[7] As we will see in Chapter 2, Justice Neil Gorsuch hid Christian discovery behind citations. As Newcomb pointed out, the religious foundation of the law "is seldom, if ever, explicit. . . . [It] remain[s] out of sight, below the level of conscious awareness. With few exceptions, [it is] never brought into contemporary discussions of the law."[8] Angelique EagleWoman, speaking of Canada and the United States, similarly said, "What is often glossed over in the property law introductory lesson is the Christian formed 'doctrine of discovery' that continues in full force in both countries."[9]

The opinions in *McGirt* and *City of Sherrill* demonstrate another important point: Christian discovery doctrine in federal anti-Indian law spans the so-called liberal-conservative political spectrum in the United States. *Sherrill* was written by the liberal Ruth Bader Ginsberg, *McGirt* by the conservative Neil Gorsuch. As Professor Bethany R. Berger wrote, "The more liberal members of the Court . . . not only joined, but at times led, the charge against tribal interests." She added, "Something beyond a liberal-conservative bias is going on here."[10]

The chapters in this book present four interrelated arguments:

1. Federal anti-Indian law is an *exception from the rule of law*—it is a claim of unlimited U.S. power.
2. Federal anti-Indian law has facilitated the genocide and attempted genocide of Native peoples.
3. The doctrine of "tribal sovereignty" in federal anti-Indian law is really nonsovereignty—it is a relic of Native original free existence restricted and dominated by the U.S. claim of "plenary power."
4. Federal anti-Indian law remains the basis for the ongoing U.S. invasions of Native lands and domination of Native peoples.

To say all this somewhat more fully, federal anti-Indian law is not ordinary law. It is the *suspension* of law—an assertion by the U.S. government of unlimited authority over Native peoples and lands. The trilogy of decisions written by John Marshall assigned Native peoples and lands to the arena of U.S. congressional politics, thereby sanctioning whatever federal policies that a majority in Congress might concoct. This is what permitted and sanctioned "Indian removal." Marshall ignored ordinary common law principles of land ownership and instead adopted what the law professor Kent McNeil has shown to be a misunderstanding of English law and Crown powers.

As we will see, the suspension of law—the *exception*—has made federal anti-Indian law a jurisprudential mess. Its legal theories are ambiguous and contradictory. Legal terms like "trust relationship" and "government-to-government relations" have meanings in federal anti-Indian law diametrically opposed to what they mean in ordinary law. This has been pointed out at the highest level of the U.S. judiciary by Justice Clarence Thomas, who said in *United States v. Lara* (2004), "Federal Indian policy is, to say the least, schizophrenic."[11] Professor Angelique EagleWoman applied that same label in her critique of U.S. restraints on Native economies when she said that "federal policies schizophrenically have swung between imposing greater federal control of tribal resources and at the same time declaring a policy of tribal self-determination."[12] Professor Bryan Wildenthal, in the conclusion to *Native American Sovereignty on Trial*, his compilation of these cases, said, "As the twenty-first century dawns, the story of Indian tribal governments and their place within the U.S. constitutional framework is becoming ever more complex and paradoxical."[13]

This book will show that the often-noted confusion in federal anti-Indian law arises from trying to view the field as a set of legal rules when federal anti-Indian law is in fact the suspension of law and rules—an *exception* from the rule of law.

When we unpack the legal system that has entrapped and entangled non-state so-called tribal peoples worldwide, we will reveal a way forward for humanity in this twenty-first-century moment of awareness that life on Earth is imperiled by dysfunctions of legal, political, and economic principles based on domination. In the final chapter, I take a global view, drawing some lessons from the long struggle for Native survival and opening a vista for humanity to rearrange our relations with each other and with the planet that we share with the rest of Creation.

Despite the massive pressures arrayed against them, Indigenous peoples still exist, through what the Anishinaabe professor and writer Gerald Vizenor called "survivance"—survival and resistance.[14] The Osage/Cherokee law professor Rennard Strickland lauded Native peoples for having "learned the lesson of building and rebuilding a civilization, of adapting, of changing, and yet of remaining true to certain basic values regardless of the nature of that change." He said, "At the heart of . . . Indian values is an understanding and appreciation of the timeless—of family, of tribe, of friends, of place, and of season. It is a lesson that white civilization has yet to learn."[15]

Strickland's remarks illuminate what the sociologist John Collier wrote in 1947 when he reflected on his experience as Bureau of Indian Affairs commissioner in President Franklin Delano Roosevelt (FDR)'s New Deal administration. Collier said, "The deep cause of our world agony is that we have lost that passion and reverence for human personality and for the web of life and the earth which the American Indians have tended as a central, sacred fire since before the Stone Age. Our *long* hope is to renew that sacred fire in us all. It is our only long hope. But the externals we have made our gods are in the saddle now. In our present crisis and out of our inadequacy we must try to sway the immediate event."[16]

How are timeless Indigenous values that White civilization has yet to learn to be protected in the face of federal anti-Indian law not only in the United States, but replicated throughout the world? That question guides this book. I offer it as a tool in what the Muscogee Creek medicine teacher Phillip Deere called "a rightful education."[17]

# CHAPTER ONE

# Learning in Navajoland

## An Anglo in Shiprock

I knew at the outset that living in Navajoland and lawyering for the Navajo would be a significant change in my life. This chapter tells some of the stories that deepened that change.

In September 1968, soon after I arrived in the just-opened Shiprock office of Dinébe'iiná Náhiiłna be Agha'diit'ahii (DNA) Navajo Legal Services, I got a call from Navajo District Court judge Virgil Kirk. He wanted to discuss a 1967 U.S. Supreme Court case about juvenile criminal law. The case, *Application of Gault*,[1] said juvenile defendants have due process rights: notice of charges, the right to counsel, the right of confrontation and cross-examination of witnesses, and the privilege against self-incrimination. The *Gault* case had started in Gila County, Arizona, just south of the Navajo Nation border. Judge Kirk asked me to look at whether the decision might be relevant for Navajo courts.

Only months before our meeting, the U.S. Congress had passed the Indian Civil Rights Act of 1968, which mandated the application of parts of the U.S. Constitution to "Indian tribes." It said, "The writ of habeas corpus shall be available to any person, in a court of the United States, to test the legality of his detention by order of an Indian tribe."[2] It was an edict from the U.S. Congress saying that U.S. courts could oversee the decisions of tribal courts. I didn't immediately grasp the stark presumption of U.S. domination inherent in the act, but I could see that U.S. law was colliding with Navajo ways. As Professor Wenona Singel later put it, "The Indian Civil Rights Act represent[ed] Congress's attempt to impose liberal democratic ideals on Indian nations."[3]

What happened next is that learning about Navajo culture gave me the opportunity to see America from outside. Later, I also learned something about my profession: "The Navajo word for lawyer is 'aha'diit'aahii, which means 'one who can never lose an argument,' or 'one who pushes out with words' (the deeper meaning)."[4]

## "Tribes"

Judge Kirk's question opened a door for me into the inner workings of a non-Western, nonstate society. I began to see fundamental differences between *state* systems of law and *nonstate* ways of life. What started out as my effort to understand Navajo society resulted in a deeper understanding of Western civilization. It educated me about what "society" means and who (or what) "I" am.

My education happened by listening and watching how people related to each other and how others related to me. An example: One day I spoke to a group of parents at Teec Nos Pos about the possibility for them to take control of the local school, replacing the U.S. Bureau of Indian Affairs. Frank Begay, a Navajo Tribal Court advocate, was translating. An older man, he was also the go-to person for other advocates who needed help with translating. He once came up with a Navajo way to express the puzzling concept of "beyond a reasonable doubt"; he said that it meant the jury had to go "one step further" before they could find someone guilty. When I finished my talk to the parents, several people spoke up. Frank leaned in and told me, "They want to know more about you." Thinking that I had been unclear in describing the case or how DNA lawyers might work with them, I began to say more about DNA and legal services. Frank stopped me. "That's not what they're asking about. They want to know more about *you* personally: Where were you born? Do you have brothers or sisters? Things like that."

I still feel a surge of emotion as I recall the event. I was flabbergasted. I felt shock and surprise. I felt embarrassed. I was thrilled. I had learned to isolate professional work and personal life; this was ordinary in American society and emphasized in legal education. I suddenly knew that these people were paying attention to *me*—not just as their lawyer, but to me as a human being. I felt alive, and I loved it. From that time on, I worked with Frank as much as possible, because he was older and more traditional than other advocates, and he was with me for that first experience of being cared about as a person, not just as a lawyer. We traveled to meetings sometimes an hour or more away, and he told me stories about the places we passed, about the lives of people, about what it means to be human in the Navajo world, and about skin-walkers (a malevolent entity that can assume an animal disguise) and how to avoid them. Later, I learned how rare it was for a non-Navajo to be privy to this world.

What started as my efforts to understand Navajo society resulted in a sharp re-evaluation of some basic U.S. legal concepts. I saw old cases in a new light such as the (in)famous 1819 case, *Dartmouth College v. Woodward*, where the U.S. Supreme Court said that a corporation is an immortal, "artificial being" with legal rights. Chief Justice John Marshall (about whom we will learn much more later) offered the truly bizarre statement that a corporation's "immortality no more confers on it political power . . . than immortality would confer such power . . . on a natural person."[5]

Marshall thus accomplished with the edict of law what Mary Shelley's Dr. Frankenstein[6] had tried to do only a year earlier—create a being by human ingenuity. One crucial difference between Dr. Frankenstein's creation and the creation of the court is that the "monster" had feelings and thought about life; he expressed bewilderment at the notions of "laws" and "property" and even showed compassion for the colonial "discovery" of Native peoples!

I heard of the discovery of the American hemisphere and wept . . . over the hapless fate of its original inhabitants. . . . For a long time I could not conceive . . . why there were laws and governments; but when I heard details of vice and bloodshed, my wonder ceased and I turned away with disgust and loathing. . . . The strange system of human society was explained to me. I heard of the division of property, of immense wealth and squalid poverty, of rank, descent, and noble blood. . . .What did this mean? Who was I? What was I? Whence did I come? What was my destination? These questions continually recurred, but I was unable to solve them.[7]

In sharp contrast to the monster's feelings, as the Supreme Court emphasized in 1886, "it is impossible to conceive of a corporation suffering an injury or reaping a benefit. . . . The legal entity, the metaphysical being, that is called a corporation, cannot feel."[8] The *Dartmouth College* decision was the beginning of a chain of decisions that have made corporations into "persons" in U.S. law, up to and including the 2010 decision in *Citizens United v. Federal Election Commission*[9] that said that corporations have "free speech" rights.

In 1926, the philosopher John Dewey acknowledged that the creation of corporate persons created a dilemma for legal theory. He said that law was having trouble rationalizing the difference between "legal persons" and "natural persons," raising confusion about what "personhood" means. Dewey urged lawyers not to worry about having no theory of what it means to be a person. He said, "Courts and legislators do their work . . . sometimes without any conception or theory at all." He said it would be best to abandon "*any concept of personality*" and just get on with the business of establishing "rights."[10] That is the approach the Supreme Court has taken, going so far as to decree in 2014 that a corporation has religious freedom.[11]

In short, the more I thought about Navajo kinship and community, the more I realized how thoroughly U.S. law has cannibalized humanity, leaving immortal metaphysical monsters in its wake. As I reflected on these strange doctrines, I began to understand the depth of the antagonism between states and tribal societies. I also realized that the collapse of the distinction between humans and corporations was a major factor behind social problems in state "civilization."

Years later, after I started teaching, I discovered an important book specifically about the conflict between Navajo kinship and U.S. law—Leonard B. Jimson's *Parent and Child Relationships in Law and in Navajo Custom*. Jimson's book was originally part of the Ramah Navajo School Board's bicultural approach to education; it became an important part of U.S. congressional debates that led to the 1978 Indian Child Welfare Act.[12]

Jimson spelled out the differences between U.S. and Navajo family cultures through the testimony of an expert witness in a 1969 Arizona case in which the state welfare department wanted to terminate the parental rights of a Navajo father. The witness's testimony on behalf of the father emphasized the differences between Navajo family structure and that of ordinary, middle-class Americans. The difference, he said, "is the relationship of the child to a number of caring people. In general, the relationship to aunts and uncles is much more important in the Navajo family than it is to the middle-class American family. A great deal more responsibility is given to other members of the extended family, and there is considerable attachment of the child to the entire group."[13]

Yet another book, *Childhood in an Indian Village*, by Wilfred Pelletier, though not written by a Navajo author, illuminated much that is common to nonstate tribal societies everywhere: a way of life built from everyone's relations to each other and to nature. Pelletier recounted his life in the Odawa village of Wikwemikong on Manitoulin Island. He said, "I remember as a child a different kind of organization existing, and I have come to call it now 'community consciousness.' That community can exist and function and solve all its problems without any kinds of signals, like a school of fish. All of a sudden you see them move: they shift altogether. That is exactly the way most Indian communities function."

In the face of this deep structure among the Odawa people, Pelletier recalled "the Department of Indian Affairs coming and telling us we have no organization. The local priest or minister will come and tell us we have to be organized. The Recreation Department will come along and say there's no organization in this community. And when they come it's like shooting a goose in a flock of geese. When you hit him you disrupt the pattern. . . . I know that in one community where there are 740 people (about two-thirds of them children) there are 18 organizations. There are 3 churches that all have 2 or 3 organizations, and there is also a community development officer who has a number of organizations behind him, and they are in such conflict that the community cannot function."[14]

In 1974, the anthropologist Stanley Diamond offered a theoretical approach to these personal insights into nonstate societies. In "The Rule of Law versus the Order of Custom," Diamond argued that law, as a statist system of organization, is inherently opposed to nonstate, customary societies. "The relation between custom and law," he wrote, "is basically one of contradiction, not continuity. . . . Law and custom both involve the regulation of behavior but their characters are entirely distinct. . . ." He said that state legal systems "cannibalize" nonstate societies whenever they interact.[15]

In 1954, a group of American anthropologists convened in Detroit to discuss how anthropology was being used by the U.S. government in Native land cases. Reading their proceedings, I discovered the term "tribe" itself is an artifact of state antagonism toward nonstate societies. The noted anthropologist A. L. Kroeber introduced this fact when he questioned the government's naming of Indigenous peoples as "tribes." He said that the "usual conventional concept of tribe . . . appear[s] to be a White man's creation of convenience for talking about Indians, negotiating with them, administering them." Kroeber asked, "How does this interpretation affect the pending Indian land claim cases?" He suggested, "It might affect them adversely, because . . . 'tribe' is often an administrative fiction . . . a construct of our convenience and imagination imposed and impressed on [the Indian]."[16]

In 1975, the anthropologist Morton Fried developed Kroeber's point in more depth in *The Notion of Tribe*. Fried explained the term "tribe" arose as a concept to facilitate state domination of nonstate peoples. He said, "The invention of the state, . . . a tight, class-structured political and economic organization . . . began a process whereby vaguely defined and grossly overlapping populations were provided with the minimal organization required for their manipulation, even though they had little or no internal organization of their own other than that based on conceptions of kinship. The resultant form was that of the tribe."[17]

In short, the term "tribe" arose as a word used by state systems to name peoples whose social organizations are not "state-like." The term spread through the efforts of colonizers, missionaries, land speculators, armies, and other invaders from the world of states to describe the target of their extermination and assimilation efforts—nonstate societies.

We can see this process at work in the history of federal anti-Indian law. The 1887 General Allotment Act[18] (the Dawes Act, named after its chief sponsor, Senator Henry Dawes of Massachusetts) is a prime example. Senator Dawes and others referred to tribal society itself as the "Indian problem." The Allotment Act, therefore, attacked this problem by breaking up Indigenous peoples' communal existence. Homelands were converted into homesteads, *peoplehood* into personhood. In the process, by design, allotment "freed" millions of acres of "excess" Indigenous lands for White owners.

The Allotment Act was an explicit assault on the extended family, as Jimson describes it—an effort to impose the Western notion of individualism and nuclear family, the idea that a family consists of one woman, one man, and their children, living in one residence. As Professor Kristen Carpenter emphasized in "Real Property and Peoplehood," her study of relationships between human beings and land, the individualist paradigm of property does not support peoplehood.[19] The historian Rose Stremlau said, "The allotment debates were not about land; they were about the kind of societies created by different systems of property ownership."[20] In short, the purpose of the Dawes Act was not simply to gain White access to Indigenous lands; it was to destroy Indigenous *peoples* and assimilate Indigenous *persons* as individuals into U.S. society.

President Theodore Roosevelt made this goal clear in his 1901 State of the Union address. He praised the Dawes Act for targeting tribal ways of life. He said, "The General Allotment Act is a mighty pulverizing engine to break up the tribal mass. It acts directly upon the family and the individual. . . . The Indian should be treated as an individual—like the white man."[21]

It is important to understand that statist attacks on nonstate societies are not always overtly violent. Indeed, federal anti-Indian law has imposed statist forms even in its comparatively "progressive" eras. President Franklin Delano Roosevelt (FDR)'s 1934 Indian Reorganization Act[22] is an example. The act stopped the allotment process; but as its name indicates, it was an effort to reorganize Indigenous nations. A key provision encouraged Native peoples to replace their traditional governments with a council format modeled on standard American business corporation structure. Among other things, this was intended to facilitate tribal approval for the U.S. government and corporations to have access to Native lands. As Professor Angelique EagleWoman put it, "A primary purpose of the IRA was to reorganize Tribes to provide a means for federal negotiation over tribal resources, and the establishment of federally-recognized tribal governing councils accomplished this end."[23]

After FDR's death, the U.S. Congress resumed the effort begun in the Allotment Act to extinguish Indigenous peoples. The goal was presented as an issue of establishing individual equality. Thus, the 1953 House Concurrent Resolution 108 mandated "as rapidly as possible, to make the Indians . . . subject to the same laws and entitled to the same privileges and responsibilities as are applicable to other citizens of the United States."[24] The disguise was thin, however, and the effort quickly became known for what it was, "termination." Similar termination projects continued through the 1960s, with sixty separate actions against tribes, affecting more than three million acres of Indigenous lands.

In 1970, eight months after the American Indian Movement (AIM) occupied Alcatraz Island in San Francisco Bay to reclaim it as Indigenous land, President Richard Nixon ordered a formal halt to termination policy. In rhetoric echoing FDR, Nixon called the new U.S. policy "self-determination without termination." Nixon promised to create a relationship between Indigenous peoples and the United States between the "extremes" of "termination" on one side and "excessive dependence" on the other.[25] The result was the 1975 Indian Self-Determination and Education Assistance Act,[26] in which Congress declared its "commitment to . . . permit an orderly transition from the Federal domination of programs for, and services to, Indians to effective and meaningful participation by the Indian people in the planning, conduct, and administration of those programs and services." Though presented as tribal self-determination, the goal was still to assimilate tribes into a "normalized" relationship with America. Self-determination in practice meant tribal officials making contracts with U.S. agencies to administer federally funded programs. It was another form of reorganization.

In 1983, Standing Rock lawyer and theologian Vine Deloria, Jr., and political scientist Clifford Lytle assessed the results of Nixon's self-determination without termination policy. They reported that Indigenous nations continued to exist but had been transformed. They were assimilated to the framework of states and municipal governments seeking federal funds. In the process, Deloria and Lytle said that Indigenous people as individuals had also been widely assimilated. They wrote, "Local institutions that served Indians were in a much stronger position even though they now resembled the local units of government that served other Americans and possessed little that was distinctly Indian. Indians themselves had assimilated to a significant degree."[27] Nixon's policy might well have been called "Indian self-termination."

The long campaign against tribalism continues in twenty-first-century America, not only in federal anti-Indian law, but as a misplaced epithet in popular debates about extreme partisanship ripping American society apart. For example, former president Barack Obama said, "We're fighting against . . . being selfish, being tribal, being divided and seeing others as an enemy." He equated tribalism with a "mind-set—of 'what's in it for me' and 'to heck with everybody else.'"[28] Similarly, Eduardo Porter, the author of *American Poison: How Racial Hostility Destroyed Our Promise*, used the word "tribal" throughout his analysis of a U.S. society fractured by racism. He told a reporter that he saw the current moment as "a tribal inflection point."[29]

But the problem with America is that it is not a community. It is a corporate state, with a centralized, hierarchical political-economic system based on capitalist competition rather than cooperation. In this vein, Vine Deloria, Jr., described American towns by saying, "Very few political subdivisions are in fact communities. They are rather transitory locations for the temporary existence of wage earners."[30] The anthropologist Colin Turnbull said, "In the sense that [a] tribe is a vast, extended family . . . it is obviously . . . not a mere conglomeration of individuals who happen to live in the same territory."[31] Professor EagleWoman's 2008 study of tribal economics demonstrated how Native peoples have survived U.S. efforts "to boil down the Tribal existence to corporate shareholders and managers."[32]

Turnbull also said, "'Tribalism' generally comes under fire from all sides without recognizing the force to unity that lies in the ability of tribal peoples to recognize the validity of other ways of life and thought in other people, rejecting them for themselves at the ritual level while co-operating at an economic or political level."[33]

America's political fractures are not tribal—far from it. They arise from an ideology of individualism, a denial of reciprocal relations. The mindset of "What's in it for me?" that Obama decried is the opposite of tribalism. If Obama and other commentators understood tribalism, they would discover that it actually is what they say they want for America—a lived experience of togetherness, of all of us being related to each other and to the world. As the humanities professor James Axtell put it, summarizing what Europeans said about their experiences living among Native peoples, "They found Indian life to express a strong sense of community, abundant love, and uncommon integrity . . . [as well as] social equality, mobility, adventure . . . the most perfect freedom, . . . ease of living, the absence of . . . corroding solicitudes."[34] Contemporary diatribes against tribes have forgotten this long-existing perspective, that tribal life is more humane than state civilization.

The earliest contacts between colonial invaders and Native peoples illustrate Axtell's point. The Puritans, for example, were embarrassed by the fact that so many of their kind fled to the Indians, while so few Indians wanted to adopt Puritan life. Sebastian Junger, in his book, *Tribe: On Homecoming and Belonging*, quoted Ben Franklin bemoaning that White captives "liberated from the Indians" and returned to "stay among the English . . . take the first good opportunity of escaping again" to their Native communities. On the other hand, Franklin said, "When an Indian child has been brought up among us . . . if he goes to see his relations . . . there is no persuading him ever to return."[35]

Junger also recounted that when Colonel Henri Bouquet, a Swiss mercenary under British general Jeffrey Amherst, attacked the Odawa chief Pontiac's forces (after delivering smallpox-infected blankets to Fort Pitt)[36] and demanded the return of White "captives," Native families had to bind those people and forcibly bring them in. Many later escaped and returned to the Native communities where they had come from.

Junger said that the colonials gravitated to the "intensely communal nature" of Indian life: Not only the "rough frontiersmen," as he put it, but also "the sons and daughters of Europe" were drawn to the natural sociability of Indian life and against "the material benefits of Western civilization." He quoted the French immigrant writer Hector Saint John de Crèvecoeur, saying, "Thousands of Europeans are Indians, and we have no examples of even one of those Aborigines having from choice become European. There must be in their social bond something singularly captivating and far superior to anything to be boasted of among us."[37]

Junger undertook his study of the contrasts between tribal life and American civilization to diagnose difficulties experienced by American soldiers returning to civilian life after combat. He discovered that Native traditional ceremonies, economies, and even relationships to war produce social solidarity, heal psychic wounds, and maintain community relations. America, he said, doesn't have such healing ways or a sense of solidarity. He described America as "a society that is basically at war with itself." He concluded that a "sense of solidarity is at the core of what it means to be human," and "tribes" provide that core.[38]

At the close of the nineteenth century, Friedrich Nietzsche perceived civilization as a kind of monster. He described the state as "the new idol." His philosophical novel, *Thus Spoke Zarathustra*, proclaimed: "State? What is that? Well then, open your ears to me, for now I shall speak to you about the death of peoples. State is the name of the coldest of all cold monsters. Coldly it tells lies too; and this lie crawls out of its mouth: 'I, the state, am the people.' That is a lie! It was creators who created peoples and hung a faith and a love over them: thus they secured life."[39]

In sum, what I discovered from my own experiences and from studying is that tribalism as a lived experience is the opposite of selfishness. It is coexistence. Tribal strength is demonstrated in the ability of Indigenous peoples to survive generations of termination and extermination programs. Tribes survive in the twenty-first century because they are communities, peoples. They are still under attack by the "cold monster."

## Injustice

My work in Shiprock wasn't all about legal philosophy. Yet even what would otherwise be ordinary cases made me think twice about how law affected my Navajo clients. Two cases stand out in my memory: the car dealers and the trading post owner.

There were no car dealers in Shiprock. Navajos who bought cars went primarily to the nearby town of Farmington, New Mexico, where they were treated as second-class citizens, only tolerated for the money they might spend. The dealers routinely got away with wantonly unconscionable sales practices, extracting usurious amounts of money from Navajo buyers. One common method was contracts with balloon payments, involving a long series of small monthly payments followed by an enormous final payment, the "balloon." The description of the balloon was typically concealed in the contract behind complicated legalese. The result was that a buyer would be attracted by the affordable monthly payments but be unable to meet the final payment. The balloon payment contract is almost a guarantee of default.

In my New Haven work, I had seen furniture store contracts with balloon payments structured to allow the repossession of every item of furniture the buyer bought if default occurred on any single item. In Farmington, the car dealer would repossess the vehicle, put it back on the lot, and sell it again to another unsuspecting buyer. Each vehicle was a kind of rolling gold mine, extracting wealth from our clients, producing profit until it literally fell apart. Even a crash produced profits because the contracts required buyers to purchase insurance to cover any outstanding payments.

We knew that balloon payments had been successfully challenged in other jurisdictions as "unconscionable" under the Uniform Commercial Code.[40] We painstakingly gathered evidence and prepared a New Mexico state court class action against one of the biggest dealers to stop their use of these contracts.

When building a class action lawsuit, it takes time to gather clients. Among the many people who came to the office after car repossessions—sometimes with dealers' demands for continuing payments after repossession to fulfill the terms of the contract!—we began to work with a few whom we felt would be best able to withstand the difficulties of a trial. Many of our clients spoke only Navajo—and, indeed, we thought this might weigh as a special factor showing unconscionability in the actions of greedy car dealers. To build a group of plaintiffs, we worked with Tribal Court advocates who were fluent in English and Navajo and extremely creative at explaining legal concepts that are exotic even to Anglos.

The class action provoked an immediate response from the Farmington bar association. At one bar luncheon, the attorney for the biggest dealer railed at me for being an agitator, stirring up Navajos who had never complained before and who were in fact grateful for the services provided by his client. I was taken aback by his personal animosity, having been conditioned at Yale to seeing the law profession as a kind of club, where friendships (or at least civility) prevailed despite diverging client interests. The local district attorney (an example of the professional ideal—he implemented due process practices to respect criminal defendants' rights well before the U.S. Supreme Court mandated them) came to my defense. He counseled me not to worry, saying that a lawyer always takes his client's cases personally. I knew that I was taking my client's cases personally, too; but I expected to be able to discuss the case professionally with my adversaries.

When we got to court, the car dealer's attorney opened his argument by saying that we were violating rules of legal ethics. I knew that legal services programs had been attacked on various ethical grounds, typically "vexatious litigation" and other professional evils with ancient names like "barratry," "champerty," "solicitation," and "maintenance." The charges always boiled down to a complaint that legal services lawyers were stirring up litigation that would not have happened otherwise, and the litigation was supported by the programs rather than the clients. None of these challenges had succeeded, and I was confidently prepared to argue that professional ethics did not prevent DNA from providing legal services.

As I listened to the lawyer, I began to puzzle out what he was really saying. He was talking about the paper our complaint was printed on! I suddenly remembered the New Mexico Bar Ethics Committee had recently received a protest that DNA was engaged in advertising, in violation of the American Bar Association (and New Mexico Bar Association) prohibition on advertising (a prohibition that would be successfully challenged in later years but remains an area of controversy).[41]

The protest said the English translation of "Dinébe'iiná Náhiitna be Agha'diit'ahii" on our letterhead and court documents—"lawyers who work for the economic revitalization of the people"—constituted advertising. He said that the phrase was descriptive of all lawyers and therefore could be advertised by no specific one. DNA's program director argued the phrase was *not* descriptive of all lawyers, and in any event, it was only the translation of a name. The Bar Ethics Committee decided that the translation was unethical and could no longer be displayed anywhere.

In short, while I was prepared to argue every aspect of the case, I was flabbergasted to have to defend our legal stationery. The car dealer attorney said that our complaint was a clear violation of the ethics ruling and should be dismissed immediately. I pointed out that the Ethics Committee had made its ruling after our complaint was filed, and I asked for leave to refile on blank stationery so the case could go forward in its place on the docket. Instead, the judge granted the motion to dismiss.

My district attorney friend urged me not to give up fighting the car dealers and the local prejudice against Navajo litigants. But I knew that it had already cost our clients time and effort to prepare the case, and this judicial rebuff would make them reluctant to stay the course. After all, they still needed to deal with the car dealers. I grappled with how to explain what happened, especially since for them, the whole Anglo legal process looked like an invasion from another world.

Fortunately, another event occurred in the legal world: the Navajo Nation enacted a law banning self-help repossession of automobiles—the typical situation, in which the dealer simply finds and tows away the car. The law required a Navajo Court order to allow repossession. We still nurtured the idea of filing a class action in state court against the dealers, but now we had a more accessible remedy: we could challenge balloon payment contracts and other such devices in Navajo Court, blocking repossession in the meantime.

Like other legal remedies, the new Navajo law would be effective only to the extent that it could be enforced. Car dealers continued their old ways, and many clients were not even aware of the new law; by the time a client found out about the requirement for a court order, the car was back on the lot in Farmington, out of Navajo Court jurisdiction.

One afternoon, one of my favorite clients, a man whose energy and enthusiasm for life were palpable, arrived in the office, agitated and out of breath. He said that he might be in trouble. He had been riding from Farmington into Shiprock with his brother and saw a tow truck with his pickup hitched to it, heading toward Farmington. He told his brother to turn around and give chase; they came abreast of the tow truck and forced it to stop. My client told me that he pulled out a gun and ordered the driver to unhitch the pickup, which the man did. He then watched the truck drive away and drove his own pickup to my office. I was elated; at last, self-help on our side of the law! It was unorthodox, to be sure, but it saved the truck and gave us a chance to enforce the new law. Within the day, I got a call from the car dealer himself, spluttering, "Your guy pulled a gun on my guy!" and demanding satisfaction. I relied on attorney-client privilege and said I could not talk about what happened, but I assured him that if he again attempted to repossess any vehicle without an order from Navajo Court, we would take steps to impound his tow truck. Later, I told my client that I thought he was safe, but we should be prepared to enforce the Navajo law if there were another attempt. I never heard of another attempt, and I like to think of this as the only case I won on the repossession issue.

By the time I started working on the trading post case, I was disabused of my notions of a professional community and a judiciary interested in substance as much as paper; but I was still determined to litigate. The trader case started when an old man came to the office with his wife and daughter. Only the daughter spoke English. Working with them and a Navajo Court advocate, I gathered the story. The old man had gone to a trading post with his daughter to get needed goods. Upon seeing him, the trader yelled and demanded payment of an old debt, and then physically attacked him, knocking him to the ground. Fearful for her father's safety, the daughter helped him into their vehicle and drove away. She took him to the hospital, where his cuts and bruises were treated. A few days later, a state magistrate court summons arrived in their mail, announcing a civil action by the trader to collect the alleged debt. She and her father came to our office to get help.

I shared their outrage. The father was a small man, thin and fragile with age. The father and daughter acknowledged their debt, but we agreed that no debt could justify assault and battery. We determined to fight back by counterclaiming for damages from the tort of assault and battery, including punitive damages to deter this kind of abuse. Our preparation took many weeks and involved friends and other members of the family who could serve as witnesses. Everything had to be translated back and forth to be sure that we all understood each other and how the case would proceed. Their fear of the trader and of the legal system added to the emotional strain of preparing for the hearing.

The trial on the trader's complaint took place before a state magistrate in Farmington. We could have moved to dismiss the trader's state court complaint under the 1959 Supreme Court decision in *Williams v. Lee*, stating that state courts do not have jurisdiction over civil suits against Indians where the cause of action arises on an Indian reservation.[42] But we wanted to sue the trader for his tortious acts, and there was at the time no decision upholding Tribal Court jurisdiction over non-Natives in tort cases. This issue would not be resolved until 2016, when a decision by the 5th Circuit Court of Appeals in *Dolgencorp, Inc. v. Mississippi Band of Choctaw Indians* ruled that such a case "may be vindicated by individual tribe members in tribal court"; that decision was affirmed by an equally divided Supreme Court.[43] We will look at that case in Chapter 5.

We arrived at the magistrate's court early and calmed ourselves on the steps outside. The case went smoothly, with our witnesses and translators speaking clearly and to the point. We admitted the debt and asserted a counterclaim that more than offset it. At the conclusion of the hearing, the magistrate said, "I believe what you have told me, that the trader beat you, knocked you to the ground, and injured you. But I cannot award you any damages. You must pay the debt." The magistrate continued, "The old man didn't have any out-of-pocket monetary damages. He has no job and therefore lost no wages. His health care for the cuts and bruises was at the Indian Health Service, which cost him no money. Having suffered no loss of money, he cannot demand money damages. With no out-of-pocket damages, he cannot claim punitive damages or damages for pain and suffering. This is the rule I will apply."

We were stunned—not only that we lost the case, but that we lost it in this way, to have suffered the beating and then the injustice of a decision based on money and money alone. I can still recall walking out of the room and into the street, the father and daughter and the rest of the group all speaking Navajo, all stunned. I knew that my role as their attorney was to say, "Don't worry. We'll appeal." But I couldn't do it. I couldn't promise justice. I felt bankrupt, with nothing to offer. Indeed, I felt that suggesting an appeal would rub salt in their wounds. There was so much work preparing for the case, in reliance on my offer to defend and counterclaim. The daughter looked at me and knew that I could not encourage her father to put more faith in the state's legal system. I was at the end of my own rope. I knew from these and other cases that the overwhelming weight of the law was not on my clients' side.

I began to see my legal services role as a part in a morality play produced by the War on Poverty. I was the attorney wearing the hero's white hat, working for the poor Navajo. I was part of a package deal from the United States, which also provided the laws, courts, police, and jails and maintained the economic system that extracted wealth from the Navajo. Law was still all about money. I had gone to Shiprock looking for a chance to use law to do something for people, but now I felt helpless. I encountered the old philosophical questions, now merged with history, anthropology, economics, law practice, and personal experience. When the Yale Law School placement office called me about a teaching job at the University of Massachusetts Amherst, I decided that might give me a chance to step back from practice, take a deeper look at law, and come at it another way.

In April 1974, a few years after I left Shiprock, the bodies of three Navajo men were found in separate locations in the rugged terrain near Farmington. The men had been severely beaten, tortured, and burned. An Advisory Committee to the U.S. Commission on Civil Rights visited the area in the aftermath. The committee held hearings and conducted independent investigations of the social and economic relationships between Farmington and Navajo people.

In July 1975, the Advisory Committee issued its report, examining "issues relating to community attitudes; the administration of justice; provisions of health and medical services; alcohol abuse and alcoholism; employment; and economic development on the Navajo Reservation and its real and potential impact on the city of Farmington and San Juan County." The letter of transmittal summarized the conclusion: "From testimony of participants during a 3-day open meeting in Farmington and from extensive field investigation, the Advisory Committee has concluded that Native Americans in almost every area suffer from injustice and maltreatment."[44]

Injustice, maltreatment, termination, colonization, domination: How is it Native peoples still exist?!

# CHAPTER TWO

# "Indians"

## Survivance

Native peoples have so far managed to surprise everyone who predicted their demise. This chapter explores how they did that in the face of those who tried to bring about that demise.

In 1994, Anishinaabe White Earth Ojibwe author Gerald Vizenor repurposed an old legal term—"survivance"—to define a combination of Indigenous *survival* and *resistance*. Vizenor added a new word of his own making—"postindian"—and used the two words to critique conventional discussions about Native peoples.[1] He said that the dominant discourse about Native peoples is a discourse of domination. In particular, he attacked the word "Indian," saying that it is inextricably tied to subjugation, assimilation, and simulation. He said that it is a word from the vocabulary of "manifest manners," which, like "manifest destiny," subordinates Native peoples to White Christian civilization. "Indian," he said, is a "simulation in the literature of dominance."[2]

In plain language, there is no such entity as "Indian" except among the peoples of the Indian subcontinent. Christopher Columbus knew that; he just didn't know where he was when he "discovered America." The ensuing "misrecognition of natives as *indians* is both oppressive and a prison of false identities."[3]

Vizenor's critique also applies to "Native American" as one of the "notions and misnomers that are read as the authentic."[4] In the 1960s, Americans tried again to make the "Indian problem" go away by linguistically incorporating Indigenous peoples into America—"Native Americans," to mix with all the other "hybrid Americans." The Santee Dakota poet, musician, and activist John Trudell responded to this by saying, "They change the name and treat us the same." John also spoke to Natives who were willing to adopt the new labels: "We're too busy trying to protect the idea of a Native American or an Indian—but we're not Indians and we're not Native Americans. We're older than both concepts. We're the people. We're the human beings."[5] Columbus introduced generic "Indians" to the world, and America was named for Amerigo Vespucci, another Italian navigator. Both "Indian" and "Native American" are colonizer names—manifest manners.

Vizenor made clear that survival and resistance are not just a matter of names: "Survivance is greater than the right of a survivable name. Survivance stories are renunciations of dominance, detractions, obtrusions, the unbearable sentiments of tragedy, and the legacy of victimry." Vizenor added that "Indian" has a "curious sense of legal standing."[6] That curious standing is federal anti-Indian law. However, contradicting the U.S. claim of land ownership inherent in that law, Vizenor said, "Survivance is the heritable right of succession or reversion of an estate."[7]

The anthropologist Jonas Bens sidestepped these considerations in his investigation of what he called "indigeneity" and the "Indigenous paradox." He said that "indigeneity comes into being when native communities engage with the law." Bens assumed that Indigenous peoples have no alternative to the system of dominance and therefore must present themselves as simulations. He said, "Native communities . . . depend on the settlers' legal system" and must therefore "play Indian." He said, "The indigenous nations are stuck with this. . . . That is the Indians' 'tough luck.'"[8]

To follow Vizenor is to challenge the dominating legal system, not to go along with it. The challenge begins with rejecting manifest manners and manifest destiny, revealing their genocidal impulses, and insisting on the reality of Indigenous peoples' original free existence. Survivance is the assertion of Native self-determination.

## Legalized Genocide

Indigenous peoples have lived in what is now called "the Americas" for thousands of years. Archeologists continue to push the date farther and farther back with radiocarbon tests of plant remains when artifacts are discovered. In May 2004, Professor Albert Goodyear unearthed material from along the Savannah River in South Carolina that were tested at the University of California at Irvine and shown to be at least 50,000 years old,[9] well prior to the last Ice Age more than 20,000 years ago, which the Bering Strait land bridge theory relies on to say that the continent was once "empty." Indeed, after Vine Deloria, Jr.'s devastating critique in *Red Earth, White Lies: Native Americans and the Myth of Scientific Fact*, the Bering Strait theory has become widely mocked as the BS theory.[10]

Indigenous peoples generally just say that they have lived here since time immemorial. Christianity was not even a dream for most of this time. The fifteenth-century Christian colonizers who claimed discovery of the so-called New World were in fact encountering a very old world. The phrase "New World" is a misnomer, another simulation; the colonizers came from a group of nations far younger than the Native nations they encountered. The colonizers' religion, which commanded them to colonize and subdue (in ways we will examine later, in Chapter 7), could only claim a couple thousand years of history. Indigenous spiritual teachings existed for thousands of years before that.

The continued existence of Indigenous peoples in the twenty-first century around the world testifies to their cultural strength, which has sustained them through centuries of genocidal attacks. U.S. history reverberates with these attempted extinction events—diseases accidentally and intentionally inflicted, wars of genocide and removal, coerced and induced assimilation, and imposition of a legal framework for domination, often in the guise of "protection" but in fact as claims of U.S. "plenary power" or "sovereignty" over Native peoples.

Attorney and adjunct professor David Coventry Smith emphasized the ongoing assault of U.S. law against Native peoples in his 2014 review of "emerging issues in Tribal-State relations." He said, "The majority of Americans live in the misguided belief that depriving Indians of the ownership, use, and benefit of their lands was merely an unfortunate episode in American history, an artifact of a racist past. However, the fact remains that the challenges facing Indian nations in maintaining the sovereign right to control their own lands is no less imposing today than in past centuries." Smith emphasized, "Today tribes are fighting battles both inside and outside the courtroom they have not experienced since the 1800s, testing not only their right to exercise ownership of their land and their sovereign status, but questioning their very right to exist."[11]

Smith's assessment echoed what Federal District Court judge Royce C. Lamberth said in 2007 in *Cobell v. Norton*, a many-years-long class action lawsuit challenging the U.S. government's ongoing mismanagement of Indigenous people's lands and the revenue derived from allotting those lands, starting with the 1887 Dawes Act, which (we saw in Chapter 1), was a major attack on "tribalism." Judge Lamberth indicted the government, saying, "For those harboring hope that the stories of murder, dispossession, forced marches, assimilationist policy programs, and other incidents of cultural genocide against the Indians are merely the echoes of a horrible, bigoted government-past that has been sanitized by the good deeds of more recent history, this case serves as an appalling reminder of the evils that result when large numbers of the politically powerless are placed at the mercy of institutions engendered and controlled by a politically powerful few."[12]

Judge Lamberth's statement got him removed from the case.

In 1986, Professor Rennard Strickland (Osage/Cherokee) raised a critique of federal anti-Indian law as being legalized genocide. In "Genocide-at-Law: An Historic and Contemporary View of the Native American Experience," he wrote, "In nineteenth century attack[s] on the Native American, the law was both a formal and an informal instrument of genocide. . . . These were legally enacted policies whereby a way of life, a culture, was deliberately obliterated."[13]

The historian Carroll P. Kakel III charged, in his 2013 comparative study *The American West and the Nazi East*, "Much Nazi genocidal violence and many of the events we have come to call the Holocaust were a radicalized blend of several forms of mass political violence whose patterns, logics, and pathologies can be located in the early American project"[14] of extreme violence against Native peoples.

American studies professor David E. Stannard pointed out that the Creek, Seminole, and Cherokee death rate during the official U.S. "Indian Removal" campaigns "was equal to that of Jews in Germany, Hungary, and Rumania between 1939 and 1945."[15]

In 1945, the attorney Ernest L. Wilkinson referred to the Nazi's use of U.S. "Indian policy" when he testified before the U.S. House Committee on Indian Affairs. He said, "The historic parallel between what Hitler has done, and what we did to Indian tribes, has been seized upon as late as last year by none other than Adolf Hitler himself to justify his invasion of Czechoslovakia and of Poland."[16]

In her February 2016 blog, "Honoring Native American Voices: Recognizing Tragic History and Praising Brave Spirits,"[17] Lia Mandelbaum discussed not only how the Nazis borrowed U.S. technologies of extermination, but also the daily life consequences of what she called the "ongoing genocide" of Indigenous peoples.

In 2013, the United Nations (UN) Permanent Forum on Indigenous Issues issued the *Study on the Impacts of the Doctrine of Discovery on Indigenous Peoples*. The report said, "The Doctrine of Discovery . . . has been used as a framework for justification to dehumanize, exploit, enslave and subjugate indigenous peoples and dispossess them of their most basic rights, laws, spirituality, worldviews and governance and their lands and resources. Ultimately it was the very foundation of genocide."[18]

## Confession of Genocide

The most astounding evidence of federal anti-Indian law as genocide comes from the U.S. government itself, in a brief filed by the U.S. Department of Justice in a 2018 U.S. Supreme Court case, *Carpenter v. Murphy*.[19] The case involved a challenge to Oklahoma state criminal jurisdiction in

Muscogee Creek territory. Before we examine that legal brief, let us review what "genocide" means.

The term "genocide" was coined in the early twentieth century by Raphael Lemkin, an international lawyer who later became an advisor to Nuremberg War Crimes chief prosecutor and U.S. Supreme Court justice Robert H. Jackson in the war crimes trials of Nazis accused of genocide during World War II.

Lemkin developed the underpinnings of the concept of genocide at a 1933 conference in Madrid, in a report titled *Acts Constituting a General (Transnational) Danger Considered as Offences Against the Law of Nations*. He said that the offenses, which he called "acts of barbarity," included "acts of extermination directed against . . . ethnic, religious or social collectivities whatever the motive (political, religious, etc.)." He said that acts of extermination included not only massacres and pogroms aimed at killing people, but "actions undertaken to ruin the economic existence . . . of a collectivity"[20]—in other words, acts aimed at killing *peoples*.

The first time that the word "genocide" appeared in print was Lemkin's 1944 publication for the Carnegie Endowment for International Peace, titled *Axis Rule in Occupied Europe*. There, he elaborated the *group* nature of genocide, the targeting of *peoples*. He said, "By 'genocide' we mean the destruction of a nation or of an ethnic group. . . . Genocide . . . [means] a coordinated plan of different actions aiming at the destruction of essential foundations of the life of national groups, with the aim of annihilating the groups themselves. The objectives of such a plan would be disintegration of the political and social institutions, of culture, language, national feelings, religion, and the economic existence of national groups. . . . Genocide is directed against the national group as an entity." He added, "Genocide has two phases: one, destruction of the national pattern of the oppressed group; the other, the imposition of the national pattern of the oppressor. This imposition, in turn, may be made upon the oppressed population which is allowed to remain, or upon the territory alone, after removal of the population and the colonization by the oppressor's own nationals."[21]

We can now return to the 2018 U.S. brief in *Carpenter v. Murphy*. The case arrived in the Supreme Court after the Tenth Circuit Court of Appeals ruled that Oklahoma had no criminal jurisdiction over a Native person in Creek lands because those lands are "Indian Territory." Despite the familiar rhetoric that the United States has "trust responsibility" for its "Indian wards," the U.S. brief disputed the Tenth Circuit decision and supported Oklahoma's claim of jurisdiction. The United States said that there was no "Indian Territory" because there was no Muscogee Creek nation. The brief explicitly presented a 100-year history of actions by the U.S. Congress to "disestablish" the Muscogee Creek Nation—to "overthrow . . . the communal system of land ownership" and to "extinguish the tribal titles."

The brief opened with the heading, "Congress Abolished the National Territory of the Creek Nation." The Justice Department said that Congress had intended a "complete transformation" of the Creek (Muscogee) Nation and the other "Five Civilized Tribes"—Cherokee, Chickasaw, Choctaw, and Seminole Nations. The brief used verbs ranging from "dismantle" to "abolish" to "extinguish" and said, "Congress broke up the Creek Nation's territory, substituting individual for communal ownership and distributing the proceeds to individual Indians." It said Congress "made members of the Creek Nation citizens of the United States; eliminated the Creek Nation's tribal courts; [and] provided for the dissolution of the tribal government, divestment of tribal property, and distribution of tribal funds."[22]

The Justice Department emphasized the extinguishment intent, saying, "Congress's goal was not simply to open Indian lands to non-Indian settlement, but rather to clos[e] the history of these [Indian] nations." The brief described the congressional actions in terms explicitly identified as genocidal by Lemkin's definition, saying, "The object of Congress from the beginning has been the dissolution of the tribal governments, the extinguishment of the communal or tribal title to the land, the vesting of possession and title in severalty among the citizens of the tribes, and the assimilation of the peoples and institutions of this Territory to our prevailing American standard."[23] In short, the Justice Department confessed that the United States intended to kill the Creek nation and argued that it had succeeded.

When we read the brief in light of Lemkin's words, we see clearly that it was a confession of attempted (and in the brief's terms, successful) genocide: As Lemkin wrote, "By 'genocide' we mean the destruction of a nation or of an ethnic group. . . . Genocide . . . [means] a coordinated plan of different actions aiming at the destruction of essential foundations of the life of national groups, with the aim of annihilating the groups themselves. The objectives of such a plan would be disintegration of the political and social institutions, of culture, language, national feelings, religion, and the economic existence of national groups. . . . Genocide is directed against the national group as an entity." The brief gave no indication of whether Justice Department lawyers were aware of the significance of their statements.

In one especially startling passage, the Justice Department relied on the historical resistance to genocide by the Creek Nation to prove the fact of the U.S. genocide effort! It said that the "Creek Nation . . . recognized that Congress intended to disestablish its historic territory." The brief then quoted an 1893 statement by "a Creek Chief [who] observed that Congress's 'unwavering aim' was to 'wipe out the line of political distinction between an Indian citizen and other citizens of the Republic' so that the tribal governments could be 'absorbed and become a part of the United States.'" The brief also cited an 1897 Muscogee Nation statement that "objected to Congress's proposed 'disintegrating' of 'the land of our people' so that it could 'be transformed into a State of the Union'"; the statement said that this would mean "the civil death of the Muscogee Nation." The brief admitted that the

Muscogee "sought . . . to 'preserve . . . unimpaired' their 'chief safeguard, the national title to [their] land.'"[24]

The Justice Department pointed out that at least one U.S. political figure at the time was outraged by these genocidal efforts. It quoted an 1898 statement by Tennessee senator William Bate, who said that the United States was "sweep[ing] all the laws of the Indians away, all their courts of justice, all their juries, all their local officers, and all the rights they have under [their] treaties. . . . We go along and encroach upon them inch by inch, Congress after Congress, until at last you have got to the main redoubt, and here it is destroyed."[25]

The brief did not quote the further remarks of Senator Bate, which eerily prefigured the Nazi concept of a "final solution." He said, "I wish to enter my protest. I think it is doing a very marked injustice to the Five Civilized Tribes. . . . [T]his bill violates [their] treaties. We have for the last few years, especially since the establishment of the Dawes Commission I think in every Congress, more or less violated the treaties. This, however, seems to be the consummation of it, the finality of it. . . . I for one, sir, desire to enter my protest against it from a high moral standpoint, as well as a legal and political standpoint."[26]

Strange as it seems, when the Muscogee Creek filed an amicus brief in the *Carpenter* case supporting the Tenth Circuit's ruling, it did not call out the U.S. confession of attempted genocide. Instead, avoiding any deep critique, the Muscogee brief simply disputed whether the U.S. Congress had in fact succeeded in its efforts to commit genocide against the Creek Nation. The basic Muscogee argument was that the genocidal power inherent in federal anti-Indian law had not been used to its fullest extent *yet*; some remnants of Muscogee self-government still existed. The brief said, "Every original attribute of the government of the Creek Nation still exists intact which has not been destroyed or limited by act of Congress."[27] The Muscogee brief actually stated that the United States may, so long as it makes its intentions clear, commit genocide against a Native nation.

To be sure, the Muscogee brief did not use that awful word. Rather, in a series of Orwellian touches, the brief characterized the U.S. actions as forms of congressional "oversight" that made "significant adjustments to [Muscogee] land ownership"! It said, "The Creek Nation, like many tribes, suffered significant insults to its authority during the allotment era." It added, "Congress . . . imposed significant restrictions on the Nation's government, including abolishing its courts" and "substantially diminished" the Nation's authority by subjecting its laws to federal "oversight." However, the Muscogee brief concluded that "such oversight is a staple of federal-tribal relations."[28] Wow! So true; but not protested.

They not only failed to critique the attempted genocide, they agreed that "the metes and bounds of tribal sovereignty are Congress's to adjust."[29] One wonders at the reluctance of Indigenous nations to call genocide by its name and to critique doctrines of domination.

The Tenth Circuit rejected the U.S. assertion of "extinguishment" and agreed with the Muscogee that the United States had not (yet) "terminated" their national existence. The court did not challenge the U.S. claim of a *right* to kill the Muscogee, only that the right had not yet been exercised. When Oklahoma appealed to the U.S. Supreme Court, the newly appointed justice Neil Gorsuch recused himself because he had been involved with the case in the Tenth Circuit. The court deadlocked at 4–4 and sent the case back to the lower court for reargument.[30]

In the meantime, a second case on the very same issues, *McGirt v. Oklahoma*,[31] made its way from the Tenth Circuit to the Supreme Court. With Gorsuch now participating, the Supreme Court reached a 5–4 decision affirming the Tenth Circuit. The majority opinion, written by Gorsuch, ruled that Oklahoma did not have criminal jurisdiction in Muscogee Creek territory because Congress had not (yet) disestablished the Muscogee nation. The *Carpenter* case was immediately closed based on the *McGirt* decision. But that's not the end of the story.

So much hoopla and media excitement surrounded the *McGirt* decision that few people realized what the opinion really said. Lots of people were thrilled to read Justice Gorsuch's opening line, "On the far end of the Trail of Tears was a promise."[32] The temptation was great to think that *McGirt* had closed the door on the genocidal era of "Indian Removal." But *McGirt* didn't close that door. In fact, as we will see, the opinion explicitly left the door open for the U.S. Congress to kill the Muscogee Nation.

Despite widespread public pronouncements calling *McGirt* a landmark decision, the case did not transform federal anti-Indian law. In fact, the decision explicitly affirmed the federal anti-Indian law doctrine of U.S. domination over Native peoples. Gorsuch said that the Creek Nation still existed only because Congress had not yet exercised the power to kill it. He said, "This Court long ago held that the Legislature [Congress] wields significant constitutional authority when it comes to tribal relations, possessing even the authority to breach its own promises and treaties." Gorsuch did not directly name the root of this supposed "authority," but he cited *Lone Wolf v. Hitchcock*, the 1903 Supreme Court decision that exalted "Christian discovery" into a claim of "plenary power over . . . Indians."[33] He added a further citation to Emory Washburn's 1868 *Treatise on the American Law of Real Property*, which said, "The Christian nations that planted colonies . . . recognized no seisin [ownership] of lands on the part of Indian dwellers."[34]

In fact, the majority opinion and the dissents in *McGirt* agreed on the U.S. claim of plenary power over Native peoples. They all said that the U.S.

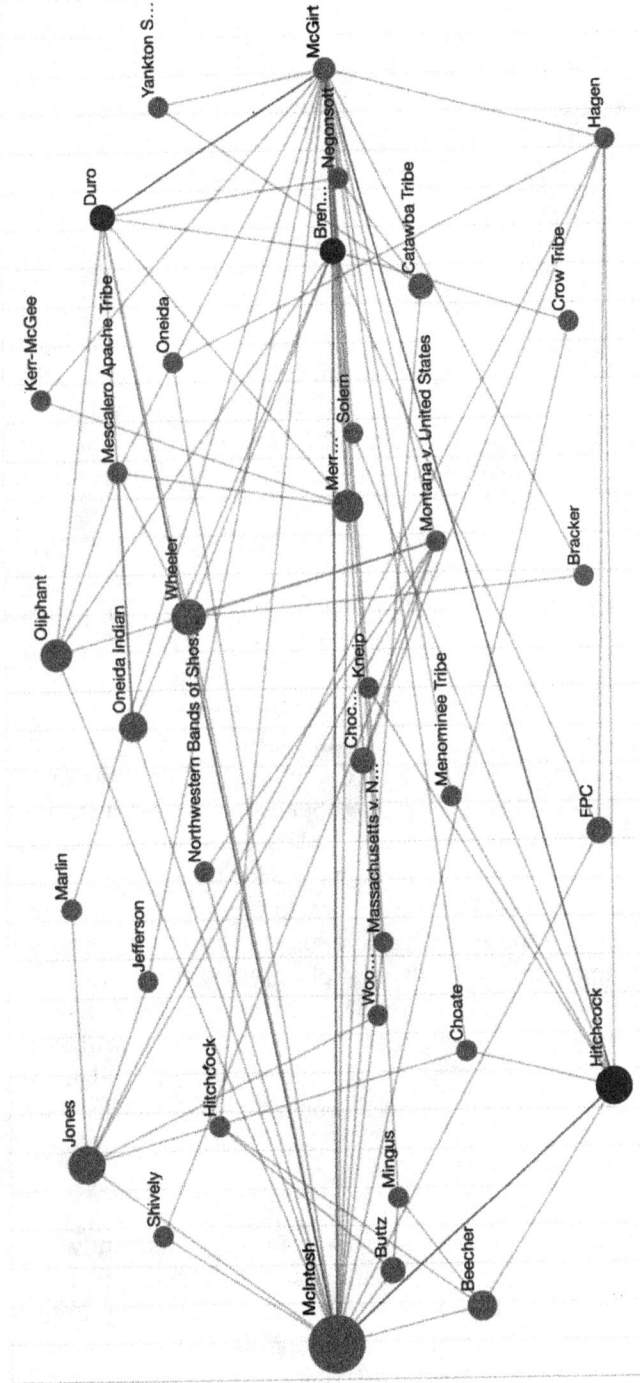

Map showing *McGirt* citations traced to *Johnson v. McIntosh*. (Created by the author at the Supreme Court Mapping Project, University of Baltimore School of Law)

Congress can do as it wished with Native peoples and their lands. The only difference between the majority and dissents was whether Congress had or had not already disestablished the Creek Nation. The majority said no. The dissents said yes. Gorsuch made the point absolutely clear, He wrote, "Of course, . . . Congress remains free to [take action] . . . about the lands in question at any time. It has no shortage of tools at its disposal."[35] In short, *McGirt* as a whole said that Congress could do the dirty deed whenever it wished.

Moreover, the technical point in the *McGirt* decision was that criminal jurisdiction in the case belonged to the federal government rather than Oklahoma. Gorsuch pointed out that the 1885 Major Crimes Act had imposed U.S. jurisdiction over certain crimes committed by Native persons in "Indian country." Therefore, Gorsuch wrote, Oklahoma had no criminal jurisdiction. In other words, what the *McGirt* decision did was to affirm U.S. power as opposed to Oklahoma power. It bypassed Muscogee criminal jurisdiction altogether, since that already had been "clearly extinguished" by the Major Crimes Act.

Anyone who reads the decision closely can see this. But somehow, the public response to the *McGirt* decision was like the observers in the folktale "The Emperor's New Clothes."[36] They pretended not to see, or, perhaps, they had no confidence in their own eyes. Either way, they avoided seeing the emperor's nakedness.

When the *Carpenter v. Murphy* case was scheduled for reargument before *McGirt* came along, Professor Ronald Mann called it "the single hardest case of the [Supreme Court] term." The hard question, he said, was the "conundrum" of determining when the United States has disestablished a Native nation. He said that the "settled regime" in U.S. law was that Congress must make a "clear statement" of disestablishment. He said that the Tenth Circuit decision indicated that Congress might have to use "a multi-factored arrangement . . . based on a loose amalgam of historical practice."[37] Mann didn't suggest any critique of the U.S. claim of plenary power; he only questioned how to determine whether the power has been exercised in a given case.

As a consequence of not seeing the emperor's nakedness, neither the court nor the public arrived at the time and place where Robert Williams said that doctrines of domination, "once revealed, would shame those who cite them."[38]

## Genocide Denied

Closing one's eyes to genocide happens surprisingly frequently. A particularly jarring example occurred in Gary Anderson's 2014 book *Ethnic Cleansing and the Indian: The Crime That Should Haunt America*. Despite chapter titles pointing to "penetration," "invasion," "stealing," "removal," and "land grab," Anderson's central argument was that genocide did *not* occur! This view grossly undermined what was otherwise an excellent recounting of anti-Indigenous history in America.

Early in the book, Anderson foreshadowed his conclusion with the bizarre statement, "Indians' survival had much to do with the implementation of [a] dominating policy of ethnic cleansing."[39] Read that again—Anderson suggested a benign aspect of ethnic cleansing: it *prevented* genocide!

Anderson repeatedly concluded his descriptions of U.S. army and militia violence against Indigenous peoples with the statement that these were "war crimes" and "crimes against humanity," but "not genocide." He wrote, "Genocide will never become a widely accepted characterization for what happened in North America, because large numbers of Indians survived and because policies of mass murder on a scale similar to events in central Europe, Cambodia, or Rwanda were never implemented."[40] This statement begged so many questions! Does acceptability govern the work of a historian? Does it matter whether the proper term to describe history "will never become widely accepted"? Is there a numerical balancing test for genocide?

Anderson dismissed a number of historians who use "genocide" to describe American history by commenting that they "devalue what actually happened to people who experienced organized, policy-driven genocide in central Europe, Cambodia, Rwanda, and even perhaps Darfur."[41] He added, "Some scholars consider it an affront even to use the term 'holocaust' . . . to describe anything other than what happened to Jews in central Europe."[42]

Anderson's privileging of some victims of mass violence was a perverse form of "political correctness." One should indeed think carefully about using charged words like "genocide" and "holocaust"; but in the end, one does a disservice to humanity and to scholarship to pretend that "holocaust" is a noun meaning a singular event, rather than a verb referring to an action, a repeatable and repeated event.

To borrow rhetoric once applied to Mahmoud Ahmadinejad, the president of Iran from 2005 to 2013, Anderson is a "genocide denier." I mean this literally, based on his stated thesis that U.S. attacks on Indigenous nations were not really genocide. I mean it figuratively, too, based on the similarity of his arguments to the arguments of those who are regarded as Holocaust deniers.

The U.S. Holocaust Memorial Museum states: "Some Holocaust deniers argue that, since there is neither a single document that outlines the Holocaust nor a signed document from Hitler ordering the Holocaust, the Holocaust itself is a hoax."[43] Anderson reflected this line of thought in his arguments about official U.S. government statements. He admitted that a long list of American leaders—including George Washington and generals William Tecumseh Sherman and Philip Sheridan—called for the extermination of Indigenous peoples. He argued, however, that official government policy documents generally avoided the use of that awful word, and some massacres were the work of fighters "completely out of control" of their superiors. He concluded, therefore, that the mass killing of Indians was not genocide because it was not policy-driven.

The Holocaust Museum also states, "Holocaust deniers cite uncertainty about the exact number of deaths . . . as proof that the whole history of the Holocaust has been fabricated." Anderson explicitly raised the numbers question. He asked, "As the number of dead declines, does genocide still occur?" He asked, "Wounded Knee might constitute a crime, but was it 'genocide'?"[44] Again, his argument echoed the argument of Holocaust deniers.

Anderson's own evidence showed that Indigenous peoples were subjected to what the Holocaust Museum describes as "systematic, bureaucratic, state-sponsored persecution and murder."[45] Anderson's reluctance to use that definition of genocide to define American history undermines the usefulness of his book.

Anderson said that the word "holocaust" derives from a Hebrew and Yiddish root meaning "catastrophe" or "destruction."[46] Perhaps he considered this an argument for restricting its use to the Jewish experience. However, according to the Holocaust Museum, "'Holocaust' is a word of Greek origin meaning 'sacrifice by fire.'"[47] The burning of the Pequot village by English invaders in 1637—which Anderson minimized as "perhaps a war crime"—is a literal "holocaust" by the Greek meaning.

The Nazis believed that Germans were racially superior and the inferior Jews, Gypsies, and others were a threat to German civilization. Hitler aimed to remove Jews, whom he often referred to as "vermin."[48] This Nazi rhetoric precisely mirrored U.S. rhetoric that targeted Indigenous peoples as a lower race that should be removed so that the superior White race could grow and prosper. Correspondence between Lord Jeffrey Amherst, the commander-in-chief of British colonial forces, and Colonel Henri Bouquet during the summer of 1763 referred to Indigenous peoples as vermin and called for their "total extirpation."[49] Anderson acknowledged parallels between Nazi anti-Semitism and U.S. anti-Native policies and practices, but he repeatedly argued that the two were fundamentally different.

Ian Kershaw, in "Improvised Genocide? The Emergence of the 'Final Solution' in the 'Warthegau,'"[50] said that as late as July 1941, the Nazis "still looked to a territorial solution, envisaging the removal of . . . Jews to a massive reservation in the east—somewhere beyond the Urals." But the worsening war situation precluded that plan and prompted the program for elimination. Kershaw described the Nazi territorial solution as "a different form of genocide in the long run."[51] In contrast, Anderson said that "Indian removal," the U.S. territorial solution, was not genocide at all because it did "not result in the utter destruction of the Indians." Would he dare say of the Jews there was no Holocaust because there are still Jews left in the world? Anderson even applauded what he called the "moral restraint" of "Indian Removal," which he said, "to some degree prevent[ed] genocide."

Anderson rested a large portion of his denial of genocide on a linguistic claim. He said, "It is presumptive . . . to use modern terms to describe past . . . realities."[52] By "modern terms," he apparently meant the definition of "genocide" introduced into international law by the 1948 UN Convention on the Prevention and Punishment of the Crime of Genocide. But Anderson had no problem applying even more modern terms to arrive at his conclusions about ethnic cleansing, using definitions from the 1998 and 2002 Rome Statute of the International Criminal Court.

For reasons that remain personal and impenetrable, Anderson wrote a book of more than 400 pages filled with details about the principal actors in U.S. efforts to eliminate Indigenous peoples, only to make the case that this was not genocide. To do this, he employed two parallel rhetorical strategies: one was to interpret the Genocide Convention more narrowly than the text itself states, and the other was to insist U.S. anti-Indigenous policies and programs were somehow moral and unintentional.

Article II of the 1948 UN Convention on Genocide states, "Genocide means any of the following acts committed with intent to destroy, in whole or in part, a national, ethnical, racial or religious group, as such: (a) Killing members of the group; (b) Causing serious bodily or mental harm to members of the group; (c) Deliberately inflicting on the group conditions of life calculated to bring about its physical destruction in whole or in part; (d) Imposing measures intended to prevent births within the group; (e) Forcibly transferring children of the group to another group."[53]

Given that Anderson's own evidence demonstrated all these elements of the definition of genocide, why did he sidestep the obvious conclusion? Indeed, if we include the forced sterilization of Indigenous women and the transfer of Indigenous children to non-Indigenous families by state agencies (which is what the 1978 Indian Child Welfare Act[54] was supposed to prevent), we have to conclude that genocide is still going on, albeit without mass murder.

## With Friends Like These . . .

Hard as it may be to acknowledge genocidal actions against Native peoples, it is harder to acknowledge that a great deal of harm has been done in the name of help. Supposed "friends of the Indian" have driven U.S. policy back and forth in different modes of damaging "help" over the years since Christian colonizers first arrived. Indeed, the theme of "help" was portrayed in the first seal of the Massachusetts Bay Colony in 1629, which presented an image of an Indigenous person saying, "Come over and help us."

Professor Kristina Bross described the image as "ventriloquism."[55] She said that the image of Natives calling for the colonizers to come was "an echo of

The 1629 Massachusetts Bay Company seal. (Massachusetts Archives)

the Pauline dream of the welcoming Other, taken from *Acts* 16: 9–10 [of the Christian Bible]." It put words from the Bible into Native mouths, imagining the Natives as willing recipients of Christian colonization. It also implied that the real sufferers were the Puritans, who, like Paul, were persecuted for their missionary efforts.

In 1902, then–Lieutenant Colonel Richard Henry Pratt, founder of the notorious Carlisle Indian Industrial School program that seized Native children from their families to forcibly integrate them into American society, spoke at the Lake Mohonk Conference of Friends of the Indian about his boarding school project. He explained the purpose of taking Indigenous children from their homes (many never to return because they died at the school) as being necessary for "Indian progress." Pratt's vision of progress is that Native children would be "freed" from tribal lives. They would become individuals assimilated into U.S. society, "civilized," and Christian. He described his plan as a program to "destroy racism and classism," as if the independent existence of Native peoples somehow violated notions of equality.[56]

Pratt had expressed his viewpoint infamously in an earlier speech at the 1892 Annual Conference of Charities and Correction, when he quoted U.S. army general Philip Sheridan, who said, "The only good Indian is a dead one." Pratt remarked, "In a sense, I agree with [Sheridan's] sentiment, but only in this: that all the Indian there is in the race should be dead. Kill the Indian in him, and save the man."[57]

Sheridan and Pratt both targeted the existence of Indigenous peoples. Sheridan wanted to accomplish this by killing as many Indigenous people as he could. Meanwhile, Pratt wanted to accomplish the goal by killing Indigenous *ways*—languages, rituals, clothing, family ties, social relations, and other characteristics—starting with the children.

As we saw in Chapter 1, President Theodore Roosevelt trumpeted the same theme in his 1901 Message to Congress, where he called allotment "a mighty pulverizing engine to break up the tribal mass"[58] and praised the effort to forcibly assimilate Native people into American society. Roosevelt also reportedly said at the death of Geronimo in February 1909, "I don't go so far as to think that the only good Indians are the dead Indians, but I believe nine out of every 10 are. And I shouldn't like to inquire too closely into the case of the tenth."[59]

A key part of Pratt's critique of Native societies was the fact that Indigenous peoples hold land in common. He told the conference, "In dealing with the Indian the eternal thing with us is his property. Property is the stumbling block all the time, and I am glad to see any steps taken to get it out of the way." He tied together his distaste for communal land with an acknowledgment allotment would "free" Native land to fulfill American greed. He said, "The Indian's property and our greed for it stands in the way of the Indian's progress."[60]

This critique of communal property ownership continues with twenty-first-century "friends of the Indian." For example, *The New Trail of Tears: How Washington Is Destroying American Indians*,[61] a 2016 book by American Enterprise Institute resident fellow Naomi Schaefer Riley, framed the problem as a matter of "equal rights" for "all citizens," echoing Pratt's rhetoric. Her approach explicitly aimed to separate Indigenous *persons*, as individuals, from Indigenous *peoples*. The title of one chapter put it as "The Tribe vs. the Individual." And the title of Riley's concluding chapter said it all: "Native Americans as Americans." Riley actually praised the Dawes Act's effort to destroy Indigenous peoples by breaking up communal tribal ownership. Her perspective presented an individual civil rights concern of equality for *persons* instead of Indigenous *peoples*' self-determination.

Similarly, the Citizens Equal Rights Alliance/Citizens Equal Rights Foundation (CERA/CERF),[62] a Wisconsin-based organization, billed itself in favor of "Many Cultures—One People—One Law." Their mission statement echoed Riley's and Pratt's theme: "It is . . . CERF and CERA's mission to ensure the equal protection of the law as guaranteed to all citizens by the Constitution of the United States." This is an ironic statement in light of the fact that two of the three total references to Native peoples in the U.S. Constitution, including the Fourteenth Amendment, exclude "Indians" from the number of people counted for representation in Congress.

CERA/CERF offers an array of position papers with tantalizing titles on "sovereignty," but it ultimately grounds its program in an attack on "collective sovereignty." The program aims for the same goal as the Dawes Act and the boarding schools—to extinguish Indigenous *peoples* and assimilate individual Native *persons*.

President Franklin Delano Roosevelt is usually seen as a friend of Natives because his appointment of the sociologist John Collier as commissioner of Indian affairs in 1933 led to a self-proclaimed "New Deal for Indians." The

1934 Indian Reorganization Act disavowed the destructive Allotment Act, which broke up Native communal landholding into nuclear households and handed "surplus" Native lands to non-Natives. But Roosevelt's reorganization carried its own version of assimilation; it pushed Native peoples to replace their many different traditional governments with a standardized business corporation model of Tribal Councils, under federal supervision, in order to make it easier for Indigenous lands and peoples to become part of the U.S. national economic system. Despite halting the allotment of Native lands, the New Deal did not disavow the U.S. claim to own Native lands and have plenary power over Native peoples.

Commentators sometimes describe "friends of the Indian" as "well-intentioned." Whatever else that means, it provides a good example of the phrase, "With friends like these, you don't need enemies."

## Indian Claims Commission

Every U.S. program supposedly designed to "help" Natives has actually aimed to terminate the independent status of Indigenous *peoples* and assimilate Native *persons* as individuals in American society. Each successive U.S. effort raised the promise of a "final solution" to the "Indian problem" that would consummate the U.S. claim of ownership of Indigenous lands and domination over Indigenous peoples. I use the phrase "final solution" advisedly, considering its notorious association with the Nazi genocide project. But, as we have seen, the word "genocide" precisely characterizes U.S. actions toward Indigenous peoples.

The Indian Claims Commission provides a prime example of extinguishment disguised as assistance. It is frequently cited as a "pro-Native" project and sometimes even described as a "reparations" program.[63] The truth of the matter is quite different.

In 1928, Lewis Meriam, vice president of the Brookings Institution, presented a report to Hubert Work, the U.S. secretary of the interior. Funded by the Rockefeller Foundation and titled *The Problem of Indian Administration* (also called the *Meriam Report*), it presented a devastating critique of conditions on reservations in the wake of allotment and the disarray of federal programs aimed at reservation land management, education (boarding schools), and health care. Meriam forced a confrontation with the Bureau of Indian Affairs, but he did not challenge the underlying federal assimilation and extinguishment policies. Instead, he investigated "what remains to be done to adjust the Indians to the prevailing civilization." He said, "The object of work with or for the Indians is to fit them either to merge into the social and economic life of the prevailing civilization as developed by the whites or to live in the presence of that civilization at least in accordance with a minimum standard of health and decency." He cautioned that "allotment of tribal holdings will continue," but it should proceed with more education in order to attain the goal of assimilation: "The ultimate goal is to advance the Indian to the point where he is competent to take care of himself and to manage his own property."[64]

President Herbert Hoover responded to the *Meriam Report* with a request to Congress for emergency funds for food and clothing. He also requested that Commissioner of Indian Affairs Charles J. Rhoads undertake administrative reforms. But deep cross-currents swirled in Congress; reactions ranged from insistence on allotment on one side to support for a stabilized Native land base on the other side. The election of President Franklin Roosevelt and his appointment of John Collier as commissioner of Indian affairs in 1933 captured the federal agenda with the New Deal for Indians and the Indian Reorganization Act, which, as we have seen, put an end to allotment efforts but also encouraged a move away from traditional Native governments.

After the death of Roosevelt and the departure of Collier in 1945, allotment and termination forces again took control of the federal agenda. A series of explicit "Indian termination" initiatives quickly emerged in the U.S. Congress. One of them, the 1946 Indian Claims Commission Act,[65] is not typically viewed as part of the termination movement. In fact, the Claims Commission is often viewed as "pro-Indian" because it allowed Indigenous peoples to sue the United States for compensation for prior land takings. But that was only on the surface. The deep purpose of the Indian Claims Commission was to certify U.S. claims of title to Indigenous lands and to encourage the breakup of Indigenous peoples by closing the books on their ownership of land.

The 1945 testimony of Lynn Adams, special attorney for the Chickasaw Indians, to the House Committee on Indian Affairs during hearings on the Claims Commission bill shows how far termination and assimilation had already entrapped Native peoples. He said, "I think it would be very beneficial to the State as a whole to have those claims heard, because the Indian himself, until that claim is over with, is a little reluctant to give up a lot of his tribal connections, and he does not assimilate himself well with the people of the State."[66] Similarly, in hearings before the U.S. Senate Committee on Indian Affairs in June and July 1946, Oklahoma congressman William Stigler (speaking apparently as an assimilated Native: "having Indian blood myself") testified, "I think this bill will go further than anything that has been done in the last twenty-five years. At least, in order to bring about the opportunity to wind up the affairs of some of the tribes that should have been wound up years ago."[67]

After the commission was created and some of its decisions were appealed to the U.S. Court of Claims, the court acknowledged the termination and assimilation purpose of the commission. In a 1953 decision, it said, "The obvious . . . desire on the part of Congress . . . [was] to establish a means whereby Indian claims against the United States should be finally and expeditiously settled . . . with the hope that a fair and complete settlement of such claims would ultimately reduce the cost to the Government of aiding the various tribes. It was anticipated that with the settlement of these claims, many Indians would abandon their connection with the tribes and their dependence upon the United States. It was intended, in order to effect this end, to give the Commission the broadest possible powers."[68]

But one power was not given to the commission: It was not empowered to acknowledge or affirm continuing Native land ownership. It was authorized only to provide compensation for U.S. taking of Native lands. The history professor Harvey D. Rosenthal, the author of *Their Day in Court: A History of the Indian Claims Commission*, described the commission's facade of compassion for Natives as follows: "A familiar pattern. . . . An aroused Congress cloaking its own interests in a rhetoric of generosity toward the Indian."[69] Not surprisingly, when the commission included a condensed version of Rosenthal's study as a "Historical Survey" in the published *Final Report of the Indian Claims Commission*, it omitted this statement.[70]

The Claims Commission was actually a belated outgrowth of the *Meriam Report*. In a section titled "Indian Tribal Claims Against the Government," Meriam discussed the existence of Native land claims against the United States. His analysis was entirely in line with the extinguishment/assimilation agenda, saying, "The existence of these claims is a serious impediment to progress. The Indians look forward to getting vast sums from these claims. . . . They will hardly knuckle down to work while they still hope the government will pay what they believe is due them. Some Indians . . . are maintaining their tribal connections . . . because they have rights under these claims."[71] The report also recommended the creation of a special expert staff in the Interior Department to make the land claim problem go away.

When Congress held hearings on the proposed Claims Commission, no one suggested that it was the United States that was making "claims" on land. Witnesses testified about "clouds" on U.S. land title. A cloud on title is a legal uncertainty about who owns land. They said that these clouds were "a serious hindrance to development in many parts of the country." The House report put it this way: "It is essential that the jurisdiction to hear claims . . . be broad enough to include all possible claims. . . . [because] the chief purpose of the [Act is] to dispose of the Indian claims problem with finality." The House committee members apparently felt no hesitation about speaking of a final solution, even as Nazi "final solution" war crimes were being revealed and prosecuted. They said the Claims Commission "would, in the judgment of all who have studied the [Indian] problem, expedite its final solution."[72]

U.S. president Harry Truman's statement on signing the act left no doubt that the desired end point was extinguishment of Indigenous *peoples* and assimilation of Indigenous *persons*. Like Richard Henry Pratt before him and the twenty-first-century "friends of the Indian" after him, Truman expressed the goal using the language of equal rights. He said, "With the final settlement of all outstanding claims which this measure ensures, Indians can take their place without special handicap or special advantage in the economic life of our nation and share fully in its progress."[73]

Three years later, Truman sharpened the point when he vetoed a bill intended to rehabilitate the Navajo and Hopi nations. He said, "Ultimate acceptance of State jurisdiction is a logical consequence of our policy of assisting the Indians to develop their natural talents and physical resources in ways that will enable them to participate fully in our free, but vigorously competitive, society. . . . . . In the long run, this process of adjustment to our culture can be expected to result in the complete merger of all Indian groups into the general body of our population."[74]

In short, the dual purposes of the Indian Claims Commission were individual assimilation and tribal dissolution. Its decisions foreclosed further arguments about Indigenous land ownership—arguments that "clouded" U.S. title claims. As the Tenth Circuit Court of Appeals explained in a 1987 decision denying Navajo Nation land title, the Claims Commission Act reflected a congressional policy that "tribes with valid claims would be paid in money. No lands would be returned to a tribe. . . . They either get an award in cash or their case is dismissed and they do not get anything."[75] Native peoples were recognized only as having claims, not ownership.

The Western Shoshone ran into this barrier in 1976, a decade earlier than the Navajo, when they tried to stop a Claims Commission proceeding after realizing that the commission would not allow them to assert their continuing ownership. They petitioned for a stay of the proceedings. This was opposed both by the United States and by a "Western Shoshone Identifiable Group" that the commission had designated as the official representative of the Western Shoshone.[76] The Western Shoshone thus found themselves opposed not only by the United States, but by a creation of the Claims Commission using their own name! Elmer R. Rusco pointed out that a majority of the Western Shoshone were never represented by any party to the Indian Claims Commission proceedings.[77] Nevertheless, the commission denied the request for a stay and continued the process of decreeing a final solution. The Western Shoshone refused to accept the commission's offer of a money payment, stymieing the final solution until a special congressional act was passed in 2004, forcing a distribution of the money.[78] In Chapter 4, we will look at how the U.S. Supreme Court applied federal anti-Indian law "trust doctrine" to achieve "finality" in the *Western Shoshone* case.

Coincidental with the creation of the Indian Claims Commission, the U.S. Congress undertook a series of reorganizations of its committee structure, supposedly to "streamline" the "management of Indian Affairs." Rosenthal said that the reorganizations showed "the intimate connections between Indian claims . . . and the desire of the government to terminate its . . . relationship with the Indian tribes."[79] Professor David Wilkins said that even those committee reorganizations that "did not directly focus on indigenous peoples . . . adversely affected Native rights."[80]

The Claims Commission Act was quickly followed by other laws and policies aimed at extinguishment in the guise of bringing help and equality. In 1950, the Bureau of Indian Affairs instituted a relocation program to move Indigenous people away from reservations to urban areas where jobs were supposedly available. On August 1, 1953, House Concurrent Resolution 108 mandated "as rapidly as possible, to make the Indians . . . subject to the same laws and entitled to the same privileges and responsibilities as are applicable to other citizens of the United States."[81] On August 15, 1953, Public Law 280 imposed state jurisdiction over "Indian reservations."[82] On August 3, 1956, Public Law 959 established vocational training to undergird the bureau's relocation program.[83]

David Wilkins pointed out the insidious financial transfers involved in these programs. He said that the costs of termination programs were supported in part by Indian Claims Commission settlement payments: "The government would appropriate money won in court by the Indians to finance its ultimate goal of gradually severing all remaining federal trust and treaty obligations to tribes. Tribes, in effect, were to pay for their own termination."[84]

Having stripped away the rhetoric of friendship from federal anti-Indian law, we are ready to plunge into the doctrinal depths—the case law that created and continues to undergird the system of domination.

# CHAPTER THREE

# Federal Anti-Indian Law

## A Semantic World

Law professor Robert M. Cover famously wrote in 1986, "Legal interpretation takes place in a field of pain and death."[1] The way I sometimes put it is that law and force are intimately intertwined; the phrase "law enforcement" captures that truth. Without force, law is just words; but without words, law is just violence. You might see this clearly in criminal law, which was the focus of Cover's article; but, as Cover himself made clear, "All law which concerns property, its use and its protection, has a similarly violent base." We have seen that this applies to federal anti-Indian law, with its history of violent land acquisition. On the other hand, as Cover suggested, the "violent foundation is [sometimes] not immediately at issue." This also applies to federal anti-Indian law, where words and interpretations often intentionally hide its inherent violence.

This chapter excavates the foundational cases of federal anti-Indian law and pulls aside the veil of their words to try to expose the violence.

In 1965, just as I was starting Yale Law School, the U.S. Supreme Court issued a decision directly affecting the Navajo Nation, *Warren Trading Post v. Arizona Tax Commission*.[2] Four years later, practicing in Shiprock, we Dinébe'iiná Náhiiłna be Agha'diit'ahii (DNA) lawyers saw the *Warren* case as an important precedent. We were enthusiastic about the court's statement that Navajos were "free to run the reservation and its affairs without state control."[3] We ignored the deeper meaning of the case.

The *Warren* case was a state tax dispute brought by a trading post operating in Navajoland against the Arizona Tax Commission. The Navajo Nation was not involved in the case. When the Arizona courts approved the state tax, the trading post appealed to the U.S. Supreme Court, which struck the tax down. In an opinion written by Justice Hugo Black, the Supreme Court said, "No burden shall be imposed upon Indian traders for trading with Indians on reservations except as authorized by Acts of Congress."[4]

We ignored the fact that the Supreme Court was not really upholding the authority of the Navajo government, but rather asserting U.S. power over Navajoland. The Court said that the trading post operated in Navajoland under a federal license and under "comprehensive [federal] statutes and regulations." It added, "Congress has taken the business of Indian trading on reservations so fully in hand that no room remains for state laws."[5] The *Warren* case was really a decision about U.S. power pitted against Arizona power. Navajo power was left hanging.

In Shiprock, we quoted the Court's statement, "The Federal Government [permits] the Indians largely to govern themselves." What we ignored was the underlying legal theory that Navajo self-government depended on U.S. permission. The tenuousness and ambiguity of this U.S. permission was clear in a footnote in the decision, which said, "Certain state laws have been permitted to apply to activities on Indian reservations, where those laws are specifically authorized by acts of Congress."[6]

In 1968, a U.S. Supreme Court fishing rights case, *Menominee Tribe of Indians v. United States*,[7] again displayed how federal anti-Indian law leaves Indigenous peoples hanging between state and federal government claims of control. The question in the *Menominee* case was whether Menominee hunting and fishing rights were abrogated when the U.S. Congress enacted the Menominee Indian Termination Act of 1954.[8] The act transferred title to Menominee lands to the state of Wisconsin and extended all Wisconsin laws to govern the Menominee. The Menominee sued the United States in the U.S. Court of Claims for compensation for taking away their treaty-recognized hunting and fishing rights.

The Court of Claims said that the Termination Act did not abrogate Menominee hunting and fishing rights; therefore, the United States owed no compensation. The court said that it was the state of Wisconsin that was responsible for any interference with Menominee hunting and fishing rights. Meanwhile, the Wisconsin Supreme Court decided that the Termination Act *did* abrogate Menominee fishing rights. The U.S. Supreme Court took the case to resolve the conflict between the Court of Claims and the Wisconsin Supreme Court.

In an opinion by Justice William O. Douglas, the Supreme Court distinguished between "treaty rights" and "termination." Douglas quoted a statement in the Congressional Record by Senator Arthur Watkins, the leading proponent of termination, saying that the Menominee Termination Act "in no way violates any treaty obligation with this tribe."[9] Although this sounds favorable to the Menominee, it is a strange statement because the treaty in question—the Treaty of Wolf River, enacted in 1854—guaranteed the Menominee "a permanent home . . . as Indian lands are held" on lands where they agreed to move.[10] So this act clearly did violate Menominee land rights. Watkins's statement was mendacious, to say the least; but it fit his general view that termination meant "liberation" and was "in their best interest."[11]

Douglas used Watkins's statement to parse the fishing rights dispute. He pointed to Public Law 280, a separate congressional act passed a year before the Termination Act, which authorized Wisconsin and other states to assert their jurisdiction over "Indian country." Unlike the Termination Act, which didn't mention fishing rights, Public Law 280 preserved the rights to hunt, trap, and fish. In a remarkable feat of doctrinal legerdemain, Douglas mixed the two acts together and came up with a decision that Menominee fishing rights had slipped through a crack in Watkins's liberation scheme. He said, "The two Acts read together mean to us that, although . . . all tribal property was to be transferred to [the state], the hunting and fishing rights granted or preserved by . . . Treaty . . . survived."[12] Although the decision protected Menominee fishing rights, it illuminated the inherent instability of federal anti-Indian law treatment of U.S. treaties with Native nations; they are not regarded as binding agreements, but rather just as historical incidents to be interpreted in light of the ongoing U.S. drive toward domination.

In 1942, the U.S. Department of the Interior issued a *Handbook of Federal Indian Law,* the field's first-ever compilation, now regarded as its "bible."[13] The work was authored by Felix Cohen, the principal architect of President Franklin Delano Roosevelt's Indian Reorganization Act. Department solicitor Nathan Margold wrote the introduction to the *Handbook,* where he said that the field encompassed "the federal law governing Indians."[14] Margold's definition called attention to the fact that, despite its name, "federal Indian law" is not Native law, but rather law for the United States to use to control Natives. Margold did not question the rightness of this control; he simply praised Cohen for the arduous work of compiling the precedents.

When we enter the realm called "federal Indian law," we need to keep this in mind: we are entering a semantic world created by the United States to control Native peoples and claim their lands. However, because of the power of language (especially legal language), control can be presented as "guardianship," or even "liberation." But it nevertheless is a claim of domination.

## Christian Discovery

There's a wonderful dialogue in Robert Heinlein's classic science fiction novel *Stranger in a Strange Land,* which illuminates the legal history that we are about to explore. Two of the main characters, Jill and Ben, are pondering a possible lawsuit about who owns the planet Mars: is it the Martians or one

of the colonizers from Earth? The latter possibility shocks Jill. She says, "Ben
. . . This notion of a single man *owning* a planet . . . it's fantastic!" Ben replies,
"Don't use that word to a lawyer; straining at gnats and swallowing camels is
a required course in law schools."

Ben then explains how legal doctrine works. He says, "Besides, there is
precedent. In the fifteenth century the Pope deeded the western hemisphere
to Spain and Portugal and nobody cared that the real estate was occupied by
Indians with their own laws, customs, and property rights. His grant was
effective, too. Look at a map and notice where Spanish is spoken and where
Portuguese is spoken."

Jill, still astonished, says, "Yes, but—Ben, this isn't the fifteenth century."
Ben replies, "It is to a lawyer, Jill."[15]

Federal anti-Indian law is indeed rooted in fifteenth-century papal
decrees. The foundation was set in the Marshall trilogy—*Johnson v. McIntosh*,
*Cherokee Nation v. United States*, and *Worcester v. Georgia*. It's called the "Marshall trilogy" because Chief Justice John Marshall wrote the opinions; but as
my historian friend Steven Schwartzberg observed, given what Marshall
wrote, they should be known as "Marshall's War." Marshall created a *jurisprudence of domination* rooted in a property law concept that the United States
owns Native lands "discovered" by the Christian colonizers and has a right
of "ultimate dominion" over Native peoples living on these lands.

Heinlein's character Ben is correct: This property doctrine was set forth in
fifteenth-century papal bulls and the decrees of colonizing Christian monarchs. The Portuguese crown used the doctrine of Christian discovery first, in
order to ensure their dominance over the African slave trade. The Spanish were
next, using it to claim ownership of the New World, which they announced in
their infamous *Requerimiento* (Requirement) of 1513 as a demand for Native
obedience to the pope as "lord of the world" and to King Don Fernando and
Queen Doña Juana as "lords, in his place." The *Requerimiento* said that Native
disobedience would be met with "war against you in all ways and manners that
we can, [to] subject you to the yoke and obedience of the Church. . . . We shall
take you, and your wives, and your children, and shall make slaves of them,
and as such shall sell and dispose of them . . . and we shall take away your
goods, and shall do you all the mischief and damage that we can."[16]

In short, the origin story of Christian discovery is not pretty. The ugliness
of the doctrine and an increasing desire to hide it are part of the reason why
federal anti-Indian law appears so complex and peculiar. The Marshall trilogy decisions are still routinely cited in the twenty-first century, but their
religious foundation is embarrassing, and therefore bowdlerized or concealed
entirely. What remains is a mind-boggling array of rules and subrules with
no explanation other than a repeated claim of U.S. title and dominion.

For example, as we saw in the introduction, when the Supreme Court
denied Oneida Nation title and sovereignty over its ancestral lands in 2005

in *City of Sherrill v. Oneida Indian Nation*, Justice Ruth Bader Ginsberg avoided any reference to religious metaphysics. The closest she came to naming the conceptual foundation of federal anti-Indian law was a statement concealed in a footnote, where she wrote, "The English possessions in America were claimed by right of discovery. . . . Under the 'doctrine of discovery,' . . . fee title to the lands occupied by Indians when the colonists arrived became vested in the sovereign—first the discovering European nation and later the original States and the United States."[17]

Judicial sensibilities were less acute in 1955, during the case of *Tee-Hit-Ton v. United States*,[18] when the U.S. Department of Justice filed a brief against the Tee-Hit-Ton. It cited both the Bible and the papal bulls and succeeded in persuading the U.S. Supreme Court to rule that the Tee-Hit-Ton did not hold title to their own ancestral lands.

Today, the doctrinal foundation of federal anti-Indian law—the U.S. claim of ownership by "Christian discovery"—is so seldom explored that the ownership claim appears as a simple commonplace in mainstream news articles. For example, on December 3, 2020, in an article about the controversial border wall between the United States and Mexico, the Associated Press reported President-elect Joe Biden "will inherit a massive wall-building effort that accelerated in [outgoing president Donald] Trump's final year." In a passing remark, the article said that the border wall project was easier to do in some areas because "the construction . . . has taken place in wildlife refuges and Indigenous territory that already belongs to the U.S. government."[19] The article did not discuss how Indigenous territory "belongs to the U.S. government."

Soon, we will look further at *Tee-Hit-Ton* and other cases relying on the Marshall trilogy and see how Christian discovery doctrine is actively used into the twenty-first century. But first we embark on a deep dive into the Marshall trilogy itself to see how the doctrine was created.

## Into the Abyss

The German legal theorist Carl Schmitt wrote in 1925, "An abyss separates us from the time when international law textbooks still spoke of Christian international law, and the right of Christian nations."[20] Schmitt obviously wasn't aware that U.S. anti-Indian law still stands on the far side of the abyss, proclaiming the right of Christian nations over Native peoples.

Political science professor Anna Jurkevics dated Schmitt's abyss to "around 1900," when the European-centered order based on colonialism "crumbled."[21] The Marshall trilogy of cases establishing Christian discovery in U.S. law were decided three-quarters of a century prior to that crumbling, and yet U.S. law has yet to cross the abyss.

## Johnson v. McIntosh

*Johnson and Graham's Lessee v. William McIntosh,* decided March 10, 1823,[22] was the first case in the Marshall trilogy. By declaring that the United States held title to all Native lands, the *Johnson* decision also created a new field called "federal Indian law," although that label would not actually be used until the U.S. Department of the Interior published Felix Cohen's *Handbook of Federal Indian Law* in 1942.

The case was a dispute among competing non-Native land speculators, each claiming ownership of Indigenous land. Although ownership of Indigenous land was at stake, no Indigenous nation was party to or participated in the case. And there was another nefarious aspect: the plaintiff and defendant connived to get it to court. They were not actually adversaries, but conspirators in what Professor Lindsay Robertson called "a collusive case, an attempt by speculators in Indian lands to . . . win a judgment from the Supreme Court recognizing their claim to millions of acres."[23]

To prevent the Court from discovering their collusion, the conspirators filed something called a "case stated," which today is called a "joint stipulation of facts." They did this to force the Court to choose between their competing legal theories even though there was no actual land dispute. They wanted the Court to settle a question that was crucial for all land speculators: How could non-Natives acquire ownership of Native lands under U.S. law?

The first stipulation in the case stated harked to the earliest colonial days. It said that in 1609, King James I of England granted to the earl of Salisbury and his associates land to establish "The Treasurer and Company of Adventurers and Planters of the City of London, for the first Colony in Virginia." The stipulation said that the parties were quarreling about lands within the royal grant. They also stipulated that the specific lands they were each claiming were within the Illinois and Piankeshaw nations, who "neither acknowledged nor owed any allegiance or obedience to any European sovereign or state whatever," including the king. They thus framed the legal issue as a question of the power of English royal prerogative versus the land rights of independent, sovereign Native peoples.[24]

The plaintiffs, Johnson et al., said that they had purchased the lands in a 1773 contract with the Illinois and a 1775 contract with the Piankeshaw. They said that both nations held title to their lands "by occupancy [which title] is to be respected, as much as that of an individual, obtained by the same right, in a civilized state." The only question, they said, was whether they as individuals could purchase that title or whether purchasing land from Native nations was "the exclusive prerogative of government."[25]

The plaintiffs' purchase contracts showed what they meant by the two alternative modes of purchase; they covered both bases. In doing so, they displayed the confusion of late-eighteenth-century English property law, which was teetering between feudal and market conceptions of land. In a verbose clause with many now-arcane verbs, the contract said that the Illinois and Piankeshaw nations "grant, bargain, sell, alien, enfeoff, release, ratify, and confirm to the [purchasers] their heirs and assigns, equally to be divided, or to George III, then King of Great Britain and Ireland, his heirs and successors, for the use, benefit, and behoof of all the [purchasers], their heirs and assigns, in severalty, by which ever of those tenures they might most legally hold."[26] In short, and in plainer English, the contracts said that they purchased title either directly, as individual buyers in an open market, or indirectly, as a feudal transaction via the English Crown—whichever one of these modes might be "most legal."

McIntosh, the defendant, avoided all this confusion. He claimed that he got title to the land in 1818 by a grant from the U.S. government. He sidestepped the plaintiffs' question of whether they, as individuals, could purchase title to Native land; he just argued that Indigenous nations had no title to sell. Period. He said that the colonizers, acting on behalf of the Crown, had already acquired title to all Indigenous lands as soon as they "discovered" the continent. He elaborated his argument by saying this principle was recognized by all "the civilized powers of Europe [who] . . . have uniformly disregarded [the Natives'] supposed right to the territory." He said, "The whole theory of . . . titles to lands in America, rests upon the hypothesis, that the Indians had no right of soil as sovereign, independent states. Discovery is the foundation of title, in European nations, and this overlooks all proprietary rights in the natives."[27]

McIntosh bolstered his discovery argument by saying that Native peoples were inherently inferior to the civilized colonizers. He added that their inferiority had legal consequences: "They are of that class who are said by jurists not to be citizens, but perpetual inhabitants with diminutive rights. The statutes of . . . all the . . . colonies, and of the United States, treat them as an inferior race of people."[28] In short, McIntosh said that the Illinois and Piankeshaw only *inhabited* the land; they did not *own* it.

With the stipulation of facts and the competing arguments in place, Chief Justice Marshall began the Court's opinion. He opened with the plaintiffs' question of whether their private purchase from the Illinois and the Piankeshaw nations "can be recognised in the Courts of the United States." He phrased it as the question: What is "the power of Indians to give, and of private individuals to receive, a title" to land? He ignored the alternative feudal mode of transfer. He then said, "The title to lands . . . depend[s] entirely on the law of the nation in which they lie."[29] Since the lands in dispute were in the Illinois and the Piankeshaw nations, it seemed that Marshall might next inquire about what their property laws were. But he ignored that question too.

Instead of examining Illinois and Piankeshaw laws, Marshall turned to the defendant's argument that "discovery is the foundation of title"[30] and adopted it, devoting his entire opinion to the proposition that "discovery gave exclusive title to those who made it" and asserting "the universal recognition" of this "principle."[31] He also adopted the defendant's Native inferiority argument and took it one step further, talking not only about the inferior character of Natives, but about their religion. He said, "The character and religion of the [Indigenous] inhabitants afforded an apology for considering them as a people over whom the superior genius of Europe might claim an ascendency."[32]

Marshall elaborated the meaning of this "ascendency," saying, "The potentates of the old world found no difficulty in convincing themselves that they made ample compensation to the inhabitants of the new, by bestowing on them civilization and Christianity" in exchange for claiming title to their lands. He described this as an outgrowth of the Christian colonizers' "right of acquisition."[33]

Marshall's rhetoric about exchange echoed the Puritan clergyman John Cotton's famous 1630 sermon, delivered to the Puritans as they boarded ship for the New World. Cotton preached to them, "Offend not the poore Natives, but as you partake in their land, so make them partakers of your precious faith: as you reape their temporalls, so feede them with your spirituals."[34] Marshall and Cotton alike referred to Christianity as both a *rationale* for colonial domination and a *compensation* for colonial domination! That theme was repeated by Georgia senator John Forsyth, speaking in the U.S. Senate in 1830 in favor of the genocidal Indian Removal Act. Forsyth said, "All Christendom seems to have imagined that by offering . . . immortal life, promised by the Prince of Peace to fallen man, to the aborigines of this country, the right was fairly acquired of disposing of their persons and their property at pleasure."[35]

Marshall referred to the papal bull authorizing Spain's Christian colonization and claim of ownership in the New World. He emphasized English monarchs relied on Christian discovery doctrine even more than the Spanish. He said, "No one of the powers of Europe gave its full assent to this principle, more unequivocally than England. . . . So early as the year 1496, her monarch granted a commission to the Cabots, to discover countries then unknown to *Christian people*, and to take possession of them in the name of the king of England." He said, "To this discovery the English trace their title."[36]

Marshall repeatedly stressed the Christian basis of the property doctrine that he was creating, saying, "The right of discovery given by [King Henry VII's] commission [to John Cabot—aka Giovanni Caboto, another Italian navigator], is confined to countries 'then unknown to all Christian people' . . . thus asserting a right to take possession, notwithstanding the occupancy of the natives, who were heathens, and, at the same time, admitting the prior title of any Christian people who may have made a previous discovery." Marshall stressed Christianity yet again in referring to the 1578 royal charter to Sir Humphrey Gilbert, renewed to Sir Walter Raleigh, and

James I's charter of 1606 to Sir Thomas Gates and others. He said that these charters gave "a right to take possession, notwithstanding the occupancy of the natives, who were heathens."[37]

Marshall then came to the ultimate question whether this doctrine of Christian discovery was part of U.S. law. He answered yes, "unequivocally": "The United States . . . have unequivocally acceded to that great and broad rule by which its civilized inhabitants now hold this country. They hold, and assert in themselves, the title by which it was acquired. They maintain, as all others have maintained, that discovery gave an exclusive right to extinguish the Indian title of occupancy, either by purchase or by conquest."[38]

In short, the *Johnson* decision said the United States had a "right" of Christian domination over non-Christian peoples, and this right automatically transformed Native peoples into "occupants" of their lands. Marshall concluded the opinion by saying that the plaintiffs' purchases from the Illinois and the Piankeshaw were invalid, and McIntosh's claim based on a U.S. grant was valid, because the United States, as heir to the discoverers, held title and could grant it to another. He wholly ignored the implications of the feudal language in the plaintiff's contract that would have made *them* the heirs to the English discoverers since their purchases preceded the formation of the United States. Marshall's aim from this case forward was to achieve federal dominance over all matters connected with Native peoples and lands. If that meant illogical leaps and diversions, so be it.

It's not as if Marshall were blind to the questionable nature of the doctrine of Christian discovery and the illogic of his opinion. He described the doctrine as an "extravagant . . . pretension of converting the discovery of an inhabited country into conquest." He elaborated the "extravagant pretension," saying, "this restriction [of Native ownership] may be opposed to natural right, and to the usages of civilized nations, yet, if it be indispensable to that system under which the country has been settled, and be adapted to the actual condition of the two people, it may, perhaps, be supported by reason, and certainly cannot be rejected by Courts of justice."[39]

To say the least, it was odd to say that a "pretension" cannot be questioned, especially if it "may be opposed to natural right, and to the usages of civilized nations" and it was only "perhaps" rational. And as for his statement that the pretense was "adapted to the actual condition of the two people," who can say? There were no Indigenous parties in the case to present evidence of their "condition."

Note again that Marshall did not say that Christian colonizers *conquered* Indigenous peoples; he said that they *pretended to have conquered*—"the pretension of converting discovery . . . into conquest." In Chapter 4, we will return to the legal and geopolitical significance of the difference between discovery theory and conquest. For now, though, it is sufficient to understand that a *pretense* lies at the roots of U.S. property law.

As we dig into the legal theory of the *Johnson* decision, it is necessary to remember that Marshall wrote the opinion in the context of the English common law of property. Although English conceptions were teetering between feudal and market relations, a key maxim of the law said, "Possession is nine-tenths of the law." The maxim meant that *actual occupancy* of land created a presumption of title. As Sir William Blackstone explained in his historic eighteenth-century common law treatise *Commentaries on the Laws of England*, "Actual possession is, *prima facie*, evidence of a legal title in the possessor. . . . Without such actual possession no title can be completely good."[40] As the law professor Kent McNeil explained in his 1989 *Common Law Aboriginal Title*, the common law rule meant that "since the indigenous people were in occupation, the presumptions of possession and title would be in their favour."[41]

This is why the plaintiffs in *Johnson* pointed out that the Illinois and Piankeshaw nations had possession of their lands: Native occupancy raised a property law presumption of Native title, which the Natives could transfer to the plaintiffs. Land speculators were all troubled by the fact that Native peoples were in possession of the land. Otherwise, there would have been no reason for the *Johnson* litigation.

Only a year before the *Johnson* decision, the Supreme Court had explained the common law maxim of possession in the case of *Ricard v. Williams*. Justice Joseph Story, who was also on the Court for the *Johnson* decision, wrote the opinion. He described the maxim this way: "Undoubtedly, if a person be found in possession of land, claiming it as his own, in fee [title], it is *prima facie* evidence of his ownership."[42]

The common law maxim of possession still exists in the twenty-first century—for non-Native land. A 2006 case, *Willcox v. Stroup*, in the Fourth Circuit Court of Appeals put it this way: "That possession is nine-tenths of the law is a truism hardly bearing repetition. Statements to this effect have existed almost as long as the common law itself. . . . The common law has long recognized that actual possession is, *prima facie*, evidence of a legal title in the possessor. . . . The presumption of law is that the person who has possession has the property."[43]

Marshall simply ignored the common law maxim; or, to put it technically, he created an *exception* to exclude Indigenous peoples from the law. The exception was that Natives were not capable of ownership because of their "character and religion." They were uncivilized heathens. For these reasons (though he said that it might not be reasonable), Marshall said that Native people's presence on the land did not constitute *possession*; they were merely *occupants*. By declaring an exception from the common law of property, Marshall converted Native landowners into tenants, a crucial step in establishing a U.S. empire spanning the continent.

In 2006, Professor Ken MacMillan argued that ordinary common law property rules "could not . . . establish . . . the legal foundations of empire. . . . Instead," he said, "the crown derived its authority from absolute prerogatives."[44] Marshall's exception explicitly adopted English imperial claims and royal prerogatives. He wrote, "The power now possessed by the government of the United States to grant lands, resided, while we were colonies, in the crown, or its grantees. . . . All our institutions recognise the absolute title of the crown, subject only to the Indian right of occupancy, and recognise the absolute title of the crown to extinguish that right."[45]

Kent McNeil's close analysis of the common law casts doubt on this expansive reading of Crown power. He wrote, "As against a subject who is in possession, the Crown must prove its present title just like anyone else."[46] The feudal system, he explained, differentiated between "lordship" and "seisin": The "lord" had rights to feudal services—knight service, for example—while "seisin" was the right to possess the land itself. In a nutshell, McNeil wrote, "The Crown would . . . be entitled to whatever services . . . might be due, but it would have no right to the land."[47] Thus, regarding royal grants, he said, "A grant by the Crown of lands held of it is always a grant of lordship, though on its face it may look like a grant of the soil."[48] McNeil concluded, "Chief Justice Marshall's . . . decisions . . . ignored common law principles and constructed a vague theory of Indian title on the basis of doubtful premises [sic] drawn to some extent from his own perceptions of international law. In effect, what Marshall did was invent a body of law which was virtually without precedent."[49]

Although Marshall described the exception as an extension of the feudal power of the English Crown, his definition dispensed with common law protections against the Crown described by McNeil: "The fiction of original Crown ownership cannot generally be used to support a Crown claim against persons who are in occupation (and therefore presumed to be in possession) because the law deems a Crown grant to have been made in those circumstances."[50]

Marshall's phrasing of the exception excluding Native peoples from the ordinary rules of land law was blunt, yet also subtle; he introduced the positive-sounding phrase "Indian title" as a camouflage for the negative phrase "mere occupancy." His rhetoric had the effect of hiding the exception. This has led countless commentators, lawyers, and scholars to praise Marshall for recognizing Native rights because he said, "It has never been contended, that the Indian title amounted to nothing."[51] It may be true that mere occupancy is not "nothing," but it is not title either. And without ownership of their lands, "Indian title" is not Native sovereignty.

The anthropologist Jonas Bens exemplified the effort to find a silver lining in *Johnson*. He went so far as to say, "I take the liberty . . . of characterizing *Johnson v. McIntosh* as an indigenous rights case, because what became case law in *Johnson* is . . . the idea that the Indian tribes are sovereign nations."[52] Bens's statement flies in the face of Marshall's explicit insistence that Natives' "rights to complete sovereignty, as independent nations, were necessarily diminished . . . by the original fundamental principle, that discovery gave exclusive title to those who made it."[53]

Bens didn't see that Marshall's exception from the common law deprived Native peoples of land *and* sovereignty. In fact, Bens argued the opposite— that the Marshall trilogy cases reveal "the unbroken sovereignty of indigenous communities after colonization." Having said this, however, Bens confusedly recognized that there is an exception at work, saying that Native peoples were "somehow diminished in terms of their sovereignty." At another point in his analysis, Bens said, "A sovereign entity is governed only by its own rules or by rules derived indirectly from its own sovereignty."[54] His failure to see the exception is what made all this confusion possible.

Commentators frequently fall prey to the conventional hagiography of John Marshall as a "friend of the Indians." It is not unusual to find Marshall lauded as the "greatest judicial advocate of Indian sovereignty."[55] It has been said that Marshall wrote the *Johnson* opinion unthinkingly and created legal doctrine "completely incidentally . . . with no sense of depth of impact."[56]

The truth of the matter is that *Johnson v. McIntosh* is *not* "a story of unintended consequences," nor is it "a doctrine intended to be of limited application."[57] Marshall's careful parsing of Christian discovery, his vigilance in tracing the doctrine to support a U.S. crown, and his insistence on absolute U.S. dominion over Indigenous lands all demonstrated a clear intention to legalize U.S. domination over Indigenous peoples. Moreover, *Johnson* and the Marshall trilogy as a whole have as much to do with the battle between federal and state powers as they do with Indigenous peoples. To put it another way, what was at issue in the cases was White colonizer power systems competing for political-economic control of an emerging empire. Native lands were the object of that struggle and Native peoples the plaything. Marshall defined the exception to fit that scheme.

The beatification of Marshall as the "definer of a nation"[58] indicates the context in which the trilogy of Native cases were decided. Marshall celebrated federalism as a basis for national cohesion and westward expansion of the United States into an empire. He led the Supreme Court through a convoluted period of postrevolutionary politics to establish the notion of a supreme constitutional law to protect federal supremacy and the security of private property derived from his interpretation of crown power.

Eric Cheyfitz viewed the *Johnson* decision as "the work of an imperial culture." He said that Marshall's opinion evinced "a need to repress a truly threatening opposition"—namely, Indigenous kinship modes of landholding. These presented "a powerful . . . critique of . . . expansive, acquisitive capitalism . . . that Marshall . . . with . . . the dream of empire boiling in [his] brain could not afford to entertain."[59]

In 1903, the Supreme Court carried the *Johnson* "right of discovery" beyond a claim of title to Native lands to include a right to "interfere with or determine" the "Indian occupancy" itself. The case in question was *Lone Wolf v. Hitchcock*. Justice Edward White, who would later become chief justice of the Court, wrote a unanimous opinion giving discovery doctrine a name that it still carries—"congressional plenary power." He cited *Johnson* and said, "Plenary authority over the tribal relations of the Indians has been exercised by Congress from the beginning." He said that no matter how "sacred" the occupancy of the Natives might be, it did not block the power of the U.S. Congress over their lands. He also ruled that the power was not limited, even by treaties the United States made with Native peoples: "When . . . treaties were entered into between the United States and a tribe of Indians it was never doubted that the power to abrogate existed in Congress." In an oblique reference to the religious basis of the doctrine, White added, "It is to be presumed that in this matter the United States would be governed by such considerations of justice as would control a Christian people in their treatment of an ignorant and dependent race."[60] In 1979, Judge Philip Nichols, Jr., of the U.S. Court of Claims, said, "The day *Lone Wolf* was handed down, January 5, 1903, might be called one of the blackest days in the history of the American Indian, the Indians' *Dred Scott* decision."[61]

Ultimately, as subsequent case law has developed it, Marshall's exception created an entirely new juridical zone unknown to the common law and the English Crown: a zone of absolute, unlimited power in the name of U.S. sovereignty. Moreover, despite the phrasing "congressional plenary power," the exception is a judicial creation—an assertion of supreme judicial power. As Supreme Court justice William Rehnquist put it in 1978, treaties and legislation form "the backdrop for the intricate web of judicially made Indian law."[62]

In 1991, the attorney Mark Savage demonstrated that the judicial web was made up out of whole cloth. He said, "Examination of the text of the Constitution, the intentions of the Framers, contemporary notions about sovereignty, the records of the Continental Congress, and contemporary treaties with Native American Nations makes it clear that the Constitution has never granted to the United States a plenary power over Native Americans."[63]

Not coincidentally, the *Johnson* decision had personal significance for Marshall's property interests. Although it is often passed over in hagiographies of Marshall, he was a well-known land speculator and, as Lindsay Robertson put it, was "guided by his own interests at the time the case . . . came before him."[64] Specifically, *Johnson's* adoption of Christian discovery doctrine assured the Marshall family of title to thousands of acres of land in Virginia and Kentucky under a 1649 grant by King Charles II to Lord Fairfax. The smoking gun in the opinion is the passage referring to "the sale of that country which now constitutes Kentucky, a country, every acre of which was then claimed and possessed by Indians."[65] By the end of the 1780s, Marshall claimed ownership of over 200,000 acres in Kentucky, and his father and his brothers claimed about

twice that amount.[66] *Johnson v. McIntosh* thus involved corruption and conniv-
ance not only by the parties, but by the chief justice himself. Corruption was
part and parcel of the extravagant pretension of Christian discovery.

As Professor Walter Echo-Hawk put it, "A judicial conflict of interest . . .
should have disqualified Marshall from participating in the *Johnson* case. . . .
[He had] enormous property or financial interests at stake in the outcome of
*Johnson* that compelled him to side with M'Intosh; and that is precisely what
he did."[67]

Marshall's corrupt role as a judge speculating in Native lands put him in
the company of "virtually every prominent leader during the Revolutionary
War and first and second-generation American politicians." Echo-Hawk
pointed out, "Schoolbook fixtures like George Washington, John Marshall,
Thomas Jefferson, Andrew Jackson, as well as most of the governors, judges,
and legislators of the thirteen states were heavily involved in the buying, sell-
ing, investing in, or otherwise acquiring . . . Indian land."[68] *Fletcher v. Peck,*
the notorious Yazoo lands case,[69] where the entire Georgia legislature but
one had been bribed to approve a speculative transaction in Native lands,
resulted in a Supreme Court opinion by Marshall that upheld the transaction. George Washington revealed his corruption in a letter quoted by Echo-
Hawk: "notwithstanding the [1763 Royal] Proclamation that restrains
[purchases of Native lands] at present . . . I can never look upon the Proclamation in any other light (but this I say between ourselves) than as a temporary expedient to quiet the Minds of the Indians . . . Any person therefore
who neglects the present opportunity of hunting out good Lands and in
some measure marking and distinguishing them for their own (in order to
keep others from settling them) will never regain it."[70]

Echo-Hawk said that land speculation drove the U.S. economy of the
time. To put a finer point on it, the United States was itself a land office business following the pattern set by the Virginia Company and other colonial
companies, whose charters established joint-stock enterprises to colonize
Native lands "not . . . possessed by any *Christian* prince or people."[71] Contrary to the stereotypical image of the colonizers as simple farmers looking
for land, Kent McNeil pointed out, "Most of [the colonial charters] were
granted during the seventeenth century when the great landholders in England were still essentially feudal lords, and . . . generally covered immense
regions. . . . Clearly, the grantees were not simple farmers who were going to
the New World to cultivate the soil themselves. They were lords on a grand
scale." McNeil quoted the 1745 English Chancery decision in *Penn v. Lord
Baltimore*, a case involving the boundary between Pennsylvania and Maryland, where the court said, "This is a question between feudatory Lords, proprietors of provinces."[72] Briefly put, the colonies were *companies*; their
progeny after the American Revolution was a confederation of state companies followed by a federal company that persists to this day.

This perspective on the United States as a land-appropriation business sheds new light on the constitutional scholar William F. Swindler's editorial note to his collection of Virginia constitutional documents. He wrote, "The first successful English colony in North America was also the site of the first permanent government, and hence the constitutional history of Virginia is essentially the constitutional history of the nation."[73]

In short, Marshall invented the exception in *Johnson* to confirm for the United States the land-appropriation business model of royally chartered joint-stock companies. He did this to benefit himself and similarly situated "founding fathers" who were amassing the equivalent of feudal estates that they could turn around and sell. He did it to ensure the business of the United States itself, describing the cessions of state land claims to the nation, including Virginia's cession of claims to Illinois and Piankeshaw country, as having "granted a productive fund to the government of the Union."[74]

As Professor Colin Calloway explained, "The Indian policy of the new nation was essentially land policy." He said, "The nation's security, prosperity, and future depended upon converting Indian country into American real estate, creating a national market in Indian lands, and turning Indian homelands and hunting territories over to commercial agriculture and economic development." For example, he cited the fact that "the United States would spend $5 million, almost five-sixths of the total federal expenditures for the period 1790–96, fighting the Indian confederation [defending the Ohio River], and it needed land sales to foot the bill."[75]

Joel Richard Paul wrote that at the time Marshall wrote the *Johnson* opinion, the phrase "extravagant pretense" was "in common usage in America and Britain to describe any false idea worthy of debunking."[76] Emer de Vattel, the famous eighteenth-century international law scholar, debunked "the dangerous error or extravagant pretense of those who . . . extravagantly set [themselves] up as defenders of the cause of God . . . [and] of a people not committed to their superintendency."[77]

Whether or not Marshall was aware of Vattel's critique (and he was certainly aware of Vattel and of the epithet "extravagant pretense"), he took the occasion of the second decision in his trilogy, *Cherokee Nation v. Georgia*, to build the next step in federal anti-Indian law by declaring a U.S. "superintendency" over Indigenous nations.

## Cherokee Nation v. Georgia

On January 1, 1831, the U.S. Supreme Court decided *Cherokee Nation v. Georgia*.[78] The decision declared that Indigenous nations are not independent, but rather "domestic dependent nations" under U.S. domination, which Marshall said "resemble[d] [the relation] of a ward to his guardian." The basis for the decision was Christian discovery doctrine: "They occupy a territory to which we assert a title independent of their will."[79]

As we have discussed, there were no Native parties in *Johnson v. McIntosh*, when the court adopted Christian discovery. That decision applied directly only to non-Native land speculators. Marshall took the opportunity in *Cherokee Nation* to turn Christian discovery doctrine directly against a Native nation and to make a pronouncement that would attack all Native nations.

The *Cherokee Nation* case was brought by John Ross, the principal chief of the Cherokee Nation, in an effort to enforce Cherokee treaties with the United States and protect Cherokee territory from armed invasion by the state of Georgia. Between 1828 and 1830, the Georgia legislature enacted a series of laws claiming jurisdiction over Cherokee lands and parceling out those lands to Whites by lottery. The legislation also purported to abolish the Cherokee government. It declared Cherokee laws "null and void and of no effect, as if the same had never existed,"[80] and made it a "high misdemeanor punishable by imprisonment . . . at hard labor for four years, for the Cherokee to call a council"[81] or take any other governmental action under their own laws.

These legislative acts were the culmination of efforts beginning in 1802, when Georgia ceded to the United States a large portion of territory that the state claimed under a 1732 charter from England's King George II (territory that became Alabama and Mississippi). The Georgia cession contained language committing the United States to "extinguish Indian title" to the remaining lands in Georgia "as early as the same can be peaceably obtained, on reasonable terms."[82] When the Cherokee were still in possession of their ancestral lands thirty years later, Georgia took matters into its own hands.

The Cherokee Nation responded by suing the state directly in the U.S. Supreme Court, asking for an injunction. They said that the suit came within the power of the court under the U.S. Constitution to enforce treaties as part of what the Constitution called the "supreme law of the land." They added that they could bring the case directly to the Supreme Court (known as the court's "original jurisdiction") because it was a "controversy between a State . . . and a foreign State."

Jonas Bens described the Cherokees' approach to the Supreme Court as a "change [in] their political strategy" following President Andrew Jackson's refusal to deal with them on an intergovernmental basis and enforce the treaties. He added that the Cherokee found it "insufficient to deal with the United States merely 'from the outside,' government to government, as a foreign state would do; rather, they had to become engaged in the internal political processes of the Union."[83] Bens referred to Cherokee political efforts as "playing Indian," saying, "They 'play themselves' for the nonindigenous audience and engage in an 'indigenous performance.'"[84]

But in the lawsuit itself, the Cherokee presented their case as a government-to-government matter. They presented the lawsuit as a sovereign treaty partner seeking enforcement of treaty terms. They were not "playing" at anything. As Bens ultimately acknowledged, their "strategy was to address the Supreme Court directly about the enforcement of treaty rights."[85] Glen Coulthard described a similar strategy in the 1975 Dene Declaration, which demanded recognition from the Canadian state, saying that it "sought to protect the intricately interconnected social totality of a distinct mode of life. . . . George Barnaby wrote . . . 'The land claim is our fight to gain recognition as a different group of people—with our own way of seeing things, our own values, our own life style, our own laws. . . . [It] is a fight for self-determination using our own system with which we have survived till now.'"[86]

As part of their defense of separate national identity, the Cherokee explicitly attacked the doctrine of Christian discovery. They said that it violated the natural law of nations. In an echo of how the Piankeshaw and Illinois were described in *Johnson*, they described themselves as "a foreign state, not owing allegiance to the United States, nor to any state." They said that they had existed on their lands "from time immemorial . . . [as] a sovereign and independent state." They emphasized, "Long before the first approach of the white men of Europe . . . the Cherokee nation were the occupants and owners of the territory . . . the sole and exclusive masters, governed, of right, by no other laws, usages, and customs [than their own]."[87]

They ridiculed royal grants to colonize Cherokee lands issued by "the monarch of . . . islands on the eastern coast of the Atlantic ocean" under a "pretended title by . . . discovery" and said such grants have "no effect in divesting the prior title of the Indian[s]." They described the theory of title by discovery as "wild and chimerical." They said that the Cherokee and other Indigenous nations who were "in possession of the country" had "both the exclusive right to their territory and the exclusive right of self-government within that territory." William Wirt, one of their attorneys, referred to the Christian discovery papal bull as "the monstrous pretensions of Pope Alexander."[88]

Georgia refused to participate in the court proceedings. The state filed no answer to the Cherokee complaint and sent no lawyer to represent it. In fact, it took advantage of the lawsuit to issue statements denying the power of the U.S. Supreme Court over *any* acts of the state, inflaming secessionist, antifederal sentiment throughout the South.

Marshall opened his *Cherokee Nation* opinion by acknowledging "the character of the Cherokees as a State as a distinct political society, separated from others, capable of managing its own affairs and governing itself."[89] He then shifted his attention to the clauses in the U.S. Constitution that the Cherokee said authorized the lawsuit. He asked, "Is the Cherokee Nation a foreign state in the sense in which that term is used in the Constitution?" He said that this is "a question of much . . . difficulty."[90]

The difficulty of the question, Marshall said, arises from "the condition of the Indians in relation to the United States." In phrases clearly showing federal anti-Indian law as an exception from ordinary law, he said, "The relation of the Indians to the United States is marked by peculiar and cardinal distinctions which exist nowhere else." Indeed, he said that the relation "is perhaps unlike that of any other two people in existence."[91]

Marshall explicitly described the "peculiar" relation in terms of the Christian discovery exception. He put it this way: "It may well be doubted whether those tribes which reside within the acknowledged boundaries of the United States can, with strict accuracy, be denominated foreign nations. . . . They occupy a territory to which we assert a title independent of their will."[92] In short, Marshall's definition of "peculiar" was a straight reiteration of the *Johnson v. McIntosh* Christian discovery claim of title to Native lands.

Having declared that the Cherokee Nation was not independent because the United States claimed title to their lands, Marshall then said that the Cherokee Nation was not legally qualified to sue the state of Georgia in the Supreme Court because it was not a "foreign state." If the Cherokee wanted to sue Georgia, it would have to file in a lower court, perhaps even a Georgia court, and then appeal to the Supreme Court. He denied its request for an injunction and dismissed the case. He washed the court's hands of the matter, saying, "If it be true that the Cherokee Nation have rights, this is not the tribunal in which those rights are to be asserted."[93]

Marshall coined a metaphor for the U.S. claim of domination that persists to this day. It was another way of describing the exception. He said, "Indians . . . may more correctly, perhaps, be denominated domestic dependent nations. . . . Their relations to the United States resemble that of a ward to his guardian."[94] His hesitant phrasing of this ward/guardian metaphor— "may . . . perhaps"—echoed his tentative language in *Johnson* that Christian discovery "may, perhaps, be supported by reason."[95] But, as in *Johnson*, Marshall was adamant in his conclusion about total U.S. domination: "The Indians . . . and their country are . . . completely under the sovereignty and dominion of the United States."[96]

Marshall's metaphorical formulation of U.S. domination as guardianship persists in federal anti-Indian law today as one of its most versatile dresses, invoked whenever the United States decides to take any action regarding Native lands and peoples. The "ward/guardian" phrase has become "trust relationship"; and "domestic dependency" has become "government-to-government relation." Despite the modernized lingo, the insistence on U.S. domination remains unchanged.

Marshall's opinion pulled off another rhetorical trick that also still resonates today. He framed his denial of Cherokee independent nationhood (and therefore the denial of Supreme Court jurisdiction)—the exception—within a discussion of the U.S. Constitution. This rhetorical strategy has persuaded many observers to discuss federal anti-Indian law not as an exception from law, but as if it were a branch of ordinary constitutional law.

In 2002, Supreme Court justice Stephen Breyer spoke to the Georgia Historical Society about Marshall's purported constitutional analysis in *Cherokee Nation*. Breyer pointed out that Marshall's reason for dismissing the case, because the Cherokee Nation was "not a foreign state," ignored an entirely different constitutional basis to take the case. Breyer pointed to the opening lines of the judicial power section of the Constitution—Article III, Section 2—that say, "The judicial power shall extend to all cases . . . arising under this Constitution, the laws of the United States, *and treaties*." He pointed out that this treaty clause in Article III was "strangely absent" from Marshall's opinion.

Breyer added that Marshall also ignored the part of Article III, s. 2, that says the Supreme Court "shall have original jurisdiction" (meaning cases brought directly in the court) in "all cases . . . in which a state shall be party." He reminded his audience that both parts of Article III were present in the case: "The Cherokees . . . argued that their case arises under a treaty" and that the State of Georgia was "a party"; therefore, he said, the case met the constitutional requirements for original jurisdiction in the Supreme Court.

In fact, in oral argument in *Cherokee Nation*, John Sergeant, one of the Cherokees' attorneys, made the very same argument as Breyer. He said that the Cherokee Nation was a foreign nation, but that factor wasn't necessary because Georgia—a state—was a party to the case. Sergeant argued, "The original jurisdiction of the supreme court . . . depends upon the fact that a state . . . is a party." He added, "It matters not who may be the other party."[97] As Breyer commented to the Georgia Historical Society, "Chief Justice Marshall did not describe the flaw, if any, in this jurisdictional logic."[98]

As Justice Breyer said, Marshall wholly ignored the treaty basis for jurisdiction, neither discussing it nor pointing out any flaw. He simply skipped the opening sentence of Article III, referring to "cases arising under . . . treaties," and jumped to the closing sentence, referring to "controversies . . . between a State . . . and foreign states." Marshall devoted his entire *Cherokee Nation* opinion to analyzing only that closing clause.

The phrasing of Article III, unlike many other parts of the Constitution, is not ambiguous; it does not require deep interpretation to discern the intent of the framers about the scope of U.S. judicial power. As Breyer noted, it opens by saying, "The judicial power shall extend to all cases, in law and equity, arising under this Constitution, the laws of the United States, and treaties." The article then lists a variety of other cases under U.S. judicial power, including cases "affecting ambassadors" and involving "maritime jurisdiction." It adds a series of "controversies," including "between a state . . . and foreign states." Article III then says, "In all cases affecting ambassadors, [etc.], and those in which a state shall be party, the Supreme Court shall have original jurisdiction." So there we have it: Article III refers to "cases arising under . . . treaties" and to "cases in which a state shall be a party." The literal constitutional text ties Supreme Court jurisdiction to "cases" between "parties." *Cherokee Nation* was a "case arising under a treaty" and a "case in which a state is a party." As Breyer pointed out, the Constitution provided jurisdiction for the Court to take the case.

The only possibility for ambiguity in Article III is whether a "case" is the same as a "controversy." No one has ever clarified the distinction between case and controversy. In fact, the two words are almost always used together, as in the rule that U.S. courts do not decide hypothetical questions, but only questions that arise in a "case or controversy." As Professor Charles Alan Wright, the author of a major treatise on federal procedure, said, "The two terms can be used interchangeably."[99]

Actually, since the *Cherokee* case is covered by clauses using the same word, "cases," we can ignore the possible ambiguity about "controversies." It is irrelevant. Nevertheless, there is a reason to explore the possible ambiguity. In doing so, we will expose incoherence and mendacity in Marshall's denial of jurisdiction to hear the Cherokee case.

If we assume for the sake of discussion that there is an ambiguity about whether a "case" is a "controversy," we will see that Marshall's exclusive focus on the difference between a "state" and a "foreign state" was wholly irrelevant. The Article III phrase referring to "states" and "foreign states" is in the clause following the word "controversies," whereas the original jurisdiction clause begins with the word "cases." Marshall pretended to be doing a close reading of the Constitution, but he did not pay attention to where the crucial words appear. Despite his reputation for rhetorical skill, there was no coherence in his analysis.

The driving force in Marshall's analysis (if we can call it that, given its incoherence) was his determination to apply Christian discovery doctrine directly to a Native nation. The only way that he could do that was *not* to take the Cherokee case—to banish it. Banishment ramified the *Johnson* property law exception into a constitutional exception. In short, *Cherokee Nation* built Christian discovery into a two-faceted exception.

Marshall's mendacity (what else to call it?) becomes even more obvious when we take a short detour to compare his *Cherokee Nation* analysis of original jurisdiction in Article III with another of his opinions on the same article—*Cohens v. State of Virginia*, decided in 1821. The *Cohens* case was brought to the Supreme Court on appeal; in other words, it was not brought originally in the Supreme Court. *Cohens* did not involve a treaty, but it was a case invoking the laws of the United States and was thus covered by the same opening clause—"arising under this Constitution, the laws of the United States, and treaties." And, as the case name indicates, a state was a party.

In 1994, Professor James Pfander studied the *Cohens* decision in his critique of the notion that Supreme Court original jurisdiction does not extend to cases arising under the Constitution and treaties. Recall that this was a key part of Marshall's argument in *Cherokee Nation*—namely, that the treaty was not a basis for suing Georgia directly in the Supreme Court.

Pfander began by saying, "The Court and most scholars have long assumed" that the first clause of Article III does not provide original jurisdiction. He said that this assumption "is difficult to sustain in light of the text."[100] He pointed out what we have already seen and what Justice Breyer pointed out—that the text of Article III does not exclude the category of cases under treaties from the category of cases in which a state is a party. The text also does not require cases arising under treaties to come to the Court only on appeal.

Pfander said that the debates during the drafting of the U.S. Constitution confirmed the literal reading of the text. He said, "The framers intended the term 'cases' to apply . . . to all disputes that touched upon subjects of national concern"[101] (i.e., disputes "arising under this Constitution, the laws of the United States, and treaties"). Professor Charles Wright's *Federal Practice & Procedure: Jurisdiction* supported Pfander's view, saying that a literal reading is the "better view" of Article III.[102]

We do not need to explore this Article III issue for itself. We only look at it to emphasize that the supposed constitutional restriction that Marshall said blocked the Cherokee lawsuit is a nonliteral reading of the text, not in accord with the constitutional debates. We use this insight to set the stage for a further analysis of Marshall's mendacity. Bear with this discussion for a moment.

It was Marshall who initiated the nonliteral reading of Article III. He did it in an incidental remark in the *Cohens* case. Although *Cohens* was a case about the Supreme Court's *appellate* jurisdiction [cases on appeal, as opposed to cases originating in the court], Marshall digressed from the subject to talk about original jurisdiction. It was there that he presented his nonliteral reading, which became the dominant reading, saying, "The constitution declares the jurisdiction, in cases where a State shall be a party, to be original, and in all cases arising under the constitution or a law, to be appellate." (He did not quote the entire "arising under" clause, which, as we have seen, includes treaties.) As was his style, Marshall simply asserted this nonliteral reading of Article III as if it were self-explanatory, despite its obvious deviation from the text.[103]

Here's the strange part that reveals Marshall's mendacity. Before he made these remarks, he pointed to a possible loophole in a nonliteral reading of Article III: What happens, he asked, if a state is a party *and* the case arises under the Constitution, U.S. laws, and treaties? "What rule is applicable to such a case?" He answered his question by saying that it would be "the duty of the court . . . to construe the constitution as to give effect to both provisions, as far as it is possible to reconcile them, and not to permit their seeming repugnancy to destroy each other." He said, "We must endeavor so to construe them as to preserve the true intent and meaning of the instrument."[104] In other words, Marshall said that he would find a way to bend his interpretation of Article III to take such a case.

Now, as we noted previously, *Cohens* was an appeal to the Supreme Court from a Virginia court. Virginia argued that the Supreme Court did not have appellate jurisdiction over the case because Article III mandates "original jurisdiction" when a state is a party; thus, the state said that the appeal should be dismissed.

But Marshall wanted to take the case. He acknowledged that the appellant Cohens framed the issue as "arising under the laws of the United States," which he had already said could be brought only by appellate jurisdiction. He then reconciled that little problem by going through a convoluted *negative* analysis of Article III; he focused on what the text did *not* say. He said that it "does *not* say that . . . appellate jurisdiction shall *not* be exercised in cases where, from their nature, appellate jurisdiction is given, whether a State be or be not a party."[105] In other words, Marshall said that it didn't matter that a state was a party, even though he had just said a state party called for original jurisdiction. Based on this negative analysis, he rejected Virginia's argument and took the *Cohens* case.

The point here is that if Marshall had wanted to take the Cherokee case, he could have gone through the same kind of negative analysis to get around his nonliteral reading of Article III. He could have said, "Article III does *not* say that treaty cases shall *not* be brought under original jurisdiction, where, from their parties [i.e., a state is a party,] original jurisdiction is given." Such a negative analysis would have provided a basis to accept the Cherokee case. But Marshall was not interested in taking that case.

Marshall also could have borrowed another statement he made in *Cohens*, where he said that the court must be ready to deal with "cases . . . of direct legislative resistance . . . opposing the . . . government." He said that the government must be able "to protect itself and its laws." Compare the issues in the two cases to evaluate what Marshall regarded as "resistance opposing the government."[106] *Cohens* arose from a District of Columbia lottery ticket seller marketing tickets in Virginia. *Cherokee Nation* arose from Georgia's invasion of the Cherokee Nation in violation of U.S. treaties. Marshall apparently thought that the lottery business in the District of Columbia had a greater significance than U.S. treaties with Native nations.

Yet another of Marshall's statements in *Cohens* would have supported taking the *Cherokee* case despite his nonliteral reading of the foreign state clause. In *Cohens*, Marshall referred to the "very important part" of Article III, section 2—the "cases arising under" clause—and said that the purpose of that clause was "to give jurisdiction where the character of the parties would not give it."[107] It was somehow "very important" to Marshall to take jurisdiction over the state of Virginia in *Cohens,* even though it conflicted with his nonliteral reading of the article, and yet it was not important to take jurisdiction in *Cherokee Nation*.

Marshall's overall rhetorical approaches to *Cohens* and *Cherokee Nation* are sharply contrasting. He opened his *Cherokee Nation* opinion with a perfunctory expression of sympathy: "If Courts were permitted to indulge their sympathies, a case better calculated to excite them can scarcely be imagined." He closed it with a stony-hearted conclusion: "If it be true that wrongs have been inflicted, and that still greater are to be apprehended, this is not the tribunal which can redress the past or prevent the future."[108]

Compare that language with his full-throated championing of the importance of taking the *Cohens* lottery case, where he said, "The judiciary cannot . . . avoid a measure because it approaches the confines of the constitution. We cannot pass it by because it is doubtful. With whatever doubts, with whatever difficulties, a case may be attended, we must decide it, if it be brought before us. . . . Questions may occur which we would gladly avoid; but we cannot avoid them. All we can do is, to exercise our best judgment, and conscientiously to perform our duty."[109]

Marshall's rhetoric in both cases displays what Pfander called "vintage Marshall": "great rhetorical power, invocation of the constitutional text less as the basis of decision than as a peg on which to hang a result evidently reached on other grounds . . . a tendency to resolve difficult questions by aggressive assertion of one side of the case, and an absolute certainty in the correctness of his conclusions."[110]

What Breyer called the "strange absence" of any discussion of Article III treaty-based judicial power was not an oversight. Marshall intentionally ignored the treaty clause; he didn't want to take the Cherokee case. He had a mission to accomplish, and it required a dismissal on grounds that would apply the doctrine of Christian discovery to a Native nation. He mined treaty language throughout the opinion to support his conclusion that the Cherokee did not constitute a foreign state, but he ignored the treaties as a basis for jurisdiction. In ignoring them, Marshall made them something less than international agreements among independent nations; they became historical incidents in an all-consuming U.S. drive toward continental domination. In short, Marshall placed the Cherokee treaties in the exception that he had created in *Johnson*. Professor Mark Rifkin says that in *Cherokee*, "the concept of *nationhood* works as a discursive placeholder . . . that simultaneously recognizes and evacuates Cherokee sovereignty while cutting off an avenue for political redress."[111]

There's an intriguing twist in the history of these two cases: What Marshall said about "ward/guardian" and Article III were extraneous remarks; they were not actually necessary to the decisions—they were digressions. In legal jargon, they were "dicta"—remarks that a judge makes in passing. But in each instance, Marshall's dicta became dogma. As Pfander said, the "poorly thought out" *Cohens* remarks about original jurisdiction became "bedrock limits" in Article III jurisprudence: "The clear text of the Constitution has been submerged under the weight of two hundred years of precedent."[112] Similarly, Marshall's infamous "ward/guardian" metaphor in *Cherokee Nation*—Native peoples "may, perhaps, be denominated domestic, dependent nations"—has become a bedrock doctrine of federal anti-Indian domination of Native peoples.

Jonas Bens not only provided an example of taking the dicta as dogma, but he also misread the dicta. He said that the "remarkable phrase 'domestic dependent nation' . . . actually acknowledged the sovereign character of the Indians with the word 'nation.'" In fact, as we saw, Marshall's "domestic" label explicitly denied that the Cherokee are foreign; and his assertion that the United States holds a title against their will explicitly claimed U.S. ownership of Cherokee lands. Bens subsequently came close to recognizing that there is an exception at work. He said, "'Domestic dependent nation' grammatically embodies what I [call] 'the indigenous paradox': the Cherokees are foreign and domestic at the same time."[113] He added that the Cherokee were "neither a foreign state nor part of the United States but something in between."[114]

The *Cherokee Nation* decision was not unanimous. Two justices—Smith Thompson and Joseph Story—took issue with Marshall's extension of the exception. Their dissent said that the Supreme Court did have jurisdiction to hear the Cherokee case. They based their conclusion on the writings of the influential eighteenth-century international law scholar Emer de Vattel, *The Law of Nations: Or, Principles of the Law of Nature Applied to the Conduct and Affairs of Nations and Sovereigns.*[115]

Vattel discussed rules for "unequal alliances." He wrote, "A weak state, that, in order to provide for its safety, places itself under the protection of a more powerful one without stripping itself of the right of government and sovereignty, does not cease on this account to be placed among the sovereigns who acknowledge no other power."[116] To determine whether a nation deserves to be called an independent sovereign state, Vattel said that it is "sufficient . . . that . . . it govern[s] itself by its own authority and laws."[117]

According to Vattel's test, said Thompson and Story, "It is not perceived how it is possible to escape the conclusion that [the Cherokee] form a sovereign state."[118] The fact that the Cherokee had "yield[ed] up by treaty, from time to time, portions of their land" did not remove their "sovereignty and self-government over what remained."[119]

Thompson and Story did not challenge the Christian discovery exception itself. They passed over that subject, saying, "It does not fall within the scope and object of the present inquiry [i.e., their dissent] to go into a critical examination of the nature and extent of the rights growing out of [Native] occupancy."[120] Had they wanted to critique those concepts, they could have again quoted Vattel, who sharply challenged "those ambitious Europeans who attacked the American [i.e., Native] nations, and subjected them to their insatiable avidity of dominion, in order, as they pretended, for civilizing them, and causing them to be instructed in the true religion; these usurpers, I say, grounded themselves on a pretence equally unjust and ridiculous."[121]

Rather than critique the Christian discovery exception and the notion of "mere occupancy," Thompson and Story sidestepped it. They said, "It is immaterial whether [the Cherokee have] a mere right of occupancy or an absolute right to the soil. The complaint is for a violation, or threatened violation, of the possessory right. And this is a right, in the enjoyment of which they are entitled to protection."[122] By steering clear of the occupancy doctrine while arguing for jurisdiction, they maneuvered within the exception. Nevertheless, their dissent shows us what was thinkable in the early development of the exception—what forks in the road were *not* taken.

One year later, in *Worcester v. Georgia*, the final case of the trilogy, Marshall intensified the exception to consolidate ultimate dominion and absolute ultimate title to Native lands in the federal government, thus coordinating federal anti-Indian law with his overall drive toward federal supremacy.

## *Worcester v. Georgia*

On January 1, 1832, the U.S. Supreme Court issued the last decision in the Marshall trilogy, *Worcester v. Georgia*.[123] Marshall's opinion in the case completed the foundation of federal anti-Indian law. He used *Worcester* to position Indigenous lands and peoples under exclusive U.S. control, excluding the states from asserting their own Christian discovery claims. This double supremacy— over Indigenous peoples and over the individual states—was a major advance toward Marshall's federalist goal of creating a national government in dominant control of the continent, which, as the law professor Craig Joyce put it, was "the organizing principle of Marshall Court jurisprudence."[124]

The *Worcester* opinion also defined a limited domain of Indigenous internal affairs, which Marshall described as an arena for Natives' "self-government so far as respected themselves only." This aspect of the opinion confuses many readers, especially those who would like to find a silver lining in the Marshall trilogy—a last-minute change of heart on Marshall's part as he watched "Indian removal" in progress. We will examine this confusion next.

The *Worcester* case, like *Cherokee Nation*, arose from Georgia's invasion of Cherokee lands. This time, the plaintiffs were American citizens, Samuel Worcester, from Vermont, and Elizur Butler, from Connecticut. They were missionaries to the Cherokee sent by the American Board of Commissioners for Foreign Missions to spread Christian civilization.

Georgia saw the missionaries as interlopers and charged them with the crime of "residing within the limits of the Cherokee Nation without a [state] license. . . . [and] without having taken the oath to support and defend the Constitution and laws of the State of Georgia." The potential penalty was four years of hard labor in the penitentiary. Georgia governor George Gilmer offered to pardon the missionaries if they took the required oath. They refused.

The missionaries protested that Georgia had no jurisdiction over them. They said that they were in Cherokee territory, "under the authority of the President of the United States . . . and with the permission and approval of the . . . Cherokee Nation, and in accordance with the humane policy of the Government of the United States for the civilization and improvement of the Indians." They continued that Cherokee treaties with the United States "acknowledge the . . . Cherokee Nation to be a sovereign nation, authorised to govern themselves and all persons who have settled within their territory."[125]

The county judge rejected the missionaries' arguments, and a jury took only fifteen minutes to convict them, whereupon the judge sentenced them to the maximum: four years of hard labor in the penitentiary. Worcester and Butler appealed to the U.S. Supreme Court, represented by a local lawyer, Elisha Chester, and William Wirt and John Sergeant, the two lawyers who had handled the *Cherokee Nation* case. Marshall's opinion voided the convictions and sentences.

The *Worcester* case epitomized the fact that the battle for supremacy over Native lands was a contest between the federal government and the states. The *Johnson* and *Cherokee Nation* decisions had already declared that Native peoples did not have title to their lands—they fell into an exception from property law. The issue remaining to be decided in *Worcester* was which colonizer government controlled that exception.

Marshall began his opinion by distinguishing the *Worcester* case from *Cherokee Nation*, saying that the case involved "the personal liberty of a citizen." He added that the case also involved "the rights, if they have any, the political existence of a once numerous and powerful people [i.e., the Cherokee]."[126]

Marshall tried to skate by the troublesome political issue lurking in the appeal: the scope of federal power over the states, especially the question whether the U.S. Supreme Court had the power to review state court decisions. The issue had been brewing for some time and was escalating among the Southern states into talk of secession. He simply asserted, without explanation, "It is . . . too clear for controversy" that the Court had jurisdiction in the case, and therefore "the duty . . . however unpleasant" to decide whether the Georgia law was valid.[127] His words tossed gasoline on the fire of the secession movement.

Marshall next presented a superficial history of Indigenous nations. He wrote, "America, separated from Europe by a wide ocean, was inhabited by a distinct people, divided into separate nations, independent of each other and of the rest of the world, having institutions of their own, and governing themselves by their own laws."[128]

Of course, it was not America that was inhabited, because "America" came into existence only after the arrival of the colonizers. The *Oxford English Dictionary* traces the name "America" to the 1507 German mapmaker Martin Waldseemüller's book *Cosmographiae Introductio*. Waldseemüller Latinized the name of Amerigo Vespucci, the Italian explorer who navigated the coast of South America in 1501. This may seem a trivial point, but it illustrates the dilemma of finding the appropriate language to talk about Indigenous peoples. Marshall's description muddled the fact that Indigenous peoples preexisted the United States and its claim of sovereignty. Indigenous peoples are not occupying the United States; the United States is occupying Indigenous territories.

More muddle followed, as Marshall offered an account of "discovery" fraught with racial and cultural prejudice. He wrote, "After lying concealed for a series of ages, the enterprise of Europe, guided by nautical science, conducted some of her adventurous sons into this western world. They found it in possession of a people who had made small progress in agriculture or manufactures, and whose general employment was war, hunting, and fishing."

Note his adjectives: Europeans were "enterprising, scientific, adventurous." Natives were of "small progress," and their "general employment was war, hunting, and fishing" rather than the supposedly higher pursuits of agriculture and manufacturing. Never mind that war, especially civil war, continuously preoccupied Christian European monarchs (as well as the United States, which was shortly going to enter its own civil war). [129] And never mind that hunting was a special domain of royal power in Europe, where the king's hunting rights superseded every other use, even the ordinary activities of people who lived in the forests.[130] And never mind that fishing was a special area of concern among competing Christian colonizers along the coasts of the continent. To cite one example, the English were careful, when making their claims to Newfoundland, not to tread on French, Portuguese, and Spanish fishing interests.[131] In short, Marshall ignored real history in his fantasy of Christian Europeans discovering something that had been concealed. Indigenous lands were certainly not concealed from the Indigenous peoples whose homes they were.

The most persistently confusing language in the *Worcester* opinion came next, when Marshall appeared to question the doctrine of Christian discovery. He wrote, "It is difficult to comprehend the proposition that the inhabitants of either quarter of the globe could have rightful original claims of dominion over the inhabitants of the other, or over the lands they occupied, or that the discovery of either by the other should give the discoverer rights in the country discovered which annulled the preexisting rights of its ancient possessors." He asked: Did the Christian "adventurers . . . acquire . . . a rightful property in the soil, from the Atlantic to the Pacific, or rightful dominion over the numerous people who occupied it?"[132]

Many readers take Marshall's acknowledgment of the original free and independent Indigenous existence (however distorted) and his questioning of discovery rights as evidence that he was backing away from the extravagant pretension of Christian discovery that he had declared in *Johnson* and affirmed in *Cherokee Nation*. This is wishful thinking, belied by Marshall's statements that followed.

Marshall immediately answered his question about the rightfulness of discovery, saying, "But power, war, conquest, give rights, which, after possession, are conceded by the world, and which can never be controverted by those on whom they descend."[133] With this answer to his own question, Marshall not only held onto Christian discovery doctrine, but cleaned up his depiction of it in *Johnson* as an extravagant pretension—the "pretension of *converting the discovery of an inhabited country into conquest.*"[134] In *Worcester*, he depicted the U.S. claim of title to Native lands as an actual conquest. Marshall thus intensified rather than diminished his assertion of U.S. domination. He added that this "glance" at history "might shed some light on existing pretensions."[135]

The next parts of the *Worcester* opinion have also confused readers. Marshall described the right of discovery as "the sole right of acquiring the soil." He said that this right "could not affect the rights of those already in possession . . . as aboriginal occupants," and that discovery "gave the exclusive right to purchase, but did not found that right on a denial of the right of the possessor to sell."[136] Lindsay Robertson, for example, asserted that Marshall thereby "dismantle[d] the discovery doctrine by overruling that part of the doctrine assigning fee title to the discovering sovereign."[137]

Again, this reading misapprehends the decision. Marshall's apparently pro-Native statements about possession and occupants did not diverge from the decision in *Johnson*. Indeed, Marshall had already said in *Johnson*, "It has never been contended, that the Indian title amounted to nothing." But he made clear that "Indian title" did *not* mean ownership of land. He said, "The claim of government extends to *the complete ultimate title,* charged with this right of possession, and to the exclusive power of acquiring that right."[138] Nothing in *Worcester* retreated from that claim. As Paul Finkelman put it, Marshall's "opinion in *Worcester v. Georgia* . . . is sometimes seen as a failed attempt to gain a measure of justice for the Cherokee and by extension all Indians—but the thrust of that opinion was to protect the rights of the national government to enforce treaties against the states and not to respect the rights of indigenous peoples."[139] In this, he echoes Rifkin, who says, "The use of Cherokee nationhood as a jurisdictional cipher [in *Cherokee Nation*] also holds true in *Worcester v. Georgia*, except the latter case is concerned with preserving treaty relations in order to assert the supremacy of federal acts over those of the states."[140]

Robertson's reading of *Worcester* is quite common among legal scholars who say that Christian discovery doctrine only means U.S. power over the *transfer* of Native lands—the "exclusive power of acquiring" Native land. We need only a bit of economic theory to unpack what this supposedly limited power means. It is what economists today call "monopsony." The *Oxford English Dictionary* defines "monopsony" as a market in which a single buyer controls trade. This is precisely what the "exclusive power of acquiring" created. Marshall said that the U.S. government is the only lawful buyer of "Indian occupancy." This in fact was Marshall's crucial economic move in *Worcester*: elaboration of the property law exception to exclude the states from any role in the market for Native lands.

A federal monopsony is precisely what happened. The United States used its claim of sole power to acquire Native lands to transfer those lands to non-Native settlers and land speculators. It did this through grants, allotments, leases, and other arrangements, including outright awards of Native lands to soldiers and assignment as collateral for U.S. debts. As Supreme Court justice John Catron explained in the 1839 case of *Clark v. Smith*, "Grants . . . after the Revolution, were made for lands within the Indian hunting grounds . . . [to pay] officers and soldiers of the revolutionary war . . . and extinguish . . . the arrears due the army. . . . It was one of the great resources which sustained the war."[141] As we saw, Marshall had already acknowledged as much in *Johnson*—that state cessions to the United States of their claims to Native lands (exactly like the one involved in Georgia) "granted a productive fund to the government of the Union."[142] Marshall used his *Worcester* opinion to put a lock on that fund.

Law professor Eric Kades described Marshall's decree "as a means of expropriating Indian land at minimal cost. Just as sellers can charge more when they are monopolists without competitors, so too buyers can pay less when they are monopsonists without competing bidders."[143]

In 1862, the United States distributed nearly 11 million acres from 245 Native nations to the states for "land grant colleges" pursuant to the Morrill Act, "Donating public lands to the several states and territories which may provide colleges for the benefit of agriculture and the mechanic arts."[144] A 2013 public radio documentary called it "An Audacious Act: How a High School Dropout Helped Educate America."[145] But the audaciousness of the Morrill Act is the fact that it seized Native lands, declared them "public," and gave them away to raise money for state colleges. The celebration of the act conveniently ignores this. As the historian Robert Lee and his team explained in their groundbreaking "land grab universities" statistical study, "It's a common misconception that the Morrill Act grants were used only for campuses.

In fact, the grants were as big [as] or bigger than major cities, and were often located hundreds or even thousands of miles away from their beneficiaries." In short, the land grants were a form of speculative investment; for example, "For every dollar the United States claims to have spent to purchase Dakota title, the Morrill Act heaped $250 into the University of Minnesota's coffers— a return of 250 to 1."[146]

Kades said that the monopsony inherent in Christian discovery doctrine "ensured that Europeans would not transfer wealth to the tribes in the process of competing against each other to buy land."[147] James Warren Springer didn't use the technical term "monopsony," but he came to the same conclusion: "It is a reasonable generalization to say that land purchases from Indians were a governmental monopoly."[148]

Stuart Banner studied the same monopsony condition in New Zealand, where *Johnson v. McIntosh* was copied as the rule for dealing with Maori lands. Banner said, "Economic theory predicts that the government would realize a tidy profit in these roles, and in fact such was the case. By 1844, the government had paid slightly more than £4,000 for land, but had realized over £40,000 in land sales."[149] He also explained that the *Johnson* ruling "was defended primarily on paternalistic grounds . . . [that] Government was needed as a mediator between greedy buyers and easily duped sellers. . . . The argument contained a great deal of hypocrisy . . . as was frequently noted at the time. . . . All the problems the Maori had in negotiating with private purchasers—the inability to predict future prices, the failure to understand what the British meant by a sale, and so on—were accentuated when the Maori sold to the government, because the government faced no competition that might have pushed prices higher. . . ."[150] Banner's economic analysis demolished any notion that the *Johnson* ruling "protects" Natives.

In short, Marshall's *Worcester* decision did not pull back from the property law exception declared in *Johnson*. To put it the other way around, the federal anti-Indian law definition of "Indian title" as nontitle—as the *exceptional* "mere right of occupancy"—constituted the U.S. claim of ultimate land title and continental sovereignty. The declaration of exclusive U.S. power to acquire Native occupancy consolidated rather than contradicted the exception.

Close reading of yet other language in *Worcester* helps dispel any confusion that may still linger about Marshall's supposed relinquishing of U.S. claims of power over Native peoples. Perhaps his most famous statement, celebrated by readers who praise Marshall's professed "sympathy" for the Cherokee, is the following:

> The Cherokee Nation . . . is a distinct community occupying its own territory . . . in which the laws of Georgia can have no force, and which the citizens of Georgia have no right to enter but with the assent of the

Cherokees themselves, or in conformity with treaties and with the acts of Congress.[151]

Wishful thinkers love the opening phrases. But the crucial words followed the conjunctions "or . . . and": The sentence said that Georgia has no right to enter Cherokee territory except by Cherokee assent *or* by treaty *and acts of Congress.* The final clause empowering Congress made clear that Marshall was not relinquishing the claim of overriding U.S. power. *Worcester* can be described as a victory for the Cherokee only in the limited sense that it protected them from Georgia. As to the United States, they had no protection. They remained in the exception. Professors Carole Goldberg and Kevin Washburn said, "Although [*Worcester*] was a victory for Indian sovereignty, the Court's decision made clear the Cherokee's rights depended entirely on the largesse of the federal government."[152] But it is a mistake to define "sovereignty" as "dependent" on another government.

Nowadays, the U.S. claim of domination is frequently described as "congressional plenary power." As we saw earlier, this phrase was coined in 1903 by Edward White in *Lone Wolf v. Hitchcock.* Justice White understood the significance of Marshall's "or . . . and"—these words preserved a U.S. claim of domination over Native peoples. The *Lone Wolf* decision said that the description of "Indian occupancy" as a protected right does not apply to the United States; it does not limit "the power of Congress to administer the property of the Indians."[153]

If we take Marshall's "or . . . and" as a kind of small print, we can say that in *Worcester,* "the large print giveth, and the small print taketh away."[154] Or we could describe Marshall's language the way that an Illinois judge in a 1955 case described a deceptive purchase order defrauding a small manufacturer who thought that he had a contract with General Motors. The judge said that the purchase order was "artfully prepared" and had "the indicia of a binding and enforceable contract," but it was not a contract. He said, "Behind the glittering façade is a void." The judge was apparently reluctant to charge General Motors with fraud, so he said it this way: "This agreement was made in the higher echelons of business, overshadowed by the aura of business ethics. To say the least, the agreement was deceptive. In a more subterranean atmosphere and between persons of lower ethical standards it might, without any strain on the language, be denominated by a less deterged appellation."[155]

Either way we describe Marshall's rhetoric, it demonstrates an important point about reading cases. It is not enough to read cases like a story, even though there is a story in every case; as S. F. C. Milsom explained—one needs to take a mathematics or scientific approach, reading slowly, "thinking each sentence through in relation to the last and then again in relation to the next."[156] Read in this way, Marshall's "or . . . and" functions like Boolean operators determining the logic of his opinion.

Marshall's rhetoric fools a lot of readers. It has enough glitter to fool even as perceptive a historian as Claudio Saunt, who described *Worcester* as "a complete legal victory for the Cherokees." He added, however, "The consequences were far from clear."[157]

In short, the seemingly pro-Native language in *Worcester* actually reinforced Christian discovery doctrine, which *Worcester* itself framed as the ultimate right of domain of the colonizing potentate who made the discovery. Justice John McLean's concurring opinion in *Worcester* affirmed this close reading of Marshall's words. McLean stated the basic Christian discovery exception in blunt language: "At no time has the sovereignty of the country been recognized as existing in the Indians. . . . They may not be admitted to possess the right of soil."[158]

The true significance of the *Worcester* decision lay in Marshall's careful parsing of the U.S. and state claims—what we might call the topology of jurisdiction over Native lands. His aim was to close the loophole that he had left in the *Johnson* opinion—the one that allowed states to claim discovery title to Indigenous lands, which was precisely what Georgia was doing in *Worcester.* Marshall left open the loophole for state jurisdiction in *Johnson* intentionally, to validate state grants of Native lands to pay soldiers for their service in the Revolutionary War—so-called bounty lands. Connecticut, Georgia, Maryland, Massachusetts, New York, North Carolina, Pennsylvania, South Carolina, and Virginia all engaged in the bounty lands practice. In Virginia, for example, a noncommissioned militia officer serving a three-year enlistment was entitled to 200 acres. The Continental Congress also made use of bounty lands, as decreed by "the financier of the Revolution" Robert Morris, superintendent of finance.[159]

As Lindsay Robertson explained, "Marshall intended *Johnson v. McIntosh* to settle . . . the problem created by Virginia's grant of military bounties to lands still in possession of the Chickasaws."[160] *Johnson* said that Virginia's bounty land grants were valid because the state had inherited the English Crown's Christian discovery claim of title and could pass it to militia veterans. Robertson noted that Marshall's personal interest in this provision: "Marshall had served as an officer in the continental line, and as such, was a beneficiary of the Virginia legislature's grant of lands."[161] In short, Marshall could not have denied state jurisdiction in *Johnson* without undermining his own land claims and breaking political promises to his compatriots. So much for the U.S. Supreme Court justice most often rated as "greatest" (despite the fact he has also been called crafty and hedonistic).[162]

Marshall had left open the same loophole for state power prior to the trilogy. In an 1810 case, *Fletcher v. Peck,* his decision allowed land speculators to claim title to Yazoo Nation lands despite the fact that the Yazoo people still lived there (and despite massive corruption between the speculators and the Georgia legislature). Marshall's *Fletcher* opinion said, without any explanation at all, "Indian title . . . is not such as to be absolutely repugnant to seisin in fee [full ownership] on the part of the state."[163] In those few words, he heartened speculators in Native lands everywhere. By the way, Joseph Story, who was appointed to the Supreme Court in time to participate in *Johnson*, was one of the attorneys for the speculators.

In *Worcester*, Marshall was not preoccupied with personal interests to stop him from denying state power over Native lands. His own land claims had already been protected. He was free to assert exclusive U.S. power and close the loophole that he had left open in *Fletcher* and *Johnson*. Marshall therefore wrote, "Indian territory [is] completely separated from that of the States, and . . . all intercourse with them shall be carried on exclusively by the government of the Union."[164] In short, after *Worcester*, only the United States could use the Christian discovery doctrine.

The contest between state and federal claims of ultimate dominion over Native lands began well before the *Worcester* case. In fact, it was going on prior to *Johnson*. States began claiming power over Native lands immediately after the 1783 Treaty of Paris ended the American Revolutionary War. By 1822, a year prior to the *Johnson* decision, state claims were playing out in the U.S. Congress, specifically focusing on Georgia. A House Select Committee was appointed to investigate the conflict between U.S. treaties with the Creek and Cherokee Nations, on one hand, and the 1802 Georgia land cession agreement with the United States, which had committed the United States to "extinguish Indian title . . . as early as the same can be peaceably obtained, on reasonable terms," on the other. The Select Committee was charged "to take into consideration the treaties made by the United States with the Creek nation of Indians . . . and . . . the Cherokee nation of Indians . . . and also the articles of agreement and cession between the United States and the State of Georgia . . . and to report whether the said articles have been executed according to the terms thereof, and the best means of executing the same."[165]

The committee presented its report on January 7, 1822, entitled, *Extinguishment of the Indian title of land in Georgia*. It was a resounding affirmation of Georgia's claim of dominion over Native lands. The report said, "The United States have no jurisdiction over the country, or interest in the soil of the lands belonging to the Indians within the limits of Georgia." It also attacked what it called a federal plan to civilize the Indians by upgrading "Indian occupancy" to standard fee-simple ownership. The report said, "It will be necessary for the United States to relinquish the policy which they seem to have adopted with regard to civilizing the Indians, and rendering them permanent upon their lands, and changing their title by occupancy into a fee-simple title."[166]

The controversy continued in Congress after *Johnson*. On December 18, 1823, a "memorial and remonstrance" of the Georgia legislature was submitted to the U.S. Senate Committee on the State of the Republic, similarly titled

*Extinguishment of the Indian title of lands in Georgia.* Georgia reiterated what the House Select Committee had said earlier: "The State of Georgia is vested with the ultimate title to all the lands within her territorial limits; . . . the claim of the Indians is, consequently, restricted to a mere temporary usufructuary right."[167] (A "usufruct right" means a right to enjoy the fruits of someone else's land.)

Given this long, contentious background, it is not surprising that Georgia strongly resisted the *Worcester* decision. Governor Wilson Lumpkin ignored it altogether and refused to release Samuel Worcester and Elizur Butler from their hard labor. Moreover, Marshall's opinion immediately inflamed secessionist movements throughout the region. The possibility that the United States might try to enforce the court's order to release the missionaries provoked formidable public responses in the newspapers and official maneuvers behind the scenes. Ultimately, northern liberals persuaded Worcester and Butler to accept a pardon from the governor to avoid exacerbating the threat of Southern secession. The missionaries did so, ending the conflict between the U.S. Supreme Court and the state. As we know, their move did not avoid secession and civil war, nor did it ward off the invasion and dispossession of Cherokee territory.[168]

Ironically, and contrary to notions that Marshall was pro-Native in *Worcester*, his declaration of exclusive federal power to deal with Indigenous peoples accomplished only one sure thing—it erected a scaffold for U.S. "congressional plenary power," the doctrine that the Congress has full control over Indigenous peoples and lands that have been excepted out of ordinary law. Marshall's opinion celebrated the 1819 Indian Civilization Act[169] as an example of congressional power, saying it promoted "those humane designs of civilizing the neighbouring Indians which had long been cherished by the Executive."[170] Marshall said that the missionaries were "performing, under the sanction of the chief magistrate of the union, those duties which the humane policy adopted by congress had recommended."[171] He never mentioned the 1830 Indian Removal Act,[172] the inhumane and genocidal congressional policy enacted the year before *Worcester* and also celebrated by the executive, despite the fact that the Removal Act far surpassed the Civilization Act in public and political controversy. Removal was strangely invisible in Marshall's opinion.

Marshall's insistence on paramount U.S. jurisdiction mirrored a core concern of the English Crown in its colonizing projects. As Ken MacMillan explained it, "The crown was especially concerned to ensure that its *imperium*, or independent and absolute sovereignty, and its *dominium*, or right to possess and rule territory under its jurisdiction, were fully and legally expressed."[173] The English Crown insisted on absolute royal prerogative and plenary power. Marshall, like those fifteenth-century Christian monarchs, denied the states' competing claims for *imperium* and *dominium* over Native peoples and lands. *Worcester* positioned the United States as the recipient of Crown claims, setting a legal foundation to create an American empire out of Native lands.

Marshall's move in *Worcester* to close the door to state jurisdiction over Indigenous lands has not lasted. A 2001 U.S. Supreme Court case, *Nevada v. Hicks*,[174] pushed the door back open. The *Hicks* case arose when Nevada officials invaded Fallon Paiute–Shoshone lands to investigate an alleged state hunting violation by Floyd Hicks, a Fallon Paiute–Shoshone man. After Hicks won in both district and circuit courts, Nevada appealed to the Supreme Court. Justice Antonin Scalia wrote the Court's opinion reversing the lower courts. Scalia upheld Nevada jurisdiction on one hand and limited the jurisdiction of the Fallon Court on the other hand.

Scalia nodded in the direction of the *Worcester* decision and said, "Though tribes are often referred to as 'sovereign' entities, it was long ago that the Court departed from Chief Justice Marshall's view that the laws of [a State] can have no force within reservation boundaries. . . . Ordinarily, it is now clear, an Indian reservation is considered part of the territory of the State."[175]

Scalia thus summarily tossed aside Marshall's seemingly pro-Native language in *Worcester*. He did so by emphasizing the fundamental exception rooted in the Christian discovery doctrine, which he defined as "the dependent status of the tribes" and U.S. power over the scope of "tribal self-government."[176] Tossing *Worcester* aside enlarged the exception so that Native peoples could now be dominated by states, as well as the United States.

The fundamental exception created in the Marshall trilogy persists into the present day, with mutations, as the court develops retail exceptions within the wholesale exception of the domination matrix.

# CHAPTER FOUR

# The Domination Matrix

## Engulfed by "Discovery"

We are now prepared to go deeper into the matrix of words and violence that constitute federal anti-Indian law. Now we will burrow into the philosophy behind the exception and explore the interpenetration of exception and land appropriation. We will see the confusion and contradiction that result from trying to hide the exception, and uncover the jurisprudential crisis federal anti-Indian law produces at the core of U.S. law and order.

As we saw, the *Johnson v. McIntosh* decision placed U.S. land law on the foundation of the Christian discovery claim of domination over Native lands and peoples.

In 1888, Professor Burke A. Hinsdale pointed out that Christian discovery was "so thoroughly . . . carried out" in U.S. land law that even "the Indian landowner, as well as the white one, holds ultimately by right of discovery!" Using the phrase "Indian title" to mean the original Native ownership of their lands (as we have seen, federal anti-Indian law uses "Indian title" to mean "mere occupancy"), Hinsdale added, "There is not an Indian in the United States who holds the soil on which he lives, his farm, if he has one, his interest in the reservation on which he lives, if in tribal relations, by an original Indian title."[1] In short, Hinsdale said, all land titles in the United States rest on Christian discovery.

The deeper implications of Hinsdale's insight about the totalizing effect of Christian discovery land law are illuminated by the German legal scholar Carl Schmitt's study of "land-appropriation." Schmitt wrote, "Not only logically, but also historically, land-appropriation . . . constitutes the . . . source of all further concrete order and all further law."[2] Briefly, the federal anti-Indian law exception underlying U.S. appropriation of Native lands constitutes the source of the entire U.S. system of law and order.

## Sovereign Exception

The peculiar characteristics of federal anti-Indian law might seem to mark it as a field apart from the rest of U.S. law. In fact, as we will see, federal anti-Indian law actually constitutes the ontological foundation of the U.S. claim to continental sovereignty.

We have seen federal anti-Indian law routinely described as exceptional. In fact, the exceptional quality of federal anti-Indian law is so often noticed that to point it out seems insipid. For example, in his book, *American Indian Law in a Nutshell*, Ninth Circuit Court of Appeals senior judge William Canby wrote, "The independence of the tribes is subject to exceptionally great powers of Congress to regulate and modify the status of the tribes."[3] Professor David Getches, reviewing a book about water rights, said, "Indian law . . . is exceptional, with its often uncontextualized results [and] its relative timelessness."[4] In her review of land law, Professor Jessica Shoemaker said, "Indian law is always postured as the exception to 'regular' rules. . . . In land tenure specifically, many property law terms have unique meanings that depart from conventional understandings."[5]

From the foundation cases forward, U.S. courts have made this exceptionalism into a mantra. Thus, as the Ninth Circuit said in 1991, "Because of the unique legal status of Indians in American jurisprudence, legal doctrines often must be viewed from a different perspective from that which would obtain in other areas of the law."[6] And the U.S. Supreme Court had said 100 years earlier, "The relation of the Indian tribes living within the borders of the United States has always been an anomalous one and of a complex character."[7]

But the exceptional quality of federal anti-Indian law is not simply a matter of having rules that don't apply in other fields or having inconsistent precedents. As Professor Philip P. Frickey put it, responding in part to what Professor Frank Pommersheim called the "poverty of theory" in the field,[8] we must "recognize . . . the exceptionalism of the field [is] significantly more fundamental than precedential inconsistency."[9] Briefly, the exceptionalism of federal anti-Indian law consists of the fact that the conceptual structure of the field differs from the rest of law, as well as differing in fact from the rule of law.

Frickey said that the incoherence of the field stems from a root "antimony," which he described as the attempt to "justify . . . colonialism in the pursuit of constitutionalism." Of the early cases, he said, "The rule of law did double work, providing the glue holding the republic together while legitimating the displacement of indigenous institutions to make room for it."[10] What emerges from this insight is that federal anti-Indian law operates at an *ontological* level—at the level of the creation and definition of the United States itself. In a nutshell, the judicial creation of federal anti-Indian law was coextensive with the creation of federal sovereignty. One might say that U.S. sovereignty was created on the back of the federal anti-Indian law exception.

In 1922, Schmitt published *Political Theology*, which opens with the famous statement, "Sovereign is he who decides on the exception."[11] His immediate concern was the precarious status of the Weimar Republic, but his analysis of the concept of exception as a suspension of law carried out by the state to preserve itself illuminates the origin of federal anti-Indian law. He said, "The state suspends the law in the exception on the basis of its right of self-preservation." Schmitt added, "What characterizes an exception is principally unlimited authority."[12]

As we saw, Chief Justice John Marshall's opinion in *Johnson v. McIntosh* created just such an exception when he described Christian discovery doctrine as a matter of U.S. self-preservation, saying that it was "indispensable to that system under which the country has been settled"; he described it in terms of unlimited authority—a claim of "absolute ultimate title" that "cannot be questioned."[13] To rephrase Frickey, federal anti-Indian law is the ontological glue holding the United States together via a displacement of Indigenous peoples.

Let me pause for a moment to clarify what I mean by "ontology." As the *Stanford Encyclopedia of Philosophy* says, "Ontology . . . is a big word in philosophy, and different philosophers have used [it] in different ways."[14] The simplest definition is "ontology" is the study of "being," of what exists and how different entities that exist relate to each other. A classic example is the question of whether there is a god and, if so, how that relates to the rest of existence. For our purposes, the question is whether "Indians" exist and, if so, how they relate to the United States.

It may seem strange to ask whether "Indians" exist, since we know there are peoples in existence who are called by that name. But remember Gerald Vizenor's discussion of "survivance," where he referred to the word "Indian" as a "simulation in the literature of dominance."[15] We know that the American use of the word "Indian" is a result of the fact that Christopher Columbus didn't know where he was or what he had "discovered." "Indian" is thus a simulation; it is not something that actually exists, except where it is not a simulation, as in the Indian subcontinent.

Federal anti-Indian law deploys the simulation "Indian" as a generic name for the Indigenous peoples of the continent. "Indians" functions as an ontological category around which U.S. law constructs an array of relationships to other entities—"citizens," "states," "the United States," and, most important, "property." In federal anti-Indian law, we approach "ontology" as it is used in information science, where it refers to the conceptualization of a "domain of discourse."[16] Thomas Gruber, a computer scientist credited with giving the term a technical definition for information science, explained, "Ontology" is a "body of formally represented . . . objects, concepts, and other entities that are *presumed to exist* in some area of interest and the relationships that hold among them."[17]

Gruber's definition illuminates the ontological function of the presumption originated by Marshall in his infamous trilogy. Using Gruber's terms, Marshall created an "explicit specification of a conceptualization. . . . [of a] set of objects, and the formalized relationships among them, . . . reflected in [a] representational vocabulary"[18] called "federal Indian law." Marshall's vocabulary incorporated Columbus's geographical mistake, mixed in Christian presumptions of domination, and declared an exception from the rule of law, a juridical zone "marked by peculiar and cardinal distinctions which exist nowhere else."[19]

Professor Frickey, despite his general clarity, missed this ontological function when he wrote, "Chief Justice Marshall in *Cherokee Nation v. Georgia* acknowledged that 'the condition of the Indians in relation to the United States is perhaps unlike that of any other two people in existence.'"[20] The verb "acknowledged" masked the fact that Marshall's opinion *declared* the "condition of the Indians." It was not an acknowledgment, but rather a *presumption in a representational vocabulary.*

Frickey made the same mistake when he went on to say, "The tribes were within the boundaries of . . . the United States." The phrase "were within" is another aspect of Marshall's representational vocabulary—his conceptualization of the exception as incorporating Native peoples. Frickey combined these misreadings by saying, "In light of these characteristics, the Court called tribes 'domestic dependent nations . . . in a state of pupilage. Their relation to the United States resembles that of a ward to his guardian.'"[21] On the contrary, and to be ontologically clear, it is not "in light of these characteristics" that Marshall came up with domestic dependency; rather, "domestic dependency" was his shorthand phrase for the characteristics that he presumed were in the representational vocabulary that he was constructing. To borrow again from information science, Marshall's purported "characteristics" of Native peoples were actually "formally represented . . . concepts . . . *presumed to exist* . . . in [a] representational *vocabulary.*"[22] Marshall's "Indian" vocabulary was simultaneously the vocabulary of U.S. sovereignty.

The ontological significance of federal anti-Indian law as coextensive with U.S. sovereignty claims is generally obscured by conventional views of the field, which, as Professor Bethany Berger said, usually see "Indian law cases . . . [as] an obscure backwater in the Supreme Court docket." She noted that U.S. Supreme Court justices have described "Indian law cases . . . as 'pee wee' and even 'chickenshit' cases" (quoting Justices John Marshall Harlan and William J. Brennan).[23] The law professor Joseph William Singer similarly pointed out, "American Indian legal issues are generally treated as a specialized field whose principles are irrelevant to the core of United States property law." He went on to say, "To the extent the rules of Indian property differ from rules concerning non-Indian property, they are understood as exceptions to basic principles."[24]

But Singer dug deeper and raised an ontological question. He said, "These exceptions . . . are not thought to affect the integrity of the core principles. But what happens if we take the law of American Indian property as a central concern rather than as a peripheral one? What happens if it is the first thing we address, rather than the last?" Singer answered his own question: "If we start our analysis of the relation between sovereignty and property by asking how the law treats the original possessors of land in the United States, we learn some valuable lessons about property law generally."[25]

Professor Milner Ball took a similar approach in his 1987 study *Constitution, Court, Indian Tribes,* saying,

> Because we say we have a government of laws and not men, we hold our government to be limited and to have no unlimited power. If the federal government nevertheless exercises unrestrained power over Indian nations, then what we say is not true, and we have a different kind of government than we think we have. . . . The Court is regarded as the institution of restraint and a protector of rights. If the Court restrains neither Congress nor itself in taking away tribal rights, then we are confronted by a fundamental contradiction between our political rhetoric and our political realities.[26]

Briefly put, when we see federal anti-Indian law as the starting point of U.S. law and order, we reveal what has been concealed by the rhetoric of peculiarity.

Frickey framed this contradiction between rhetoric and reality as a "normative dilemma." He said, "Chief Justice Marshall seemed to recognize the core normative dilemma of building constitutionalism on a foundation of colonization." Frickey went on to repeat a common form of wishful thinking among federal anti-Indian law writers—namely, that John Marshall perceived the dilemma and had a "desire to mediate colonialism and constitutionalism."[27] In fact, as we have seen, Marshall had no such thing in mind, aside from surface rhetoric.

Because normativity is a common theme in discussions of federal anti-Indian law, we need to pause to explore its meaning and to see that it is an inadequate framework for a theory of the field. "Normativity," wrote the philosophy professor Roberto Farneti, "concerns . . . phenomena that . . . occur within the space of reasons [and] . . . give us our bearings. . . . Normativity, therefore, concerns the capacity to act on reasons."[28] One may easily see that Marshall and his fellow judges and land speculators acted normatively: they expressed reasons to support their title claim. "Christian discovery" was the normative framework.

To refer to a "normative dilemma" in federal anti-Indian law is thus a retrospective evaluation. Marshall made conscious normative choices. To the extent that he felt any dilemma, he set it aside, as in his dismissal of "natural right, . . . usages of civilized nations, . . . and reason."[29] He freed federal anti-Indian law from those alternative norms.

In the exception, Schmitt said, "The decision frees itself from all normative ties and becomes in the true sense absolute."[30] Marshall's rhetoric exemplified this. He disconnected Christian discovery from ordinary normative ties, describing it as "extravagant"—opposed to natural right, perhaps supported by reason, and so on—and yet necessary for the United States to exist and have an absolute title to lands.

In the framework of Christian discovery, Native lands appeared as *normatively uncharted territory*. The colonists projected their Christian reasons and norms into an "uncivilized wilderness," where, as Marshall put it, "some new and different rule" had to be laid down. That rule was the exception placing Native peoples in a juridical zone where norms were imposed from the outside. Simply put, federal anti-Indian law is a system of normative domination based on norms of domination.

Carl Schmitt explained, "The exception appears in its absolute form when a situation in which legal prescriptions can be valid must . . . be brought about. . . . For a legal order to make sense, a normal situation must exist, and he is sovereign who definitely decides whether this normal situation actually exists."[31] Applied to federal anti-Indian law, we can say that Marshall decided that the Christian discovery exception was the normal situation. To say it paradoxically, Marshall declared the normality of the exception.

Now that we can see federal anti-Indian law as a space outside ordinary law, we can understand why trying to analyze it as a set of legal rules produces complex muddles. But the muddles become coherent when we see the purported rules as the product of a claim of unbounded domination. In short, federal anti-Indian law is not a set of legal rules. It is the suspension of rules—a suspension of the rule of law in the claim of U.S. sovereignty.

Conventional definitions of sovereignty fail us in trying to understand this situation. Sovereignty is typically spoken of as a quality possessed by someone—a ruler of one sort or another. But sovereignty is an *action* rather than a static condition. Sovereignty is a *claim* of dominance over others. It is an exertion of force in a field of forces.

As Professor Mark Rifkin put it, "It is not that sovereignty exists as a possession. . . . Sovereignty is what is tactically produced through the very mechanism of its self-justification."[32] Political science professor Daniel Philpott said, "Understanding sovereignty, then, involves understanding claims to it."[33] As a claim, sovereignty necessarily presupposes an *other*, who acquiesces in or resists the claim. The political theorist Joan Cocks wrote, "Without an actual, potential, or imagined competitor, no assertion of sovereignty would ever have to be made."[34] One might say that no assertion of sovereignty would ever *need* to be made.

Luke Sunderland, professor of medieval literature, in his study of baronial resistance to assertions of royal power in the Middle Ages, said that since sovereignty is a claim, it is "always subject to counter-claim." Rebel barons over whom would-be kings claimed sovereignty fought those claims and denounced royal pretensions. They sought "a sustainable outside space" beyond the claims of the monarchical powers, who, in turn, kept expanding their claims.[35]

John Marshall aimed at two "others" in making the U.S. claim to continental sovereignty: Indigenous peoples and the individual states. Both resisted, giving the United States excuses and occasions for enlarging its claim of sovereignty into a claim of empire.

As we have seen, the anthropologist Jonas Bens described the situation of Native nations—"legally incorporated and excluded at the same time"[36]—as a "paradox." This sounds very much like a description of the exception, except that for Bens, the paradox is a procedural matter that arises when Native peoples go to a U.S. court and thereby "subject themselves to . . . foreign rule."[37] But the paradox of simultaneous inclusion/exclusion—the exception—exists whether or not Native peoples go to court. Indeed, the exception was originally defined in a case with no Native parties—*Johnson v. McIntosh*. The federal anti-Indian law exception, as an ontological phenomenon, a domain of discourse accompanying the action of asserting U.S. sovereignty, does not depend on or arise from Native actions. It is a unilateral assertion of U.S. domination denying Indigenous sovereignty.

Nearly every federal anti-Indian law case is concerned with sovereignty. One practitioner's guide to "effectively representing Indian tribes" warned, "One of the most universal issues affecting tribes is sovereignty protection. Tribes have a paramount interest in protecting their inherent authority, and maintaining their ability to exercise their sovereign powers."[38] Carl Schmitt said, "A jurisprudence concerned with ordinary day-to-day questions has practically no interest in the concept of sovereignty. Only the recognizable is its normal concern; everything else is a 'disturbance.'"[39] Schmitt's designation of the concept of sovereignty as a disturbance illuminates the problematic character of federal anti-Indian law, even as such law illustrates the disturbing character of the concept of U.S. sovereignty.

A federal judge in a 1973 case involving Blackfeet sovereignty stated the federal anti-Indian law exception baldly: "The blunt fact . . . is that an Indian tribe is sovereign to the extent that the United States permits it to be sovereign—neither more nor less."[40] The judge emphasized, "The word 'sovereignty' . . . as applied to Indian tribes . . . means no more than 'within the will of Congress.'"[41]

The Blackfeet case arose from a conflict between the Blackfeet Nation and the U.S. Federal Bureau of Investigation (FBI). The FBI raided a small gambling operation licensed by the Blackfeet Nation and seized its slot machines. The Blackfeet Tribal Court ordered the agents not to remove the machines from Blackfeet territory and cited the U.S. attorney for contempt when he went ahead and authorized the removal. The U.S. attorney appealed the contempt citation to the U.S. District Court, which, as we just saw, ruled against the Blackfeet. The judge said that the Blackfeet had no power to license gambling in the first place and thus no power to hold U.S. officers in contempt.

But the judge said that he had sympathy (we've heard that before) for the Tribal Court judges. He said that he could "understand the pressures [of] political urgings for the exercise of tribal sovereignty," especially because of "the complex problems of jurisdiction which plague tribal courts."[42]

When the FBI insisted on an injunction against the Blackfeet, the Blackfeet upped the ante and challenged the U.S. claim of plenary power over Indigenous peoples on the ground that it had no basis in the U.S. Constitution. The judge responded that U.S. power over Indigenous nations "is not dependent upon specific constitutional grant"; he then issued the injunction.[43] He thereby restated in its simplest form the ontology of the federal anti-Indian law exception: Natives are subject to U.S. domination, regardless of the so-called founding documents of the United States. This is a prime example of what Professor N. Bruce Duthu called the "potentially lethal traces of colonizing agents . . . [in] the substantive body of federal law [that] sets the . . . contours" of Indigenous self-governance.[44]

John Sergeant, one of the attorneys for the Cherokee Nation in the Marshall trilogy cases, raised the earliest challenge to the ontology of federal anti-Indian law in his argument to the Supreme Court in *Cherokee Nation v. Georgia*. He said that if the Cherokee were not a "foreign" nation, this would mean that their people would be domestic (i.e., they would be U.S. citizens). However, Sergeant argued, "they certainly are not citizens; and if they be not aliens, what are they? Out-laws. Declared outlaws, without a nation, and without protection." He told the court, "Public law abhors such a state of existence."[45]

In fact, however, Sergeant precisely defined the situation created for Indigenous peoples by the doctrine of Christian discovery. They are in the exception, a special juridical zone outside ordinary law. Federal anti-Indian law does not abhor that situation; it created and maintains it. The situation is the ontological ground of the U.S. claim of continental sovereignty. In Schmitt's terms, it is the "normal situation" that allows the U.S. legal order "to make sense."[46]

In 1898, the U.S. Court of Claims also ran into the ontology created by the exception when a U.S. citizen in Nebraska filed a complaint demanding compensation under the Indian Depredation Act of 1891 for damages to his property. He said that Dull Knife's and Little Wolf's bands of Northern Cheyenne had "taken and destroyed 40 horses, 1 mule, and 40 steers, of the value in the aggregate of $3,750" as they made their way back to their ancestral lands after escaping from U.S. army confinement. The court said that the Indian Depredation Act was limited to damages caused during times of peace, and thus the question was whether the Cheyenne were "at peace" at the time of the damages. Chief judge Charles C. Nott said that the facts showed that Dull Knife and Little Wolf were in a state of war that commenced when U.S. troops fired on them, which Nott described as "one of the many mistakes, military and civil, which have been the fatality of our Indian administration."[47]

Judge Nott went on to say that the difficulty of defining the legal status of the Cheyenne bands "illustrates the extraordinary difficulties which the court has had to encounter in dealing with these Indian depredation cases."[48] He said, "The so-called bands were not . . . bands in a tribal, political, or military sense, but simply parties who lived, as it were, in separate hamlets on the reservation."[49] Nott elaborated his point in language that clearly evoked the exception, saying:

> These Indians . . . occupied an anomalous position, unknown to the common or the civil law or to any system of municipal law. They were neither citizens nor aliens; they were neither free persons nor slaves; they were the wards of the nation, and yet, on a reservation under a military guard, were little else than prisoners of war while war did not exist. Dull Knife and his daughters could be invited guests at the table of officers and gentlemen, behaving with dignity and propriety, and yet could be confined for life on a reservation which was to them little better than a dungeon, on the mere order of an executive officer.[50]

He concluded, "It is impossible to define their status from a legal point of view."[51]

Carl Schmitt followed his famous formulation of sovereignty—"Sovereign is he who decides on the exception"—by saying, "It is precisely the exception that makes relevant the subject of sovereignty, that is, the whole question of sovereignty."[52] The Italian philosopher Giorgio Agamben elaborated Schmitt's perspective of the link between "exception" and "sovereignty." He said, "What is at issue in the sovereign exception is . . . the very condition of possibility of juridical rule and, along with it, the very meaning of State authority." The state of sovereign exception, Agamben said, "creates and guarantees the situation that the law needs for its own validity."[53]

Viewed through this lens, the function of the Christian discovery exception in federal anti-Indian law was (and is) to create the condition of possibility and the meaning of U.S. sovereignty claims. The federal anti-Indian law exception "guarantees the situation" that the United States needs in order to make its claim of continental sovereignty.

Professor Frickey captured part of the picture when he wrote, "Federal Indian law . . . [is] the law governing the historical and ongoing colonial process underpinning the United States." He described this as "a largely overlooked, little-understood paradox."[54] As we have seen, however, the situation seems paradoxical only when one does not see the exception as the *ontological foundation* of U.S. sovereignty. To repeat Thomas Gruber's information science definition of ontology, the exception creates a domain of discourse, a "body of formally represented objects, concepts, and other entities that are *presumed to exist* and the relationships that hold among them."[55] Within the juridical space of the federal anti-Indian law exception, the "ongoing colonial process" is not a paradox; it is "the situation [U.S.] law needs for its own validity."[56]

The exception operates as an "inclusive exclusion,"[57] excluding Natives from the category of independent sovereignty so that Indigenous lands may be included under the U.S. sovereignty claim. In Agamben's terms, the juridical realm of the exception constitutes "in its very separateness, the hidden foundation on which the entire political system rest[s]."[58] Mark Rifkin, following Agamben, put it this way: "The production of [U.S.] national space depends on coding Native peoples and lands as an exception."[59] He added, "The supposedly underlying sovereignty of the US settler-state is a retrospective projection generated by, and dependent on, the 'peculiar'-ization of Native peoples."[60]

Schmitt also said, "The exception . . . confirms . . . the rule, which derives only from the exception."[61] Or, as Agamben translated it, "The rule . . . lives off the exception alone."[62] This becomes obvious when we examine U.S. Supreme Court decisions that try to fit federal anti-Indian law within the U.S. constitutional framework, to make it seem part of the ordinary rule of law, to make the U.S. sovereignty claim seem ordinary, to normalize the entire edifice.

From John Marshall forward, neither the Supreme Court nor lower courts have been able to do this. Federal anti-Indian law decisions constantly spill over into what Marshall himself called "peculiar and cardinal distinctions which exist nowhere else." Each decision is unavoidably entangled with the indeterminacy of the exception. We can now better understand the significance of the Ninth Circuit's statement in 1980 that "unusual, ironic and paradoxical situations are more the rule than the exception where federal Indian law is concerned."[63]

In 1886, in *United States v. Kagama*, the Supreme Court confronted the predicament head-on and conceded to the exception. The case involved criminal charges brought by the United States against a man named Kagama (alias Pactah Billy) for the murder of a man named Iyouse on Hoopa Valley Nation land. The issue was whether the United States had jurisdiction to bring criminal charges in Hoopa territory. In an opinion by Justice Samuel

Freeman Miller, the Court said that it could not find any provision in the Constitution authorizing U.S. jurisdiction. Miller wrote, "We are not able to see in . . . the Constitution . . . any delegation of power to enact a code of criminal law [over Indians]." But Miller was undaunted. He simply embraced the exception, saying, "This power . . . arises, not so much from . . . the constitution . . . as from the ownership of the country . . . and the right of exclusive sovereignty which must exist in the national government, and can be found nowhere else."[64] The Court upheld U.S. criminal jurisdiction on this basis.

As Milner Ball said, ordinary U.S. constitutional law defines the federal government as having limited powers, powers delegated to it in the Constitution. Justice Miller could not confine federal anti-Indian law within the Constitution because it is an exception from the constitutional structure. Miller's statement, "The right of exclusive sovereignty . . . must exist in the national government," precisely matches Agamben's description of the exception as "the situation that the law needs for its own validity . . . the condition of possibility of juridical rule." Miller did not consider whether U.S. power was limited to dealing with the Hoopa as an independent nation because that would undermine the U.S. claim of sovereignty.

In 1991, a century after *Kagama*, the Supreme Court again squarely confronted the impossibility of normalizing federal anti-Indian law within U.S. constitutional law. The case, *Blatchford v. Native Village of Noatak & Circle Village*, involved a lawsuit by Noatak and Circle Villages against an official of the state of Alaska. The Villages filed their lawsuit in the U.S. District Court for the District of Alaska, which dismissed the case. The Villages appealed to the Ninth Circuit Court of Appeals, which reversed the district court. Alaska then appealed to the Supreme Court, which, in an opinion written by Justice Antonin Scalia, reversed the Ninth Circuit and upheld the district court's dismissal.

Scalia said that the reason for the dismissal was that the state of Alaska had immunity from the Villages' federal lawsuit. He added that the state's immunity was embedded in the Eleventh Amendment to the Constitution, which says, "The Judicial power of the United States shall not be construed to extend to any suit . . . commenced or prosecuted against one of the United States by Citizens of another State, or by Citizens or Subjects of any Foreign State."

The Villages pointed out that the Eleventh Amendment only restricts suits by individuals—"citizens or subjects." The Villages said that they were not individuals, but sovereign entities; their argument echoed the Cherokee position in *Cherokee Nation v. Georgia* 160 years before.

Scalia rejected their argument. He agreed with them that the letter of the Eleventh Amendment says "citizens or subjects," but, Scalia went on to say, there are "postulates which limit and control" the literal words. This was a surprising and strange statement for a self-proclaimed strict reader of the Constitution. The postulate that Scalia came up with was, "States of the Union . . . shall be immune from suits . . . save where there has been a surrender of this immunity" in the Constitution. Scalia said the states could not possibly have surrendered their immunity from suit by a Native nation because the "tribes . . . were not even parties" to the Constitution.[65]

Scalia's constitutional postulate put the federal anti-Indian law exception on full display, as follows: The fact that the Eleventh Amendment doesn't refer to Native nations doesn't matter because they aren't part of the constitutional structure; in fact, Scalia said, the Eleventh Amendment blocks Native lawsuits *because* Natives aren't part of the constitutional structure. Scalia's postulate, like Justice Miller's explanation in *Kagama*, was an admission that federal anti-Indian law arises outside of and in opposition to the U.S. Constitution. Simply put, federal anti-Indian law is not constitutional law, despite oft-repeated claims to the contrary by politicians, judges, and others concerned to normalize the field.

In 1997, the exception was visible yet again in the Supreme Court case of *Idaho v. Coeur d'Alene Tribe.*[66] This time, the Court formulated the exception as an exception to the *original* exception! The case arose when the Coeur d'Alene Nation sued the state of Idaho in U.S. District Court. The issue, as in *Blatchford*, was whether Idaho was immune from being sued by an Indigenous nation in federal court. As before, the Supreme Court, in an opinion by Justice Anthony Kennedy, said that the state had immunity under the terms of the Eleventh Amendment to the U.S. Constitution.

Kennedy cited Scalia's *Blatchford* opinion, but he made his own effort to rationalize the exception. Before we look at what he said in his opinion, recall the decision in the Marshall trilogy case of *Cherokee Nation v. Georgia*, saying the Cherokee could not sue Georgia in the U.S. Supreme Court because Indigenous peoples do not have the status of foreign nations. That definition of the exception did not bother Justice Kennedy. Without so much as a nod in the direction of the original formulation of the exception, he said that the Coeur d'Alene could not sue Idaho in federal court because "Indian tribes . . . *should be accorded the same status as foreign sovereigns.*"[67] It is possible that neither Kennedy nor his clerks were well versed in the Marshall trilogy; we'll see in the next section that Justice Stephen Breyer couldn't recall the *Cherokee Nation* formulation during an oral argument in a different case. Nonetheless, the *Coeur d'Alene* decision demonstrated what Carl Schmitt said: "The rule derives from the exception."[68] *Coeur d'Alene* and *Cherokee Nation*, taken together, show that within the domain of the exception, there are only exceptions—the exception is the rule. The rule in a case will be formulated in whatever way serves the purpose of the exception, even if the rule in one case is transparently contradictory to the rule in another case. The exception remains consistent.

Some observers have picked out various Supreme Court decisions that they suggest placed constitutional limits on the plenary power exception. They point to *United States v. Alcea Band of Tillamooks* (1946), where the Court said, "The power of Congress over Indian affairs may be of a plenary nature; but it is not absolute."[69] That line was quoted in *Delaware Tribal Business Committee v. Weeks* (1977), when the Court said that it would "scrutiniz[e] Indian legislation to determine whether it violates the equal protection component of the Fifth Amendment."[70]

Close analysis, however, dispels any suggestion that the exception was restricted in these decisions. First, the Supreme Court expressly disavowed the constitutional implications of the *Alcea* language in 1955, in its *Tee-Hit-Ton v. United States* decision, when Justice Stanley F. Reed referred to *Alcea* as "one opinion in a case decided by this Court that contains language indicating that unrecognized Indian title might be compensable under the Constitution." Reed said that the *Alcea* case was brought under an act of Congress, not the Constitution, and added that, when the case came back to the Court five years later, "This Court unanimously held that none of the former opinions in Vol. 329 of the United States Reports [the volume containing the *Alcea* decision] expressed the view that recovery was grounded on a taking under the Fifth Amendment."[71]

Despite the *Tee-Hit-Ton* disavowal, Justice Brennan quoted the *Alcea* language in his *Delaware Tribal Business* opinion. He said that there is a "question [about] . . . what judicial review of [a congressional act] is appropriate in light of the broad congressional power to prescribe the distribution of property of Indian tribes." He said, "The general rule . . . ordinarily requires the judiciary to defer to congressional determination of what is the best or most efficient use for which tribal funds should be employed." He concluded, "The standard of review . . . is that the legislative judgment should not be disturbed as long as the special treatment can be tied rationally to the fulfillment of Congress' unique obligation toward the Indians."[72]

As Robert Miller put it, the decision called for "the lowest level of judicial constitutional review—rational basis review." He added, "Notwithstanding that level of judicial review . . . no act of Congress has ever been overturned for exceeding its plenary power in the Indian law arena."[73] This is not surprising because, to the extent that the *Alcea* language survived *Tee-Hit-Ton*, the *Delaware Tribal Business* decision made clear that the supposed constitutional limit on plenary power, the "special treatment" of Native peoples, is tied to the plenary power exception itself—"Congress' unique obligations"! Once again, as Schmitt said, the rule lives off the exception.

A 1958 federal district court decision involving an 1868 treaty between the United States and the Standing Rock Sioux provided an even more Byzantine explanation of the federal anti-Indian law exception than we have yet seen.[74] The case concerned a land acquisition program by the U.S. secretary of the army to construct Oahe Dam and Reservoir on Standing Rock and Cheyenne River lands. Standing Rock and Cheyenne River sued to block the land taking. The decision was a prelude to events that came to a head more than fifty years later, when the Dakota Access oil pipeline invaded Standing Rock and Cheyenne River territory in 2016.

The 1958 case arose when the United States moved to take Standing Rock land. It was titled *United States v. 2,005.32 Acres of Land, More or Less, Situate in Corson County, South Dakota; and Sioux Indians of Standing Rock Reservation, et al., and Unknown Owners.*[75] Standing Rock and Cheyenne River claimed that their land was protected by treaty. Chief Judge George Mickelson of the U.S. District Court for the Northern Division of South Dakota acknowledged that the 2,000-plus acres of land were in fact part of "a vast reservation set aside for the Sioux Nation by a treaty between the United States and the Sioux on April 29, 1868 . . . set apart for the absolute and undisturbed use and occupation of the Indians."

Judge Mickelson said that the question in the case was whether the secretary of the army had "sufficient authorization from Congress to acquire this tribal land." He began his answer with "a recitation . . . [of] certain principles of law . . . [to] assist in placing the issue here in its proper perspective." His statement of principles was a straightforward recitation of the federal anti-Indian law exception: "Congress has the power to authorize the taking of Indian tribal lands . . . [and] Where there is a treaty with Indians which would otherwise restrict the Congress, Congress can abrogate the treaty in order to exercise its sovereign right."[76]

Having stated the question and principles (i.e., the exception), Judge Mickelson leaped to what he called the "obvious" answer, saying, "Congress has the authority to condemn the [land] in this case, and this can be done even though it is in abrogation of the treaty provisions."[77] Once again, the exception was the rule.

Then he tried to explain the exception. He said that this is "not to say that the treaty provisions are to be ignored, but instead . . . to require that there be clear Congressional action which indicates an intention to abrogate . . . the treaty." He added, "Manifestly, this must be so if the treaty is to have any meaning at all."[78] Read that again: The treaty can't be ignored, but it can be clearly abrogated; and this gives the treaty meaning. What?

He tried harder, getting more convoluted: "By the very existence of the treaty, providing that the reservation land be set aside for the absolute and undisturbed use and occupation of the Indians . . . a special situation has been created. . . . [The Treaty] contain[s] solemn promises to the Indian people by the government of the United States . . . that . . . stand as the highest expressions of the law regarding Indian land until Congress states to the contrary."[79] This time, Mickelson came very close to actually naming the exception: a treaty guarantee of absolute and undisturbed use is *not* a guarantee of absolute and undisturbed use; it only creates a "special situation" (the exception) in which the guarantee of absolute and undisturbed use may be abrogated, so long as the abrogation is clear. That's a mouthful.

Judge Mickelson's valiant attempt to define the exception as an act of domination that is not an act of domination was an explanation worthy of *Alice in Wonderland*: "If I had a world of my own, everything would be nonsense. Nothing would be what it is, because everything would be what it isn't. And contrariwise, what it is, it wouldn't be. And what it wouldn't be it would. You see?"[80]

Mickelson's convoluted reasoning provided yet another textbook example of Carl Schmitt's assertion, "The exception does not only confirm the rule; the rule as such lives off the exception alone."[81] In federal anti-Indian law, only the exception exists; the seeming rules are only its reflections in a hall of mirrors.

Having tried to explain how federal anti-Indian law works, Judge Mickelson went back to the secretary of the army's argument that the federal Flood Control Act of 1944 abrogated the treaty and authorized the Army Corps to take Standing Rock and Cheyenne River lands. The Standing Rock and Cheyenne River lawyers had already agreed with the federal anti-Indian law exception, but they argued that the Flood Control Act had not "clearly" abrogated the treaty. The power of the exception is such that even lawyers who argue for Native nations get caught up in it; we will see other examples of this phenomenon later in this book.

Mickelson agreed with Standing Rock and Cheyenne River. He said that the words of the act showed that Congress wanted "voluntary negotiations to be made in relation to tribal lands," not a unilateral taking. He referred again to the exception, which he called "the peculiar situation of the Indians which has resulted in a guardian-ward relationship,"[82] and said that the U.S. guardian was "obliged to indicate" when it wanted to take the property of its ward. He said that it had not indicated a taking in the Flood Control Act.

Having delivered a win for Standing Rock and Cheyenne River, Judge Mickelson closed his opinion with a helpful reminder to the Army Corps of how the United States could undo the victory. He did this by restating the exception: "In order to emphasize the issue in this decision, we wish to restate that the authority of Congress to exercise the right of eminent domain over Indian tribal lands is not questioned. We are granting the motion of the Tribe because of a lack of exercise of this authority. The matter can be speedily remedied by bringing it to the attention of the Congress."[83]

This is precisely what happened. Congress quickly asserted its claimed right of domination under the federal anti-Indian law exception. On September 2, 1958, barely seven months after Judge Mickelson's decision, it enacted Public Law 85–915, the Oahe Dam Act, "to provide for the acquisition of lands by the United States required for the reservoir created by the construction of Oahe Dam on the Missouri River and for rehabilitation of the Indians of the Standing Rock Sioux Reservation in South Dakota and North Dakota." The text of the act said, "Approximately 55,993.82 acres of land . . . are hereby taken"[84] (almost thirty times the original claim!). Not even two weeks after Congress passed the Oahe Dam Act, the Eighth Circuit Court of Appeals vacated the District Court's order blocking the taking, saying that the issue was now "moot."[85]

The Oahe Dam Act appropriated money "in consideration" of the taking; but the act also said, "No part of [the] funds shall be used for . . . the purchase of land by the tribe except for the purpose of resale to individual Indians in furtherance of the rehabilitation program authorized by this section." In other words, in keeping with the 1950s termination policy of breaking up Native peoples and allotting lands to individuals, the money could not be used to purchase other Standing Rock or Cheyenne River land, but only for "individual . . . rehabilitation."[86]

Oahe Dam was constructed, displacing thousands of Standing Rock and Cheyenne River people from tens of thousands of acres of their land, including their most productive agriculture and most fruitful medicinal plant–gathering areas. The huge reservoir that was created backed up over 200 miles of the Missouri River, flooding additional land. It is that body of water through which the Dakota Access Pipeline (DAPL) was built in 2017, sparking worldwide protests and support for Indigenous land rights. Actions took place inside and outside the courts. Litigation over the pipeline continues in 2022.

In 1997, Professor David E. Wilkins wrote, "'Federal Indian law' as a discipline having coherent and interconnected premises is wholly a myth."[87] We are able to penetrate the myth and arrive at an understanding of the confusion when we realize that federal anti-Indian law consists of an exception from the rule of law—a suspension of law. We then understand why analyzing the cases as if they displayed a set of rules—even contradictory rules—leaves everything in a theoretical mess. Carl Schmitt addressed this by saying in creating the exception, "Authority proves itself not to need law to create law. . . . What characterizes an exception is principally unlimited authority. . . . The state remains, whereas law recedes."[88] Ultimately, as Eric Cheyfitz and Shari M. Huhndorf put it, "The . . . incoherence [of federal anti-Indian law] is a mark of its violence, of the genocide by other means it visits on the tribes."[89]

Professor Matthew Fletcher's 2008 article, "The Supreme Court and the Rule of Law: Case Studies in Indian Law,"[90] provided an example of the muddle that arises from trying to view federal anti-Indian law as a set of rules. Fletcher opened the article by saying that the "principles" of the Marshall trilogy "form the basis for Indian law today." He closed by saying that *Johnson v. McIntosh* exercised the "power" of "divestiture" against "tribal sovereignty."[91] These two characterizations of the founding case in federal anti-Indian law can be reconciled only if the "principles" are the principles of divestiture, of domination; but Fletcher didn't go there. He asserted that the U.S. Supreme Court has developed "a settled common law of federal Indian law," following this by saying that the court has engaged in a "decades-long assault on the rule of law in federal Indian law cases."[92] Again, he did not take the step of saying that the settled law of federal anti-Indian law *is* an assault on the rule of law.

Instead of coming to what seemed like obvious conclusions about the nature of federal anti-Indian law, Fletcher fell into the netherworld of the unnamed exception: on the one hand, he said, "Indian law jurisprudence has degraded into a jumble of confusion and obfuscation since the late 1980s"[93]; on the other hand, he said, "much of the whole field from 1832 to 1959 is obfuscated by poorly reasoned decisions and racism."[94] Despite the fact that these timelines left fewer than twenty years of nonobfuscation in a nearly 200-year period, he said that the rules "appeared to have been settled law for long periods of time."[95] He then almost acknowledged the exception when he concluded that sentence by saying that the "settled law" lasted only "until the Court announced new principles that contradicted the settled law." He added, "It was easier for the Court to subvert the rule of law in these cases, because no explicit precedent appeared to be on point."[96] In short, Fletcher skated all around the evidence of the exception and ignored his hunch that there is no rule of law in federal anti-Indian law.

Instead, Fletcher offered a simple win-lose test for determining whether federal anti-Indian law decisions abide by the rule of law. He said, "In the past two decades, tribal interests have lost 75 percent of their cases before the Supreme Court, reversing the prior trend of the Court's findings in favor of tribal interests in slightly more than half its cases. Where is the rule of law here?" He did not indicate what he meant by the "prior trend," nor how a win-loss chart can define the rule of law.

Only in his final sentence did Fletcher finally allude to the absence of the rule of law in federal anti-Indian law. He said, "Federal Indian law offers a frightening glimpse of the future of the Supreme Court's view of the 'rule of law.'"[97] In this sentence, he echoed Milner Ball: "If the Court restrains neither Congress nor itself in taking away tribal rights, then we are confronted by a fundamental contradiction between our political rhetoric and our political realities."[98]

In short, as Joseph Singer suggested, we must start with federal anti-Indian law. When we start there, with the frightening glimpse, the fundamental contradiction, we penetrate the morass of rules to the exception. The exception is our starting point to clarify what otherwise appears as an impenetrable thicket.

Giorgio Agamben said that the foundational link between land appropriation and law is "even more complex than Schmitt maintains." He described
the exception as "a fundamental ambiguity, an unlocalizable zone of indistinction." Agamben said that the unlocalizable zone of indistinction acts as "a
principle of . . . infinite dislocation."[99] In federal anti-Indian law, this infinite
dislocation manifests as the principle that Native peoples may be moved and
removed, terminated and extinguished at the will of the United States. Federal anti-Indian law is an inherently paradoxical and contradictory juridical
space, which is what Judge Mickelson was trying to get his head around
when he struggled to explain the "special situation." Even a treaty guarantee
of land—a solemn promise forever—may be revoked, despite the fact that
the U.S. Constitution includes "all Treaties made, or which shall be made,
under the Authority of the United States," within the "supreme law of the
land."[100]

In a chilling remark that illuminates the creation of the reservation system, Agamben added, "When our age tried to grant the unlocalizable a permanent and visible localization, the result was the concentration camp." He
added, "The juridical constellation that guides the camp is . . . martial law
and the state of siege."[101]

## Land Appropriation

In 1950, Carl Schmitt published *The Nomos of the Earth in the International
Law of the Jus Publicum Europaeum*, exploring the global "division and distribution of land" as the origin of law and order. He wrote, "Every . . . ontological judgement derives from the land. . . . Land-appropriation [is] the primeval
act in founding law." Land appropriation "constitutes the original spatial
order, the source of all further concrete order and all further law." Land
appropriation is "the reproductive root in the normative order of history. . . .
All further property relations," Schmitt wrote, and "all subsequent law and
everything promulgated and enacted thereafter as decrees and commands"
are derived from this "radical title."[102]

With this perspective in mind, we turn to the famous book written in 1833
by Justice Joseph Story, *Commentaries on the Constitution of the United States*. A
member of the Supreme Court throughout the Marshall trilogy, Story published the book one year after the final case in the trilogy. In Book I, *History of
the Colonies*, Chapter I, "Origin of the Title to Territory of the Colonies," Story
said that the origin of the English claim of title to its colonies was the "right
of discovery" proclaimed in Henry VII's 1495 commission to John Cabot,
"to subdue and take possession of any lands unoccupied by any Christian
Power."[103] Story commented, "In respect to countries, then inhabited by
the natives, it is not easy to perceive, how, in point of justice, or
humanity, or general conformity to the law of nature, it [title by discovery]

can be successfully vindicated." He added that there was "no doubt" the Natives of the continent were the original "absolute proprietors of the soil."[104]

Story then spelled out how the doctrine of Christian discovery justified setting aside justice, humanity, and the law of nature to make a claim of colonizer title. He said that the colonizers "found little difficulty in reconciling themselves to the adoption of any principle, which gave ample scope to their ambition . . . their interests, their prejudices, and their passions." He explained, "The Indians were a savage race, sunk in the depths of ignorance and heathenism." Indeed, he said, if Indigenous peoples were not "extirpated for their want of religion and just morals, they might be reclaimed from their errors" and exchange "their wild and debasing habits for civilization and Christianity."[105] Story explicitly disputed any notion that the colonists conquered the Natives, saying, "They claimed an absolute dominion over the whole territories afterwards occupied by them, not in virtue of any conquest of, or cession by, the Indian natives, but as a right acquired by discovery."[106] He said all these principles were "discussed at great length in the celebrated case of *Johnson v. M'Intosh*." He added that the *Johnson* opinion was "more clear and exact than has ever been before in print."[107]

Story pointed to the papal grant that Marshall referred to in *Johnson*. This was the 1493 bull *Inter Caetera,* issued by Pope Alexander the Sixth,[108] which granted Ferdinand and Isabella, sponsors of "our beloved son, Christopher Columbus," ownership of all land Columbus might discover, "so far as it was not then possessed by any Christian prince." Story said that this papal authority to dominate Indigenous peoples was "for the purpose of overthrowing heathenism, and propagating the Catholic religion."[109]

Story summarized the doctrine of Christian discovery as follows: "The title of the Indians was not treated as a right of propriety and dominion; but as a mere right of occupancy. As infidels, heathen, and savages, . . . [they] were not allowed to possess the prerogatives belonging to absolute, sovereign and independent nations." He concluded with the extraordinary statement that Native "territory . . . was, in respect to Christians, deemed, as if it were inhabited only by brute animals."[110]

Story said that the language of the papal bulls set the mode of legal reasoning that had been adopted by all Christian monarchs to justify their colonial enterprises. He emphasized that England followed the papal doctrine even after breaking with the papacy. In saying this, Story followed not only John Marshall, but John Dee, a key advisor to Queen Elizabeth I, who explained to Her Majesty that despite excommunication by the pope, she had "the natural and divine obligation of Christian monarchs to bring all infidels and pagans into a state of Christianity."[111]

In short, Joseph Story illuminated the U.S. claim of title to Native lands as a *land appropriation* under the rubric of "Christian discovery." He showed that, to use Schmitt's words, Christian discovery is the "primeval act" in founding federal anti-Indian law. To follow and paraphrase Schmitt further, Christian discovery "constitutes the original spatial order [of the United States], the source of all further concrete order and all further law." Christian discovery is "the reproductive root in the normative order of [U.S.] history." Finally, "all further property relations" and "all subsequent [U.S.] law and everything promulgated and enacted thereafter as decrees and commands" are derived from this Christian discovery claim of "radical title." Ultimately, federal anti-Indian law and claims of U.S. sovereignty are joined at the hip, conceptually and historically.

In 1888, Burke A. Hinsdale examined the question of "why the Christian powers rested their claims on discovery, and not on conquest." The answer, he said, was that "discovery . . . would reach much farther than conquest." Conquest was a factual matter, a result of a war; it required an invading force to actually establish itself. Discovery, in contrast, was a symbolic assertion requiring only symbolic acts, as when Columbus, "clad in shining vestments, bearing a drawn sword, caused a cross to be erected while he repeated in Latin a prayer," and claimed the land that he called San Salvador ("The Savior"). The royal grants of land extending from ocean to ocean did not reflect ignorance of geography, Hinsdale said, but rather were a way of claiming territories that had not yet even been encountered, let alone could be claimed to have been conquered. In short, the doctrine of discovery had distinct advantages over factual conquest as a doctrinal basis for claiming title to land.[111]

Hinsdale pointed to a further advantage of discovery over conquest. He said, "To claim by discovery was more dignified than to claim by conquest, since the latter would be a recognition of the savages as enemies."[112] To understand his meaning, we need to recall that Christian discovery originated in the international law of Christendom, the *respublica Christiana*, with what Carl Schmitt referred to as "its profound distinctions between different types of enemies and, consequently, various types of wars . . . based on profound distinctions between human beings and on great disparities in their status."[113] To put it simply, an attack on savages did not have the same dignity as a war against a just enemy; it was demeaning for a Christian to fight against a savage. A dignified conqueror wanted an honorable enemy. Thus, as Hinsdale said, "To claim by conquest. . . .would be a recognition of the savages as enemies," a higher status than they deserved. It might even suggest that the Natives were full human beings.

Story's *Commentaries* support Hinsdale's analysis. In closing Book I with a "General Review," he took pains to insist again that colonial title claims were *not* rooted in conquest. He emphasized, "The Indians could in no just sense be considered a conquered people, who had been stripped of their territorial possessions by superior force." Instead, he said, "they were considered as a people, not having any regular laws, or any organized government; but as mere wandering tribes."[114]

Once again, we see Christian discovery doctrine is more than a legal theory of property; it lies at the core of an *ontological matrix—a metaphysics of being:* being human, being Indigenous, being civilized, being Christian, being heathen, being capable of owning land, being capable of sovereignty. When we parse federal anti-Indian law at this level, we are engaging in what Steven Newcomb called "cognitive legal studies."[115]

Schmitt's words quoted at the beginning of this section provide a precise philosophical definition from which to understand the land-appropriation doctrine of Christian discovery: it is the root of every ontological judgment in American culture—the order of things, so to speak—including America's self-image as a nation with a divine mission. As the origin of the U.S. claim to land, it is the source of all further concrete order and all further U.S. law—not only U.S. federal anti-Indian law, but U.S. property law and U.S. sovereignty claims. This fundamental intertwining of legal and cultural domains accounts for the intense anxiety encountered in discussions of Indigenous peoples in relation to the United States. Logically and historically, federal anti-Indian law carries significance far beyond relations of the United States to Native peoples. A challenge to Christian discovery and U.S. appropriation of Native lands amounts to a metaphysical crisis for America.

Before we dive into this crisis, we will explore one of the most common—and commonly misunderstood—masks for the doctrine of Christian discovery, the so-called trust doctrine.

## Untrustworthy Trust Doctrine

While "plenary power" is the most common name for the federal anti-Indian law exception, the so-called trust relation is the most common mask. "Trust" implies that the domination inherent in the exception is really a form of "protection."

In a 1975 law review article, Professor Reid Chambers phrased the trust doctrine as a commonplace, saying, "It is generally accepted that the United States owes fiduciary duties to American Indians."[116] In 1984, a "Note" in the *Harvard Law Review* revisited this theme, saying, "moral rhetoric suffuses federal Indian law." It added, "For a century and a half, the President and Congress have explicitly invoked morality or used moral terminology to justify actions with legal consequences for American Indians." It added, "The trust doctrine purportedly follows from normative principles."[117] In 1987, the U.S. Senate Select Committee on Indian Affairs declared emphatically, "The trust relationship is one of the primary cornerstones of Indian law."[118] The committee's rhetoric came from the 1982 edition of Felix Cohen's *Handbook of Federal Indian Law.*[119]

As we saw, the root of the trust doctrine is *Cherokee Nation v. Georgia*, in which Chief Justice Marshall said that Native peoples' relation to the United

States "resembles that of a ward to a guardian."[120] Technically, Marshall's metaphor was only dicta—a remark he made in passing that was not necessary to the decision—whereas the decision was about what the Cherokee were *not* (a foreign nation), and the negative answer showed the exception in action. But Marshall's extraneous image of what the Cherokee *were* quickly became dogma.

In 1987, Professor Milner Ball sharply criticized the trust doctrine, saying that although "much has been made of fiduciary duties owed to Indians by the United States," the reality is that the trust doctrine reflects the same "ethnocentrism that also produced the notions of superiority and unrestrained plenary power."[121] Ball said that the way the United States uses the "trust doctrine," with its purported normative morality, "appears in fact primarily to give moral color to depradation [sic] of tribes." He concluded that, in practice, "the trust doctrine is not a limit on plenary power and instead makes exercises of plenary power seem the right thing to do."[122] Professor Ball's assessment was spot on: "The trust doctrine is not a new game but a new way of shuffling the old deck."[123] We saw this earlier in rhetoric surrounding the Indian Claims Commission.

The close reading of cases that follows will demonstrate federal anti-Indian law trust doctrine as the exception at work, revealing that the "trust" is not actually trustworthy.

In 2011, the case of *United States v. Jicarilla Apache Nation* disposed of a breach-of-trust action filed against the U.S. Department of the Interior by the Jicarilla Apache Nation in the Court of Federal Claims. The Jicarilla said that the department owed them money damages for mismanagement of their natural resources—timber, gravel, oil, and gas. The department was managing Jicarilla resources as the self-proclaimed U.S. trustee for the Jicarilla—resources to which the United States also claimed to hold title as part of its claim of title to all Native lands. The department deposited proceeds from the sales of resources into trust funds held by the U.S. Treasury. The Jicarilla demanded to see Interior Department management documents. The Court of Federal Claims and the Court of Appeals granted access to some of the documents, but the department appealed to the U.S. Supreme Court, which reversed the lower courts. We will now examine what Justice Samuel Alito said when he delivered the Court's opinion.

Alito began by saying that the issue involved "the nature of the trust relationship between the United States and the Indian tribes." He added that under ordinary trust law, a trustee "could not withhold . . . [these documents] from the beneficiaries." However, Alito continued, "the relationship between the United States and the Indian tribes is distinctive."[124] He elaborated on this "distinction," saying, "Congress may style its relations with the Indians a 'trust' without assuming all the fiduciary duties of a private trustee, creating a trust relationship that is 'limited' or 'bare' compared to a trust relationship between private parties at common law."[125]

Alito explained further, "The difference between a private common-law trust and the statutory Indian trust follows from the unique position of the Government as sovereign."[126] "Unique, distinctive": These are metonyms for "exception." Alito was simply describing the federal anti-Indian law Christian discovery exception, without naming it as such.

The difference that Alito mentioned between federal anti-Indian law trust and ordinary trust law is stark. The best way to see it is by comparing Alito's language in *Jicarilla* to the definition of normal trust responsibility stated in 1928 by Supreme Court justice Benjamin Cardozo when he was still chief judge of the New York Court of Appeals. Cardozo described the norms that guide and control trustees in ordinary law. He said that a trustee is held to something stricter than honesty. He said, "Many forms of conduct permissible in a workaday world . . . are forbidden to those bound by fiduciary ties. A trustee is held to something stricter. . . . Not honesty alone, but the punctilio of an honor the most sensitive, is . . . the standard of behavior." Cardozo added a special warning against making exceptions in trust law: "Uncompromising rigidity has been the attitude of courts of equity when petitioned to undermine the rule of undivided loyalty by the disintegrating erosion of particular exceptions."[127]

Alito, in sharp contrast to Cardozo, emphasized that the federal anti-Indian law trust is not based on undivided loyalty to the Native beneficiaries, but rather on a U.S. claim of plenary power bound only by its own interests. He said, "Throughout the history of the Indian trust relationship, we have recognized that the organization and management of the trust is a sovereign function subject to the plenary authority of Congress." Congress, he wrote, has "plenary authority to divest the tribes of any attributes of sovereignty . . . plenary authority to legislate for the Indian tribes in all matters, including their form of government . . . plenary authority over the Indians and all their tribal relations, and full power to legislate concerning their tribal property."[128]

Alito emphasized that in the exercise of its so-called trust responsibility, the ultimate loyalty of the U.S. trustee is to itself. He said, "The Government has often structured the trust relationship to pursue its own policy goals. Thus, while trust administration relat[es] to the welfare of the Indians, the maintenance of the limitations which Congress has prescribed . . . is distinctly an interest of the United States."[129]

In plain language, what Alito was saying was this: federal anti-Indian law trust doctrine is a thoroughgoing exception from the normal trust law requirement of undivided loyalty to the beneficiary.

Alito continued his explanation of the federal anti-Indian law trust exception by unabashedly listing the vagaries and volatility of policies and programs imposed on Native peoples by the U.S. trustee. He echoed Interior solicitor Nathan R. Margold's 1942 definition of federal anti-Indian law as "the federal law governing Indians," saying, "Congress has structured the trust relationship to reflect its considered judgment about how the Indians ought to be governed."[130] He expressed no qualms about this U.S. domination and went on to provide examples.

"For example," Alito wrote, "the *Indian General Allotment Act* of 1887 . . . was a comprehensive congressional attempt to change the role of Indians in American society. . . . Congress aimed to promote the assimilation of Indians by dividing Indian lands into individually owned allotments. The federal policy aimed to substitute a new individual way of life for the older Indian communal way." He continued, "The *Indian Reorganization Act* of 1934 . . . marked a shift away from assimilation policies and toward more tolerance and respect for traditional aspects of Indian culture. . . . The Act prohibited further allotment and restored tribal ownership." Subsequently, he said, Congress decided to enable "tribes to run health, education, economic development, and social programs for themselves."[131]

Alito concluded that federal anti-Indian law trust doctrine "authorizes the adoption on the part of the United States of such policy as their own public interests may dictate."[132] He summed up the *Jicarilla* decision with a full-throated embrace of the exception: "The control over the Indian tribes that has been exercised by the United States pursuant to the trust relationship—forcing the division of tribal lands, restraining alienation—does not correspond to the fiduciary duties of a common-law trustee. Rather, the trust relationship has been altered and administered as an instrument of federal policy."[133]

He could have been channeling Carl Schmitt: "The state suspends the law in the exception on the basis of its right of self-preservation. . . . What characterizes an exception is principally unlimited authority." In the exception, said Schmitt, "the decision frees itself from all normative ties and becomes in the true sense absolute."[134] Alito's *Jicarilla* opinion demonstrated this absolutely.

The *Jicarilla* case was not the first to distinguish between federal anti-Indian law and ordinary trust law. In 1980, in *United States v. Mitchell,* the Supreme Court, in an opinion by Justice Thurgood Marshall, ruled that the trust doctrine inherent in the 1887 General Allotment Act, which took land from the Quinault and other Native peoples, was a "limited trust . . . that does not impose any duty upon the Government." The dissenting justices—Byron White, William J. Brennan, Jr., and John Paul Stevens—pointed out that this means that the federal anti-Indian trust doctrine "is not a trust as that term is commonly understood."[135]

In 2009, in *United States v. Navajo Nation,*[136] the Supreme Court denied a Navajo claim for damages based on breaches of U.S. fiduciary duties regarding coal mining royalties. The Court, in an opinion by Justice Scalia, said that the United States had no fiduciary duty to the Navajo, even though it had "comprehensive control" over coal mining on Navajo land. Scalia's denial of fiduciary responsibility flew in the face of a finding in the case by the Federal Court of Claims "that the United States violated the most fundamental fiduciary duties of care, loyalty and candor." The Court of Claims added, "Were this a court of equitable jurisdiction considering a private trust, plaintiffs might easily qualify for remedies typically afforded wronged beneficiaries."[137] Yet again, the exception was hiding in plain view.

A most bizarre example of the exception at work in the federal anti-Indian law trust relationship occurred in 1985, in *United States v. Dann*. The case started when the United States accused two Western Shoshone sisters, Mary and Carrie Dann, of trespassing on U.S. public land by grazing their cattle without a federal permit. The Danns replied with two arguments: Contrary to federal anti-Indian law, they said that the land belonged to the Western Shoshone Nation as possessors from time immemorial; alternatively, they argued, they had occupancy rights under federal anti-Indian law. The United States replied that any title that the Western Shoshone ever had, of any sort, had been extinguished in a prior Indian Claims Commission proceeding.

The *Dann* case went back and forth twice between the federal district court, which ruled against the Danns, and the Ninth Circuit Court of Appeals, which favored them. The Ninth Circuit, in an opinion by Judge Canby, said two things: One, title to Western Shoshone lands could not have been extinguished by the Indian Claims Commission because "the title issue in this case was neither actually litigated nor actually decided in the proceedings before the ICC."[138] Two, regardless of the Claims Commission proceeding, the Western Shoshone had never actually been paid any compensation by the commission.

Most amazingly, Judge Canby turned Christian discovery doctrine back on itself by looking at the practical litigation effects of the doctrine: He wrote, "The Government consistently maintained that the Indians never owned the lands they claimed and therefore . . . the question of title-extinction never arose."[139] In other words, Canby said that Western Shoshone title had never been litigated or decided because the United States simply declared itself the owner and refused to litigate the issue! The United States was suddenly trapped by its reliance on Christian discovery doctrine.

While all this was going on, the Danns and other Western Shoshone were actively trying to remove their lands from the Indian Claims Commission proceeding. The commission rejected their efforts and continued the proceeding to a final judgment award. Nonetheless, Canby said, no award had ever been actually paid to the Western Shoshone; and so long as they have not been paid, they may still assert their title arguments. He added that a Claims Commission proceeding is not final "until the Commission has filed its final report with Congress *and the Indians have actually been paid the compensation owed them.*"[140]

Briefly put, the Ninth Circuit decision in *Dann* opened a door in federal anti-Indian law to actually litigate the question of who owns Western Shoshone lands. But when the United States appealed to the Supreme Court, that door was quickly slammed shut.

In an opinion written by Justice William Brennan, the Supreme Court reversed the Ninth Circuit. Brennan noted, but passed over, the question of whether Western Shoshone title had ever actually been litigated or decided by the Indian Claims Commission. He ignored the fact that the Western Shoshone had tried to stop the commission proceedings in order to protect their land. Instead, he focused on the commission's decision that the United States had taken Western Shoshone land and awarded $26 million to the tribe as compensation. Brennan said that the award itself meant that title was extinguished, despite the fact the Western Shoshone had refused any money from the commission. Here's where things got interesting.

Brennan started explaining the decision by saying that the "chief purpose" of the Indian Claims Commission Act was "to dispose of the Indian claims problem with finality." He went on to say that requiring actual payment to the Western Shoshone would "frustrate" that purpose. He tried to make the situation look like ordinary trust law, saying, "Funds transferred from a debtor to an agent or trustee of the creditor constitute payment, and it is of no consequence that the creditor refuses to accept the funds from the agent." Then he worked the magic of the exception. He said that the award of the Indian Claims Commission "placed the Government in a dual role with respect to the Tribe: the Government was at once a judgment debtor, owing $26 million to the Tribe, and a trustee for the Tribe. . . . The Indian Claims Commission ordered the Government *qua* judgment debtor to pay $26 million to the Government *qua* trustee for the Tribe as the beneficiary."[141]

In short, Brennan put two hats on the United States: Under one hat, it was a *debtor* who owed money to the Western Shoshone; under the other hat, it was a *trustee* who accepted the money on behalf of the Western Shoshone. Presto! Federal anti-Indian law to the rescue: "Once the money was deposited into the trust account, payment was effected." Milner Ball called Brennan's opinion in the *Dann* case a "bookkeeping" maneuver and said, "Besides serving as an extraconstitutional moral excuse in the familiar ways, the trusteeship may always provide cover for novel operations against tribes."[142]

Brennan's two hats explanation would be preposterous in ordinary trust law. Judge Cardozo, who so strongly emphasized the high duties of a trustee, dealt in a 1926 case specifically with "dual interests," where he said that only by "uncompromising rigidity has the rule of undivided loyalty been maintained against disintegrating erosion."[143] As opposed to uncompromising rigidity and undivided loyalty, the federal anti-Indian law exception allowed Brennan to be incredibly flexible.

Brennan understood that the decision went against the rules of ordinary trust law, so he went on to explain how federal anti-Indian law differs from ordinary trust law. His explanation presented the exception: "The principles of payment under the common law of trust *as they have been applied to the context of relations between native American communities and the United States* require that we hold that payment occurs . . . when funds are placed by the United States into an account in the Treasury of the United States for the Tribe."[144]

The untrustworthiness of "trust" doctrine raises the question why Native litigants rely on rather than challenging the doctrine when they sue the United States. As Ball pointed out, the doctrine would carry "a fundamental threat," even if trust litigation were successful. "To bring suit on the trust requires acceptance of the premises of the trust—that the United States is a trustee for the tribes and can legitimately claim such power over them and their resources." To use trust doctrine means "indirectly embracing the degrading ethnocentrism that supports the theory."[145] We will look at litigation tactics and strategies in Chapter 5.

But first, we will investigate the jurisprudential crisis arising from the conflation of "fiduciary duty" and "plenary power."

## Legal Schizophrenia

Ironically, the forbidding adjectives used to describe federal anti-Indian law—"complex," "confusing," "contradictory," "peculiar," "obscure," "unmanageable," and so on—are almost always followed by positive assertions of the importance of the field. A typical example is the 2017 statement by the Judicial Branch of California: "The field of Federal Indian law . . . is incredibly complex . . . involving issues of real property, international law, administrative law, constitutional law, water law, federal jurisdiction, procedure, contracts, criminal law, etc., . . . [with] significance for everyone."[146]

The rhetorical pattern was set in 1942 by U.S. Interior Department solicitor Nathan R. Margold's introduction to Felix Cohen's *Handbook of Federal Indian Law*. He wrote, "The federal law governing Indians is a mass of statutes, treaties, and judicial and administrative rulings, that includes practically all the fields of law known to textbook writers." Margold added enigmatically, "In each of these fields the fact that Indians are involved gives . . . a new quirk which sometimes carries unpredictable consequences."[147]

In 1954, U.S. Supreme Court justice Felix Frankfurter echoed the theme in his foreword to a special issue of the *Rutgers Law Review* memorializing Felix Cohen. Frankfurter praised Cohen's *Handbook*, describing it as a "forbidding task of bringing meaning and reason out of the vast hodge-podge of treaties, statutes, judicial and administrative rulings, and unrecorded practice in which the intricacies and perplexities, the confusions and injustices of the law governing Indians lay concealed." He added, "Only a ripe and imaginative scholar with a synthesizing faculty would have brought luminous order out of such a mish-mash."[148]

Lawyers and judges generally prefer to ignore the thorny jurisprudential problems underlying these characterizations—the fact that "tribal sovereignty" is a negative concept and federal anti-Indian law "trust" is joined at the hip with a claim of "plenary power." Their reluctance to engage with philosophy, let alone critique the exception, demonstrates the accuracy of Carl Schmitt's description of the concept of sovereignty as "a disturbance" in the day-to-day flow of litigation. Federal anti-Indian law lawyers learn to live with what Margold called the "quirks," even when the quirks are as obvious and consequential, as in the *Coeur d'Alene* case, when the Supreme Court contradicted its own theories of "tribes" and the U.S. Constitution.

But in 2004, U.S. Supreme Court justice Clarence Thomas broke the silence and addressed the "quirkiness" of federal anti-Indian law. In a forceful concurring opinion in *United States v. Lara,* he attacked both the plenary power and tribal sovereignty doctrines, breaking open the exception and calling for a discussion of the forbidden topic.

*Lara* was a thorny jurisdictional case. Billy Jo Lara was a Turtle Mountain Chippewa living among the Spirit Lake Sioux. After Lara's repeated run-ins with the law, Spirit Lake authorities ordered him away and sent officers to escort him out of Spirit Lake. Lara resisted the police, and at his trial in Tribal Court, he pleaded guilty to striking a police officer, who was also a federal employee. Lara served ninety days in jail. Subsequently, the United States brought its own charges against him for striking the officer. Lara argued that this was double jeopardy and appealed, saying that he had already served time for the crime.

When the Supreme Court put the *Lara* case on its calendar, Professor Frank Pommersheim predicted that the decision would be "important, and arguably very potent"; but he added, "it is unlikely to get to the heart of the problem."[149] He underestimated Justice Thomas.

The Supreme Court upheld the separate prosecutions in an opinion by Justice Steven Breyer, who said that the U.S. Congress has "plenary power" to contract or expand "tribal jurisdiction" and in this case it had expanded it as a power independent of the United States. Therefore, Breyer said, Lara was not actually charged twice with the same crime but rather was charged for two separate crimes committed in one act—a "tribal" crime and a "federal" crime.

Justice Thomas leaped into the fray with his critical concurring opinion. He said that he felt obliged to agree with the court majority that Billy Jo Lara had not been subjected to double jeopardy because the precedents of federal anti-Indian law include the congressional power to expand tribal jurisdiction as described by Justice Breyer. However, Thomas added, "The time has come to reexamine the premises and logic of our tribal sovereignty cases."[150]

Thomas echoed Solicitor Margold and Justice Frankfurter, saying that there are "tensions" and "confusion" in federal anti-Indian law. But he was not satisfied to leave it there. He dug into it. He said that the trouble arises from "two largely incompatible and doubtful assumptions." One assumption, Thomas said, is the plenary power doctrine—the notion that the U.S. Congress "can regulate virtually every aspect of the tribes without rendering tribal sovereignty a nullity." The other assumption, he said, is the tribal sovereignty doctrine that says, "Indian tribes retain inherent sovereignty to enforce their criminal laws against their own members."[151]

Thomas attacked both doctrines. First, he said, "I cannot agree . . . that the Constitution grants to Congress plenary power [over] tribal sovereignty." Next, he added, "In my view, the tribes either are or are not separate sovereigns, and our federal Indian law cases untenably hold both positions simultaneously."[152] His critique became incendiary: "Federal Indian policy is, to say the least, schizophrenic. And this confusion continues to infuse federal Indian law and our cases."[153] Thomas summarized his critique by saying the United States "cannot simultaneously claim power to regulate virtually every aspect of the tribes through . . . legislation and also maintain that the tribes possess anything resembling 'sovereignty.'"[154]

Thomas concluded by calling for a "more critical" examination of federal anti-Indian law. The starting point, he said, was to "carefully follow . . . our assumptions to their logical conclusions and . . . identify . . . the potential sources of federal power to modify tribal sovereignty."[155] He left unstated the possibility that there may be *no* acceptable source of U.S. power to modify Indigenous sovereignty.

In 2016, Justice Thomas spoke again. And again he used a concurring opinion to call out the contradiction between the tribal sovereignty and plenary power doctrines, which he described as "a central tension within our Indian-law jurisprudence."[156]

The case, *United States v. Bryant*, was another criminal prosecution, this time under the U.S. Violence against Women Act,[157] which made it a federal crime for any person to commit "a domestic assault within . . . Indian country" if the person had at least two prior convictions for domestic violence in any court, including a "tribal court." The case involved Michael Bryant, Jr., a Northern Cheyenne man who had multiple convictions for domestic assault under Northern Cheyenne law. Using the Violence against Women Act, the U.S. attorney charged Bryant with a federal crime in U.S. court. Bryant argued that his prior convictions in the Northern Cheyenne court could not be used to trigger the federal law because he had not had legal counsel in tribal court, and therefore those convictions did not count as valid "prior convictions." He cited the Sixth Amendment right "to have the Assistance of Counsel for his defense." The district court ruled against him; on appeal, the circuit court ruled for him. The case then went to the U.S. Supreme Court.

Justice Ruth Bader Ginsberg wrote the opinion, in which she repeated the well-worn rhetoric about confusion in federal anti-Indian law. She said that the difficulty in this case was due to the "complex patchwork of federal, state, and tribal law governing Indian country, [which] has made it difficult to stem the tide of domestic violence experienced by Native American women."[158] Ginsberg bobbed and weaved through the "complex patchwork" and arrived at a decision affirming Bryant's federal conviction.

Justice Thomas had his opening. He began by concurring with the decision, as he had in *Lara*, "because our precedents dictate that holding."[159] Then he again challenged the coherence of the precedents. On the one hand, Thomas wrote, federal anti-Indian law doctrine says, "Tribes [hold a] status as separate sovereigns pre-existing the Constitution." On the other hand, he pointed out, a contrary doctrine says, "Congress [holds] plenary power over Indian tribes." Not satisfied this time with pointing out the contradiction, Thomas called for an inquiry into the theory of sovereignty, saying, "I continue to doubt whether *either* view of tribal sovereignty is correct."[160]

Thomas offered a historical diagnosis of the problem. He wrote, "Indian tribes have varied origins, discrete treaties with the United States, and different patterns of assimilation and conquest." The U.S. Supreme Court precedents, he said, "have made it all but impossible to understand the ultimate source of each tribe's sovereignty and whether it endures."[161] He then pointed to the plenary power doctrine, saying, "Congress' purported plenary power over Indian tribes rests on even shakier foundations. No enumerated power . . . [in the Constitution] gives Congress such sweeping authority."[162]

Thomas said until these central contradictions are cleared up, federal anti-Indian law "will remain bedeviled by amorphous and ahistorical assumptions about the scope of tribal sovereignty . . . and the fiction that Congress possesses plenary power over Indian affairs." Moreover, he said, if these confusions remain, federal anti-Indian law "will continue to be based on the paternalistic theory that Congress must assume all-encompassing control over the 'remnants of a race' for its own good."[163]

Justice Thomas's critiques stand out for two reasons. First, he sits on the court that originated and maintains the exception and its contradictory and confusing doctrines of federal anti-Indian law; second, he minced no words about it. Contrast his description of federal anti-Indian law with a typical clichéd commentary from the legal profession: "American Indian law cases . . . are interesting because of the inherent complexities in navigating the complicated landscape of federal Indian law. . . . The practice area requires mastery of many complex and continually changing areas of law."[164] The profound turmoil of doctrine that Thomas identified at the core of federal anti-Indian law belies the blandness of "interesting inherent complexities."

Justice Thomas's critique echoed the Standing Rock Sioux historian Vine Deloria, Jr.'s 1971 description of federal anti-Indian law in his book *Of Utmost Good Faith*. Deloria wrote, "Using a number of illogical and irreconcilable theories of ward-dependent nation, plenary powers of Congress, and treaty abrogation the court skips along spinning off inconsistencies like a new sun exploding comets as it tips its way out of the dawn of creation."[165]

In 1972, in *God Is Red*, Deloria went beyond pointing out internal contradictions. He traced federal anti-Indian law to its roots in Christian discovery doctrine, a topic that Justice Thomas managed to sidestep (although the inquiry that he proposed would necessarily lead there). Deloria wrote, "The reaction of the Christian nations to the discovery of the New World and its potential riches was one of unmitigated greed." He added, "The Christian church saw a means of directing the invasion of the new lands by placing its imprimatur on exploitation, in effect taking a percentage of the loot in return for blessing the enterprise."[166]

It remains to be seen whether Justice Thomas or any other justice will confront Christian discovery doctrine head-on and follow a critique of federal anti-Indian law to its logical conclusion: termination of the exception that denies Native land ownership and full self-determination. At a minimum, Thomas's voice is the clearest signal, at the highest level, that federal anti-Indian law is in a state of crisis.

It is getting increasingly hard to avoid deep philosophical discussion about federal anti-Indian law that would reveal the crisis. Contradictions are increasingly apparent, and efforts to hide the exception produce further "quirks."

Moreover, because federal anti-Indian law provides the ontological matrix of U.S. land appropriation claims, the doctrinal crisis spirals into a deep anxiety about U.S. sovereignty.

## Sovereign Anxiety

Professor Mark Rifkin said that the United States has not found an acceptable "normative foundation on which to rest the legitimacy" of its claim of sovereignty over Native lands and peoples: "The legitimacy of [U.S.] . . . jurisdiction remains a nagging source of anxiety."[167] His comments echo what James Gordley called, in another legal context, a "doctrinal crisis."[168]

Gordley's diagnosis of doctrinal crisis focused on contract law, but he said that the same situation faced property law. He said that the crisis arose from the fact the doctrines in these fields emerged from sixteenth- and early-seventeenth-century metaphysical syntheses that had become "all but unintelligible."[169] He quoted David Hume, for example, whose 1739 *Treatise of*

*Human Nature* said that the rules that "determine property . . . are principally fix'd by the imagination, or the more frivolous properties of our thought."[170] Gordley said that judges and lawyers nevertheless tried to use the old doctrines until finally, in the twentieth century, the crisis was recognized.

Similarly, federal anti-Indian law doctrines rest on a philosophical basis in Christian discovery that is all but unintelligible to modern thinking. Yet no acceptable substitute has been found. The philosophical foundation of federal anti-Indian law is a special embarrassment in a legal system that supposedly separates religion from law. The stakes are high.

The doctrinal crisis in federal anti-Indian law becomes more acute as critics of Christian discovery become more vocal and widespread. Religious groups, even some Christian churches, have joined the fray, calling for an end to Christian discovery doctrine, although none of them has acted to systematically transfer ownership of their property to the Indigenous peoples from whom it was taken.[171] Some have focused on demanding that the Vatican renounce the fifteenth-century papal bulls that articulated the doctrine. Some Indigenous litigants have attacked the doctrine in court. Meanwhile, Indigenous struggles on the ground, such as the Lakota at Standing Rock, directly reject the U.S. domination of Native lands based on the doctrine.

In 1993, Steven Newcomb asked whether federal anti-Indian law could sustain itself if the old ideas were brought to light: "Should the United States continue to assert a plenary dominion over Indians and an underlying vested property right in Indian lands based on the historical fact that Indian people were not Christians at the time of European arrival? Should Indian nations and peoples be denied under United States law their rights to 'complete sovereignty' and an exclusive right of territory in their lands on the basis of Christianity?"[172] Newcomb wrote that failing to confront and supplant the foundation of federal anti-Indian law "is to suggest that federal Indian law will always rest on a subjugating religious ideology."[173]

Gordley said that jurists responding to "a doctrinal crisis" may "wonder . . . if it [is] possible to have coherent legal doctrine."[174] Justice Thomas may be in this camp. What he might do to resolve the confusion in federal anti-Indian law is not clear. Contrary to some expectations about his conservative politics, his suggestions were not simply anti-Native. In his *Bryant* opinion, he suggested paying attention to "tribes' distinct histories. . . . to understand the ultimate source of each tribe's sovereignty and whether it endures."

On March 23, 2021, during oral argument in *United States v. Cooley*, it became clear that Thomas was not the only justice aware of a doctrinal crisis. *Cooley* involved the question of whether tribal police officers may detain or search non-Natives suspected of violating state or federal law on public highways running through reservations.[175] Commenting on the argument, Professor Elizabeth A. Reese said that it "revealed a court that seems deeply conflicted on just about every aspect of this case from top to bottom." Under the headline, "Court Struggles with the 'Indefensible Morass' it's Made in Indian Law," Reese said that the justices' questions showed their concern for "tribal sovereignty in theory vs. practice," adding that the "particular combination of facts and law has the potential to provoke both internal conflicts for individual justices and to create strange bedfellows across the court."[176]

For example, she pointed to the fact that the court's struggle to find an acceptable theory for federal anti-Indian law was made most obvious by questions from two justices usually found on opposite sides of the political spectrum, Samuel Alito and Stephen Breyer.[177] Alito asked the U.S. deputy solicitor general Eric Feigin to provide a "general test for distinguishing between those aspects of sovereignty that tribes retained and those that they did not." And Breyer posed essentially the same question to Eric Henkel, the attorney for Cooley: "What exactly do you think the tribal officer can do and what can't he do and why?"[178]

The answers shed no light. Feigin replied to Alito, "I don't think I can do a better job than the Court did in . . . other cases, which is they retain the inherent authority so long as it's not inconsistent with the overriding interests of the federal government." For his part, Henkel replied to Breyer, "The tribal officer needs to first ascertain Indian status when we're—when we're on non-tribal lands, like we are—. . . I think there's a—I think—yeah, I think there's a number of ways that he or she could do that."[179]

One aspect of the argument was clear: There was no indication that the justices or the attorneys were inclined to investigate the foundation of the doctrinal crisis—the federal anti-Indian law exception and the doctrine of Christian discovery. The closest the argument came to the question of Native land title and territorial jurisdiction was the following exchange between Justice Elena Kagan and Attorney Henkel:

ELENA KAGAN: Mr. Henkel, the government relies in some significant measure on the idea of cross-enforcement authority, in other words, the belief that sovereigns generally have the power to respond to potential violations of another sovereign's laws. Are you contesting that that authority generally exists, in other words, outside the Indian context, or are you accepting that but just saying it's—it's different in the Indian context?

ERIC R. HENKEL: I—I'm not accepting that, no. I—I think the first place to start is a line of analysis that this Court gave in *Plains Commerce Bank*, where the Court expressly rejected, you know, drawing some sort of parallel between tribal authority and what state and federal authorities they can do. Those—that line of argument, this Court said, completely overlooks the very reasons that cases like *Montana* and *Oliphant* and this one even exist, which is that the sovereign authority of Indian tribes is limited in ways state and federal authority is not. And the—and the way that it's more limited is because they are not full territorial sovereigns.

They do not have authority over all who come within their borders. So I think, when you start from that proposition and then you're—any analysis—any analogy to, you know, state authority to enforce federal law and—and vice versa, I mean, there's—there's no comparison right out of the gate because states and federal authorities are full territorial sovereigns.

Justice Thomas entered the fray and opened a path for deeper analysis when he asked the U.S. deputy solicitor, "Could you discuss [the *Lara* case] just a bit?"[180] As we saw earlier, *Lara* was the case where Thomas character- ized U.S. law related to Native peoples as "schizophrenic." No one in the *Cooley* case took advantage of Thomas's opening to question the exception, the extravagant pretension that the United States owns Native lands and has dominion over Native peoples. Professor Reese suggested that the overall tenor of the argument showed a likelihood that the Court would uphold tribal police power in the case, but "the path they choose to get there could vary dramatically, with equally dramatic implications for tribal sovereignty."[181]

As it turned out, the Court unanimously agreed, in an opinion by Justice Breyer, that the tribal police officer had authority to detain the non-Native driver. Breyer opened with the familiar statement of the exception—namely, the "sovereignty that the Indian tribes retain is of a unique and limited charac- ter."[182] He then gave a quick tour of the indeterminacy of the rules developed in the exception. On the one hand, he wrote, "A tribe could not exercise criminal jurisdiction over non-Indians." On the other hand, this "general proposition was not an absolute rule." He pointed out, as if this would clear up the confu- sion, that the court had "repeated [the] proposition and exceptions in several cases."[183] Perhaps trying to channel Carl Schmitt, Breyer added, "We have pre- viously warned that the . . . exceptions are 'limited' and 'cannot be construed in a manner that would swallow the rule.'"[184] As Schmitt said, however, "The exception . . . confirm[s] the rule; the rule . . . lives off the exception."

The confusion in the *Cooley* case paled in comparison with the fracturing of the Fifth Circuit Court of Appeals in *Brakeen v. Haaland* one month later (April 26, 2021). Sixteen judges, two short of the entire bench, issued a total of 325 pages of conflicting and overlapping opinions trying to decide a case about the constitutionality of the Indian Child Welfare Act and the validity of implementing regulations promulgated by the Bureau of Indian Affairs. We do not need to delve into the substance of the case and the narrow area of agreement that produced an en banc majority for a limited range of issues to see the chaos. It is demonstrated by a simple list of the separate opinions:

Dennis, Circuit Judge, filed an opinion concurring in part and dissenting in part, in which Stewart and Graves, Circuit Judges, joined, and Wiener,

Higginson, Southwick, and Costa, Circuit Judges, joined in part, and Owen, Chief Judge, joined in part.

Duncan, Circuit Judge, filed an opinion concurring in part and dissenting in part, in which Smith, Elrod, Willett, Engelhardt, and Oldham, Circuit Judges, joined, and Jones, Southwick, Haynes, Circuit Judges, joined in part, and Owen, Chief Judge, joined in part.

Haynes, Circuit Judge, filed an opinion concurring in part.

Owen, Chief Judge, filed an opinion concurring in part and dissenting in part.

Wiener, Circuit Judge, filed an opinion dissenting in part.

Costa, Circuit Judge, filed an opinion concurring in part and dissenting in part, in which Owen, Chief Judge, and Wiener, Higgenson, and Southwick, Circuit Judges, joined in part.[185]

The list speaks for itself: federal anti-Indian law is in crisis, and the self-proclaimed sovereign is anxious.

The crisis arising from the exception has spread far beyond the United States. A 1996 United Nations (UN) statement merged the exceptional definition of Indigenous peoples as subject to state domination in the following definition: "Indigenous communities, peoples and nations are those which, having a historical continuity with pre-invasion and pre-colonial societies that developed on their territories, consider themselves distinct from other sectors of the societies now prevailing in those territories, or parts of them. They form at present non-dominant sectors of society."[186]

The law professor S. James Anaya, who would later be appointed UN special rapporteur for Indigenous peoples, distilled the UN definition as follows: "The term indigenous refers broadly to the living descendants of preinvasion inhabitants of lands now dominated by . . . settler societies born of the forces of empire and conquest."[187]

But the United Nations acknowledged that Indigenous peoples resist domination, saying that they "are determined to preserve, develop and transmit to future generations their ancestral territories, and their ethnic identity, as the basis of their continued existence as peoples, in accordance with their own cultural patterns, social institutions and legal systems."[188]

In 2007, the Christian discovery exception became subject to worldwide critique when the UN General Assembly adopted the Declaration on the Rights of Indigenous Peoples. Article 3 of the declaration condemned "all doctrines, policies and practices based on . . . national origin or racial, religious, ethnic or cultural differences."[189]

In 2014, the UN Permanent Forum on Indigenous Issues intensified the critique in a *Study on the Impacts of the Doctrine of Discovery on Indigenous Peoples.* The study said, "The Doctrine of Discovery . . . has been used as a framework for justification to dehumanize, exploit, enslave and subjugate indigenous peoples and dispossess them of their most basic rights, laws, spirituality, worldviews and governance and their lands and resources. Ultimately it was the very foundation of genocide."[190]

Steven Salaita took advantage of international attention to these issues and suggested an "inter/national" process of negotiation.[191] But international negotiation has yet to displace the role of litigation; court challenges remain a crucial avenue for action. In the next chapter, we investigate the possibilities and pitfalls of that path.

# CHAPTER FIVE

# Revoking Christian Discovery Doctrine

## Lawyers and Litigants

We are accustomed to lawsuits as a normal part of life, but we rarely pause to consider what it means to litigate a case. We know that some cases affect only the people in the lawsuit, while others affect thousands and even millions of people. Cases that change the law itself, like the famous case that overturned the racist doctrine of "separate but equal," are in the latter category. This chapter focuses on litigation that aims to change federal anti-Indian law.

Court challenges to federal anti-Indian law depend on the willingness of litigants and lawyers to shoulder a complex and even hazardous burden. Criticism of the doctrine of Christian discovery constitutes a kind of lèse majesté: an affront to the pretension of U.S. sovereignty. Even when the emperor wears no clothes—when courts declare his "trusteeship" to be "bare"—he insists on his prerogatives as the Christian dominator.[1]

In 2006, Richard B. Collins and Karla D. Miller asked "why there were few tribal lawsuits" to enforce their rights.[2] Their answer included demoralization resulting from colonial domination and racial hostility, and the inordinate complexity of federal anti-Indian law. They nevertheless emphasized the "obvious importance" of defending Native rights, saying that failure to litigate has "negative consequences for those whose rights lie dormant."[3]

In 2012, Professor Walter Echo-Hawk called for a "focused national legal movement" in federal anti-Indian law. He called it the "mother of all campaigns," in which "strategists should develop . . . legal, legislative, and social strategies implemented through a coordinated program of public education, national litigation, and legislation."[4] Echo-Hawk noted that the twentieth-century challenge of the National Association for the Advancement of Colored People (NAACP) to "separate but equal" required years of advance discussion.

The political analyst Juan Williams's biography of Thurgood Marshall, the lawyer who organized that challenge and argued *Brown v. Board of Education* before the Supreme Court (and who would later be appointed to the Court), described how Marshall had to bring together lawyers and political leaders who proposed varying, even contradictory strategies. Indeed, not all Black leaders were interested in the challenge because they "feared that demands for integration might anger white state officials and lead them to cut back already meager funding for existing black schools."[5] Echo-Hawk pointed out a similar hesitancy to rock the boat among "scholars . . . concerned about the colonial stigma of the foundational principles in federal Indian law . . . who remain cautious about departing from them for fear of unraveling the fabric of that body of law."[6]

An important factor fueling the Black civil rights litigation was the geopolitical Cold War rivalry for the allegiance of Third World countries. The Soviet Union's promotion of worldwide awareness about American racial discrimination gave energy to the challenge and provided political space for the U.S. Supreme Court to reassess fundamental racism in U.S. law. A similar geopolitical space appears to be opening in the twenty-first century for Indigenous challenges to US law. When U.S. president Joe Biden declared in April 2021 that the 1915 Ottoman attack on Armenians constituted genocide, Turkish president Tayyip Erdogan sharply responded, "The U.S. president has made baseless, unjust, and untrue remarks about the sad events that took place in our geography over a century ago. . . . If you say genocide, then you need to look at yourselves in the mirror and make an evaluation. The Native Americans, I don't even need to mention them, what happened is clear."[7]

In January 2021, the U.S. State Department issued a determination that the People's Republic of China "has committed genocide against the predominantly Muslim Uyghurs and other ethnic and religious minority groups in Xinjiang." Secretary of State Mike Pompeo added, "I believe this genocide is ongoing."[8] In March 2022, China responded with a sharp challenge to what it called "the American Genocide of the Indians." The statement, issued by the Chinese embassy in Washington, D.C., said, "The slaughter, forced relocation, cultural assimilation, and unjust treatment the United States committed against American Indians have constituted de facto genocides. These acts fully match the definition of genocide in the UN Convention on the Prevention and Punishment of the Crime of Genocide, and have continued for hundreds of years to this day. It is imperative that the U.S. government drop its hypocrisy and double standards on human rights issues, and take seriously the severe racial problems and atrocities in its own country."[9]

Prominent commentators seized on the issue, exemplified by an October 2021 essay in *Foreign Policy* magazine called, "The United States Must Reckon with Its Own Genocides," marking Indigenous Peoples Day in the United States. The authors said, "Just as Canada is reckoning with its genocidal history of colonization, so must the United States. This is not only a moral necessity at home but one vital if Washington wants to be a credible opponent of abusive regimes worldwide." They called out the boarding schools designed to "kill the Indian, save the man" as "assimilationist ambitions [that] were explicitly genocidal." They also noted, "Americans have begun to engage with their country's history of slavery and racism. . . . But there has been no similar epiphany when it comes to the legacy of the genocide against Native Americans." In a conclusion explicitly echoing the Cold War theme surrounding the *Brown* decision, the authors said, "There is . . . a steep international price to this failure to recognize U.S. history. . . . Without international faith in America's moral purpose, the country will never again enjoy the alliance of goodwill and just purpose that constituted the free world."[10]

Yet another source of political space to challenge federal anti-Indian law arises from increasing global concern with ecological crises and social justice. There is increasing awareness that environmental damage from corporate-state extraction projects especially affects Indigenous lands. This awareness, coupled with widespread racial justice protests against continuing systemic racism, brings Indigenous rights issues into public discussion. These pressures have already led to the elimination of "Indian" mascots for American sports teams and the removal or reinterpretation of statues of historic colonizers and slaveowners. These actions indicate an auspicious social-political context for litigation.

The present context also includes efforts to persuade the Holy See to revoke the fifteenth-century papal bulls underlying Christian discovery.[11] While church revocation would not have a direct effect on U.S. law, it would signal a moral, political, philosophical, and theological environment that is conducive to legal change. A further factor in the present context is the work of truth and reconciliation commissions in various countries, which, however limited, indicate efforts to come to terms with repressive histories.

On the other hand, the fact that large numbers of Native people have adopted Christianity, either outright or in combination with traditional spiritual practices, adds a complication to the task of challenging Christian discovery doctrine in U.S. law. For example, in 2013, the Crow Tribal Legislature passed a resolution "To honor God for his great blessings upon the Crow Tribe and to proclaim Jesus Christ as Lord of the Crow Indian Reservation."[12] That resolution indicated successful Christian colonization and undercut community support for a critique of Christian discovery doctrine.

As with the Black civil rights struggle, it will take more than an array of single challenges to overturn the doctrine of Christian discovery. It will require lawyers and litigants to take a strategic approach, coordinating the efforts of many people—and Peoples.

## Black and Red: Two Dominations in U.S. Law

Let us take a closer look at the historic challenge to "separate but equal" to clarify the similarities and differences between that campaign and an Indigenous challenge to federal anti-Indian law.

In 1954, the U.S. Supreme Court overturned the racial segregation doctrine of "separate but equal" in the case of *Brown v. Board of Education*.[13] The *Brown* decision was immediately seen as a major historical event, both by those who applauded it and those who resisted it. Today, the *Brown* case occupies a legendary, even iconic, place in American life. A 2006 *New York Times* article described *Brown* as "a sacred text in the American legal canon."[14] Racism against Blacks still exists in twenty-first-century America, but the U.S. legal system no longer explicitly authorizes it.

In sharp contrast to *Brown*, the 1955 case of *Tee-Hit-Ton Indians v. United States*[15] upheld the federal anti-Indian law doctrine that the United States owns Native lands and therefore may take them without paying compensation. The *Tee-Hit-Ton* decision was hardly reported at the time, and it remains almost unknown to the general public, although it is in continuous use as a kind of "sacred text" in federal anti-Indian law, having been cited in 130 cases, up to and including a September 2, 2020, federal district court decision;[16] the theology that it upholds is the theology of domination, not freedom. Indeed, the *Tee-Hit-Ton* decision marked the start of increased emphasis on the founding decision of *Johnson v. McIntosh*. In the 131 years before *Tee-Hit-Ton* (1823–1954), *Johnson* was cited in 153 cases, an average of little more than one time per year; in the sixty-five years since *Tee-Hit-Ton* (1956–2022), *Johnson* was cited 204 times, an average of over three times per year.

The day after the *Brown* decision, the *New York Times* blared a front-page banner headline, "High Court Bans School Segregation."[17] The day after *Tee-Hit-Ton*, the *Times* simply included the name of the case on page 41, in a fine-print listing of the previous day's Supreme Court decisions.

Between 1954 and 2017, *Brown v. Board of Education* was discussed in nearly 9,000 articles in the *New York Times*. In the same period, the *Times* mentioned *Tee-Hit-Ton Indians v. United States* only once, in a 1957 column by Arthur Krock praising the author of the opinion in the case, Justice Stanley Reed, on the occasion of Reed's retirement. Krock referred to *Tee-Hit-Ton* as a "good example of Justice Reed's dissents that became the law of the land." Krock unapologetically described the case as deciding that "the United States owed no compensation [to anyone] for seized Indian lands."

The difference in attention to the two cases reflects a complexity of America's self-image. Both *Brown* and *Tee-Hit-Ton* were decided in the mid-twentieth century, when America projected itself as the world champion of freedom against the totalitarian evils of Soviet Ccommunism. In that context, the *Brown* case could be celebrated as a "win," but *Tee-Hit-Ton* couldn't.

In an amicus brief filed with the Supreme Court in *Brown*, the U.S. Department of Justice explicitly invoked the Cold War to support overturning "separate but equal." It said, "It is in the context of the present world struggle between freedom and tyranny that the problem of racial discrimination must be viewed. The United States is trying to prove to the people of the world, of every nationality, race, and color, that a free democracy is the most civilized and most secure form of government yet devised by man."[18]

The U.S. brief quoted President Harry S. Truman's 1948 civil rights message to Congress, which criticized discrimination based on race, religion, color, or land of origin and came down heavily against segregation, calling its eradication a question of "national importance," part of "an affirmative government obligation to insure respect for fundamental human rights." It said the "subordinate position occupied by Negroes in this country as a result of governmental discrimination . . . presents an unsolved problem for American democracy."[19]

Although the *Brown* decision was met with immediate, widespread, and violent resistance to desegregation in several parts of the United States, the overall trajectory of public opinion since 1954 is unmistakably self-congratulatory: America prides itself on the elimination of legalized discrimination against Blacks; America does the right thing; America is just and fair; in America, everyone has a chance to prosper; everyone has equal rights. In short, the *Brown* civil rights decision fits quite comfortably within America's self-congratulatory story.

In contrast, the *Tee-Hit-Ton* decision—to the extent that anyone even thought about it in terms of national image—was problematic. Krock's eulogy of Justice Reed missed that point (or maybe he shared Reed's antipathy to Native peoples). The court's approval of the United States taking Native lands without having to pay compensation presented an image of unfairness, double-dealing, bad faith, injustice, and continuing colonialism. *Tee-Hit-Ton* reaffirmed a dishonorable side of American history—U.S. colonialism, wars against Native peoples, and "termination" projects.

*Tee-Hit-Ton* blindsided legal scholars. One professor called it a "feat of judicial legerdemain."[20] Another said it "sent shockwaves throughout Indian country."[21] The professors did not expect a 1955 U.S. Supreme Court decision to affirm fifteenth-century Christian religious discrimination, especially just thirteen months after the Court overturned segregation, with its roots in fifteenth-century slavery doctrines. The professors had been lulled by the *Brown* decision, which was decided by the same justices who decided *Tee-Hit-Ton* (except for Robert Jackson, who died in October 1954 and had not yet been replaced). The professors apparently expected a parallel move in relation to Native peoples, even though the U.S. Department of Justice had given fair warning in its *Tee-Hit-Ton* brief—filed just 127 days after the *Brown* decision—that the United States was not on the same page in Indigenous rights as in African American civil rights.

The U.S. brief in *Tee-Hit-Ton* opposed the Tee-Hit-Ton tribe's argument that it owned its ancestral homelands and the United States owed it compensation for taking timber from its lands to supply pulp paper mills. The brief said the Tee-Hit-Ton didn't own any land, let alone the timber. It expressly relied on the doctrine of Christian discovery. The brief quoted papal bulls, and even the Christian Bible. It said, "The Christian nations of Europe acquired jurisdiction over newly discovered lands by virtue of [fifteenth-century] grants from the Popes, who claimed the power to grant to Christian monarchs the right to acquire territory in the possession of heathens and infidels."[22] The brief added that the U.S. government had succeeded to the rights of colonial Christian monarchs and concluded that it is "plain that the Indians retained only a right of occupancy through the grace of the sovereign."[23] Professor Nell Jessup Newton rephrased it as "the whim of the sovereign."[24]

In its *Brown* brief, the United States had called for an end to legal doctrines denying Blacks equal status with Whites. Ironically, those doctrines were rooted in the same fifteenth-century papal decrees and religious colonialism that the U.S. brief affirmed in *Tee-Hit-Ton*. The *Brown* brief said, "The color of a man's skin—like his religious beliefs, or his political attachments, or the country from which he or his ancestors came to the United States—does not diminish or alter his legal status."[25]

In its *Tee-Hit-Ton* brief, the United States turned sharply away from an effort to position itself as the guardian of freedom and equality in the modern world. The brief noted, "Principles of natural law, and abstract justice, are appealed to by some, to show that the Indian tribes . . . ought . . . to be regarded as the owners of the . . . soil they occupy." The brief rejected those arguments. It said, "The fundamental principle, that the Indians had no rights, by virtue of their ancient possession, either of soil or sovereignty, has never been abandoned."[26]

Rutgers law professor Earl Maltz compared the two decisions, saying, "*Tee-Hit-Ton* minimized the import of the injustices inherent in the process by which the nation was established," while "the *Brown* Court sought to eliminate practices that the dominant political faction viewed as aberrational."[27] He ignored the fact that racial segregation—indeed slavery—was as inherent in the nation's founding as was dispossession of Native peoples; it was declared aberrational in 1954 only because it embarrassed the United States in the Cold War.

In short, in its rivalry with the Soviet Union for the allegiance of the Third World, the United States positioned itself as the guardian of Black people in a nation of freedom, justice, opportunity, and equality. The U.S. position on Indigenous rights occurred in another dimension altogether—namely, the centuries-long Christian European war to own the world. In *Brown*, the court overturned the separate but equal doctrine because it obstructed the Cold War quest of the United States to dominate international politics. In *Tee-Hit-Ton*, there was no comparable political pressure to abandon the doctrine of Christian discovery. Indeed, a rejection of that doctrine would have threatened a core U.S. geopolitical interest—the claim of ownership of the American landmass, with its many sites of strategically important industrial resources. Taken together, *Brown* and *Tee-Hit-Ton* demonstrate American history as a *mission to dominate the world*.

## Indigenous Rights Are Not Civil Rights

The sharp contrast between the U.S. briefs in *Brown* and *Tee-Hit-Ton* highlights the way that legal doctrines are entangled with political, social, economic, and historical agendas. The agendas for civil rights law and federal anti-Indian law are different. Although some observers try to apply civil rights theory to Native cases, federal anti-Indian law is not fundamentally a civil rights issue. As the Yankton/Standing Rock attorney and theologian Vine Deloria, Jr., explained in *Behind the Trail of Broken Treaties*, "Few people [in America] were able to . . . recognize that if the United States and its inhabitants . . . regarded the Indians as another domestic minority group, the Indians did not see themselves as such."[28]

To put it in a nutshell, federal anti-Indian law affects the status of Native peoples as *sovereign political entities separate from the United States*; civil rights law focuses on the equality of *individual persons as citizens of the United States*.

Critiques placing federal anti-Indian law within a civil rights framework quickly become problematic. In fact, they easily play into the U.S. project to extinguish Native *peoples as nations* by assimilating individual Native *persons as citizens*. The 1924 Indian Citizenship Act, for example, is often described as an affirmation of Native civil rights. In fact, it was part and parcel of the federal program to assimilate Natives as *individuals* into U.S. society and pave the way for the termination of Native *peoples* as separate political entities.

Harold L. Ickes, secretary of the U.S. Department of the Interior, wittingly or unwittingly fostered confusion between Native rights and civil rights in his foreword to Felix Cohen's *Handbook of Federal Indian Law*, in which he said that the Department of the Interior has "the obligation . . . to protect and safeguard the rights of our oldest national minority."[29] Similarly, Commissioner of Indian Affairs John Collier characterized the Indian Reorganization Act as changing "the sort of treatment dominant groups give to subject groups."[30] While Collier acknowledged that domination is inherent in federal anti-Indian law, his phrasing suggested that Native rights are akin to civil rights.

Conflating Native rights with "minority" rights obscures a critical legal issue. To state it baldly, Native rights are not minority rights. Minority rights—civil rights—refers to the equality of individual citizens under the U.S. Constitution. Native rights, in contrast, are *group rights* and not based on the U.S. Constitution. Native rights are extraconstitutional because Native nations existed before the Constitution. As we saw, the U.S. Supreme Court acknowledges this fact when it wants to, as in the 1991 case of *Blatchford v. Native Village of Noatak and Circle Village*, where it referred to the U.S. Constitution as "a convention to which [the tribes] were not even parties."[31] As we also saw, the Court ignores this fact when acknowledging it would impede the claim of federal domination.

A civil rights approach is thus not only inappropriate to Native rights, it actually undermines Native rights by assimilating Native issues into the constitutional citizenship framework. This is exactly how the various "friends of the Indian" campaigns aimed to "solve the Indian problem" by absorbing Native *persons* and extinguishing Native *peoples*. Briefly, federal anti-Indian law and civil rights law rest on fundamentally different legal concepts. Clarity on this distinction is crucial. As Steven Curry wrote, "The racializing of communal identity [i.e., applying race theory to Native nations] has been used as a policy designed to destroy indigenous communities."[32]

Having distinguished between civil rights and Native rights, it is nonetheless important to recognize the pervasiveness of racial terminology in federal anti-Indian law. As Professor Stacy Leeds put it, laws affecting Black people, like the infamous *Dred Scott* decision,[33] are identical to laws affecting Native peoples in their reliance on racism. *Dred Scott* referred to Blacks as "a subordinate and inferior class of beings . . . subjugated by the dominant race"; *Lone Wolf v. Hitchcock*,[34] where the court declared "plenary power," referred to Native peoples as "an ignorant and dependent race." Leeds pointed out the "ultimate similarity" of the two decisions as "classify[ing] the white Christian inhabitants of the United States as a race that rightfully dominates the ignorant, inferior, subordinate, and dependant [sic] African and Indian races."[35] Professor Leeds provocatively described the continuing presence of racist thinking in recent cases. She said the 1978 Supreme Court decision in *Oliphant v. Suquamish Indian Tribe*[36] prohibiting tribal court criminal jurisdiction over non-Natives relied on the principle that "Brown people don't put white people in jail." She translated the 2001 decision in *Nevada v. Hicks*[37] that said that tribal courts have no authority over state law enforcement officers as "If brown people want to sue police officers for violating their civil rights, they'll have to do it in a white court."[38]

Professor Leeds concluded by saying, "The majority of Indian law decisions from Chief Justice Marshall's trilogy to *Lone Wolf* to the Rehnquist Court are premised on notions of racial supremacy of the United States over the perceived inferiority and dependency of Indian people. Until we can discuss this openly in the Indian law circles, in the mainstream legal community, and in our classrooms, an Indian law *Brown v. Board of Education* decision will not be possible."[39]

It will help provoke the necessary open discussion to see the first cited use of the term "racism" in the *Oxford English Dictionary*. It points to remarks made by one of the most infamous self-appointed "friends of the Indian," U.S. army officer Richard Henry Pratt, the founder of the infamous Carlisle Indian Industrial School—a boarding school founded in 1879 for Native children forcibly taken from their homes. Pratt spoke at the 1902 Lake Mohonk Conference of Friends of the Indian, an organization with an outright assimilationist agenda.

Pratt said, "Segregating any class or race of people . . . kills the progress of the segregated people . . . Association of races and classes is necessary in order to destroy racism and classism." He explained how his Carlisle School combated the "racism" of federal policy, which allowed Native nations to exist apart from American society. Pratt's "anti-racism" program aimed at extinguishing Native nations and peoples.[40] His methods (and the methods of all Indian boarding schools) required the forcible removal of Native children from their families and destroying their community bonds. Pratt's program was to break the transmission of Native languages and traditions, with the goal of incapacitating Native cultures and political structures through a multi-generational process.

Professor Leeds emphasized, "I am not suggesting that Indian people seek integration into the American political process, but that an Indian law *Brown v. Board of Education* would put an end to the Court's reliance on race-based rationales for the divestiture of tribal autonomy and self-determination rights."[41] Similarly, Professor Ralph Johnson and E. Susan Crystal, an attorney, conclude their survey of "Indians and Equal Protection" by saying that "special deference should be accorded tribal laws designed to further tribal self-determination or to preserve ancient customs and traditional values."[42]

Briefly, despite the obvious racism in federal anti-Indian law, a critique relying on civil rights theory runs the risk of supporting anti-Native individualist assimilation agendas. Federal anti-Indian law must be critiqued on different grounds. Native "equality" occurs at the level of *nationhood*.

## Crossing the Abyss

It is one thing to criticize legal doctrine in a book. It is another to challenge it in court. An entrenched doctrine is hard to dislodge. The difficulty is epic when the doctrine was created at the foundation of the field and has been used for decades and centuries.

In 1906, Professor Henry S. Redfield described an entrenched legal doctrine as "an active and conquering force," almost impossible to dislodge.[43] He wrote those words as part of a project to improve law school education—more specifically, to prepare lawyers to "make war" for their clients.

In the early 1970s, the Otoe Missouria/Osage attorney Francis Browning Pipestem[44] coined the phrase "Briefcase Warriors" to describe his hope that Indigenous law school graduates would take on the role of protecting Indigenous peoples. The National Native American Law Students Association (NNALSA)[45] and the Native American Rights Fund (NARF)[46] followed Pipestem's vision of organizing Indigenous students and lawyers to argue for Indigenous rights.

The premise of the "Briefcase Warrior" vision was that U.S. law could somehow be used to undergird rather than undermine the survival of Indigenous nations, and U.S. law could be a tool for Indigenous sovereignty rather than U.S. domination. As Deloria urged in a 1970 *New York Times* article, "The Indian revolution [is] well under way and . . . someone had better get a legal education so that we could have our own legal program."[47]

For a while, the plan seemed to be working. In 1987, nearly twenty years later, Professor Charles Wilkinson confidently declared, "Most branches of Indian law have stabilized." He predicted that "tribes can begin to withdraw from the judicial system and [concentrate] . . . on creating workable islands of Indianness."[48] In 1991, Professor Rennard Strickland (Osage/Cherokee) said that Indigenous lawyers and non-Indigenous colleagues were using law "to help shape an economic and political revolution which has drawn tribes into the courts as well as the congress to address the full range of Native issues."[49]

But in 2003, barely more than a decade after these confident and hopeful assessments, Professor Bryan Wildenthal said that the "vision of legal stability no longer appears true, if it ever was. The law governing Indian nations and their relationship with the United States continues to evolve in dramatic and unpredictable ways."[50]

In 2013, another decade later, *Indian Country Today* reported that the scene had radically changed from the heady days when briefcase lawyers were imagined as the way to tame an aggressively hostile legal regime. At the National Congress of American Indians 70th Annual Convention in Tulsa, Oklahoma, Richard Guest, NARF's lead staff attorney in Washington, DC, "sounded the alarm." Guest was reported as saying, "We've had one win and nine losses in front of the [Chief Justice John] Roberts court. And our message . . . is . . . today: Stay out of the courts!"[51]

In short, forty years after the celebrated launch of briefcase lawyers, it appeared that they were in retreat. Federal anti-Indian law was as entrenched and anti-Indigenous as it ever was. The political hopes of Natives lobbying the U.S. Congress to exercise its "plenary power" in a favorable way also had not brought about a revolution.

No wonder, then, that when an *Indian Country Today* interviewer asked John Echohawk, then executive director of NARF, "Is anyone challenging

Congress' claim to plenary power over the nations?" Echohawk replied: "Yes, but of course, under the law of this country, the way all that's been interpreted and the way it's been litigated is the tribes are domestic dependent nations and that's just the way things are and you go to court and that's what they'll tell you. The federal government has exclusive authority over all Indians, all tribes under the Constitution, basically, that takes care of everything—if you're a tribe then you're under federal jurisdiction, any tribe, anywhere, is under federal jurisdiction. Period."[52]

In 1986, when it had seemed the briefcase warriors might succeed, Strickland gave them some advice. He said, "Too much of Indian law has been reactive rather than planned. Frequently, issues that were litigated were defensive, brought under the wrong circumstances, and at the wrong place. Indian tribes went to the courts to put out fires; they were forced to the courthouse as a last ditch effort to preserve and protect."[53]

Strickland urged the development of a strategic vision. He said, "A coordinated plan—a strategy for law—ought to be a part of the long-range planning of every Indian tribe. Thinking ahead—planning ahead—offers the best hope for the years ahead. It is no secret that much of the success of the Black Civil Rights cases came from a coordinated and closely planned litigation strategy."[54]

In 2014, David Coventry Smith emphasized the importance of seeing the long view: "The history of our country's interaction with Indian nations teaches us that whenever Indian sovereignty is diminished or disregarded, both federal and state governments exploit those opportunities to gain a foothold and assert control over Indian land interests. The result is always the same for Indians—the diminished role of tribal governments, increased social disorder, impaired cultural identity, loss of economic opportunities, and increased poverty."[55]

Challenging federal anti-Indian law is especially hard because its doctrines of federal supremacy—"trust," "domestic dependent nation," and even "plenary power"—can sometimes support "pro-Indian" rulings against states and local governments. Indigenous fishing and hunting cases have been decided this way by courts blocking state action on the ground that only the United States with its "plenary power" can interfere with these Indigenous rights. I litigated a fishing rights case in that way for Michael Maxim and David Greene of the Mashpee Wampanoag. We challenged a Massachusetts town ordinance on the basis of U.S. fishing rights cases and won unanimous decisions from the Massachusetts Appeals Court and Supreme Judicial Court throwing out their convictions for fishing without town permits.[56] This fishing rights win came at the cost of accepting the doctrine of federal supremacy over Native rights to block Massachusetts interference.

The 2014 case of *State of Michigan v. Bay Mills Indian Community* provided another example of this conundrum. When the state of Michigan sued Bay Mills

Community to stop a casino operation, Bay Mills claimed sovereign immunity from a state lawsuit. In reply, Michigan argued on the basis of the federal anti-Indian law exception, saying, "Indian tribes have no rights under the United States Constitution to any attributes of sovereignty."[57] In a gross understatement, the state added, "The scope of tribal immunity is a bit muddled."

Bay Mills responded with a reminder that Indigenous sovereignty preexists the existence of both the United States and the states, saying, "Modern-day Indian tribes are self-governing political communities that were formed long before Europeans first settled in North America." But Bay Mills also bowed to the exception, saying, "Although [tribes] no longer possess the full attributes of sovereignty, they still retain those aspects of sovereignty not withdrawn by treaty or statute, or by implication as a necessary result of their dependent status."[58] Bay Mills said that its immunity from a state lawsuit had not (yet) been "withdrawn."

When the U.S. Supreme Court eventually upheld Bay Mills's immunity from suit in a 5–4 decision, many commentators described it as a "win" for Indigenous sovereignty. But in fact, the Court's decision only affirmed the exception that Bay Mills had already conceded. The Court said, "If Congress had authorized [Michigan to file this] suit, Bay Mills would have no valid grounds to object. But Congress has not done so."[59]

*Dollar General v. Choctaw Indians*[60] provided yet another example of the tactical use of doctrines of U.S. domination. The 2016 case arose after a thirteen-year-old job trainee at the local Dollar General store accused the manager of sexually molesting him and sued the company in a Choctaw court under Choctaw tort law. The Dollar General corporation (Dolgencorp) tried to block the Choctaw courts from handling the lawsuit. They argued, "Tribal court jurisdiction over nonmembers is fundamentally incompatible with the United States' overriding sovereignty."[61]

Lawyers for the Choctaw first agreed with Dolgencorp about the basic exception, saying, "Indian tribes cannot exercise power inconsistent with their diminished status as sovereigns." But they then called on a set of "exceptions" within the exception that the Supreme Court had announced in a 1981 case, *Montana v. United States*, which allowed Native nations to regulate the activity of "non-members" like Dollar General. One exception to the exception (you need a scorecard to keep track of the convolutions) said, "A tribe may regulate . . . the activities of nonmembers who enter consensual relationships with the tribe or its members, through commercial dealing, contracts, leases, or other arrangements." The other exception said, "A tribe may also retain inherent power to exercise civil authority over the conduct of non-Indians . . . when that conduct threatens or has some direct effect on the political integrity, the economic security, or the health or welfare of the tribe."[62] The Choctaw lawyers said that one or both of these exceptions applied to lessen the diminishing impact of the basic exception.

When the case got to the U.S. Supreme Court following a decision in favor of the Choctaw by the Fifth Circuit Court of Appeals,[63] a group of historians and legal scholars submitted an amicus brief in support of the Choctaw. They also began their argument by affirming "diminished tribal sovereignty," saying, "The tribes' . . . incorporation into the territory of the United States . . . restricted their exercise of separate power to the extent that it conflict[ed] with the interests of the [United States] overriding sovereignty." They then asserted a "consensual relationship" between the Choctaw and Dollar General and said, "the relevant question is whether the federal government has *withdrawn* [tribal] power [over such relationships] and the historical record shows that it has not."[64]

Ironically, only the state of Mississippi, in a joint amicus brief with Colorado, New Mexico, North Dakota, Oregon, and Washington, all supporting the Choctaw, came close to attacking the federal anti-Indian law exception of "diminished sovereignty," saying that it "cast[s] doubt on the inherent rights of all interdependent sovereigns."[65] But Mississippi did not develop the point.

A curious incident occurred during oral argument of the case in the Supreme Court. Justice Stephen Breyer could not recall the formulation of the exception doctrine of "domestic, dependent nation." He directed a question on this point to one of the Choctaw lawyers:

JUSTICE BREYER: Now, is there any—and—and what is the word in *Cherokee*? I forget. It's "something dependent nation." What kind of—it was—there are two words—

MR. KATYAL: Domestic dependent—

JUSTICE BREYER: What?

MR. KATYAL: Domestic dependent nation?

JUSTICE BREYER: Domestic? All right. So if, in fact, Tasmania had this kind of . . . situation, and an American went to Tasmania and got a reasonable judgment, I take it our courts would enforce that.

MR. KATYAL: Correct.[66]

Katyal answered correctly; the United States would treat Tasmania as an independent sovereign. But the issue is precisely that U.S. law does *not* acknowledge Native sovereignty in the way that it acknowledges Tasmanian sovereignty. The federal anti-Indian law exception of "domestic, dependent nation" puts Native nations in a distinctly different—and inferior—position to both Tasmania and the United States.

Breyer gave no explanation for his reference to Tasmania. But the reference was ironic: Tasmania has its own history of colonization and domination under Christian discovery; indeed, its name is derived from the Dutch explorer Abel Tasman, who "discovered" the island on November 24, 1642, and claimed it for the Dutch East Indian Company. Breyer's confusion symbolized the confusion inherent in federal anti-Indian law.

Justice Sonia Sotomayor's question to the Dolgencorp lawyer that concluded the oral argument suggested a clearer understanding of the U.S. claim of domination. Sotomayor asked:

> What then remains of the sovereignty of the Indians? . . . You just want to cherry pick what "sovereignty" means. Because if they're sovereign, the United States can have treaties with people that basically say it's your land, you do what you want; I'm not going to enforce your judgment if I don't think it's consistent with due process here. But we don't dictate to other sovereigns what kind of systems they should have. You're right we have the power to do that, but it's still something that we don't have to exercise.[67]

Her last sentence formulated the exception as "the power to do that" and suggested that it could somehow be abandoned. The Dollar General lawyer didn't miss a beat; his reply was a straight affirmation of the exception: "I will be brief. The difference is the dependent sovereignty of the Indian tribes."

Ultimately, the Supreme Court became deadlocked. Justice Antonin Scalia died two months after the oral argument and before the decision could be announced; the court was left with eight justices, who divided 4–4. The legal result of a divided Court is that the lower court decision stands (here, the Fifth Circuit affirming the district court).

It is dangerous to take a Native case to what the U.S. Supreme Court itself calls "the courts of the conqueror." The dangers associated with challenging entrenched doctrine scare most litigators (and even some academic commentators) away from direct attacks on the foundation doctrine of Christian discovery. However, while embracing U.S. domination may provide *tactical* leverage in an argument against a state or in gaining a political concession from Congress, the tactic must be used very carefully lest it wholly undermine the *strategic* goal. As Milner Ball cautioned, using trust doctrine means "indirectly embracing the degrading ethnocentrism that supports the theory."[68]

## Attacking Entrenched Doctrine

Challenges to Christian discovery do happen. In 1954, the Tee-Hit-Ton Tlingit said that Christian discovery doctrine is not applicable to Natives in Alaska. In 1990, the Red Lake Chippewa attacked the federal anti-Indian law doctrines of "plenary power" and "trusteeship" premised on Christian discovery. In 2001, Floyd Hicks (Fallon Paiute-Shoshone) proposed to narrow the interpretation of Christian discovery and prevent the doctrine from developing "any further." The Western Shoshone Nation in 1995–2005 and the Yakama Nation in 2019 issued direct challenges to Christian discovery in litigation.

Some challenges to federal anti-Indian law do not necessarily produce litigation. For example, the Ho-Chunk attorney Lance G. Morgan said that he uses federal anti-Indian law against itself, and that he takes advantage of its contradictions when negotiating with states on behalf of Indigenous nations. Morgan said, "The goal is not to get the Supreme Court or Congress to see the light and overturn the last two hundred years of precedent. The goal is to change the system by coopting it."[69] The danger in this approach was spelled out by the Muskogee-Creek medicine teacher Phillip Deere, who said, "Many times our Indian People . . . say that we're going to beat [the government] at his own game. But we're forgetting that we're in his ball field and he's changing the rules right in the middle of the ballgame."[70] But Morgan has achieved some success. He is now the chief executive officer (CEO) and president of Ho-Chunk, Inc., a tribally chartered corporation integrating housing, employment, and retail commercial ventures in what Kristen A. Carpenter and Angela R. Riley describe as "creating a community where people can live, work, and shop." Carpenter and Riley cite the Ho-Chunk projects as "an example of pragmatic innovation in Indian land tenure toward building a sustainable economy," undoing the damage inflicted by U.S. domination.[71]

A curious challenge to federal anti-Indian law appeared in a 2018 report by the Indian Land Tenure Foundation called *Native Land Law: Can Native American People Find Justice in the U.S. Legal System?* It proposed that lawyers simply declare that Christian discovery "has never, in fact, been the law." It recommended this despite the fact that it also said, "Courts and government officials routinely apply this mistaken and discriminatory rule and believe it to be the law."[72] The foolishness of the statement that what courts and government officials do does not constitute "law" seems obvious. Where else does one find law? And simply ignoring a doctrine does not make it disappear. As Professor Karl Llewellyn explained in *The Bramble Bush*, his famous book of advice to law students, one may regard a doctrine as a "fossil" obstructing your case; in that event, he said, "Challenge it you may. . . . But overlook it you may not."[73]

Before we look at specific litigation challenges to Christian discovery doctrine, let's look at some of the difficulties standing in the way.

## Facing the Dangers of Lawyering

The Federal Rules of Civil Procedure reinforce entrenched doctrines by making it risky for a lawyer to argue against them. Rule 11(b)(2), titled "Representations to the Court," mandates that an attorney's argument must be "warranted by existing law or by a nonfrivolous argument for extending, modifying, or reversing existing law or for establishing new law."[74] Section

(c) of this rule provides penalties for violating this mandate. The bottom line is that a lawyer planning to challenge existing law in any field must build "nonfrivolous" arguments. The safest course for a lawyer is to rely on established doctrines unless the client's aims require a challenge; and in that case, the challenge must be carefully presented so it does not appear frivolous.

*Black's Law Dictionary* defines a "frivolous" lawsuit as one that is "groundless . . . with little prospect of success; often brought to embarrass or annoy the defendant."[75] Surely a challenge to Christian discovery doctrine will "embarrass or annoy" the United States, but annoyance is not the purpose of the lawsuit. The purpose is to free Indigenous peoples from the dominating grip of fifteenth-century imperial colonial religious concepts entrenched in federal anti-Indian law.

Commentators have criticized Rule 11 for blocking vigorous creative lawyering. One commentator pointed to the fact that civil rights lawyers are more frequently penalized under Rule 11 than lawyers in other fields of law,[76] indicating greater danger in litigating about rights. Indigenous rights are not the same as civil rights, but for purposes of thinking about challenges to entrenched legal doctrine, we can compare the two.

In 1896, the U.S. Supreme Court established the segregationist doctrine of "separate but equal" in the infamous case of *Plessy v. Ferguson.*[77] The *Plessy* decision not only legitimized racial segregation in the United States, it described segregation as law "enacted in good faith for the promotion of the public good."[78] "Separate but equal" remained entrenched in U.S. law until 1954, when the Supreme Court declared the doctrine unconstitutional in the landmark *Brown v. Board of Education.*[79]

Historians give major credit for the *Brown* decision to Thurgood Marshall, the lawyer who organized litigation across the country to challenge segregation (and whom President Lyndon Johnson later appointed to the Supreme Court). Marshall deserves high praise for mounting a daunting stand against legalized racism. But there is a longer history of challenges to "separate but equal" doctrine, starting immediately after the *Plessy* decision. Those challenges illuminate the importance of creative, aggressive lawyering (and courageous plaintiffs and defendants).

In 1898, only two years after *Plessy,* Joe Smith, a railroad conductor in Tennessee, appealed his conviction for "failing, neglecting, and refusing to assign certain negroes to the car and compartment of car used on the Louisville & Nashville Railroad for colored passengers, and for permitting them to ride in the car and compartment thereof assigned to white passengers."[80] Smith, represented by the law firm Smith & Maddin, argued that the Tennessee statute mandating "equal but separate accommodations for the white and colored races" was invalid because it interfered with interstate commerce, in violation of the U.S. Constitution's provision for federal supremacy of such commerce. He said that separate cars might be valid for in-state travel, but not for passengers riding into Tennessee from out of state. Notice that his argument did not attack racism per se; it offered a partial attack under a plausible, already existing (i.e., not frivolous) theory about commerce.

The Tennessee Supreme Court rejected his argument and upheld Smith's conviction, quoting *Plessy* and saying that the statute requiring conductors of passenger trains "to assign to the car or compartments of the car . . . used for the race to which such passengers belong,"[81] was not a regulation of commerce at all, but rather "reasonable legislation under the police power to provide for the health, safety, well–being, comfort, and morals of the public."[82]

The same year, Robert and Fannie Lander, represented by the law firm of John Feland & Son, sued a railroad in Kentucky for damages for forcing Mrs. Lander to either vacate her seat in the first-class Ladies coach, for which she had purchased a ticket, or leave the train. The Landers, whom the appeals court described as "colored people," testified that when she refused, the conductor, "with two or three other men, who were also agents of [the railroad], . . . took hold of her by the arms, and shoved her up from it . . . proceeding by force of arms to remove her."[83] The bold trial judge (in Christian County Circuit Court!) instructed the jury, "The plaintiff had the right to take a seat where she did in the ladies' coach, and that any attempt . . . to make her move into . . . another coach was a violation of law and of her rights." The judge told the jury if they found that the conductor made Mrs. Lander move to another car, "The jury must find for plaintiffs the damages they have sustained." The judge added that the jury "are not confined to actual damages, but may take into consideration the humiliation and injury to the feelings of the plaintiff."[84] The jury found in favor of Mrs. Lander and awarded her damages of $125. A majority of the Kentucky Court of Appeals reversed the verdict, saying the judge's instructions to the jury conflicted with the state's law requiring separate coaches for White and Black passengers. Two of the judges filed separate opinions expressing their displeasure with the racial prejudice inherent in the state law.

In 1986, U.S. District Court chief Judge Jack B. Weinstein had these courageous challenges to *Plessy* in mind when he heard a Rule 11 complaint in *Eastway Construction Corporation. v. City of New York* asking him to sanction a lawyer for making a frivolous argument. He refused to issue sanctions. When the Second Circuit Court of Appeals told him that he had to issue a sanction, Judge Weinstein took the opportunity to make a strong statement against sanctioning lawyers for their arguments. Weinstein said that lawyers have ethical responsibilities to vigorously represent their clients, and these responsibilities require them to push the limits of Rule 11. He wrote:

> Attorneys are . . . placed in a dilemma because they have the right—in fact, they have an ethical obligation . . . to present to the court all the nonfrivolous arguments that might be made on their clients' behalf, even if only

barely nonfrivolous. They are forced by their position as advocates in the legal profession to live close to the line, wherever the courts may draw it.[85]

Weinstein added, "Sometimes there are reasons to sue even when one cannot win." He turned to the history of challenges to "separate but equal" doctrine to make his point:

> Bad court decisions must be challenged if they are to be overruled, but the early challenges are certainly hopeless. The first attorney to challenge *Plessy v. Ferguson* was certainly bringing a frivolous action, but his efforts and the efforts of others eventually led to *Brown v. Board of Education.* . . . Vital changes have been wrought by those members of the bar who have dared to challenge the received wisdom.[86]

Supreme Court justice William O. Douglas put it this way in 1973, when he concurred with the majority in *United States v. Mason* that the United States was not at fault for failing to challenge a precedent that imposed an Oklahoma tax on the estate of an Osage woman: "Supreme Court decisions are on occasion overruled and . . . the opportunity to overrule them would never arise if litigants did not continue to challenge their validity."[87] The decision reversed the Court of Claims, which had held that "there was at the very least a serious question whether [the precedent] remained viable and that, as a fiduciary for Rose Mason and her estate, the United States would have to test that issue by protesting the payment of the tax and litigating its applicability."[88] In concurring with the Supreme Court's reversal of the Court of Claims, Douglas said, "In this context at least, it is unnecessary to penalize the United States' proper reliance on our past decisions in order to re-examine them, since there is no bar to a suit by plaintiffs below directly against Oklahoma for recovery of the tax."[89]

In 1993, Rule 11 was amended to clarify that arguments for "reversals of existing law or for creation of new law" are not "frivolous" if the litigant "has researched the issues and found some support for its theories *even in minority opinions, in law review articles, or through consultation with other attorneys.*" The amendment added that arguments specifically identified as calling for a change in the law are "viewed with greater tolerance."[90]

The danger associated with challenging entrenched doctrine leads most litigators to avoid attacking or criticizing Christian discovery. The fact that "diminished" Native sovereignty and "plenary" federal power have tactical utility in a particular lawsuit further encourages a lawyer's inclination not to rock the boat by challenging the entrenched underlying doctrine. Even some academic commentators prefer to take a safe course to avoid the taint of possible frivolity. But these nonactions risk the strategic goal of revoking the Christian discovery exception.

Despite these difficulties and dangers, there are cases of creative, aggressive lawyering (and courageous plaintiffs and defendants) that provide examples worth studying.

## Tee-Hit-Ton v. United States

*Tee-Hit-Ton Indians v. United States*,[91] a case that we already discussed in some detail in the preface, was a 1955 challenge to Christian discovery doctrine by the Tee-Hit-Ton Tlingit. They demanded compensation after the United States took timber from their lands and asked for an injunction to prevent the taking of more timber. It is a major case in federal anti-Indian law because the U.S. Supreme Court affirmed Christian discovery in the face of the Tlingit's explicit call to revisit the doctrine. The court's opinion rejecting the Tee-Hit-Ton challenge is infamous.

Tlingit land rights had already been discussed in hearings of the House Committee on Agriculture during the summer of 1947, when the congressional resolution to take the timber from what the United States called the Tongass National Forest was being debated. The committee studied a letter from Secretary of Interior J. A. Krug to House Speaker Joseph Martin explaining, "If not extinguished, and if not subsequently abandoned, [Native] rights exist in some form as a valid type of land ownership." But Krug also said, "For almost twenty-five years it has been the very strong desire of all persons concerned with the development of Alaska to put [its] rich timber resources . . . to use . . . for the production of . . . paper pulp."[92] President Truman emphasized that desire in a special message to Congress in May 1948, where he said, "A special legal problem is at present hampering the development of Alaska. This is the question of whether or not Alaska natives have claims to the ownership of certain lands."[93]

Felix Cohen forcefully criticized the Tongass Act, which underlay the timber-taking. He said, "For the first time in our history, it has been decreed . . . that a government bureau may seize the possessions of Americans solely because they belong to a minority race. That is the meaning of the Tongass Act, which deprives Alaskans of their land and timber if two or more of their grandparents were Indians." Cohen's language reflected the mistaken notion that Indigenous peoples are "minorities," but he nevertheless foreshadowed what the Supreme Court would do when it got the case.[94]

As expected, when the Tee-Hit-Ton filed their lawsuit, they said that they held "full proprietary ownership" of their lands and all the resources thereon. What distinguished their argument was a sharp attack on the Christian discovery doctrine. They said that it could not possibly be applicable to Tlingit lands because the Tlingit were in a "fundamentally different historical, political, and legal" situation than existed when the U.S. Supreme Court adopted the doctrine in 1823. They said that Christian discovery belongs to the "age of Sixteenth Century exploration and discovery which Chief Justice Marshall marked as the historical starting point" in *Johnson v. McIntosh*.[95]

Indeed, Marshall's supposedly factual history in his *Johnson* opinion bears no relation to Tee-Hit-Ton or Alaska history. There were no U.S. "wars," let alone "frequent and bloody" ones, between the Tlingit and the United States; the Tlingit did not "recede" from their lands, and their lands did not become "unfit"; the game did not "flee"; and the "soil" was *not* "no longer occupied by its ancient inhabitants."

The Tee-Hit-Ton were circumspect in their critique. They did not criticize *Johnson v. McIntosh* unequivocally. In fact, they threw their Native cousins of the nineteenth century under the bus, saying Marshall's decision was "understandable" as applied to "typical . . . Indian cases dealing with the rights of extremely primitive men who did not know what land titles were, had no sense of property in land, and had no system or standard of exchange." They insisted, in contrast, that the Tlingit had a civilization with a well-developed system of property ownership. In a deferential tone, their brief added that the Tee-Hit-Ton found "no fault either of the great judge who first stated [the doctrine] . . . or of the present generation of his brethren on the bench who inherited" it.[96]

The U.S. brief not only flatly rejected the Tee-Hit-Ton overture to rethink old doctrine, but also forcefully and unapologetically argued that Christian discovery applied to all Indigenous lands at all times. The U.S. brief was even more explicit than Marshall's *Johnson* opinion in acknowledging the religious pedigree of Christian discovery doctrine. It said, "In the latter part of the fifteenth century, the Christian nations of Europe acquired jurisdiction over newly discovered lands by virtue of grants from the Popes, who claimed the power to grant to Christian monarchs the right to acquire territory in the possession of heathens and infidels." The brief added, "There never has been any question . . . [in either] the very early decisions of this Court [or] the more recent ones . . . of the paramount right of the United States to extinguish the Indian right of occupancy at will, by treaty, purchase, conquest, or the exercise of complete dominion adverse to the right of occupancy."[97]

Acknowledging that some readers of Marshall's *Worcester* opinion might imagine that the decision imposed some limitations on U.S. power over Indigenous lands, the brief said, "While the opinion in the *Worcester* case contains some language which might indicate that the United States could extinguish 'Indian title' only by purchase, the opinion also recognized the existence of the power, which Chief Justice Marshall had earlier defined in *Johnson v. McIntosh*, . . . 'to extinguish the Indian title of occupancy, either by purchase or by conquest. . . .'"[98] As we saw in our discussion of *Worcester*, this is indeed what Marshall said.

New Mexico and Utah submitted amicus curiae ("friend of the court") briefs expressing alarm about the implications of the U.S. position. Utah urged the court to reverse the denial of compensation to the Tee-Hit-Ton, saying that the federal government has a "duty to clean up a situation which it has permitted to develop during a century of holding the Indian problem within its own, exclusive jurisdiction. An important part of cleaning up that problem consists of settling for the taking of Indian title on a fair and just basis."[99] New Mexico criticized the federal government's "stock defense that original Indian title is not compensable" and added that "the Tee-Hit-Ton Indians should be dealt with as if the claimant were a non-Indian invoking the jurisdiction of the Court of Claims."[100]

Justice Stanley Reed wrote the court opinion. He parroted the U.S. brief, saying, "No case in this Court has ever held that taking of Indian title or use by Congress required compensation." In the most infamous paragraph in his infamous opinion, Reed said, "It is well settled that . . . the tribes who inhabited the lands . . . held claim to such lands after the coming of the white man, under . . . permission from the whites to occupy." He said that this permission could also be called "original Indian title." Under either label, he continued, it "means mere possession not specifically recognized as ownership by Congress." Emphasizing the federal anti-Indian law definition of "tribal sovereignty" is not actually sovereignty, he said, "After conquest they were permitted to occupy portions of territory over which they had previously exercised 'sovereignty,' as we use that term. This is not a property right but amounts to a right of occupancy which the sovereign grants . . . which right of occupancy may be terminated and such lands fully disposed of by the sovereign itself without any legally enforceable obligation to compensate the Indians."[101]

Reed sidestepped the U.S. brief's direct citation of Christian religious sources, but he did cite "the great case of *Johnson v. McIntosh*" and said, "This position of the Indian has long been rationalized by the legal theory that discovery and conquest gave the conquerors sovereignty over and ownership of the lands thus obtained."[102]

In fact, the justices grappled with the wording of this sentence up to the last minute, as archives of the justices' papers reveal. In drafts circulated prior to the final opinion, the sentence referred to "Christian" discovery and conquest, to wit: "This position of the Indian has long been rationalized by the legal theory that discovery and conquest *by Christian nations* gave the conquerors sovereignty over and ownership of the lands thus obtained."[103]

Whatever the specific disagreements were about a direct quotation of the religious argument in the U.S. brief, they resulted in Reed circulating a memo to the full Court, dated February 7, 1955, the same day the Court's opinion was issued, modifying the crucial sentence. The memo is a "smoking gun" in the history of federal anti-Indian law, showing the Supreme Court's effort to conceal the religious grounds of the U.S. claim of domination over Indigenous peoples. The memo reads:

TO THE CONFERENCE

RE: No. 43, *Tee-Hit-Ton Indians v. U.S.*

If there is no objection from the members of the Conference I shall change in the final print the first sentence of the last paragraph on p. 7 to read as follows:

"This position of the Indian has long been rationalized by the legal theory that discovery and conquest gave the conquerors sovereignty over and ownership of the lands thus obtained."

It formerly read:

"This position of the Indian has long been rationalized by the legal theory that discovery and conquest by Christian nations gave these conquerors sovereignty over and ownership of the lands thus obtained."

## STANLEY REED

Reed's papers also include copies of prior drafts with margin notes addressed to him from other justices. The notes give a flavor of the discussion. For example, a copy of a prior February draft bears a handwritten note on the first page, over what appears to be Justice Tom Clark's initials: "SR: Your generous changes do not unsettle me! I duly note that this country not only is now a 'God-fearing nation' but always was a 'Christian nation'!"[104] A copy of a January draft bears an unsigned margin note at the word 'Christian' in the offending sentence, saying, "That's the stuff! Call them 'Christian' and that sanctifies everything. Marshall didn't rely much on the fact that they were 'Christian.'"[105]

Ultimately, the Court's intentional concealing of the "Christian discovery" doctrine emboldened courts throughout the U.S. legal system to rely on the foundation case of *Johnson v. McIntosh*. In a sense, *Tee-Hit-Ton* put *Johnson* through a laundromat. In the 131 years before *Tee-Hit-Ton*, courts cited *Johnson* 153 times, a rate of 1.168 per year; in the 66 years since *Tee-Hit-Ton* (up to January 2022), it has been cited in 205 cases, a rate of 3.106 per year. The laundered opinion in *Tee-Hit-Ton* put the Christian discovery doctrine on steroids.

Reed's rationale for imposing fifteenth-century Christian doctrine in the mid-twentieth century was economic: "No other course would meet the problem of the growth of the United States," which he said would be impeded if the United States were "subject . . . to an obligation to pay." He included a footnote saying that there were "claims with estimated interest already pending under the Indian jurisdictional act aggregating $9,000,000,000."[106]

Reed closed his opinion by referring to the familiar trope of judicial sympathy for Native peoples. He said there are "legal rights" and "moral deserts." He said, "We do not mean to leave the impression that the two have any relation to each other." In short, whatever the Tlingit moral deserts, they had no legal rights. He concluded, "Our conclusion does not uphold harshness as against tenderness toward the Indians, but it leaves with Congress, where it belongs, the policy of Indian gratuities for the termination of Indian occupancy of Government-owned land."[107]

The Tee-Hit-Ton challenge was even more remarkable because it was organized and propelled by a single person, William Lewis Paul, Sr. Although he would spend most of his life as an attorney for Tlingit and other Native peoples of Alaska, at the time the case was filed, he was disbarred in Alaska because of a dispute about handling client fees. The history professor Stephen Haycox suggested that the disbarment was engineered by Paul's political enemies in the Alaska Native Brotherhood and the Alaska Territorial Legislature in retaliation for his "very strong-willed, independent, and often aggressive" maneuvers.[108] Despite the fact that Paul was a founding member and president of the Alaska Native Brotherhood and a leader among the Tlingit and Haida peoples, his efforts on the *Tee-Hit-Ton* case were opposed by a majority of the Brotherhood, who were pursuing a separate case using a conventional approach. His license was reinstated twenty-two years later.[109] The attorneys of record in *Tee-Hit-Ton* were Paul's two sons, William Paul, Jr., and L. Frederick Paul.

The inherent difficulties faced by the Pauls in their solo challenge to entrenched doctrine were magnified by the fact that their adversary, the United States, was represented by its Justice Department, a mammoth organization whose budget request to Congress in 1952 for the Lands Division alone—in charge of "all civil suits and matters relating to title, possession, and use of Federal lands and natural resources [and representing] the United States in all civil litigation pertaining to Indians and Indian affairs"[110]—was more than $3.7 million.[111] It is easy to see that the Tlingit were outgunned.

## Red Lake Band of Chippewa Indians v. Swimmer

The case of *Red Lake Band of Chippewa Indians v. Swimmer*,[112] a 1990 decision by the U.S. District Court for the District of Columbia, involved a challenge to the 1988 Indian Gaming Regulatory Act, a U.S. statute establishing federal authority for "gaming activities on Indian lands."[113] The act defined three categories of gaming: traditional games, bingo and card games, and casino games. Only the first category was left under the full control of Indigenous nations; the other categories required agreement of the state that an Indigenous nation was said to be "within."[114]

Before we go any further, note again the problematic character of the view that Native nations are "included" in the United States. The assertion that an Indigenous nation is "within" a state ignores the reality that Indigenous nations preexist the states. The actual situation is that states were created within Indigenous lands. Many state organic acts explicitly acknowledge that fact and include provisions affirming that Indigenous lands are *not* part of the state. These organic acts were routinely violated, but the fact remains that it is historically and legally inaccurate to say an Indigenous nation is "within" a state.

In 1987, prior to the Gaming Act, the U.S. Supreme Court prohibited states from regulating "tribal gaming enterprises," in *California v. Cabazon Band of Mission Indians*. The Court applied the now-familiar rule of federal "plenary power" and said that gaming activities are within the realm of "tribal sovereignty . . . dependent on, and subordinate to, only the Federal Government, not the States."[115] The *Cabazon* decision concluded, "In light of compelling federal and tribal interests," California state and local efforts to regulate Cabazon gaming "would impermissibly infringe on tribal government."[116]

Note how the pro-Cabazon ruling still "lives off the exception." The opinion, by Justice Byron White, was explicit about the federal anti-Indian law exception, saying, "It is clear, however, that state laws may be applied to tribal Indians on their reservations if Congress has expressly so provided."[117] White elaborated the exception for "exceptional circumstances," when "a State may assert jurisdiction over the on-reservation activities of tribal members."[118]

Under pressure from the states, the U.S. Congress took the *Cabazon* decision as an invitation to take control of tribal gaming and diminish the concept of "tribal sovereignty." It enacted the Indian Gaming Regulatory Act under the ostensible purpose "to promote tribal economic development, self-sufficiency, and strong tribal governments."[119] The act "divided gaming into three separate classes, allowed states to prohibit class II and class III gaming if those activities were prohibited throughout a state, and required a tribal-state compact for class III gaming."[120] One does not need to do much digging to see that *state* economic development was the real purpose because prior to the act, Native nations had no obligation, let alone a requirement, to negotiate economic deals with surrounding states. The act coerced Native nations to assimilate economically with states and adopt state-style bureaucracies.

The Red Lake and Mescalero nations filed a lawsuit attacking the Gaming Act on multiple grounds. One argument stressed Indigenous independence, arguing, "The Act violates [the plaintiffs'] right to self-determination as preserved both in treaties with the federal government . . . and in aboriginal rights never surrendered to the federal government." Another argument worked within federal anti-Indian law "trust" doctrine, saying that "in passing the Act, Congress violated its federal trust responsibility to the Indians." Red Lake and Mescalero asked a U.S. District Court to block the U.S. Department of the Interior from implementing the act on their lands.[121]

The United States responded to the assertion of Native independence with the standard federal anti-Indian law "tribal sovereignty" exception, saying that "to the extent that any rights to self-determination were preserved by the Indians, whether explicitly by treaty, or implicitly by failure to surrender aboriginal rights, they are subject to complete defeasance by Congress." Within the exception, the United States argued, no matter what self-determination rights Red Lake and the Mescalero may have had, actions by Congress against Indigenous rights "do not violate the law."[122]

District Court judge Louis F. Oberdorfer quickly approved the U.S. response. He said that it "correctly asserts that under Supreme Court doctrine, Congress holds virtually unlimited power over the Indian tribes." Quoting a 1978 Supreme Court decision elaborating the federal anti-Indian law exception, he added, "The sovereignty that the Indian tribes retain is of a unique and limited character. It exists only at the sufferance of Congress and is subject to complete defeasance." He quoted U.S. District Court judge Andrew Kleinfeld in a 1988 Alaska case, who said, "As against Congress, tribal sovereignty is but a stick in front of a tank."[123]

Judge Oberdorfer addressed the Red Lake and Mescalero challenge to the "plenary power" doctrine. He said that the lawsuit was asking him to "refuse to allow Congress to assert the vast power over Indians that [the] doctrine of plenary power . . . allow[s]." He added that the challenge was "in accord with a number of authorities who criticize the doctrine of plenary power on a multitude of grounds." He again quoted Judge Kleinfeld, who said, "The doctrine of plenary power [was] . . . invented in large part to take the Indians' land."[124]

Oberdorfer quoted a number of critical law review commentaries. One said, "The doctrine of plenary power has been said to rest . . . on vague and extraordinarily unexamined foundations . . . [and] has been condemned for allowing infringement on the rights of Indians by groups eager for access to tribal and Indian resources often with disastrous impact on the tribes." Another commentary "criticized [the doctrine] as embodying the vestiges of . . . racial and cultural prejudice . . . that prompted Indians to be viewed as racially and culturally inferior and hence requiring guardianship by . . . Congress."[125]

Judge Oberdorfer also quoted a concurring opinion by Judge Philip Nichols in a 1979 U.S. Court of Claims case, where Nichols said that the invention of the doctrine of plenary power was "one of the blackest days in the history of the American Indian, the Indians' *Dred Scott* decision."[126]

After reviewing these and other criticisms of "plenary power" doctrine, Judge Oberdorfer said that he was nonetheless bound by U.S. Supreme Court decisions upholding the doctrine. He wrote:

> As disturbing as application of the . . . principle may be, however, lower federal district courts are bound by decisions of the Supreme Court. Thus, this Court is bound by the Supreme Court's clear rulings that Congress may pass laws such as the gaming legislation even if they violate treaties

with the Indians or Indians' aboriginal rights. The Indians claims to the contrary must therefore be rejected.[127]

Oberdorfer turned to the Red Lake and Mescalero argument that the Gaming Act violated federal Indian law's "trust responsibility" to the Indians. The question, he said, is "whether Congress' exercise of its plenary power was reasonably related to its trust responsibility to the [Indians]." That question, he continued, poses "a heavy burden" on Red Lake and the Mescalero because there is "a presumption of legitimacy for congressional Acts."[128] Notice that this presumption of legitimacy for congressional trustee acts is itself a violation of ordinary trust law principles. Notice also that "reasonably related" is the "test" required by the *Delaware Business* decision we looked at earlier and found to be hollow.

Moreover, the judge said, the "general deference due to Congress . . . is reinforced by Congress' careful balancing of the competing [state and tribal] interests" in the Gaming Act. "The legislative history demonstrates that Congress considered the Indians' governmental interests. . . ." In other words, again in sharp contrast to ordinary trust law, Judge Oberdorfer said that Congress only needs to *consider* Native interests; it does not actually have to *act* in their best interests. Therefore, the judge concluded, summarizing the exception, the Gaming Act did not violate "Congress' special relationship with the Indians."[129]

Oberdorfer dismissed the Red Lake/Mescalero suit. It was significant, however, that he investigated the foundation of their challenge to "plenary power" and showed that it was supported in scholarly critiques and judicial comments; he thereby protected the challenge from a charge of "frivolousness."

## Nevada v. Hicks

*Nevada v. Hicks* (2001)[130] was the case in which the Supreme Court tossed aside Chief Justice John Marshall's view in *Worcester v. Georgia* that "the laws of [a State] can have no force" within reservation boundaries. The issue in *Hicks* was whether the Fallon Paiute-Shoshone Tribal Court had jurisdiction over tort claims against Nevada game officers who twice invaded the home of a Paiute-Shoshone man and seized personal possessions in an effort to find evidence that he violated a Nevada hunting law. The officers later conceded that they found no such evidence.

Hicks's lawyers opened by asserting Indigenous independence: "The Fallon tribal court has deep historical roots in the pre-Columbian exercise of sovereignty by the country's first peoples. It is an integral part of the modern day manifestation of centuries-old authority structures that have governed the Paiute and Shoshone peoples since long before the State of Nevada was even contemplated."[131] They then added an argument within the framework of Christian discovery, saying, "Tribal authority over the activities of non-Indians on reservation lands is an important part of tribal sovereignty," but U.S. court decisions have "fashioned some boundaries for the exercise of tribal jurisdiction."[132]

The most powerful part of Hicks's brief attacked the foundation of federal anti-Indian law's "divestiture of Tribal jurisdiction." It called it "the legal fiction that the discovery of the New World by Europeans resulted in inherent limitations on tribal rights and sovereignty in favor of the European discovering nation." The brief argued that the "legal fiction" originated in "an archaic set of legal rules and principles originating in the Middle Ages and the Crusades to the Holy Lands," under which "Christian princes were authorized . . . by the Pope to undertake holy wars of conquest against the 'heathen' and 'infidel' peoples." The argument concluded, "With its roots in the same colonial era attitudes that justified slavery, the . . . doctrine of discovery remains frozen in an age of racial discrimination, . . . [and] cannot be sustained under modern principles of racial equality."[133]

Unfortunately, perhaps attempting to sweeten this bitter pill for the court, they then pulled their powerful punch. They said that their critique was aimed at what they called an "enlarged version" of Christian discovery, which they distinguished from a "limited" version of the doctrine. They said that the limited version was based on the Marshall trilogy. Under the enlarged version, they said, "The mere act of 'discovering' Indian tribes and their lands is deemed to vest the discoverer with complete sovereignty over the tribes and render the tribes' own sovereignty diminished and subjugated." We have seen that this is exactly what Marshall's *Johnson* decision stated. But Hicks's brief engaged in wishful thinking, denying that *Johnson* established "absolute sovereignty and title over lands discovered by a European nation."[134]

Briefly, Hicks's lawyers adopted an apologist's reading of the *Johnson* decision, saying that Marshall's words giving the United States "exclusive rights of territorial acquisition and colonial control over lands occupied by Indian tribes" were limited to the "minimal limitations on Indian rights and sovereignty necessarily required to effectuate the purposes of the discovery doctrine."[135] They did not explain why there was any "necessity" to restrict Native rights and sovereignty at all.

They concluded with a rhetorical flourish meant to allay any fears about Indigenous rebellion and secession: "Although historically excluded, hundreds of tribes are part of the fabric of this country."[136] In saying this, they unwittingly reflected the assimilation/termination agenda at the heart of federal anti-Indian law. Despite these limitations, however, the *Hicks* critique of Christian discovery is a noteworthy example of doctrinal challenge.

The Supreme Court rejected Hicks's effort to limit state interference with tribal lawmaking. Justice Antonin Scalia wrote: "The Indians' right to make their own laws and be governed by them does not exclude all state regulatory authority on the reservation. State sovereignty does not end at a reservation's border. Though tribes are often referred to as 'sovereign' entities, it was long ago that the Court departed from Chief Justice Marshall's view that 'the laws of [a State] can have no force' within reservation boundaries." Scalia added, "Ordinarily, it is now clear, an Indian reservation is considered part of the territory of the State."[137] Scalia didn't explain how the exception becomes "ordinary" and "clear," even as it remains an indeterminate exception whose formulation changes from case to case.

## Western Shoshone National Council

As we saw in Chapter 4, the efforts of the Dann sisters to defend their ownership of Western Shoshone grazing lands ended in a bizarre 1985 U.S. Supreme Court decision, *United States v. Dann*,[138] when the Court used the federal anti-Indian law trust doctrine to allow the United States to pay itself for taking Western Shoshone title. In 1995, ten years after the *Dann* decision, Western Shoshone chief Raymond Yowell and the Western Shoshone National Council initiated new litigation attacking the Christian discovery doctrine in an effort to undo the *Dann* decision. With help from Bob Doyle and Steve Newcomb, I helped the chief and council to file an intervention in *United States v. Nye County, Nevada*,[139] a dispute between those two parties about ownership of certain lands in ancestral Shoshone territory. The United States started the lawsuit in an effort to control what it said were federal lands; Nye County claimed ownership and started building a road.

The Western Shoshone intervention said that they, neither the United States nor Nye County, were the rightful owners of the lands; they had lived there since time immemorial. They quoted Supreme Court justice Joseph Story's acknowledgment in his *Commentaries on the Constitution* that Indigenous nations were the original sovereign proprietors of the land, and they cited early international law writers making the same point. They added that the 1863 Treaty of Ruby Valley between the Western Shoshone and the United States was not a cession of land or a relinquishment of nationhood; rather, it established the only proper basis for relations between the two nations.

Chief Judge Lloyd D. George of the federal district court denied the intervention. He said, "The Shoshone do not have a legally-protectible [sic] interest in the land" because the *Dann* decision ruled that "the Shoshone's aboriginal title has been extinguished."[140] The United States and Nye County also relied on the *Dann* decision to oppose the Shoshone intervention.

Left to right: author, Robert Doyle, and Raymond Yowell. (author photo, June 1996)

The Western Shoshone appealed to the Ninth Circuit, arguing that the *Dann* decision violated principles of ordinary property and trust law. They attacked the Christian discovery exception to ordinary law as "anathema to peace and the peaceful resolution of conflict among peoples and nations."[141] The Ninth Circuit dismissed the appeal on the ground that the United States and Nye County had settled their dispute in the meantime, and the appeal was therefore moot.[142] The unexpected Western Shoshone effort to intervene apparently had encouraged the United States and the county to conclude their litigation.

The Western Shoshone National Council also challenged the United States in international forums. In 2000, they filed an "Intervention and Appearance of the Western Shoshone National Council as *Amicus*," supporting a petition by Mary and Carrie Dann in the Organization of American States Inter-American Commission on Human Rights. The Dann sisters were asking the Commission to review the *Dann* decision. The commission's review concluded in 2002 in favor of the Western Shoshone, ruling that the legal processes in the *Dann* case "were not sufficient to comply with contemporary international human rights norms, principles and standards that govern the determination of indigenous property interests."[143] The commission exercised the only power available to it, which was to issue a set of Recommendations to the United States to "respect . . . the Danns' right to property in accordance with . . . the American Declaration [of Human Rights]."[144]

In 2005, the National Council approached another international body, the UN Committee on the Elimination of Racial Discrimination (CERD), where they filed a *Request for Early Warning and Urgent Action Procedure*.[145] In 2006, CERD issued a decision, saying, "The Committee regrets that the State party [the United States] has not . . . provided responses to the list of issues . . . as requested, and that it did not consider it necessary to appear before the

Committee to discuss the matter." It also noted "with concern" that U.S. actions regarding the Western Shoshone "did not comply with contemporary international human rights norms, principles and standards that govern determination of indigenous property interests, as stressed by the Inter-American Commission on Human Rights." The CERD urged the United States to take immediate action "to initiate a dialogue" with the Western Shoshone to find a solution that would comply with their rights to own, develop, control, and use their communal lands, territories and resources.[146] Previously, in 2001, the CERD had issued a report noting "with concern" that under U.S. law Native treaties can be abrogated unilaterally by the United States, and Indigenous land can be taken without compensation. The CERD expressed a particular concern about mining and nuclear waste storage on Western Shoshone land and stressed "the importance of securing the 'informed consent' of indigenous communities."[147]

While these international victories did not bring about a fundamental change in U.S. law, they added to the establishment of norms of international law regarding state relations with Indigenous peoples, and in this way they helped lay the groundwork for other global actions to defend Indigenous lands.

## Washington v. Cougar Den

In 2019, the Yakama Nation filed an amicus brief in *Washington State Department of Licensing v. Cougar Den, Inc.*, a case arising from an attempt by the state to tax a trucking company owned and operated by a Yakama citizen for using state highways to transport fuel to the Yakama Nation.[148] Cougar Den argued that the "right to travel" provision in the 1855 Yakama Treaty with the United States preempted the state tax. Washington State courts agreed and blocked the tax, but the state appealed those decisions. The state's position was that "longstanding rules of Indian law" controlled the issue and supported the tax.[149]

Tellingly, the United States also filed an amicus brief—in support of the state of Washington! So much for the federal anti-Indian law's "government-to-government relationship" and "trust doctrine" supposedly governing U.S. dealings with Indigenous nations.

The Yakama Nation's amicus brief attacked the Christian discovery premise of federal anti-Indian law that underlay Washington's position. It said that Washington's legal arguments were based on "the religious, racist, genocidal, fabricated doctrine of Christian discovery." It further argued that the only legitimate basis for deciding the case was the 1855 treaty, unmodified by any federal anti-Indian law rules of "interpretation." The Yakama challenge is worth reading at length. Its power comes from its directness and specificity:

> The Yakama Treaty is the organic document establishing the government-to-government relationship between the United States and the Yakama

Nation. It serves as the basis for any dispute concerning our rights. However, courts have systematically attempted to undermine our Treaty rights by imposing an imaginary prior relationship sourced in the doctrine of Christian discovery. Under that doctrine, this Court judicially manufactured an extra-constitutional congressional plenary authority to abrogate treaties and regulate Native Nations. This manufactured authority rests on the false assertion that our sovereignty and free and independent existence were "necessarily diminished" upon Christian European arrival on the North American continent [as stated in] *Johnson v. McIntosh*. . . . For nearly two centuries this Court has dehumanized original, free, and independent Nations and Peoples by issuing decisions and using language consistent with the doctrine's religious and racist foundations—*e.g.*, red man, uncivilized, barbarous, ignorant, unlearned, non-Christians, heathens, savages, infidels—all in an effort to manufacture a legal basis for the physical and cultural genocide of Native Peoples.[150]

The Yakama said that the state and U.S. positions in the case were "directly linked to the doctrine" of Christian discovery, which means that "they are asking this Court to continue wielding the sword of the religious, racist, genocidal, fabricated doctrine of Christian discovery against our People." They then offered the U.S. Supreme Court an "opportunity to repudiate the doctrine of Christian discovery." They pointed out the fact that other "troubling decisions throughout history have . . . been repudiated," as occurred with the "separate but equal" doctrine. They called on the court "to repudiate the doctrine of discovery . . . in this case and all future cases."[151]

The Supreme Court ruled for Cougar Den under the Yakama Treaty. It rejected the state and U.S. arguments in two separate opinions: one by Justice Stephen Breyer (joined by Justices Sonia Sotomayor and Elena Kagan) and another by Justice Gorsuch (joined by Justice Ruth Bader Ginsburg). Both opinions cited the Yakama amicus brief to clarify the meaning of the 1855 treaty; but neither opinion discussed the Christian discovery question. In fact, even the dissenting justices avoided talking about Christian discovery, focusing on treaty language instead.

There were two dissenting opinions in the *Cougar Den* case. One was by Justice Brett Kavanaugh (joined by Justice Clarence Thomas); the other was by Chief Justice John Roberts (joined by Justices Thomas, Samuel Alito, and Kavanaugh). The dissenters manifested a deep fear of Yakama Treaty rights, and indeed a deep fear of the Yakama themselves. They displayed fears of "Indian savagery" that characterized the colonial White image of Indigenous peoples. For example, Justice Kavanaugh said that upholding Yakama Treaty travel rights might undermine "speed limits, truck restrictions, and reckless driving laws."[152]

Justice Roberts expressed sovereign anxiety directly. He said that upholding Yakama rights will "generate significant uncertainty and unnecessary
litigation." He added, "Today's decision digs such a deep hole that the future
promises a lot of backing and filling." In what was the "hole" dug? The doctrine of Christian discovery.[153]

## International Action

Litigation challenges to Christian discovery can rely on a significant international critique of the doctrine. In 2007, the UN General Assembly adopted
the Declaration on the Rights of Indigenous Peoples, Article 3 of which con-
demns "all doctrines, policies and practices based on . . . national origin or
racial, religious, ethnic or cultural differences." It says that these doctrines
"are racist, scientifically false, legally invalid, morally condemnable and
socially unjust."[154]

Related affirmations appear throughout the Declaration, including a statement that "Indigenous peoples have the right to own, use, develop and control the lands, territories and resources that they possess by reason of
traditional ownership or other traditional occupation or use, as well as those
which they have otherwise acquired [and] States shall give legal recognition
and protection to these lands, territories and resources . . . with due respect
to the customs, traditions and land tenure systems of the indigenous peoples
concerned."[155]

The title of the UN Declaration—"Rights of Indigenous Peoples"—marks
the outcome of an argument won by Indigenous Peoples. Their insistence on
the plural form—"peoples," a term in international law that signifies collective self-determination—triggered immense resistance by some states,
including the United States, who argued for the singular form—"people"—
by saying that there are no Indigenous *peoples*, but only Indigenous *people*—
individual *persons* who are citizens of the states that claim jurisdiction over
their lands.

However, despite the recognition of peoplehood implied by the title, the
rhetoric of "self-determination," and the fact that this document emerged
from decades of Indigenous critiques of state claims to sovereignty, the Declaration did not undo the exception from the rule of law. It declares that
states shall "recognize," "establish," "implement," and "protect" Indigenous
peoples, but there is no UN mechanism to enforce any of these instructions.
The Declaration also makes no provisions for independent actions by Indigenous peoples to protect, implement, or establish their "right to self-
determination." In this sense, the Declaration maintains what political
scientist Rob Walker called the "spatiotemporal"[156] configuration of the international system of states.

In 2013, Charmaine White Face, Zumila Wobaga, spokesperson for the Sioux Nation Treaty Council at the United Nations throughout the years-long process that led to the Declaration, developed a comparative analysis demonstrating differences between the final version and the original version prepared with Indigenous representatives. She concluded that "the wording in [the final] Declaration will benefit the colonizers more than the nations it was designed for—the Indigenous Nations."[157]

One startling example she offers is Article 36. The original version focused on the "recognition, observance, and enforcement of treaties" and stated that "disputes which cannot otherwise be settled should be submitted to competent international bodies agreed to by all parties concerned." The final version says nothing about treaties, instead promising "Indigenous peoples . . . right to maintain . . . contacts . . . with their own members as well as other peoples across borders." Moreover, there is no enforcement mechanism for this right, only an exhortation that "States, in consultation and cooperation with indigenous peoples, shall take effective measures to facilitate . . . and ensure implementation of this right."[158]

As we saw earlier, the United Nations has struggled to define "Indigenous peoples."[159] Jose R. Martinez Cobo, special rapporteur of the Sub-Commission on Prevention of Discrimination and Protection of Minorities, grappled with the issue in his 1987 "Study on the Problem of Discrimination against Indigenous Populations." Note that the title refers to "populations," not "peoples"; "populations" is a demographic term. Cobo described Indigenous populations as "non-dominant sectors of society," thus positioning them as "minorities within" states rather than as independent actors. He added, "Indigenous communities, peoples and nations . . . consider themselves distinct from other sectors of the societies now prevailing in those territories."[160]

The problem is that the provisions of the Declaration depend on decisions made by member states of the United Nations. The rights of Indigenous peoples, set forth in forty-six articles, are framed within a state-centric system. The grammatical structure of the text itself signifies this—"States" (uppercase, proper noun) are superior to "indigenous peoples" (lowercase, common noun), even in stating the intended goal of the Declaration: "The recognition of the rights of indigenous peoples in this Declaration will enhance harmonious and cooperative relations between the State and indigenous peoples."[161] In short, the Declaration does not provide a self-executing platform upon which Indigenous Peoples may build international legal protections for their lands and societies. This is the Achilles heel of the Declaration.

The United States, a major opponent of the use of the plural "peoples," voted against the Declaration. In 2010, facing pressure from Indigenous peoples and embarrassment in the United Nations, it reversed its vote. The U.S. State Department announced the reversal and quoted President Barack Obama: "While we cannot erase the scourges or broken promises of our past, we will move ahead together in writing a new, brighter chapter in our joint history." The announcement continued, "It is in this spirit that the United States today proudly lends its support to the United Nations Declaration on the Rights of Indigenous Peoples."[162]

Flying in the teeth of those fine words, however, the announcement of the vote switch was accompanied by a signing statement specifying that U.S. support was limited to maintaining a diminished status for Native Peoples—the exception. It said that the concept of self-determination in the Declaration was different from ordinary self-determination: "The *Declaration's* call is to promote the development of a concept of self-determination for indigenous peoples that is *different from* the existing right of self-determination in international law." Explaining the alleged difference, the announcement said, "The Declaration's concept of self-determination is consistent with the United States' existing recognition of, and relationship with, federally recognized tribes"—that is, the exception. The announcement described the exception as a "special legal and political relationship."[163] In short, the supposed statement of support from the United States insisted that the UN Declaration had meaning only within the existing U.S. federal anti-Indian law exception.

Lest there be doubt about the significance of the exception, the announcement emphasized that the Declaration's affirmation of "free and informed consent" is a "call for a process of meaningful consultation with tribal leaders, but not necessarily the agreement of those leaders, before the actions addressed in those consultations are taken."[164]

The United States also joined other UN member-states in describing the Declaration as "aspirational" on the part of Indigenous peoples. It then made it clear that the United States had its own aspirations for the document—"aspirations that the country seeks to achieve within the structure of the U.S. Constitution, laws, and international obligations, while also seeking, where appropriate, to improve our laws and policies."[165]

Putting aside the question of whether it is ever *not* "appropriate to improve laws and policies," notice the characterization of U.S. "aspirations": namely, that the Declaration be interpreted and applied so as not to diverge from or disparage existing U.S. law—namely, the doctrine of Christian discovery. In this context, "aspiration" is equivalent to pretension; it is a restatement of John Marshall's extravagant pretensions. The Obama administration may have been embarrassed enough to switch the U.S. vote, but not to change the U.S. legal position.

The resistance of the United States and other UN member-states to the UN Declaration demonstrated what Mark Rifkin described in another context as sovereign "anxiety"—an "instability of the settler-state" arising from a "failure to find a normative foundation" for state power in relation to Indigenous Peoples. The Declaration, in its final article, reflects this anxiety explicitly and bows to states' insistence on a continuing "compulsory relation" with

Indigenous Peoples. Article 46 privileges state geopolitical claims against the possibility of "metapolitical" Indigenous challenges: It says, "Nothing in this Declaration may be . . . construed as authorizing or encouraging any action which would dismember or impair, totally or in part, the territorial integrity or political unity of sovereign and independent States."[166]

With this qualifying statement privileging member-state territorial integrity and sovereignty claims, the Declaration managed *not* to open a new chapter in world historical relations between states and Indigenous Peoples. As Sharon H. Venne (Cree), an Indigenous participant known for her struggles against state claims of domination, said about the effort to draft the Declaration, "It should have been easy for Indigenous peoples to appear at UN meetings and to be recognised as nations and peoples, using the United Nations Charter."[167] After all, she pointed out, the charter opens with a statement that the United Nations exists "to develop friendly relations among nations based on respect for the principle of equal rights and self-determination of peoples."[168]

As Mark Rifkin put it: "The topos of sovereignty designates less a content that can be replaced (a racist vision of Indian savagery, a Eurocentric resistance to Native customs) than a process of compulsory relation, one predicated on the supposedly unquestionable fact of national territorial boundaries."[169] The UN Declaration contains language replacing old notions of savagery with new notions of "rights," but ultimately it restates the "supposedly unquestionable fact of national territorial boundaries." The twenty-first-century version of the UN Declaration may thus be read as a restatement of the core issues that preoccupied Chief Justice John Marshall and the U.S. Supreme Court in the early nineteenth century. To wit: the condition of Indigenous peoples in relation to states.

The United Nations created a Permanent Forum on Indigenous Issues to provide an ongoing forum for grappling with issues raised in the Declaration. But problems persist. Although the United States failed in its effort to block the plural word "peoples" from the title of the Declaration, the issue lingers. In response to a 2014 recommendation of the Permanent Forum that its name be changed from "Indigenous Issues" to "Indigenous Peoples," the Economic and Social Council, bowing to pressure from UN member-states, said, "Further discussion is needed."[170]

A further example of limitations within the United Nations was the response to a study undertaken at the direction of the Permanent Forum in May 2014, prior to a high-level plenary meeting of the UN General Assembly billed as "The World Conference on Indigenous Peoples." The *Study on the Impacts of the Doctrine of Discovery on Indigenous Peoples, Including Mechanisms, Processes and Instruments of Redress* criticized Christian discovery as a violation of the human rights of Indigenous peoples. It made a specific recommendation for action: "The upcoming World Conference on the Rights of

Indigenous Peoples provides an opportunity . . . in the outcome document to wholly repudiate colonial doctrines and to commit to processes of redress."[171]

If the high-level meeting had really been a "World Conference on Indigenous Peoples," it would have—at least—discussed the forum's study. At most, it would have followed the study's recommendation to repudiate Christian discovery. But the high-level meeting neither discussed nor repudiated the doctrine. The conference's "Outcome Document"[172] left Christian discovery in place, without critique, as an ongoing basis for states to claim sovereignty over Indigenous lands.

In short, the Declaration on the Rights of Indigenous Peoples has not displaced the doctrine of Christian discovery exception. But despite—and perhaps because of—its limitations, the Declaration has generated continuing attention to the relations between states and Indigenous Peoples. It has at least opened a way to mount a twenty-first-century critique of the doctrine in the global political imagination. "The question remains," as Angelique Eagle-Woman said, "when the doctrine of discovery will be fully refuted and replaced with Article 26 of the United Nations Declaration on the Rights of Indigenous Peoples . . . [which] expressly provides: 'Indigenous peoples have the right to own, use, develop and control the lands, territories and resources that they possess by reason of traditional ownership, or other traditional occupation or use, as well as those which they have otherwise acquired.'"[173]

The UN Declaration came at a time when judges, lawyers, and academics in the United States were hotly contesting whether and to what extent U.S. jurisprudence ought to be open to international law.[174] One commentator suggested that the controversy itself portended "a shift of tectonic plates" in U.S. jurisprudence.[175] In 2005, an "unprecedented debate" between Justices Breyer and Scalia at American University, Washington College of Law, brought the discussion to the public.[176] The debate focused especially on constitutional issues, but it carried wider implications for legal decision-making.

Intriguingly, Justice Scalia, the opponent of relying on "foreign law" for constitutional decisions, separated out cases involving treaties. He said, "I do not use foreign law in the interpretation of the United States Constitution. Now, I will use it in the interpretation of a treaty." That attitude indicates a point of leverage to apply the UN Declaration to relations between the United States and Indigenous nations where treaties are involved. Indeed, one would be hard-pressed to deny the relevance of contemporary international law in a reassessment of federal anti-Indian law because the Marshall trilogy so clearly relied on international precedents for Christian discovery doctrine.

# CHAPTER SIX

# Federal Anti-Indian Law in the Classroom

## Teaching Federal Anti-Indian Law

Looking at how federal anti-Indian law is taught—or not taught—provides insight into the possibilities and difficulties of undoing the domination matrix. In the process, it shows how someone is taught to "think like a lawyer."

A law school classroom is a crucible in which the scholarly interests of teachers mix with pressures from the practicing bar. The topics and questions range from explicitly practical—what is the law, how is it likely to develop?—to jurisprudential—what concepts, values, and assumptions underlie the law? Every law class confronts this mixture in proportions that vary according to the interests of the teacher, the students, and even the current times. The opportunity for developing strategic approaches to overturning federal anti-Indian law domination begins in law school.

As Professor Gloria Valencia-Weber put it, "Much of what has traditionally been called Indian law are the constructs of non-Indians, built upon ethnocentric presumptions that Euro-Americans made about Indians being savages and uncivilized. That language remains in the federal law . . . since its first articulation in the Marshall Court decisions. . . . The task . . . is to 'decolonize' the laws . . . [and] to remedy the malignant results . . . [that] deny them autonomy and fairness." She added that training a briefcase lawyer "involves more than . . . producing more generic law graduates who are Indian." It requires "the environment and curriculum of the law schools . . . [to] be redesigned."[1]

Professor Rennard Strickland said that Native peoples have been exposed to "500 years of . . . a European dominated system of laws." He described federal anti-Indian law as "in flux" and said, "Dramatic shifts in the federal courts are forcing all parties to reevaluate strategies."[2] He also added, "For 200 years we have accepted as fact a doctrine which placed white American [sic] at the very center of the universe, at the heart of a divinely ordained plan. This is not a realistic world view."[3]

Before we look at how federal anti-Indian law curricula respond to these critiques, it will help to step back and look at what law schools do in general—how students learn to "think like a lawyer."

## A Jealous Mistress with a Janus Face

The study of court opinions is central to legal education. One key lesson that every law student learns is that a court opinion doesn't stand alone. Every opinion is interconnected with other opinions—those that it cites as precedent and those in which it is cited as precedent. In short, court opinions exist in *lines of precedents* in *fields of doctrines*.

Legal education—"learning to think like a lawyer"—involves immersion in case reports, precedents, and doctrines. The cognitive demands are enormous. Students must read and sift through dozens, even hundreds, of opinions; they have to determine which words are significant to the final decision and which facts are relevant to which doctrines.

One of the most famous statements about the demands of studying law was made by U.S. Supreme Court justice Joseph Story, in his 1829 inaugural address as Dane Professor of Law at Harvard University. He said, "I will not say . . . that 'The Law will admit of no rival' . . . but I will say that it is a jealous mistress, and requires a long and constant courtship. It is not to be won by trifling favors, but by lavish homage."[4]

Story's image of the law as a jealous mistress demanding all one's attention was once commonly taught to first-year students in American law schools; by now, in an era of concern for gender stereotypes, few law students hear Story's words. Nonetheless, the image of a stern taskmaster prevails in the reality of legal education. The effort to make sense of the system of precedents requires an introduction of students' minds into a cognitive framework of authority built around judges' words and decisions. Moreover, the student cannot assume that the cognitive framework is grounded in common sense or in ordinary human relations.

In Justice Story's words, the cognitive framework of law is "a system . . . built up and perfected by artificial doctrines adapted and moulded to the artificial structure of society."[5] Abraham Lincoln gave similar advice to prospective lawyers. He said, "If you wish to be a lawyer, attach no consequence to the *place* you are in, or the *person* you are with; but get books, sit down anywhere, and go to reading."[6]

Story's description of law and society as "artificial" and Lincoln's advice to ignore people and places go a long way toward explaining the difficulty of understanding law, especially for a person reared in a traditional, place-based Native society that views law as growing out of custom and morals and society as a natural phenomenon. Such beliefs may seem common sense, even to a non-Native. But legal education will quickly disabuse a student of these ideas. Law students learn that what counts as "reason" in law is what has been decided by the highest courts. High court judges' views of society are the ruling ideas, referred to as "doctrines"—literally, "teachings."

Whether in Story's words or Lincoln's, the typical law student is urged to forget about everything except what judges have said and decided. Legal education teaches students to look backward at decisions, which are called "precedents"—literally, "that which precedes." Students learn how to use what judges said in the past to build arguments to persuade a judge in the present. The conventional justification for the whole process is that it maintains consistency between present decisions and past decisions in order to ensure fairness and equal treatment. But a problem arises: concepts of fairness and equality change, so how can law change if precedents bind decision-making?

Karl Llewellyn, a famous twentieth-century law professor and scholar, offered a famous answer to this question in his 1951 introductory lectures to first-year law students, *The Bramble Bush: On Our Law and Its Study.* He said that the system of precedents is not closed and does not actually bind the present because each prior opinion is open to interpretation. He added that every court decision "is two-headed . . . Janus-faced." Janus, the ancient Roman god of gates and doorways, looks both inside and outside, forward and backward. Llewellyn said that we look to the past when we read a case; but in reading it, we can "reexamine" it, go "underneath" it and *bind it to its past,* thereby limiting or avoiding its binding effect in the present. He called this a "strict" way of reading a case because it means that we don't accept every word in a court opinion. A strict reading finds ways to disregard what a judge said in the opinion, either by showing that the judge's words were "dicta" (not relevant to the decision) or by tying the words to the specific facts of the case (they only apply to those facts). In short, a "strict" reading sorts out the words that are strictly necessary to the facts of the decision. Llewellyn said that a strict reading requires "fine . . . minds, minds with sharp mental scalpels." In contrast, Llewellyn said, a "loose" reading of an opinion can quote any and every word as may seem useful. The loose way of reading is easy, he said; there's no need for parsing or analysis. He argued, "An ignorant [or] unskillful" lawyer will find it hard to do a strict reading and will be bound by the past. In practice, Llewellyn pointed out, a lawyer or judge uses both methods, depending on the needs of the argument.[7]

As a student becomes aware of the fact that every case can be read in different ways, the indeterminacy of law appears. It startles anyone who thought that law was a certainty, authoritative, predictable. Llewellyn criticized the view that "precedent produces . . . a certainty." He emphasized law is not something "out there" that determines decisions; rather, it is a process of *argument*. He said that every case involves "matters of judgment and persuasion." He added, "People . . . who think that precedent produces . . . a certainty that [does] not involve matters of judgment and persuasion, or who think that what I have described involves improper equivocation . . . such people simply do not know our system of precedent in which they live."[8]

Llewellyn invited law students to resist the "jealousy" of law—not to follow the way of Story and Lincoln. He advised them to look outside the books, to look at persons and places, and to look at society as it is lived. Llewellyn's advice intersects intriguingly with a Native perspective pointed out by Professor John Borrows's study of Indigenous law, *Law's Indigenous Ethics*. Borrows wrote, "Reason is developed by analogy in Anishinaabe law, just as in the common law: parallel situations are correlated, dissimilar situations are distinguished. The difference is that this Anishinaabe legal process occurs by reading the land, in addition to reading past cases."[9] It may well be that Llewellyn's view of law was influenced by his experience among the Cheyenne with anthropologist E. Adamson Hoebel, which resulted in their pioneering study of Indigenous law, *The Cheyenne Way*.[10]

Llewellyn's way of studying law was called "legal realism," which says that judges don't simply apply preexisting law; they create law, and they do so not simply from books, but also from experience. Oliver Wendell Holmes, Jr., associate justice of the Massachusetts Supreme Judicial Court, inspired the legal realist view in 1897 when he insisted that statements about law are only "prophecies of what the courts will do."[11] What courts do is law, and law does not exist separate from what courts do. In 1918, when he was an associate justice of the U.S. Supreme Court, Holmes stated succinctly, "A right is only the hypostasis of a prophecy—the imagination of a substance."[12] To say there is a "right" to do something is to predict that a judge would rule in favor of doing that something—nothing more, nothing less.

Following the legal realists, we can say, first, that legal doctrine is created and maintained through argument; and second, that any particular doctrine is "real" only to the extent that it is enforced.[13] In short, legal doctrine does not exist in a true/false dimension, but rather in an accepted/unaccepted dimension. The more lawyers who argue and judges who accept and enforce the argument, the more "real" it becomes, and the harder it is to change or dismantle it.

Felix Cohen, the compiler of the original version of the *Handbook of Federal Indian Law*, the ur-text of the field, was a legal realist, and he understood all this. The history of the compilation demonstrates the force field of arguments about the relationship between the United States and Native peoples. The *Handbook* was (and is) regarded as a kind of bible for lawyers and judges in federal anti-Indian law, and it plays a significant role in legal education. But it is, like all the rest of law, open to interpretation and subject to critique, argument, and change.

In the 1940s and 1950s, legal realists in American law schools declared that all fields of law are expressions of political, economic, and personal perspectives, hiding behind apparently determinate rules. The difference is that federal anti-Indian law is not a field where politics hides behind rules. The doctrines are explicitly political, as we saw in Justice Samuel Alito's recounting of the trust doctrine (discussed in Chapter 4).

Legal realist influence declined in the face of resistance from conventional legal educators and especially from practitioners, who wanted definite—or at least finite—sets of rules.[14] The most extreme denunciation of the realist view was made by those who call themselves "textualists" or "originalists." They deny that legal rules have any indeterminacy, political or otherwise, despite the fact that even textualists and originalists find plenty to argue about on any and every precedent. If they acknowledge politics at all, they confine it to the past or cast it as an aspersion on their opponents. They are especially eager to maintain at least a public facade of regularity and order in the "rule of law."

The fact remains that there is a special pedagogical problem in teaching federal anti-Indian law. How can students be prepared to practice in a field whose doctrines are explicitly political and subject to extreme gyrations? Can a law school course be devoted to the study of *political* rules? Wouldn't that course instead belong in a department of politics or history?

The beginning of an answer to these questions is to recognize that a proper legal education actually thrives on debate, on the *indeterminacy of rules*. A law teacher takes indeterminacy in stride as grist for class discussion. Teachers and students argue about the interpretation of rules and texts without worrying that their arguments undermine the rule of law, though they may accuse their opponents of doing just that.

Briefly, although the law looks like rules when viewed from the outside, the law consists of arguments when viewed from the inside. This is especially true in the Anglo-American "adversary process," where cases are seen as contests and the parties are expected to present arguments as being one-sided as possible. Baron Patrick Devlin, a British Law Lord, promoted adversary process in his 1979 book, *The Judge*, where he said, "Two prejudiced searchers starting from opposite ends of the field will between them be less likely to miss anything than the impartial searcher starting at the middle."[15]

The pedagogical problem with teaching and learning any field of law is adequately presenting the argumentative structure of law. This means presenting the materials of law—cases, statutes, regulations, treaties, and so on—as bases for arguments. Indeed, arguments are already implicated in the teacher's selection and arrangement of materials.

There is a problem in all this for the public view of law, the "outsider" view—the need to sufficiently hide the internal argumentative process to maintain support for the law as apparently a regime of rules. The professional craft of lawyers and judges is to frame policy, process, and political purposes as arguments about "rules" supposedly derived from "doctrines." The openly political quality and the twists and turns of federal anti-Indian law make this an especially fraught process. One response is to embrace the anomalous character of the field and openly teach it as policy rather than law.

Students of federal anti-Indian law will do well to follow a legal realist method. They would look for fault lines, fracture points, places where decisions and doctrines can be limited to specific circumstances that bind them to their past and free the present from them. Students would study how Christian discovery is embedded in colonization, land speculation, and, most important, in the exception denying Native peoples full human status. They would discover that Christian discovery is ripe for being picked apart, going underneath, finding ways to set it aside as a historical anachronism— binding it to its colonial past—rather than accepting it as controlling dogma in the present.

It takes critical investigation to reveal the twists and turns of the exception and the persisting structure of the federal anti-Indian law domination matrix.

## The Importance of Books

Having said that there is more to law study than what is in books, it is important to understand the necessity of books.

In 1906, William Lile, dean of the University of Virginia School of Law, introduced a book titled *Brief Making and the Use of Law Books.* He wrote, "In the days of our grandfathers when books were few . . . the lawyer with one book was a dangerous adversary. . . . [I]n modern days . . . it is the lawyer with many books and the skill to use them whose briefs win causes in the appellate courts and furnish material for immortal opinions."[16] *Brief Making* consisted of practical advice to law students and new lawyers about how to use law books to prepare an argument.

Not until 1973, five years after I graduated from Yale, did the first casebook in the field of federal anti-Indian law appear—*Law and the American Indian,* written by Monroe Price, law professor at the University of Calfornia, Los Angeles.[17] At that time, there were "fewer than a dozen instructors . . . focused on federal Indian law" anywhere in the United States.[18] Some of the earliest teaching materials were mimeographed copies shared among the few teachers who were building a curriculum.[19]

Professor Drew L. Kershen's 1973 review of Price's casebook asked "why a course concentrating on the legal relationship between Native American peoples and the United States should be taught at all." He suggested three reasons: first, because "legal issues of the exploration for and the exploitation of mineral resources on Indian reservations seem assuredly to multiply"; second, American society is expressing "increased concern for ethnic pride and ethnic differences"; and third, "A course involving the legal problems of Native Americans can explore basic values and assumptions of the Anglo-American legal system."[20] Kershen was prescient: First, mineral extraction from Native lands increasingly produces major controversy—witness the U.S. effort to transfer Apache lands at Oak Flat to a multinational mining company, an ongoing conflict in 2021.[21] Second, racial justice issues are increasingly widely recognized; however, as we have seen, a race perspective is inadequate to understand issues facing Native peoples. Third, the combination of the first two situations is encouraging increased attention to U.S. history and law.

Kershen was also accurate in his assessment that "'Indian law' would be a challenging course to teach . . . [because] the legal problems of Native Americans have been resolved under different theories which are contradictory . . . [and] these contradictory theories have been expressed . . . with no apparent recognition . . . that the contradictions exist, or at least, no apparent attempt to reconcile or repudiate the contradictions."[22]

Until the publication of Price's *Law and the American Indian*, law students and teachers had only Cohen's *Handbook of Federal Indian Law* to guide their study, using the 1942 original, the 1958 Interior Department revision, or both. In either of its versions, the *Handbook* was not specifically designed for classroom use.

Secretary of the Interior Harold L. Ickes, in his foreword to the 1942 edition, hoped for an educational impact, saying that the *Handbook* could help "Indians themselves . . . [become] aware of [their] rights" and "should give . . . Indians useful weapons in the continual struggle that every minority must wage to maintain its liberties." But, as he also wrote, the *Handbook* was principally compiled in response to "more than a century [of appeals by] commissioners of Indian Affairs . . . for aid in reducing [the] unmanageable mass" of treaties, statutes, judicial decisions, and administrative rulings in the field.[23]

Price, in contrast, prefaced his book with an explicit call for "spurring an increase of the study of Indian legal problems."[24] His book became *American Indian Law: Native Nations and the Federal System*, which in later editions was prepared by other writers. The seventh edition was published in 2015 by Professors Carole E. Goldberg, Rebecca Tsosie, Robert N. Clinton, and Angela R. Riley. They noted that at the time of Price's 1973 edition, "Fewer than a dozen instructors . . . focused on federal Indian law. At latest count, the number was well over 100."[25]

In 1979, Professors David Getches and Charles Wilkinson, with Daniel Rosenfelt of the Interior Department Solicitor's Office, wrote another casebook, *Cases and Materials on Federal Indian Law.* They gave explicit credit to Price, saying, "His book brought the study of Indian law to the law school classroom."[26] They followed Price's pedagogical lead, designing their book "for a three-unit semester course" and recommending how instructors should use it. They noted Rosenfelt's position in the Interior Department and explicitly disavowed any connection between their presentation and the official position of the department, thus drawing a sharp line to separate their educational work from the *Handbook.* In later editions, the authors (except that Professor Robert Williams replaced Rosenfelt) said that the organization of their casebook, as distinguished from its "analytical approach," had been "adopted in . . . Felix S. Cohen's *Handbook of Federal Indian Law*,"[27] thus partially closing the circle back to the original compilation.

These casebooks thus traced their lineage to Monroe Price's 1973 book and took into account the history and continuing existence of the *Handbook.* The authors of each casebook exerted themselves to promote a positive approach to "tribal interests." In this aspect, they echoed Cohen's original New Deal views favoring "tribal self-government." The echo was not surprising since the *Handbook* had already disavowed the Indian termination policy embraced by the Interior Department's 1958 edition. The 2012 edition of the *Handbook* said that the 1958 edition was "revised for openly political purposes . . . and was never accepted as a scholarly work."[28]

In the context of legal education, the *Handbook of Federal Indian Law* loses the role of a guide and is simply another object of study. As Alaska Federal District judge Andrew Kleinfeld said in 1988, pointing to the various revisions of the *Handbook,* the different versions pose an "ideological choice."[29] The editors of the latest editions of the *Handbook* respond to all these scholarly and professional concerns and try to present the field as a coherent set of rules. As we shall see, the result is problematic.

## The Handbook and the Classroom

As we have seen, Felix Cohen's 1942 *Handbook of Federal Indian Law* occupies a special place in the history of the field. It was the first compilation of cases, statutes, treaties, agency regulations, and other materials; it still has the status of a bible even though it has gone through many revisions. The *Handbook* was a project of John Collier's administration of the Department of Indian Affairs in the New Deal, aimed at rescuing Native peoples from the outright extermination efforts of prior administrations. Cohen worked in the solicitor's office of the Interior Department as chief of the Indian Law Survey project.

As we also have seen, Cohen was a legal realist. He prepared the *Handbook* to maximize the space for arguments in favor of Native self-determination within the overall domination exception. He organized precedents in such a way as to help unbind legal arguments from doctrines intended to destroy Native peoples. To do this, he read some cases strictly, but others loosely.

Cohen's original work was displaced in 1958 shortly after his death. Franklin Delano Roosevelt (FDR) and Collier were long gone, and the United States had shifted away from the New Deal and back to an array of what were unapologetically called "Indian termination" programs. The Department of the Interior published a *Handbook* revision that was essentially a bowdlerization. It redacted much of Cohen's work and even inverted some of his analyses. The department's revision was heavily criticized by some law professors, who called it "a total bastardization" of the original work.[30]

By 1968, U.S. policy was shifting yet again, this time away from "termination" toward what President Richard Nixon called "self-determination without termination." The Congress responded by instructing the secretary of the Interior to once again revise and republish the *Handbook*.[31] The secretary commissioned a new edition, relying on a team outside the Interior Department, organized through the University of New Mexico Law School. That revision appeared in 1982.[32]

Shortly after it was published, Professor Russell Barsh cautioned that the revised *Handbook* was still presented as a "treatise." He said, "Inherent in [treatises] . . . is the tendency to establish more or less authoritative interpretations in gray areas, steering practitioners away from the disputed points that make new law. Treatises jeopardize critical thinking when they reconcile what judges have said and rationalize complexity into neat rules."[33]

We have already seen the importance of encouraging lawyers to challenge old doctrines. A related concern arises in the context of legal education. How might a teacher or student analyze the contradictions in federal anti-Indian law as they are exemplified in the various editions? One answer is that federal anti-Indian law is politics, and the changes in the *Handbook* demonstrate that fact. But this raises a conundrum: if federal anti-Indian law is essentially political, why is it in a law school curriculum? The 2012 edition of the *Handbook* confronted this "openly political" history, but it did not challenge that politics.

We turn now to the *Handbook* to further understand the possibility and the difficulty of challenging entrenched doctrines.

## Fundamental Principles?

The 2012 edition of the *Handbook of Federal Indian Law* said that before publication of the original 1942 version, the materials of the field were "a collection of loosely connected, tribally specific treaties, statutes, case decisions, and other sources." It added that Cohen "brought focus and coherence to this confusing welter of sources and, in effect, created the field."[34]

Considering the deep contradictions that we have seen, we may fairly ask whether the *Handbook* actually surmounted confusion in the field. The 2012 edition tried to answer this question by providing a short introduction to the *Handbook*, titled "What Is Federal Indian Law?" It opened by saying, "There are some fundamental principles that underlie the entire field." It then listed three principles, following each one with a brief explanation.[35] Upon close examination, though, it appears confusion remained. Let's take a look.

Fundamental principle number 1 was: "AN INDIAN NATION POSSESSES IN THE FIRST INSTANCE ALL OF THE POWERS OF A SOVEREIGN STATE."

What kind of principle is it to say sovereignty exists "in the first instance"? A statement with the phrase "in the first instance" does not constitute a "fundamental principle." It calls for an explanation. And the *Handbook*'s explanation worsened matters. In fact, the explanation contradicted the purported principle. It said, "The powers vested in an Indian nation are . . . inherent powers of a limited sovereignty that has never been extinguished." In other words, contrary to the purported "principle" that "an Indian nation possesses in the first instance all of the powers of a sovereign state," the explanation said Native Nations do *not* have "all the powers of a sovereign state," but only "a limited sovereignty." Furthermore, it said that this limited sovereignty exists at the sufferance of a power that can "extinguish" it, which a further explanation said can be accomplished by a U.S. statute or by "federal common law."[36]

We can now see that the first "principle" in the *Handbook* was a historical reference to a time *before* federal anti-Indian law! It said Native nations *were* fully sovereign *prior* to the formation of federal anti-Indian law's exception, but no longer. The explanation revealed that the actual first principle of federal anti-Indian law itself is a claim of U.S. power over Native nations, a power so extreme that it can extinguish Native sovereign existence. In short, the *Handbook*'s supposed first fundamental principle of Native sovereignty implodes when examined in light of its own explanation. It collapses into an assertion that we may translate as, "the first principle of federal Indian law is US sovereignty and Native non-sovereignty."

As we saw in Chapter 4, the actual first fundamental principle was stated by the federal district court judge in *United States v. Blackfeet Tribe* in 1973. He said, "The blunt fact . . . is that an Indian tribe is sovereign to the extent that the United States permits it to be sovereign—neither more nor less."[37]

The second fundamental principle was: "THE FEDERAL GOVERNMENT HAS BROAD POWERS AND RESPONSIBILITIES IN INDIAN AFFAIRS."

The second principle amounted to a restatement of the first; but let's unpack it anyway. The phrase "broad powers" was a gross understatement of a power that the first principle said was *total*—the power of "extinguishment." How can there be "responsibilities" that coexist with a power of extinguishment? What could possibly restrain a total power of domination?

The explanation of the second principle tried to address this conundrum by saying, "Federal Indian law is characterized by a tension between doctrines that grant the United States powers over tribes . . . and doctrines that both limit federal power and place . . . obligations on the United States." But this explained nothing. It might serve as a heading for a list of contradictory doctrines, but it left us where we started, wondering what the "principles of federal Indian law" might be that would guide the choice of contradictory doctrines. "The federal government has," the phrase in the statement of the principle, pointed to the United States as the chooser, but the explanation didn't show a principle of choice beyond U.S. fiat.

The *Handbook*'s explanation said that the doctrines supposedly limiting federal power and placing obligations on the United States "are rooted in . . . the trust relationship, a doctrine . . . that presume[s] retention of tribal sovereignty and property rights." This left us in the same position as with the first principle: the United States has power, this time as a self-declared "trustee" for "Indian wards," to choose between contradictory doctrines, including the existence or nonexistence of Native sovereignty. As we have seen, the trust doctrine is itself an instrument of U.S. power guided by U.S. interests. In short, the "broad powers" of the United States is the second principle. But wasn't that the first principle?

The third statement of principle in the 2012 *Handbook* was: "STATE AUTHORITY IN INDIAN AFFAIRS IS LIMITED."

To say something is "limited" implies ambiguity, like saying that something exists "in the first instance." What are the limits? Who and what determine them? The answers to those questions would reveal the actual third principle, if there is one.

The explanation hinted at answers when it said, "Federal supremacy . . . leaves little room for state involvement." This explanation thus repeated for the third principle what we have already discovered about the first two—namely, it collapsed the principle into a statement that U.S. power sets its own and state limits. The explanation confirmed this reading of the "principle" when it said, "Congress . . . and federal courts have granted states power . . . inside Indian country."[38]

Briefly put, the three so-called fundamental principles stated in the *Handbook of Federal Indian Law* collapsed into one actual ground rule—U.S. supremacy over Native Nations (and the states). Since this federal supremacy is guided only by what the federal power chooses to do, the one and only principle of federal anti-Indian law may also (and more accurately) be called a principle of domination. The *Handbook* thus failed in its effort to present a semblance of doctrinal coherence around a concept of inherent sovereignty for Native nations. Moreover, it disguised the single actual fundamental principle behind a thin facade of tensions and presumptions. A classic case of the emperor's new clothes.

The *Handbook* concluded its "introduction to federal Indian law" by pointing to history and politics. The closing paragraph of the introduction bears especially careful reading. It opened by saying, "The history of federal Indian law is crucial to understanding the field." It then said, "The United States has always recognized tribal sovereignty but has swung between periods when that recognition was strong and periods in which the federal government sought to limit or even abolish tribal sovereignty. This vacillation has led to conflicting lines of precedent."[39]

Here again, we see incoherence. How can "always recogniz[ing] tribal sovereignty" include "abolish[ing] tribal sovereignty"? These are polar opposites. Putting them together in a single sentence did not provide coherence nor convert them into a "principle." The phrases "vacillation" and "conflicting lines of precedent" demonstrate confusion and contradiction—the very elements that the *Handbook* had supposedly vanquished.

The final sentence of the *Handbook* introduction called for historical study to look at "the period[s] in which particular doctrines were developed and particular policies were followed."[40] A call to study legal history fits neatly within the legal realism perspective that Felix Cohen embraced. However, as the legal realism method intends, the result of studying doctrinal history is that the notion of "legal principles" fades into "politics." The *Handbook's* introduction demonstrated this: federal anti-Indian law is politics through and through.

The 2017 seventh edition of *Cases and Materials on Federal Indian Law* invoked legal realism (without using those words) by offering "innovations reflecting developments in Indian Country and in legal education more broadly." The authors said, "Beyond courtroom strategy, lawyers deal with evolving legal rules through negotiation, regulation, and reform, in tribal, state, federal, and international forums alike." They added, "Today, lawyering for tribes may occur as much in corporate board rooms and online forums, as in the courts of law or halls of Congress," and "Indian law and policy are related to governance, economics, and culture. . . . Lawyers cannot go it alone in Indian Country . . . [T]hey must work with tribal citizens, elected leaders, business people, social workers, religious leaders, and others to accomplish the work of Nation Building in the 21st Century."[41]

These innovations in legal education were already features of twentieth-century legal realism. Karl Llewellyn, for example, said that lawyers must pay attention to "all that you know of [judges], or of the trends in [the] courts, or . . . of the trend in the line of business, or in the situation, or in the times at large."[42] Oliver Wendell Holmes, Jr., insisted, "The life of the law has not been logic; it has been experience."[43] As we saw, the realist view rattles anyone who thinks that legal rules and rights exist somewhere apart from politics and economics. Legal realists view the apparent "definiteness" of law as an appearance, a facade, masking an active, malleable process. In short, legal realism does offer a powerful lens to view federal anti-Indian law.

But the question arises: if in fact there are no fundamental principles in federal anti-Indian law except for the assertion of federal supremacy, and if the exercise of this supremacy is a political function, how are law students being taught to argue in court? The starting point to examine this question is to look at how the *Handbook* and various casebooks present the foundational cases of the federal anti-Indian law matrix.

## Foundational Cases

To reiterate, we have seen that the doctrinal matrix of federal anti-Indian law was laid down in three early nineteenth-century U.S. Supreme Court cases. The decisions may be restated succinctly: In *Johnson v. McIntosh*, the court adopted the fifteenth-century doctrine of "Christian discovery" and declared that the United States holds title to all Native lands; it said that the Natives themselves are merely occupants. In *Cherokee Nation v. State of Georgia*, the court built on the *Johnson* decision to define Native Nations as "wards" under the control of a U.S. "guardian"; it denied that Native Nations have an international status. In *Worcester v. Georgia*, the court capped the previous two decisions with an assertion that the federal government has supreme power vis-a-vis the states over Native lands and peoples; it defined a domain of "internal affairs" of Native nations for "their self-government so far as respected themselves only" under "exclusive" federal control of lands. These three decisions continue to be cited in cases at all levels of the U.S. judicial system.

Strangely enough, as we have seen, the three opinions acknowledge the bizarreness of their doctrines. The *Johnson* opinion, after adopting Christian discovery, said that it was an "extravagant . . . pretension." Marshall added that the concept of "Indian title"—that is, Native inhabitants are "merely occupants" in their homelands—"may be opposed to natural right, and to the usages of civilized nations" and may "perhaps, be supported by reason." The *Cherokee Nation* opinion said that federal anti-Indian law was "marked by peculiar and cardinal distinctions which exist nowhere else." The *Worcester* opinion reaffirmed the "pretension" and "peculiar distinctions" denying Natives their "original natural rights as the undisputed possessors of the soil from time immemorial."

Interior Department solicitor Nathan Margold's introduction to Cohen's 1942 *Handbook* acknowledged the strangeness of the field. He said that federal anti-Indian law involved "a very esoteric legal problem" with roots in "the mysteries . . . [of] feudal doctrines." He added that if one digs into these roots, "endless controversy is possible."[44]

Margold suggested that federal anti-Indian law is a form of "protection of Indians"; but he also said that "to the cynic . . . [it] may frequently appear as a mechanism for the orderly plundering of the Indian"—what we call today a "protection racket." He further urged that we nevertheless view the law "charitably," saying that "the Government . . . [is protecting] the Indians against individuals who wished to separate the Indian from his possessions."[45] He ignored the fact that federal anti-Indian law itself separates Native peoples from their possessions.

The 2012 edition of the *Handbook* perpetuated Margold's approach. It first admitted, "Prior to the creation of the United States, the entire land mass it now occupies was owned and governed by hundreds of Indian tribes." It then said, "These tribes, sovereign nations under international law, were brought into the United States through a colonial process. . . ." It added that this process resulted in "intergovernmental relationships among the Indian nations, the United States, and the states of the Union." It concluded that federal anti-Indian law "is the primary mechanism for mediating" these relationships.[46]

If we break these sentences down, they present a basic question: how can the mechanism that *created* the colonial legal structure claiming ownership of Native lands also be the mechanism to *mediate* disputes arising from that structure? The *Handbook* leaped over that question. In fact, it concluded by simply accepting the colonial structure and saying, "Indian tribes . . . are within the United States and . . . subject to federal power."[47]

If we look for detailed consideration of the strange doctrines in the foundational cases, the 2012 *Handbook* provided slim pickings. It mentioned the *Johnson* case in footnotes scattered throughout the text, but it provided no thoroughgoing excavation of the decision. At one point, it said that the *Johnson* decision was based on the "rights of so-called discovering nations."[48] It did not critique the inappropriateness of "discovery" that the label "so-called" implied, although it later did use the phrase "so-called 'discovering' nation."[49]

The absence of critique of the *Johnson* decision was especially perplexing in light of the *Handbook's* opening section, which stated, "The origins of early European legal theories on colonization lie in medieval justifications for the Crusades. The most famous of these [is the bull of] thirteenth century Pope Innocent IV."[50] The *Handbook* did not take this opportunity to explore the religious basis of federal anti-Indian law.

Other references to the *Johnson* decision were also stated uncritically, and in one instance inaccurately. When the text asserted, "The United States holds title to . . . Indian property in trust for the tribes,"[51] it cited *Johnson*. But the "trust" (ward-guardian) concept was not declared until the *Cherokee Nation* case, eight years after *Johnson*.

The *Handbook* presented a fuller discussion of the "trust" doctrine in a separate section, where it appropriately separated the *Johnson* and *Cherokee Nation* decisions. Again, however, there was no critique. Indeed, the text followed Margold's 1942 lead, saying that federal trusteeship is protection, not domination. The text's phrasing of the "trust doctrine" revealed the domination, referring to the U.S. trustee as "owner" and the Natives as "occupants" of Native lands; but it did not critique the doctrine.

The text also tried to position U.S. domination in the past. It said, "The trust relationship . . . formed the linchpin for the excesses of the late 19th and early 20th century [decisions] . . . a nearly absolute and unreviewable congressional power." It then asserted that a "protective trust doctrine" had since evolved.[52] The explanation of this purported "evolution" glossed over two different concepts of trust—legal and moral. On one hand, the text admitted that Native Nation court challenges based on the trust concept "have been unsuccessful," and said that as a *legal* doctrine "the trust responsibility has never served as the basis of a judicial order." On the other hand, it said that trust as a *moral* concept provided "persuasive arguments by tribes urging passage of legislation."[53]

This glossing of the meaning of "trust" dodged the task of critically analyzing the "Christian discovery" foundation of the trust doctrine in the *Cherokee Nation* decision. Moreover, it ignored the fact that courts have repeatedly *separated* moral and legal principles in federal anti-Indian law. The most famous statement of this separation was in a concurring opinion in *Northwestern Bands of Shoshone Indians v. United States* (1945), where Justices Robert H. Jackson and Hugo Black said, "We agree . . . that no legal rights are today to be recognized in the Shoshones. . . . We agree . . . as to their moral deserts. We do not mean to leave the impression that the two have any relation to each other."[54]

As we have seen, the 1955 *Tee-Hit-Ton Indians v. United States* decision quoted this statement and affirmed it. The Court said that the United States owed no compensation when it seized Native lands, even though "the American people have compassion for the descendants of those Indians who were deprived of their homes and hunting grounds."[55] In 2011, in *United States v. Jicarilla Apache Nation*, the Court yet again underscored that it considered moral concepts irrelevant to the federal anti-Indian law "trust responsibility." Justice Alito said, "The Government's management of tribal trusts . . . represents 'a humane and self imposed policy' based on felt 'moral obligations.' . . . This . . . purpose does not imply a full common-law trust. . . . 'No trust is created [by] merely a moral obligation.'"[56]

The failure of the *Handbook* to engage in substantial criticism of the domination matrix of federal anti-Indian law was compounded by an assertion that we criticized earlier—namely, that the foundation decisions show "respect" for Native nations. For example, it said, "While refusing to accord Indian nations full sovereignty and title over their lands, the Marshall cases nevertheless accorded a great deal of respect to original Indian title."[57] Two things become apparent from this statement: first, the effort (repeated throughout the text) to find a silver lining for Natives in the context of U.S. domination; and second (and more disturbing), the masking of the domination itself.

To say that the Marshall cases respect "Indian title" does *not* mean that they respect Native *ownership*. "Indian title" is *not* ownership, as explicitly stated in *Johnson*: "Indian title" is "mere occupancy" under federal ownership. The full phrase in the *Johnson* opinion is "Indian title of occupancy."[58] In short, the Marshall cases show "respect" only for Marshall's definition of federal domination!

As we have seen, the domination inherent in the definition of "Indian title" has been repeated again and again in subsequent Supreme Court decisions. For example, in 1945, "the extinguishment of Indian title by [U.S.] sovereignty has proceeded, as a political matter, without any admitted legal responsibility in the sovereign to compensate the Indian for his loss."[59] And in 1955, "Indian title or *permission from the whites to occupy* . . . means mere possession . . . This is not a property right but amounts to a right of occupancy which . . . may be terminated and such lands fully disposed of by the [United States] without any legally enforceable obligation to compensate the Indians."[60]

The Supreme Court has also repeatedly emphasized the opposite side of the definition—namely, the U.S. claim of "title" to Native lands. As Justice Ruth Bader Ginsberg wrote in 2005, "Under the 'doctrine of discovery,' . . . 'title to the lands occupied by Indians when the colonists arrived became vested in the sovereign.'"[61] The *Handbook* ignored hundreds of plain assertions in decisions that federal anti-Indian law not only denies Native ownership, but also asserts a power to "extinguish" even the reduced "Indian title." In short, the *Handbook* contention of "respect" betrayed a total failure to analyze the doctrinal matrix of federal anti-Indian law; worse, it disguised the matrix as the opposite of what it is.

The *Handbook* reading of the *Johnson* decision adopted the notion discussed earlier, that the United States claims control over only the *transfer* of property rights in Native lands. It acknowledged, however, that even this supposedly limited claim gives the United States "vast power and a convenient way to reward favorites or to resell land at a profit."[62] As we saw earlier in Chapter 3, analyzing *Worcester v. Georgia*, Marshall's decree of "exclusive" federal control over Native land transfer created a "monopsony," a market with a single buyer. This is what the *Handbook* meant when it referred to "vast power to reward favorites or resell land at a profit." As we saw, Marshall acknowledged this power approvingly in *Johnson*, calling it "a productive fund to the government."[63] Justice John Catron referred to it in *Clark v. Smith* (1839) as "one of the great resources which sustained the [Revolutionary] war."[64]

We have seen how the U.S. monopsony over the transfer of Native lands demonstrates that federal anti-Indian law is not a peripheral field affecting only Native peoples, but rather a field that forms the foundation of U.S. land law: The nontitle of "Indian title"—the "right of occupancy"—constitutes the title claim of the United States.

The *Handbook* acknowledged that the *Johnson* ruling provided a "root of title" in U.S. land law, but it also said that this root title was "uncomplicated by differences in property concepts between Native American and European societies."[65] That statement is baffling. First, it suggested differences between Native and European (read, "Christian discoverers") property concepts are somehow resolved by subjecting Native concepts to European ones. But, as we saw earlier, the crucial difference in property concepts in the *Johnson* case was not between Natives and colonizers, but rather between the doctrine of Christian discovery and English common law. The denial of Native title under the doctrine of Christian discovery grossly violated land law principles applied by the Christian colonizers to themselves. The *Handbook* did not critique the Christian discovery exception from ordinary land law.

When Russell Barsh criticized the 1982 edition of the *Handbook*, he asked, "Is it the role of a treatise to put bad law in the best possible light, or to criticize it?" He concluded that the editors "missed . . . opportunit[ies] to take the courts to task for unprincipled and ill-suited law."[66]

The seventh edition of the casebook *American Indian Law: Native Nations and the Federal System* did criticize the *Johnson* ruling, but its critique was more distressing than the *Handbook's* absence of critique. The casebook opened its discussion of the Marshall trilogy with a quote from Corn Tassell, a Cherokee leader in the negotiations of the 1785 Hopewell Treaty.[67] Corn Tassell asked the representatives of the United States, "Under what kind of authority, by what law, or on what pretense [do you make] this exorbitant demand of nearly all [our] lands?"[68]

The casebook offered no comment on Corn Tassell's prescient phrasing—his foreseeing of the "extravagant pretension" of "Christian discovery." Instead, after extended excerpts from *Johnson*, the casebook focused on "stereotypes of savagery" in the opinion. It said, "Marshall suggested that the reason for separate autonomous treatment of Indians was that the natives were 'fierce savages.'" The text then debunked "savagery" as "European mythology."[69]

This is critical commentary, but it is nonetheless problematic. Marshall's opinion derived the rhetoric of "savagery" from the Christian discovery doctrine. In fact, the word "savage" appears only once in the *Johnson* opinion, while "heathen" appears twice and "Christian" (or "Christianity") seven times! The casebook critique of the derivative concept of "savagery" failed to give a good account even of the surface of the *Johnson* opinion.

The failure of the *American Indian Law* casebook to analyze the religious matrix of federal anti-Indian law was especially distressing because the sources that the authors cited to document stereotypes of savagery in fact document the Christian discovery doctrine underlying these stereotypes. They quoted Francis Jennings, *The Invasion of America: Indians, Colonialism, and the Cant of Conquest*, saying, "The basic conquest myth postulates that

America was . . . inhabited by nonpeople called savages. . . ." But Jennings had already explained a "Crusader Ideology" underlies the savagery myth. Savagery myths, Jennings said, were *"created by"* and were part of "one great and powerful system of myth . . . [developed by] the Christian[s] . . . of Europe."[70] In short, federal anti-Indian law stereotypes of savagery are derivatives of the underlying religious doctrine. The casebook's focus on the derivative concept obscured the basis of the *Johnson* decision and missed the analysis provided by their sources.

A separate subsection in the casebook entitled "Other Perspectives on the Doctrine of Discovery" failed even to name the doctrine—Christian discovery. And the short discussion repeatedly spoke in generic, nondoctrinal, cultural terms—"cultural racism of Europeans," "hierarchical, universalized conceptions . . . [of] European political and legal theory," and "white society's will to empire." The authors perpetuated this confusion when they presented "Euro-American civilization" and "Christianity" as two separate aspects of U.S. "Indian policy" rather than as a single complex formation called "Christian civilization," with its fundamental (and extravagant) doctrine of "title by discovery." Recall Joseph Story's explanation in his *Commentaries on the Constitution of the United States*:[71] "As *infidels, heathen, and savages*, they were not allowed to possess the prerogatives belonging to absolute, sovereign and independent nations. The territory, over which they wandered, and which they used for their temporary and fugitive purposes, was, *in respect to Christians,* deemed, as if it were inhabited only by brute animals."[72]

There is no shortage of evidence that the foundation of federal anti-Indian law is Christian discovery. No casebook is adequate to teach the field if it fails to present this material, no matter how critical it may be otherwise. As we have seen, a race-based critique illuminates but is not in itself an adequate basis for understanding U.S. law related to Native peoples.

## International Arenas

Beyond the U.S. foundational cases and doctrines, there are international concepts, conventions, and agreements with implications for teaching federal anti-Indian law. A useful casebook would include these international materials.

Thus, the 2012 *Handbook of Federal Indian Law* said, "In establishing the fundamental rules governing the relationship between Indian tribes and the United States, early United States Supreme Court cases relied extensively on international law."[73]

The important thing to keep in mind about this statement is that the literal references in the foundational cases—the Marshall trilogy—are to "the law of nations," "the rights of civilized nations," and, more specifically, "the nations of Europe." This is what Carl Schmitt, in his *Nomos of the Earth,* termed the first "world order," which arose from "the Age of Discovery, when the earth first was encompassed and measured by the global consciousness of European peoples." He added, "The first question" in this "international law . . . was whether the lands of non-Christian, non-European peoples and princes were 'free' and without authority, whether non-European peoples were at such a low stage of civilization that they could become objects of organization by peoples at a higher stage."[74] Moreover, Schmitt added, "Interstate European international law . . . arose from the disintegration of the medieval . . . order supported by empire and papacy. Without knowledge of the continuing effects of this medieval Christian spatial order, it is impossible to gain a legal-historical understanding of the international law that emerged from it."[75]

In short, the "international law" references in John Marshall's trilogy referred to a body of doctrines established by the colonizing Christian nations to govern their relations with each other as they fought over Native lands. The doctrines did not refer to laws that included the perspectives of Native nations and peoples. They arose from the "medieval Christian spatial order." It is especially strange that the *Handbook* would ignore all this in light of its prior acknowledgment that "The origins of early European legal theories on colonization lie in medieval justifications for the Crusades."

The *Handbook's* use of the phrase "Indian tribes" in its reference to "rules governing the relationship between Indian tribes and the United States" already used the cognitive framework of the "European international law" of the time, which excluded Native nations from the "family of nations." As Thomas Joseph Lawrence, whose book, *The Principles of International Law*, was quoted in the U.S. brief in *Tee-Hit-Ton*, put it, "The area within which the law of nations operates is supposed to coincide with the area of civilization. . . . We must exclude altogether from our classification such communities as the . . . Indian tribes of North America."[76]

Thus, in *Johnson*, Marshall said that the basic rule of property is "The title to lands . . . is and must be admitted to depend entirely on the law of the nation in which they lie." But he did not consider the Piankeshaw Nation (whose lands were being fought over by competing colonial speculators) as a nation whose laws governed its property. Instead, he defined "nationhood" within a discussion of colonial "discovery." He said, "The great nations of Europe . . . establish[ed] a principle, which all should acknowledge as the law."[77] That principle was Christian discovery, a "right" claimed by the only "real" nations—the colonizers.

Justice William Johnson's concurring opinion in *Cherokee Nation* elaborated the exclusion of Native nations from among the "nations" that determine "international law." He started by praising the Cherokee Nation's efforts to mimic the U.S. governmental structure, "which," he said, "certainly must be classed among the most approved forms of civil government."

But he immediately questioned whether the Cherokee Nation "can be yet said to have received the consistency which entitles that people to admission into the family of nations." In other words, even the assimilating Cherokee were not part of the family of nations; they could not participate in making international law. Justice Johnson added that Cherokee international status was not in Cherokee hands at all; rather, it was "to be determined by the executive" of the United States. "Until then," he said, "we cannot recognize it as an existing state, under any other character than that which it has maintained hitherto as one of the Indian tribes or nations."[78] Justice Johnson reiterated his point, stating it negatively, referring to "the community of nations, of whom most notoriously the Indians were no part."[79] In short, the foundational cases of federal anti-Indian law excluded Indian nations from the family of nations. The laws of Native nations were allowed no part in determining title to Native lands. Instead, the cases relied on a non-Native, Christian European international law. The *Handbook* ignored this fundamental point.

Turning to twenty-first-century international law, the *Handbook* said that there has been "increasing…attention to issues affecting indigenous peoples worldwide." It added that this attention is "just beginning to result in concrete legal tools . . . to shape federal Indian law."[80] The ensuing discussion presented an overview of various international charters and covenants. The *Handbook* did not take on the task of suggesting these "concrete legal tools" (in other words, potential arguments). Indeed, when it referred to the 2007 United Nations (UN) Declaration on the Rights of Indigenous Peoples, it missed a significant opportunity to design a tool. As we have seen, the Declaration's opening affirmations stated that "all doctrines, policies and practices based on or advocating superiority of peoples or individuals on the basis of national origin or racial, religious, ethnic or cultural differences are racist, scientifically false, legally invalid, morally condemnable and socially unjust."[81] This language certainly suggests an argument against the doctrine of Christian discovery.

The *Handbook* also did not explore powerful UN indictments of the Christian discovery doctrine—the 2010 *Study of the Impact on Indigenous Peoples of the International Legal Construct Known as the Doctrine of Discovery*[82] and the 2014 report *On the Impacts of the Doctrine of Discovery on Indigenous Peoples, including Mechanisms, Processes and Instruments of Redress*— that we examined earlier.[83] Although the latter was issued after the publication of the 2012 *Handbook*, the substance of the indictment appeared in the earlier documents, including the 2007 Declaration itself and the 2010 study.

The *Handbook* also failed to examine U.S. opposition to the UN Declaration, an opposition that revealed the invidious structure and purposes of federal anti-Indian law. As we have seen, the United States fought a losing battle against the use of the plural word "peoples" in the title of the Declaration, and when it reversed its negative vote, it did so with a signing statement insisting that the Declaration doesn't actually support international people-hood for Native nations.

The seventh edition of the casebook *American Indian Law: Native Nations and the Federal System*, by Goldberg et al., at first seemed to follow the *Hand-book* pattern when it said, "[Federal] Indian law began as part of the Law of Nations." But it immediately described that law of nations as "a colonial sys-tem that sought to place Native nations in a subordinate position in order to facilitate [their] political domination." In an additional sign of analytical strength, the authors did not confine U.S. domination to the past but rather also connected it to present-day federal anti-Indian law doctrines, even nam-ing them—"'plenary power' [and] 'domestic, dependent status' of Native nations"—and explaining their derivation from colonial domination.[84]

The connection between past and present is crucial to understanding fed-eral anti-Indian law. The situation is parallel to James Baldwin's explanation of modern racism as the "persistence of history." He wrote in 1965, "History . . . does not refer merely, or even principally, to the past. On the contrary, the great force of history comes from the fact that we carry it within us, are unconsciously controlled by it in many ways, and history is literally *present* in all that we do." He added, "It could scarcely be otherwise, since it is to history that we owe our frames of reference."[85] As we saw earlier, William Faulkner expressed it more simply: "The past is never dead. It's not even past."[86]

Since the U.S. claim of title to Native lands continues to be active legal doctrine, the colonial invasion is not confined to a bygone past. As we saw, David Coventry Smith called it a "misguided belief that depriving Indians of the ownership, use, and benefit of their lands was merely an unfortunate episode in American history, an artifact of a racist past."[87] In short, until the doctrine of Christian discovery is explicitly revoked, it will continue to func-tion underneath modern rhetoric.

In 1909, the English common law historian F. W. Maitland, speaking about rules dealing with the possession and ownership of land, famously said, "The forms of action we have buried, but they still rule us from their graves." He added, "Each of [the forms of action] lives its own life, has its own adventures, enjoys a longer or shorter day of vigour, usefulness, and popularity and then sinks perhaps into a decrepit and friendless old age."[88] Applied to federal anti-Indian law, this metaphor helps us understand why courts have gradually abandoned explicit reference to Christian discovery, preferring (as in *City of Sherrill*) to truncate the name of the doctrine. Chris-tian discovery is becoming "friendless" in its old age, notwithstanding its continued "usefulness" to the United States.

Goldberg et al., in contrast to the authors of the *Handbook*, grasped the opportunity of international condemnation to discredit the underlying colo-nial doctrine of federal anti-Indian law. Their casebook pointed to the rise of "international attention to the rights of indigenous peoples worldwide." They took this beyond a rhetorical celebration (à la the *Handbook*) to a framework for action, developing tools to litigate in U.S. courts. They said that international critique "has opened up rhetorical space for criticism of Supreme Court decisions as well as new venues for asserting Indian rights."[89]

The authors also examined the intersections of contemporary international law with laws of countries colonized by Great Britain to "provide students a broader framework within which to evaluate . . . federal Indian law." They emphasized arguments for Native peoples to be recognized as international entities, urging a clear break with the subordination rooted in colonial thought (and in present-day U.S. practice). They said, "Nineteenth century racism and colonial attitudes have no place in the modern world."[90] They also confronted the fact that U.S. abstention from international rights agreements impedes the use of those agreements in U.S. courts. As a tool to get around that roadblock, they discussed arguments based on international "customary law" ("rules that States universally abide by, or accede to, out of a sense of legal obligation and mutual concern")[91]—which the U.S. Supreme Court has said are applicable in U.S. courts.

In short, the casebook's engagement with history and international law sharply distinguished it from the *Handbook*. Texts like that of Goldberg et al. demonstrate the possibility (and necessity) of diving deeply and critically into the murky world of federal anti-Indian law to generate creative arguments for doctrinal change. Law students emerging from this kind of education are prepared to follow Professor Henry Redfield's 1906 lead—to tackle entrenched doctrine and "make war" for their clients.[92]

# CHAPTER SEVEN

# Call to Consciousness

## Challenging the World

In the introduction—the plan of this book—I said that when we unpack the legal system that has entrapped and entangled nonstate "tribal" peoples worldwide, we will reveal a way forward for humanity in this twenty-first-century moment of awareness that life on Earth is imperiled by dysfunctions of legal, political, and economic principles based on domination. I promised that the final chapter would take a global view—to draw some lessons from the long struggle for Native survival, to open a vista for humans to rearrange our relations with each other and with the planet that we share with the rest of Creation. Here is that chapter.

The foundation cases of U.S. federal anti-Indian law created a template copied around the world. As Professor Blake Watson wrote in 2011, the Marshall trilogy "not only diminished native rights in the United States, but . . . also influenced the definition of indigenous land rights in Australia, Canada, and New Zealand." Watson's examples included the 1836 citation of *Johnson v. McIntosh* by the British lawyer William Burge to argue for "a private purchase of some 600,000 acres from the Australian Aborigines was invalid as against the Crown." Watson said, "British land speculators, settlers, and government officials quoted American jurists in disputes concerning the annexation of New Zealand in the 1840s, and *Johnson* figured prominently in the colony's first judicial decision regarding Māori property rights. Likewise, when the existence and scope of aboriginal title was finally litigated in Canada in the 1880s, the *Johnson* decision played a major role."[1] In short, Indigenous peoples around the world are subjected to claimed rights of domination based on the U.S. template of exception and higher civilization.

In 1923, Indigenous peoples first formally approached the nation-states of the world to challenge this domination. The Haudenosaunee chief Deskaheh presented a petition to the League of Nations from the Six Nations Confederacy, appealing to the league to stop Canadian intrusion into their territory. He asked for "international acceptance of Six Nations political and territorial sovereignty," in opposition to Canadian policy, which was "based on the understanding that Indians were a dying race of wards to the government's guardianship."[2]

Deskaheh's petition required a complex strategy, since the league itself was a creature of imperial powers and operated "under conditions of colonial domination through the mandate system."[3] Therefore, Deskaheh coupled his request for territorial sovereignty with a plea for "protection" through enforcement of Six Nations treaties with Britain, France, and the Netherlands.

Deskaheh's appeal for treaty protection echoed the theory of "unequal alliances" articulated by the eighteenth-century international law scholar Emer de Vattel, whom Justices Thompson and Story cited in their dissent in *Cherokee Nation v. State of Georgia*. As we have seen in the discussion of *Cherokee Nation v. Georgia* in Chapter 3, Vattel said that a weaker power may bind itself to a stronger one "without stripping itself of the right of government and sovereignty." In short, Deskaheh asked Six Nations treaty partners—"stronger states"—to defend the sovereignty of the "weaker" Six Nations against Canada. When the league refused to allow the petition, Deskaheh said, "My appeal to the Society of Nations has not been heard." In the last speech of his life, he "more forcefully than ever . . . hurled defiance at big nations who disregard the claims of smaller peoples."[4]

Left to right: Phillip Deere, Grandfather David Monongye, and Tadadaho Leon Shenandoah arriving at the United Nations in Geneva, 1977. (Cover photo, *A Basic Call to Consciousness*, edited by Akwesasne Notes, Native Voices, 2005, used with permission)

In 1977, the Mohawk Nation at Akwesasne, a Haudenosaunee (Six Nations) community, revived Deskaheh's work when they sent a delegation to the United

Nations (UN) to participate in a nongovernmental organization (NGO) inquiry into the conditions of Native peoples around the world. As they put it, their presence in Geneva was to assert "a place in the international community."[5]

The Akwesasne delegation presented three position papers in a manifesto titled *A Basic Call to Consciousness*. The manifesto went far beyond anything presented to the world body before. It was not asking to participate in the global system of nation-states. It was challenging the very existence and operation of that system. The Haudenosaunee stood on Indigenous spiritual ground and presented philosophical, legal, and economic critiques of the nation-state colonial system. This was indeed a call to consciousness on a global scale. It was framed as "The Haudenosaunee Address to the Western World." It was a challenge to "the way of life known as Western Civilization."[6]

Decades before the phrase "global warming" was on anyone's lips, *A Basic Call to Consciousness* warned that the industrial exploitation and destruction of the natural world threatened the survival of life on Earth. "The way of life known as Western Civilization is on a death path on which their own culture has no viable answers. . . . The air is foul, the waters poisoned, the trees dying, the animals are disappearing. We think even the systems of weather are changing."[7]

The Haudenosaunee manifesto and the NGO inquiry ignited three decades of activism among Indigenous peoples worldwide, resulting in the 2007 UN General Assembly Declaration on the Rights of Indigenous Peoples. As we have seen, that document did not achieve the changes demanded by Indigenous peoples, let alone confront the profound crisis of life on Earth that the Haudenosaunee *Call to Consciousness* set forth.

The Haudenosaunee challenge was more than a call for a UN statement. It was a call to rethink humanity's place in the world, to understand life from an Indigenous point of view. Their call reverberates more powerfully than ever in the twenty-first century. It calls into question the deepest foundation of domination.

## A Colonial God

The Haudenosaunee *Basic Call to Consciousness* said that Western civilization "is historically and linguistically . . . commonly termed the Judeo Christian tradition."[8] In 1974, the Secwépemc Shuswap George Manuel, in his seminal book *The Fourth World: An Indian Reality*, described that tradition as follows: "The Christian view of the world, as we have received it, is a vertical triangle with each level of leadership being closer to God. The state, as we have seen it, is the perfect mirror image of this triangle." Manuel added, "This is not the shape of our world."[9]

We must understand that the Christian colonial agenda that gave birth to the doctrine of "Christian discovery" was established centuries before Christopher Columbus "discovered" the New World. The agenda began in the Bible that Columbus carried, with the "covenant" story in which God told Abraham, "Go from your country, your people and your father's household to the land I will show you. . . . To your offspring I will give this land."[10] God said, "To your descendants I give this land, from the Wadie of Egypt to the great river, the Euphrates—the land of the Kenites, Kenizzites, Kadmonites, Hittites, Perizzites, Rephaites, Amorites, Canaanites, Girgashites and Jebusites."[11]

In short, the biblical God sent His "chosen people" on a colonial mission to take other peoples' lands. God's colonization project was not simply a promise; it was a command, and God's wrath lay behind it as enforcement. The Bible says that God was angered when His "chosen people" failed to take the "promised lands." At one point, "The Lord's anger was aroused . . . because they have not followed me wholeheartedly. . . . The Lord's anger burned against Israel and he made them wander in the wilderness forty years."[12] God sent an angel to warn those who failed to oust the peoples living in the promised lands; although the colonists had subjected the Canaanites to forced labor, they had not driven them off the land. "The angel of the Lord . . . said, 'I brought you up out of Egypt and led you into the land I swore to give to your ancestors.' I said, 'I will never break my covenant with you, and you shall not make a covenant with the people of this land, but you shall break down their altars.' Yet you have disobeyed me."[13]

The Genesis story of colonial domination was embedded in an overall relationship of domination between humans and the rest of creation. The story says that in the very beginning of the world, God commanded humans, "Be fruitful and increase in number; fill the earth and subdue it. Rule over the fish in the sea and the birds in the sky and over every living creature that moves on the ground."[14]

In 1609, the English minister William Symonds relied on these passages in a sermon defending the Virginia Company. He preached that English colonizers were like Abraham in Genesis 12; they were called by God to go to Virginia.[15] In her 2012 study of how Christianity created race in early Virginia, the history professor Rebecca Anne Goetz described the London minister's words as part of "a seventeenth-century media blitz . . . to craft a theological justification for the Virginia enterprise." She said that Symonds "was fond of comparing the voyaging Englishmen to Abraham and his people. God, he said, had promised to make Abraham a great nation, and he would do the same for 'all that are of his faith and obedience.'" Symonds, she added, "also proposed a method for converting the Indians by taking Indian children captive, converting them, and then sending the young converts back to their families."[16]

The Georgia senator John Forsyth joined the conversation in 1830 when he spoke in the U.S. Senate in favor of the Indian Removal Act, arguing that the genocidal "removal" of Native peoples was authorized by the doctrine of Christian discovery. His speech tracked Genesis: "The discoverer claimed the sovereignty over the discovered country, and over everything under, upon, and above it, from the centre to the zenith. The lands, the streams, the woods, the minerals, all living things, including the human inhabitants, were all the property of, or subject to, the Government of the fortunate navigator, who by accident or design, first saw the before unknown country."[17]

In 1954, the U.S. Department of Justice took up the cause in its brief on behalf of the United States in *Tee-Hit-Ton v. United States,* demonstrating in the most direct sense that federal anti-Indian law is a continuation and fulfillment of biblical commands. The department cited passages from Genesis to support the government's argument "that the discovering nations asserted complete title in themselves, even as against the heathen natives."[18] The brief persuaded the U.S. Supreme Court to rule against the Tee-Hit-Ton. Justice Stanley F. Reed said, "After the coming of the white man," the Native peoples remained in their lands only with "permission from the whites to occupy."[19]

The U.S. position in *Tee-Hit-Ton* is evidence of the truth of Professor Chris Mato Nunpa's conclusion to his 2020 study of Christianity, the Bible, and Native genocide: "The genocide, . . . the Indigenous Holocaust in the United States, . . . was . . . the consequence of a movement of ideas, specifically, the religious ideas . . . of the genocidal commands of Yahweh, the Old Testament God; the 'chosen people' and 'promised land' ideas; the religious imperialism of Jesus Christ; and of the . . . papal bulls."[20]

The imperialism of Jesus was clearly embedded in the so-called Great Commission in Matthew, where Jesus said to his disciples: "All authority in heaven and on earth has been given to me. Therefore go and make disciples of all nations, baptizing them in the name of the Father and of the Son and of the Holy Spirit, and teaching them to obey everything I have commanded you."[21] As we saw earlier, the Massachusetts Bay Colony adopted this imagery in its seal.

The doctrinal lineage from the Bible to federal anti-Indian law is rooted in the geopolitical framework of Christendom, where church and government were one. In 1907, John Neville Figgis, the historian, political philosopher, and Anglican priest, explained, "It cannot be too often reiterated that the thinkers of the Middle Ages were not concerned with two separate and distinct societies, but merely with the relations between different officers or at most different departments of the society."[22] The political powers of Christendom, princes and popes, drew from Bible stories to make imperial claims of domination over the whole world. Christian discovery grew in that context. Strange as it seems, Christian discovery remains an active doctrine in U.S. law despite the supposed constitutional separation of church and state.

The failure to separate church and state is one of the central peculiarities of federal anti-Indian law, an element of its exceptional quality.

The seeds of Christendom were sown in the fourth-century Roman empire when Emperor Constantine decriminalized Christian practices and adopted Christianity to serve his military purposes. The story goes that Constantine, on his way to a crucial battle at the Milvian Bridge in 312 that would end a civil war and determine his emperorship, had a vision. He dreamed of a cross in the sky and the Greek words Ἐν Τούτῳ Νίκα (Latin, *in hoc signo, vinces*; English, "in this sign, conquer"). He concluded the Christian god would safeguard his army and ordered the cross adorn the shields of his soldiers. His subsequent victory tied Christianity to the Roman Empire. The growth of Christendom from those roots persisted despite efforts by Emperor Julian (361–363) to undo the linkage and reinstate the pagan gods. As the Roman Empire collapsed in the fourth and fifth centuries, Christendom continued under the jurisdiction of the bishop of Rome (the pope, the Holy See).

In his 1997 book, *The Barbarian Conversion: From Paganism to Christianity*, the medieval historian Richard Fletcher recounted the Christianization of Europe. He noted that the Christian church grew from a "predominantly urban" setting rooted in "massive confidence in the urban order of imperial Rome." The counterpart to this imperial orientation, he said, was that "the peasantry of the countryside were beyond the pale, a tribe apart, outsiders."[23] The words "heathen"—meaning "dweller on the heath"—and "pagan"— meaning "country dweller"—arose in this context. They are Christian terms for non-Christians.

By the end of the fourth century, as the church took over functions previously handled by Roman imperial offices, it faced "the challenge of the countryside"[24]—how to maintain control over the rural outsiders on whose labor the imperial establishment rested. The church's response was to undertake "conversions," a process using coercion to break "heathen" ties to the land and substitute allegiance to the church. Conversion included destruction of pagan temples and sacred sites and disruption of pagan ceremonies. As *A Basic Call to Consciousness* put it, "Christianity . . . effectively despiritualized the European world."[25]

By the turn of the ninth century, under Charlemagne, plans were made to create a specifically Christian empire—an *imperium christianum*—extending into regions far from Rome. As Fletcher put it, this was "the first time in Christian history a state-sponsored mission used the faith quite unashamedly as an instrument for . . . subjugation."[26] The methods used in Charlemagne's invasion of the Saxon peoples (in what is now Germany) became a blueprint for centuries of Christian imperialism.

The measures used against the Saxons aimed to "destabilize and dislocate the social texture of Saxon life at the most intimate levels of family existence, touching birth, marriage and death." Fletcher wrote, "It seems reasonable to infer that this tearing apart of Saxon society was deliberately intended," and added, "It is well to bear in mind that even small numbers of determined missionaries can leave an abiding impression on a defeated and demoralized population when supported by secular imperial power. . . The Spaniards were to rediscover this truth in Mexico and Peru."[27]

Indeed, the Spanish *Requerimiento*,[28] which was ordered to be read in Latin and Spanish under a notary's supervision as soon as the conquistadors encountered Natives, provides a clear example of how Christians explained their imperial claim to the "New World." It also illustrates the "vertical triangle" described by Manuel.

The *Requerimiento* opened with a description of the Spanish king and queen as "subduers of the barbarous nations." It said that "they make known to you . . . that the Lord our God . . . gave charge to one man, called St. Peter, that he should be lord and superior of all the men in the world, that all should obey him, and that he should be the head of the whole human race." It added that the pope, as successor to St. Peter, had made a "donation" of the Native lands to "the aforesaid King and Queen," who are now "the kings and lords" of these lands.[29]

The *Requerimiento* then commanded, "We ask and require you that you . . . acknowledge the Church as the ruler and superior of the whole world." The document continued, "But if you do not do this . . . we shall powerfully enter into your country, and shall make war against you in all ways and manners that we can, and shall subject you to the yoke and obedience of the Church and of their highnesses; we shall take you, and your wives, and your children, and shall make slaves of them, and as such shall sell and dispose of them as their highnesses may command; and we shall take away your goods, and shall do you all the mischief and damage that we can, as to vassals who do not obey, and refuse to receive their lord, and resist and contradict him." To top it off, the *Requerimiento* concluded, "We protest that the deaths and losses which shall accrue from this are your fault, and not that of their highnesses, or ours, nor of these cavaliers who come with us."[30]

Were the *Requerimiento* not the preface to violent subjugation of Native peoples and their lands by the Christian invaders, its preposterousness would be laughable. Indeed, the Dominican friar Bartolomé de las Casas, who became an ardent critic of the conquistadors, responded to it by saying, "I don't know whether to laugh or cry at the absurdity."[31]

By the twelfth century, the church had attained immense institutional and economic resources and was prepared to destroy any opposition to its centralized, hierarchical control of mass belief. Thereafter, wars against "pagans" and "heathens" were supplemented by wars against "heretics," people whose religious views deviated from papal subjugation. For example, at the beginning of the thirteenth century, Pope Innocent III (1198–1216) began a war against

Catharism (also known as the "Albigensian heresy," for Albi, a city in southern France where it flourished) in what is now known as southern France.

History professor Morris Berman described this campaign in his 1989 study of the relationships between culture, mind, and body in the development of Western civilization. He said, "The losses . . . during the first fifteen years . . . [of the church's war against Catharism] have been estimated to have been one million dead. . . . Whole towns, starting with Béziers in 1209 . . . were put to the sword. . . . [T]he military agents of the king and the pope went on a killing orgy . . . When Arnold Amalric (or Arnaud Aimery), Bishop of Citeaux, was asked by the crusaders what they should do with the (Catholic) citizens of Béziers, he was reported to have replied: 'Kill them all, God will recognize his own.' The new papal legate was quite happy to report to the Pope that twenty thousand people were put to death—the entire population of the town."[32]

The fact the Catharist "heresy" focused on "the Great Mother" and the "Earth Goddess" demonstrates the kind of peoples targeted by the church: peoples who affirmed the natural world, the "wild and the primitive." The destruction of the Catharists, like the earlier conquest of the Saxons, proved that church officials understood how to inflict maximum damage on social structures. A key element was to turn people against each other, to destroy kinship structures: "By 1227 the Church had instituted a primitive police system, in which people were appointed to report on their neighbors. . . . The goal was to weave a network of secrecy, suspicion, and terror, and in this the Inquisition was very successful. . . . With the added pressure of torture legalized by Pope Innocent IV in 1252, the kinship and network structure of the south simply couldn't hold."[33]

The disruption and distortion of kinship networks in so-called pagan societies presented the church with the problem of defining a new concept of social organization. In part, this was a problem of defending the church's own officers. The legal scholar Harold J. Berman's 1983 study of the formation of the Western legal tradition described the problem as follows: "The Christian clergy, . . . the monks in particular needed special protection since they were, in a sense, outside the tribal system; they were to some extent a people without kin."[34] He added that the consequent creation of a church organization outside the ancient structures of clan and kin led to the development of the "state." As he put it, "The new papal concept of the church . . . almost demanded the invention of the concept of the State."[35] In short, Christianity's forcible imposition of centralized, hierarchical authority structures to control mass belief served an imperially organized political economy. Berman concluded his book by saying, "Without the fear of purgatory and the hope of the Last Judgment, the Western legal tradition could not have come into being."[36]

In his 1973 manifesto, *God Is Red*, Vine Deloria, Jr., pointed out the sharp difference between "tribal" religions and Christianity. He wrote:

> Christianity served to transform . . . a tribal chief (*dux*) into a king (*rex*). Once converted to Christianity, the king no longer represented only the deities of his tribe: he represented, in addition, a universal deity whose authority extended to all tribes. . . . He became, in effect, the head of an empire. . . . As stated in the laws of Ethelred (about 1000 A.D.), "A Christian king is Christ's deputy among Christian people and he must avenge with utmost diligence offenses against Christ."[37]

The differences between tribal and state structures of leadership were well known to Christian missionaries; the eradication of locally rooted community leadership is what "civilization" was all about. The distinction between a Christian king and a tribal chief was the core element in the process of conversion; the strategic goal was to cannibalize ancient tribal powers for the benefit of the Christian state. Missionaries worked to displace power rooted in local social relations with power allied to imperial Christian organization. Their tactics aimed to break the bonds between a people and their leaders, between a people and their lands, between a people and their own history.

Successful conversion meant that tribal leaders no longer needed to (or could) rely on power that arose from below and around themselves, but that might (and must) assume a stance descending from above. With this, the colonial conversion was accomplished and the path to imperial resource extraction opened. Political unification under religious domination produced "the nation-state that . . . heralded the nationalisms of the modern (post-sixteenth-century) period."[38]

The next steps in political history were taken by those nation-states, defining the so-called international order of Western civilization. The religious underpinnings of that order persisted as defining elements of law. In this context, Carl Schmitt asserted, "So-called 'modern' international law—interstate European international law from the 16th to the 20th century—arose from the disintegration of the medieval spatial order supported by empire and papacy. Without knowledge of the continuing effects of [the] medieval Christian spatial order, it is impossible to gain a legal-historical understanding of the international law that emerged from it: an international law among states."[39] In Schmitt's terms, "spatial order" is the *nomos* of a social system, resting on principles of land-appropriation and including "the concrete order contained in . . . and following from" land-appropriation.[40]

As we have seen, Spain and its competitors all relied on the doctrine of Christian discovery to sustain their claims of domination over Native peoples and lands. The Christian *nomos* persisted through significant ruptures in the fabric of the church, including England's rejection of papal supremacy under Henry VIII. Schmitt described the age of Christian discovery as the era "when the earth first was encompassed and measured by the global consciousness of European peoples." He said, "For 400 years it supported a Eurocentric international law: the *jus publicum Europaeum*," also known as "*respublica Christiana* [Christian republic] and *populus Christianus* [Christian people]." Schmitt emphasized this spatial order "had definite orders and orientations. . . . The soil of non-Christian, heathen peoples . . . could be allocated . . . to a Christian prince for a Christian mission."[41] As the political science professor Rob Walker put it in 1996, "God died around the time of Machiavelli. . . . Sovereignty was . . . His earthly replacement."[42]

As we have seen, U.S. appropriation of Native lands was formulated in terms of a Christian *nomos* of the Earth, starting with "discovery" and persisting explicitly through nineteenth- and twentieth-century U.S. federal anti-Indian law projects like the General Allotment Act and the boarding schools, also aimed at tearing apart supposedly "pagan" peoples. One telltale sign of the deep Christian roots of federal anti-Indian law is that "plenary power," the common shorthand phrase for U.S. domination, is identical to the claimed power of the popes—*plenitudo potestatis*, typically translated as "fullness of power."[43]

Pier Giuseppe Monateri, in "Political Theology from Satan to Legitimacy," describes *plenitudo potestatis* as an "undefinable power to act." He traces the derivation of the concept as it entered political thought in the writings of England's King James I (1566–1625), and says that it is an example of how "canon law . . . deeply influenced conceptions of modern sovereignty." William Blackstone, Monateri says, spoke of "a necessary 'initiation' into the mysteries of the royal prerogatives," whereby one could understand the claim of unbounded power as part of the *arcana imperii*, the "mysteries" of domination known only to the Crown. "In this way," Monateri says, utilizing the concept of exception, "the exception is . . . located within the mysterious residue of indefinite power residing in the prerogatives of the Sovereign."[44]

Questioning state claims to sovereignty is what monarchs called *lèse majesté*, the treasonable act of questioning the *arcana imperii* of the Crown. Elizabeth I, for example, described her sovereignty as "something her subjects could not, and should not, ever try to interpret or understand."[45] James I deplored the "unsatiable curiosity in many men's spirits" that led them to "wade in all the deepest mysteries that belong to the persons or state of kings."[46] In 1616, James told the Star Chamber, "The mysteries of the Kings power is not lawfully to be disputed. . . . So, it is presumption and high contempt in a Subject to dispute what a King can doe."[47]

U.S. federal anti-Indian law has not abandoned the long history of Christian European jurisprudence. Neither has the international system of states rooted in the soil of the "age of discovery" been abandoned in world politics. The nation-states of the world, now assembled in the United Nations, have only nodded in the direction of abandonment; they have not yet relinquished their claims of sovereignty over Indigenous peoples and lands.

A fundamental challenge to the federal anti-Indian law exception requires a confrontation with the *nomos* containing that exception. A world not haunted by that exception requires a different *nomos*—an Indigenous *nomos* of the Earth.

## An Indigenous *Nomos* of the Earth

I was upset in August 2016 when Standing Rock filed a legal challenge to stop the Dakota Access Pipeline (DAPL)—aptly named because it wanted access to Dakota territory—from invading their lands and waters, and yet they barely mentioned their treaties with the United States and, when they did so, presented legal arguments within the framework of U.S. environmental regulations. A few people at Standing Rock shared my concerns and, together with my colleague Steven Newcomb and others, drafted an alternative legal brief framing the Standing Rock case as a defense of treaty rights. We didn't deny that U.S. environmental regulations had been distorted and ignored in the run-up to the U.S. "permit" to Dakota Access, but our approach made those arguments secondary to treaty arguments. From our perspective, the environmental regulations most relevant belonged to the Lakota/Dakota, not the United States. After several days of phone calls and emails, it was clear that our drafts were not going to produce a change of course. As it turned out, however, Cheyenne River filed a motion to intervene in the lawsuit that did raise treaty issues. (By September 2020, Standing Rock's brief for oral argument in the court of appeals showed a deeper engagement with treaty issues, though primarily presented within U.S. environmental laws.)[48]

In September, I wrote a column about this for *Indian Country Today*, titled "Memo to Briefcase Warriors: Be Bold!"[49] I criticized the approach taken in the lawsuit and praised the Water Protectors gathered to defend Standing Rock from invasion. They, at least, were standing on their own ground.

In June 2017, I wrote again about the Water Protectors. This time, I focused on TigerSwan, the company brought in by Dakota Access supposedly to provide security for the corporation against the Standing Rock defenders. Tiger-Swan arrived in the midst of violent attacks on the Water Protectors by DAPL agents and local and state police. TigerSwan claimed expertise in how to manage security without such violence; as they put it, "how to engage local communities to help navigate the diverse cultures across the globe and provide appropriate recommendations for optimal security solutions in foreign regions." I titled this article, "The Cerebral Battle of DAPL: What If Standing Rock Retained TigerSwan?"[50]

I pointed out the irony that DAPL hired a company specializing in security in "foreign regions" while the United States and DAPL were both ignoring Standing Rock sovereignty. Notwithstanding TigerSwan's invocation of "soft security" and "community engagement," the company's military surveillance tactics placed it in the posture of armed confrontation with a sovereign power. It responded to Standing Rock as a "culturally dynamic, high-threat, and politically-sensitive area." I closed my column by saying, "Imagine if Standing Rock had retained TigerSwan to defend Native territory and economic interests!"[51]

About this time, I was experimenting with Twitter, trying to learn the methods and modes of social media and also to understand its dysfunctions—the "asocial" qualities. I began to practice by engaging with Water Protector feeds. Within days of my TigerSwan column in *Indian Country Today*, I received a direct message (DM) from James Reese, chief executive officer (CEO) of the company. I was so new to Twitter that I didn't know how to deal with a DM. When I didn't do anything, I got another message, this time asking for a phone call. Reese also told me how to use DMs to keep our conversation out of public view.

A week later, we talked on the phone. He was intrigued by my suggestion that a Native nation might hire his company to protect its resources. He said that of course he'd be willing to do that. The rest of the conversation was low-key, sharing some personal thoughts; I sensed that he thought we might actually be starting to negotiate an agreement. I made it clear that I was in no position to do anything like that. I didn't respond to questions looking for an inroad to the Standing Rock legal team. The whole experience was a strange intersection of public journalism and secret operations. Surprisingly, it seemed that taking Native sovereignty seriously fit into TigerSwan's mission "to bring our international clients peace of mind." As Reese told the reporter Dan Rather in a 2012 interview, the company's work is "cerebral" preparation for the "battlefield." And "cerebral" meant studying more than relative firepower. It meant studying the big picture.[52]

DAPL's hiring of TigerSwan led me to ruminate about the big picture of Indigenous peoples around the world. We have seen how the exception functions to exclude Indigenous peoples from equal participation in international relations, while including their territories as objects of international economic extraction. Because their territories are sites of resources demanded by industrial processes, Indigenous peoples in the twenty-first century are at the bleeding edge of industrial "civilization." Indigenous territories everywhere are invaded by oil and gas pipelines, dams, mines, waste dumps, destruction of forests, and other manifestations of extractive industrial "development" that strikes at the existential bases of all life.

Standing Rock is only one of many examples of invasion. Another is Apache land at Oak Flat, which the United States designated in a 2014 statute for a "land swap" with the multinational mining company Resolution Copper.[53] The statute said that the United States "shall engage in government-to-government consultation with affected Indian tribes" and then "consult with Resolution Copper and seek to find mutually acceptable measures to . . . minimize the adverse effects on the affected Indian tribes resulting from mining and related activities on the Federal land conveyed to Resolution Copper under this section." Notice that the statute claimed U.S. ownership of the land and said that the outcome of the consultations could not stop the mine, but only "minimize" its adverse effects. The statute also mandated that the United States "shall convey" the land to Resolution Copper "not later than 60 days after the date of publication of the final environmental impact statement"—in other words, regardless of what the environmental impact statement said.[54]

On January 12, 2021, a group of Apache and other people, under the rubric Apache Stronghold, filed litigation to stop the project; oral arguments in their appeal to the Ninth Circuit was heard on October 22, 2021.[55] Efforts are also underway in Congress; the "Save Oak Flat" bill[56] was favorably voted on by the House Committee on Natural Resources on April 28, 2021.

"Economic development" presents a double-edged sword to Indigenous peoples. For example, tar sands oil extraction in Athabasca Chipewyan First Nation brought jobs and services, but also "despair." Eriel Deranger, an Athabasca spokesperson, said, "On the one hand [it] is ensuring that . . . families are fed . . . and . . . allowing new and better health facilities. . . . However it's also going hand in hand with the loss of land, the loss of culture, the loss of identity."[57]

A comparison between testimony at hearings on the land swap act and the Save Oak Flat bills highlights this tension. In 2011, testifying about the proposed land swap, the former San Carlos Apache tribal chairman Harrison Talgo told the House Natural Resources Committee, "We are in . . . desperate need of jobs and industry. . . . I believe strongly that it is possible for our traditional values to co-exist with economic progress. In fact, I don't believe one can survive without the other."[58] In 2021, testifying about the Save Oak Flat bill, Shan Lewis, vice chairman of the Fort Mojave Indian Tribe and president of the Inter Tribal Association of Arizona, told the committee, "If the land exchange . . . is not repealed, . . . the development of a massive copper mine . . . will destroy Oak Flat, leaving a crater almost 2 miles wide, and a thousand feet deep at its heart. The mine will also deplete billions of gallons of water, destroy sacred springs, and leave the natural world irreparably harmed, along with the religious freedoms and practices of those Tribal people who have relied upon the existence and health of Oak Flat for generations upon generations."[59]

Oil pipelines and copper mines are part of "development." Indeed, they are touted as essential development for the global economy. The question is whether they can be built to the satisfaction of Native peoples. UN secretary-general Ban Ki-moon addressed this issue in an August 2013 statement marking International Day of the World's Indigenous Peoples. The secretary-general pointed out, "Indigenous peoples . . . make up more than 5 percent of the world's population, some 370 million people." He said, "Indigenous peoples have made clear that they want development that takes into account culture and identity and the right to define their own priorities."[60]

The UN Global Compact, which bills itself as "the largest corporate responsibility initiative in the world," made similar remarks in its 2013 *Business Reference Guide to the UN Declaration on the Rights of Indigenous Peoples*, saying that "indigenous peoples are often particularly vulnerable to the negative impacts of commercial development and business activities." The guide elaborated on "ways business can engage respectfully and positively with indigenous peoples" and added this can "bring a range of benefits . . . [including] reputational benefits . . . recognition by investors, and the ability to partner with and learn from indigenous peoples' unique knowledge."[61]

The rhetoric of "respect" permeates contemporary corporate publicity, as in TigerSwan's promise to employ "best practices . . . [to] change the perception of foreign business and establish goodwill in new communities." TigerSwan told its corporate clients, "With minimal costs to you and your company, you can effectively establish rapport [and] support the community."

The question arises: Do efforts to "establish rapport" and "respectfully engage" with Indigenous peoples change the exceptional situation? Or do they represent only a rephrasing of the exception, as in the U.S. State Department's 2010 statement on the UN Declaration, saying that "free and informed consent" is a "call for a process of meaningful consultation with tribal leaders, but not necessarily the agreement of those leaders, before the actions addressed in those consultations are taken"? Secretary-General Ban Ki-moon's 2013 statement went beyond respect, calling on member-states of the United Nations to "take concrete steps to address the challenges facing indigenous peoples, especially their marginalization and exclusion."[62]

In 2007, the political theorist William Connolly asked whether Indigenous peoples might "participate in the . . . global assemblage [the world economy] while modifying some of its terms?" The alternative, he suggested, is that Indigenous participation might be "a co-opted movement within Empire."[63] Connolly was optimistic that "contemporary politics between 'settler' states and indigenous populations" was "a process under way that could modify state-capitalist forms of property and governance in the new world assemblage without overturning that assemblage itself."[64]

Connolly's perspective privileged capitalism as the essence of the "world assemblage." He described "the worldwide movement of indigenous peoples to govern large stretches of territory previously wrested from them" as "chart[ing] plural practices of property and governance within capitalism." In a remark that resonated with the UN Global Compact, he said, "New strategies are being proposed for indigenous peoples to participate in world capitalism in ways that stretch and pluralize the paradigmatic practices of capitalist property, ownership, territory, and sovereignty."[65]

Connolly begged the question of what the marginalization and exclusion of Indigenous peoples really means. To see it as "remediable" within the existing "assemblage" is to miss the fact that the "exclusion" is the exception adopted worldwide by colonizing states—what Carl Schmitt referred to as the Christian European *nomos* of the Earth. To terminate the exclusion would be to terminate the exception and thus "overturn the assemblage." The politics of global political-economic change are more complex than Connolly imagines.

A more penetrating way of approaching the question of Indigenous peoples in relation to the world system was offered by Mark Rifkin in 2009 when he asked, "What entities will count as polities and thus be seen as deserving of autonomy, what modes of inhabitance and land tenure will be understood as legitimate, and who will get to make such determinations and on what basis?" He explicitly framed his questions to provide "room for thinking indigeneity, the existence of *peoples* forcibly made domestic whose self-understandings and aspirations cannot be understood in terms of the denial of (or disjunctions within) state citizenship."[66] "Thinking indigeneity" means thinking outside and beyond the framework of states; it means rethinking the exception.

Fully "thinking indigeneity" means viewing reality from the perspective of the original free existence of Indigenous peoples. Professor Wenona Singel addressed these concerns in 2006 when she decried "transplanted law," the phenomenon of "Indian nations . . . incorporat[ing] non-Indian law . . . in tribal legal systems." She said that the problem becomes acute when Tribes adopt non-Native commercial law, which "may trigger . . . the introduction of new meanings, norms and values regarding relationships between individuals that may not comport with and may even directly conflict with the meanings, norms and values that are integral to the community's identity and the cohesiveness of its members' relationships."[67]

Singel's prescription was that "Indian nations . . . must confront the very difficult challenge of reforming their legal systems in a manner that is organic and appropriate to each nation's specific needs and legal institutions." At the same time, she said, "Indian nations . . . must grapple with a practical reality: the borrowing of laws from other jurisdictions is . . . often necessary to address immediate legal concerns." The goal is "to pursue self-determination without continued dependence on the control of an external colonizing nation."[68]

"Thinking indigeneity" opens the door to imagining an *Indigenous* nomos *of the Earth—a spatial order of the Earth built from the diversity of peoples* rather than the imposed homogeneity of states. Secretary-General Ban Ki-moon hinted at this in his concluding remark: "Let us create a world that values the wealth of human diversity and nurtures the potential it offers."[69]

In 2008, Angelique EagleWoman addressed the question of "tribal nation economics." She called for "economic development of Tribal Nations consistent with the tribalist economic theory."[70] She began by cataloguing the ancient trade routes and economic sophistication of Native nations prior to colonization and domination, saying, "The history and sophistication of Native commercial activities have been largely suppressed and left out of the story of the North American continent as Euro-Americans rewrote the continent's history to reflect the glorification of colonization."[71] In truth, she said, "International trade is a millennia-old tradition among Tribal Nations."[72] She cited archeological evidence of tribal peoples' trade and commercial activities going for thousands of years before colonization, including, interestingly, mining activities, such as for "copper,...obsidian, . . . mica, and galena."[73] EagleWoman said the goal is to "to re-enter commerce, both domestic and international," in order "to rebuild the historic prosperity once known on this continent by Native peoples."[74]

EagleWoman emphasized the importance of "tribalist economic theory," as opposed to the "mass commercial exploitation" that has dominated world economics since colonialism. She said, "Tribal Nations have become increasingly savvy in negotiating through Euro-American framed economic systems. This has not led to the large-scale adoption of the underlying Euro-American philosophy of full exploitation of resources. Rather, Tribes have framed their entry into global economic systems as part and parcel of tribal values,"[75] which she described as "entering into alliances, allegiances, and kinship connections"[76]—"less about creating wealth" and more about "socially responsible choices for the continued existence and cohesion"[77] of the community.

It should be obvious an economics of community cohesion is antithetical to an economics of domination. The UN Global Compact dream of incorporating Indigenous peoples into a global capitalist system is wishful thinking. As Waziyatawin and Michael Yellow Bird put it in their introduction to the 2012 *For Indigenous Minds Only: A Decolonization Handbook*, "As Indigenous peoples, we can no longer pretend that it is in our best interests to get on board with the project of modernity and economic development as a pathway to self-determination."[78]

In 1990, law professor Robert Williams emphasized Indigenous self-determination requires "means other than those provided by a conqueror's rule of law and its discourses of conquest." He said that the struggle of Indigenous peoples is "to redefine radically the conceptions of their rights and status . . . to articulat[e] and defin[e] [their] own vision within the global community." This struggle, he said, has the "potential for broadening perspectives on our human condition."[79]

In Carl Schmitt's terms, the potential that Williams identified is the possibility of a new *nomos* of the Earth, an overall change in world political economy—an *Indigenous* nomos *of the Earth*. An Indigenous *nomos* of the Earth would be a spatial reordering of humanity as a whole, working from a perspective offered by Muscogee Creek medicine teacher Phillip Deere, who said, "What we call the 'Indian way of life' is only a human being way of life."[80]

The notion that Indigenous peoples can be included in the existing order under a rubric of "multiculturalism" ignores the depth of difference between capitalism and tribalist economic theory. It is not by coincidence that the states of the world have attacked tribal economies. As EagleWoman said, this attack was "purposefully and deliberately" done.[81]

In 1974, George Manuel said that Indigenous peoples cannot "be brushed off with the multicultural broom." He spoke of "the difficulty of developing a new language" to speak the truth of Indigenous realities. He repeatedly called for something more profound than "cultural" rights. He called specifically for "recognition of native title [as] the mainspring and material base" of Indigenous existence.[82]

In 2014, the Kahnawake Mohawk anthropology professor Audra Simpson said that Indigenous peoples resisting state claims of sovereignty "find themselves in a 'nested' form of sovereignty and in politics of refusal."[83] In 2007, she wrote about how "refusal worked in everyday encounters to enunciate repeatedly to ourselves and to outsiders, 'this is who we are, this who you are, these are my rights.'"[84]

A statement issued during the 2016 Standing Rock challenge to DAPL by a group calling itself the Independent Lakota Nation exemplified Simpson's point. The statement was a Declaration on Lakota Nationhood and the Dakota Access Pipeline Conflict. In it, the group rejected the notion that its encampment required state or federal permission. It said, "We do not recognize United States or state permits to gather, pray, or otherwise demonstrate our cultural, social, and political institutions on our own aboriginal lands. This includes the permit given by the United States Government Army Corps of Engineers to the Standing Rock Sioux Tribal Government for the Sacred Stone protest encampment and/or Red Warrior encampment against the Dakota Access pipeline."[85]

The Independent Lakota Nation statement "refused" the exception and reversed the forms of "recognition." They did what the exception was intended to prevent them from doing. As Simpson said, "The state did not want Indians to remember, let alone act upon, other political traditions and authorities, to pick up weapons, to stand ground on their ground. This was not the 'culture' that multiculturalism sought to protect and preserve. This, rather, was sovereignty and nationhood, something that was and still is to say the least an uneasy fit within a state that wishes to be singular, even when it imagines itself 'federalist.'" Simpson described the "top down . . . statist forms of recognition" that create the dilemma in which Indigenous peoples find themselves; she said that the alternative is "the grounded forms of recognition that produce the authoritative nexus within the community." She described the Indigenous nexus as "a space shaped by political authority that does not derive solely from the state, but is drawn from their own traditions, their interpretations of that tradition, their shared archive of knowledge of each other, their genealogies, and their relationships with each other through time."[86]

Earlier, we used Giorgio Agamben's interpretation of Carl Schmitt's concept of the exception to illuminate the core of federal anti-Indian law—the domination of Indigenous existence. But Agamben's analysis was inadequate to explore Schmitt's concept of the *nomos* of the Earth. Agamben was concerned with the relation of individuals to the state; he saw the exception as a zone outside law created by the state. But for him, the only alternative to the exception was to be a member of the state.

Agamben did not imagine the existence of societies outside the state, non-state spaces where excluded persons were members of independent peoples. As Rifkin pointed out, Agamben had a "tendency to fetishize the relation between individuals and the state and to overlook challenges to the latter by collectives/communities."[87] As Ernesto Laclau put it in 2007, Agamben missed the fact that "we do not have lawlessness as against the law, but two laws that do not recognize each other."[88]

The Independent Lakota Nation spoke from its own sense of law, in a situation of mutual nonrecognition with the United States. As Simpson would put it, it spoke from its own existential "nexus"; the Lakota were grounded in "their own traditions, their interpretations of that tradition, their shared archive of knowledge of each other, their genealogies, and their relationships with each other through time."

The point becomes sharper when we realize that in Indigenous terms, as Eric Cheyfitz and Shari M. Huhndorf wrote, "What the West terms the law is one kind of story. . . . Western law is . . . nothing but a set of stories." These stories, however, acquire "a particular political or juridical force."[89] Professor Robert M. Cover, in "*Nomos* and Narrative," said that law exists within "narratives that locate it and give it meaning." These narratives—stories—constitute "a *nomos*—a normative universe." He added, "This *nomos* is as much 'our world' as is the physical universe of mass, energy, and momentum."[90]

Cover famously described political and juridical force in "a modern nation-state" as necessarily involving literal force: "Legal interpretation takes place in a field of pain and death." He added, "Interpretations in law also constitute justifications for violence which has already occurred . . . [leaving] behind victims whose lives have been torn apart by these organized, social practices of violence."[91]

When Vizenor repurposed the old legal term "survivance" to describe contemporary assertions of Indigenous knowledge, perspectives, and organizing abilities, he said that it involved "an active sense of presence, the continuance of native stories, not a mere reaction, or a survivable name. Native survivance stories are renunciations of dominance, tragedy and victimry."[92]

We will know when the world begins to approach an Indigenous *nomos*. As James Zion, solicitor to the Courts of the Navajo Nation for many years, suggested in 1999 that it will happen when the voices of original peoples are heard, when "instead of thinking of institutions within the state, we [are] thinking of communities."[93] That was Agamben's shortcoming—not seeing any social order outside the state.

Carl Schmitt was able to foresee a spatial order of the Earth beyond state formations. Indeed, he cautioned against appealing to a "higher" statist sovereignty of one-world government to resolve the chaos of competing state sovereignty claims. He chastised those who "rush blindly toward a single sovereign of the world." He added that that idea "certainly has a primitive simplicity, but it must not be permitted to displace other possibilities."[94]

Carl Schmitt's translator, Gary Ulmen, wrote that for Schmitt, "The new *nomos* of the earth would most likely be constituted of a . . . new pluralism—a balance of forces which could pave the way for a new international law." He said, "The new *nomos* of the earth would not be one world but a pluralistic community in unity."[95] As Steven DeCaroli said in 2007, "The task is not to justify sovereign power, but to conceive of a political community that does not pre-suppose it."[96]

The writer Tony Hillerman added to this understanding in 1997 when he shared a discussion that he had with the Navajo elder Hastiin Alexander Etcitty about anti-Native actions in the U.S. Senate. He told Etcitty that the Senate was trying to take away Native sovereignty. Etcitty replied, "The notion that any human, or group thereof, has sovereignty over any part of Mother Earth is a myth based upon the white man's Origin Story."[97]

Taiaiake Alfred (Mohawk) explained, "A crucial feature of the Indigenous concept of governance is its respect for individual autonomy. This respect precludes the notion of 'sovereignty'—the idea that there can be a permanent transference of power or authority from the individual to an abstraction of the collective called 'government'. [In] the Indigenous tradition . . . leadership is exercised by persuading individuals to pool their self-power in the interest of the collective good. By contrast, in the European tradition power is surrendered to the representatives of the majority, whose decisions on what they think is the collective good are then imposed on all citizens."[98]

An Indigenous *nomos* of the Earth would be a pluralistic world community arising from *a shared set of nonsovereign relationships* of humans to land and humans to humans. An Indigenous *nomos* would organize the Earth's spatial order around the *absence of sovereignty and the presence of diversity.* In 1997, Taino Jose Barrerio, scholar-emeritus at the Smithsonian Museum of the American Indian and longtime Indigenous activist, emphasized, "Indigenous is nearly synonymous with diversity."[99]

We now know that human diversity was an intentional casualty of Christian discovery. As Jens Bartelson said in 1995, Christianity's response to its "discovery" of the "new world" was "an effort to . . . [make] everything speak . . . with one voice."[100] Non-Christian societies were given a "choice": to assimilate to the church system and give up their independence or to be destroyed. The underlying assumption was that there is only one reality, and it is Christian. As Morris Berman put it, "This is a key feature of the modern age: the homogenization of culture, the defeat of subcultures with their alternative languages, ways of life, and modes of consciousness. Life became less diverse, and therefore less rich and more precarious."[101]

In 1979, Michael Dorris wrote, "The pre-existent variety of Native American societies . . . has been consistently obscured and disallowed. Every effort has been made to almost existentially enclose the non-Western world into a European schema, and then to blame unwilling elements for being backward, ignorant, or without vision. . . . Federal Indian policy was . . . shaped from the beginning at least as much toward deculturation as acculturation."[102]

An Indigenous *nomos* of the Earth does not necessarily require the elimination of Christianity, but only of the political and legal doctrines of domination historically rooted in Christendom. George Manuel said that Christianity might have a role in the Fourth World. He said, however, "It will be easier to believe that it can take on a shape that more closely resembles the world around us when we receive a sign that the leaders of the church have joined in the dance of life. Perhaps when men no longer try to have 'dominion over the fish of the sea, and over the fowl of the air, and over every living thing that liveth upon the earth,' they will no longer try to have dominion over us. It will be much easier to be our brother's keeper then."[103]

Felix Cohen, the architect of the *Handbook of Federal Indian Law*, once compared Native peoples to the miner's canary. He wrote, "Like the miner's canary, the Indian marks the shifts from fresh air to poison gas in our political atmosphere."[104] Cohen meant his metaphor in a political sense. He was concerned about the viability of American democracy, in which he included Native peoples. Today, we understand the metaphor literally, referring to the viability of life on Earth in the face of the dangers from "civilized" destruction of the natural world. The canary as ecological metaphor is useful because it points to the integration of traditional Indigenous lifeways with natural cycles of life. This closeness to the Earth makes them more sensitive to the poisons of industrial extraction.

In the 1970s, Native lifeways were reduced to the stereotype of an "ecological Indian" who cried about trash along the highways. As with many, if not all, representations of Native peoples in American culture, this one not only missed the truth, but it helped to cover it up. It was a so-called public service antilitter advertisement for Keep America Beautiful, an organization funded by beverage and packaging corporations.[105] It distracted attention from corporate manufacturers of throwaway products by blaming the careless consumers rather than the producers of the waste. Similar misdirection pervades the mainstream so-called environmental movement: The system of industrial extraction and production intensifies its search for profit while telling people to be better stewards of the Earth.

The rebellion of Native peoples against destruction of the natural world is a sign to the rest of humanity to take notice. This Indigenous sign has been offered before, indeed from their first encounters with colonial invaders, when it was immediately clear that Indigenous lifeways were closely integrated with the natural world. But the colonizers read this closeness to nature as a sign that Native peoples were "inferior." It was a sign that they did not take a stance of "sovereign domination" of their environment. They were "savages," without a sense of "government." They "wandered" and "merely occupied." All these notions were, in John Marshall's words, "an apology for considering them as a people over whom the superior genius of Europe might claim an ascendency."[106]

In 2021, *The Dawn of Everything: A New History of Humanity*, by David Graeber and David Wengrow, an anthropology and archaeology research team, joined the burgeoning twenty-first-century global awareness that life on Earth is in social and ecological crisis, and that crisis is tied to the system of industrial state corporate society. The authors' contribution is to help us understand why we are having such a difficult time figuring a way out of the mess. The reason, they say, is that our thinking is trapped by our belief in the story that modern corporate state society is the end-state of human evolution—the inevitable result of "progressing" from "barbarism" to "civilization." The obstacle to thinking of alternatives to the current organization of society is a belief that there is no alternative.

*The Dawn* is a detailed survey of scientific data from archaeological and anthropological investigations that have only recently become possible, including archaeobotany, deoxyribonucleic acid (DNA) analysis, "statistical frequencies of health indicators from ancient burials," and other advances. From this data, Graeber and Wengrow attack all stories of irreversible historical inevitability, whether derived from Jean-Jacques Rousseau's notion of an original human egalitarianism ruined by agricultural and metallurgy or from Thomas Hobbes's proposition of an original "nasty, brutish" humanity rescued by government.[107] They ask, "What if, instead of . . . [repeating the conventional stories], we ask how we came to be trapped in such tight conceptual shackles that we can no longer even imagine the possibility of reinventing ourselves?"[108]

The authors' core thesis is that the story of a "necessary" human evolution from "barbaric tribes" to "civilized states" was produced by European writers to rationalize the great differences between their societies and the societies "discovered" in the "New World." *The Dawn* describes this process as Europeans responding to the "Indigenous critique" provided by reports from Jesuits and other missionaries in the Northeast Woodlands region. The reports were that Native peoples are very generous with one another; that there's no one who goes hungry within their communities unless everyone is hungry; that there are no beggars within their communities and no jails. The reports also noted that Indigenous chiefs have authority only insofar as they're eloquent, and no one will do anything when ordered to do so unless they agree with it. Scandalized missionaries reported that Indigenous women had full control over their bodies; colonial authorities noted that women often took part in Indigenous governance.

Public figures in Europe directly encountered critiques from Natives visiting Paris, London, and other cities, who saw beggars in the streets and attributed this to a lack of charity on the part of the Europeans, condemning them for it. The contrasts between European hierarchy and domination, selfishness and greed, and the way of life of Indigenous peoples had a profound impact in Western thinking and was one of the major streams of thought flowing into the Enlightenment. As we saw earlier, Eric Cheyfitz's reading of *Johnson v. McIntosh* discerned Chief Justice John Marshall working to repress the Indigenous critique implicit in kinship economies and landholding principles.

In a nutshell, *The Dawn of Everything* says that the theory of human evolution from "barbarism to civilization" was developed specifically to defend European feudal societies against the overall Indigenous critique. Europeans were shaken by the unmistakable openness and fluidity of Northeast Woodlands Indigenous societies and the paradoxical (to Europeans) combination of Indigenous insistence on individual autonomy with an equally strong insistence on group solidarity. The central theme of the European arguments was that individual autonomy and self-determined group cohesion were viable only among "primitive" peoples and had to be abandoned as humans "evolved." Followers of Rousseau and Hobbes alike argued that "advanced civilization" was "necessary" in human "development" and that the life of "tribes" was doomed by this necessary "progress."

*The Dawn* notes that Europeans did not perceive such dangerous ideas from the Aztec and Inca, whose urban civilizations and empires rivaled Europe. Neither did they bother to figure out how their theory of "human progress" could explain such "advanced" Indigenous societies. The only explanation that they needed to combat such peoples was the "heathen and infidel" argument that, with religious notes, composed a hierarchical scale putting European Christendom at the top.

To borrow the words of Patrice Lumumba, an Indigenous Tetela/Bantu leader who was the first prime minister of the Democratic Republic of the Congo, describing to the Pan-African Conference in August 1960 what Africans had to do after formal emancipation from colonialism: "Sooner or later we . . . have to review everything . . . and think everything through. . . . We . . . have to create new structures . . . to revise the methods that had been forced upon us. . . . Above all," Lumumba said, we have to "rediscover our most intimate selves and rid ourselves of mental attitudes and complexes and habits that colonization had trapped us in for centuries."[109]

John Mohawk, the Seneca traditionalist, activist, and scholar, said, "The Native traditional movement is part of an international movement . . . against the abuses of the transnational corporations and toward the redevelopment of lifestyles on a human scale." He added, "The self-development of peoples is a powerful set of politics. It is the wave of the future . . . not the ghost of the past."[110]

John wrote those words in 1982. In 2012, Idle No More was founded among Treaty Peoples in Manitoba, Saskatchewan, and Alberta to protest the Canadian government's dismantling of environmental protection laws, endangering First Nations who live on the land. It is "an Indigenous-led social movement . . . led by women [calling] for 'refounded nation-to-nation relations based on mutual respect . . . a movement for Indigenous rights and the protection of land, water, and sky.'"[111] In 2016, the Independent Lakota Nation issued the Declaration on Lakota Nationhood and the Dakota Access Pipeline Conflict discussed earlier in this chapter. In 2018, the Yakama Nation filed its seminal amicus brief challenging the Christian discovery doctrine in *Washington State v. Cougar Den.*

In 2021, the Red Lake Chippewa and White Earth Ojibwe filed the case of *Manoomin v. Minnesota Department of Natural Resources* in White Earth Tribal Court: "An action for declaratory and injunctive relief to declare Manoomin, or wild rice, within all the Chippewa ceded territories is protected and possesses inherent rights to exist, flourish, regenerate, and evolve, as well as inherent rights to restoration, recovery, and preservation."[112] That case is still in progress, hitting bumps along the road. On March 10, 2022, the White Earth Ojibwe Appellate Court dismissed the Manoomin suit against Minnesota, concluding its opinion with a statement of extreme hesitancy to challenge federal anti-Indian law: "We believe that federal case law requires dismissal of this case. If we were to allow the case to proceed on its merits in the Tribal Court, and the Court granted a remedy against Appellants, and this Court affirmed such remedy, we believe that a federal court would apply the same case laws we cite to enjoin the remedy and the Tribal Court from further proceedings."[113] Undeterred, the respondents—Manoomin, the White Earth Band of Ojibwe, members of the White Earth Reservation Business Committee, tribal members, and non-Indians—moved on March 25,

2022, for reconsideration on substantive and procedural grounds, supported by a supplemental brief filed April 6.[114]

In short, Indigenous critique is active in the twenty-first century, providing humanity with the same opportunities and challenges that faced Christian European colonial powers in the sixteenth century, for shaping human societies harmoniously and sustainably.

Whether the call of Indigenous peoples today—to rid ourselves of the mental attitudes, complexes, and habits that colonization trapped us in for centuries—is heeded when it wasn't previously is an open question for the planet. It remains a call to consciousness, an opportunity to build an Indigenous *nomos* of the Earth.

# Notes

## Preface: Seeing between Worlds

1. Milner S. Ball, "Constitution, Court, Indian Tribes," *American Bar Foundation Research Journal* 1987, no. 1 (Spring 1987): 61.

2. Angelique Townsend EagleWoman, "Balancing between Two Worlds: A Dakota Woman's Reflections on Being a Law Professor," *Berkeley Journal of Gender, Law & Justice* 29, no. 2 (Summer 2014): 250.

3. Rennard Strickland and Gloria Valencia-Weber, "Observations on the Evolution of Indian Law in the Law Schools," *New Mexico Law Review* 26, no. 2 (Spring 1996): 156–157.

4. *Brown v. Board of Education*, 347 U.S. 483 (1954).

5. *Tee-Hit-Ton Indians v. United States*, 348 U.S. 272 (1955).

6. U.S. House Committee on Armed Services. *Full Committee Hearings on Review of the Administration and Operation of the Selective Service System* (HRG-1966-ASH-0025; June 22–24, 28–30, 1966). Committee Publication No. 75, 9805.

7. James Gordley. *The Philosophical Origins of Modern Contract Doctrine* (New York: Oxford University Press, 1991), 132.

8. Barack Obama. *A Promised Land* (New York: Crown, 2020), 19.

9. Laura Kalman. *Yale Law School and the Sixties: Revolt and Reverberations.* Studies in Legal History (Chapel Hill: University of North Carolina Press, 2005).

10. For fully developed versions, see "Syllabus: Legalization of American Indians (Spring 2001)," http://people.umass.edu/derrico/syllabus.html; and "Syllabus: Indigenous Peoples—Global Issues (Fall 2001)," http://people.umass.edu/derrico/syllabus470.html (accessed March 21, 2021)

11. See Paula Peters, *Mashpee Nine: A Story of Cultural Justice* (Mashpee, MA: SmokeSygnals, 2016) and the film *Mashpee Nine: A Story of Cultural Justice,* directed by Paula Peters (Mashpee, MA: Mashpee TV, 2016).

12. See *Bulletin of the Massachusetts Archaeological Society*, 43, no. 2 (October 1982), 34–37, 60–65 (respectively).

13. Public Law 101–601, 101 Congress, Session 2, An Act: To Provide for the Protection of Native American Graves, and for Other Purposes, *U.S. Statutes at Large* 104, Main Section (1990): 3048–3059.

14. *Randall Trapp, et al. v. Commissioner DuBois, et al.*, Massachusetts Superior Court (Worcester, Civil No. 95-0779), Massachusetts Appeals Court, No. 2000 -P-1640.

15. *Commonwealth of Massachusetts v. Michael J. Maxim and David S. Greene,* Barnstable County District Court, Nos. CR-95-8157 and 8158 (October 22, 1996), *reversed* by Massachusetts Appeals Court, 45 Mass. App. Ct. 49; 695 N.E.2d 212 (June 11, 1998) and Massachusetts Supreme Judicial Court, 429 Mass. 287; 708 N.E.2d 636 (April 7, 1999).

16. "A Conversation with Phillip Deere," YouTube video, an interview conducted at the 1979 Mashpee Wampanoag Sovereignty Conference, https://www .youtube.com/watch?v=_KmB1ZNOwEQ (Phillip Deere 2013 [1979]: 37:06, @25:49). (accessed February 27, 2020)

## Introduction: The Plan of the Book

1. Elizabeth A. Reese, "The Other American Law," *Stanford Law Review* 73, no. 3 (March 2021): 563.

2. *Johnson and Graham's Lessee v. McIntosh*, 21 U.S. 543, 591 (1823) (emphasis added).

3. Paul Finkelman, *Supreme Injustice: Slavery in the Nation's Highest Court.* The Nathan I. Huggins Lectures (Cambridge, MA: Harvard University Press, 2018), 237n47.

4. Steven T. Newcomb, "The Evidence of Christian Nationalism in Federal Indian Law: The Doctrine of Discovery, *Johnson v. McIntosh*, and Plenary Power," *New York University Review of Law & Social Change* 20, no. 2 (1992–1993): 304.

5. Robert A. Williams, Jr., "The Algebra of Federal Indian Law: The Hard Trail of Decolonizing and Americanizing the White Man's Indian Jurisprudence," *Wisconsin Law Review* 1986, no. 2 (1986): 242, 298 (1986).

6. *City of Sherrill v. Oneida Indian Nation,* 544 U.S. 197, 204n1 (2005).

7. *McGirt v. Oklahoma*, 140 S. Ct. 2452, 2462 (2020).

8. Steven T. Newcomb, "The Evidence of Christian Nationalism in Federal Indian Law: The Doctrine of Discovery, *Johnson v. McIntosh,* and Plenary Power," *New York University Review of Law & Social Change* 20, no. 2 (1992–1993): 305.

9. Angelique EagleWoman, "The 15th-Century Doctrine That Upholds Indigenous Land Dispossession," *The Lawyer's Daily*, LexisNexis Canada, at *1 (February 4, 2019, 2:36 p.m. EST),

10. Bethany R. Berger, "Hope for Indian Tribes in the U.S. Supreme Court? *Menominee, Nebraska v. Parker, Bryant, Dollar General* . . . and Beyond," *University of Illinois Law Review* 1901 (2017), 1911, 1913.

11. *United States v. Lara,* 541 U.S. 193, 219 (Thomas, concurring) (2004).

12. Angelique A. EagleWoman, "Tribal Nation Economics: Rebuilding Commercial Prosperity in Spite of U.S. Trade Restraints—Recommendations for Economic Revitalization in Indian Country," *Tulsa Law Review* 44, no. 2 (Winter 2008): 396.

13. Bryan H. Wildenthal. *Native American Sovereignty on Trial: A Handbook with Cases, Laws, and Documents.* ABC-CLIO's on Trial Series (Santa Barbara, CA: ABC-CLIO, 2003), 127.

14. Gerald Robert Vizenor. *Manifest Manners: Narratives on Postindian Survivance,* Bison Books print (Lincoln: University of Nebraska Press, 2010).

15. Rennard Strickland, "Genocide-at-Law: An Historic and Contemporary View of the Native American Experience," *University of Kansas Law Review* 34, no. 4 (Summer 1986): 717–718.

16. John Collier. *The Indians of the Americas* (New York: Norton, 1947), 17 (emphasis in original).

17. "A Conversation with Phillip Deere."

## Chapter 1: Learning in Navajoland

1. *Application of Gault,* 387 U.S. 1 (1967). See also Ada Pecos Melton, "Building Culturally Relevant Youth Courts in Tribal Communities," http://nc.casaforchildren.org/files/public/community/judges/July_2010/TribalYouthcourts.pdf (accessed December 17, 2019); and Jenadee Nanini, "A Tribe's Future: Native American Youth and the Right to Counsel in Juvenile Justice Systems," *Georgetown Journal of Law & Modern Critical Race Perspectives* 9, no. 1 (Spring 2017): 77–98.

2. Public Law 90–284, 90 Congress, Session 2, An Act: To prescribe penalties for certain acts of violence or intimidation, and for other purposes, *U.S. Statutes at Large* 82, Main Section (1968): 73–92.

3. Wenona T. Singel, "Cultural Sovereignty and Transplanted Law: Tensions in Indigenous Self-Rule," *Kansas Journal of Law & Public Policy* 15, no. 2 (Winter 2006): 357–368, 364.

4. James W. Zion, "Monster Slayer and Born for Water: The Intersection of Restorative and Indigenous Justice." *Contemporary Justice Review* 2, no. 4 (1999): 359, 360.

5. *Trustees of Dartmouth College v. Woodward,* 17 U.S. 518, 636 (1819).

6. Mary Wollstonecraft Shelley, *Frankenstein, or, The Modern Prometheus* (London: Printed for Lackington, Hughes, Harding, Mavor, & Jones, 1818).

7. Shelley, *Frankenstein,* 95, 114, 123, 208, 209.

8. *Santa Clara County v. Southern Pacific Railroad,* 18 Fed. 385 (1883), *affirmed,* 118 U. S. 394 (1886).

9. *Citizens United v. Federal Election Commission,* 558 U.S. 310 (2010).

10. John Dewey, "The Historic Background of Corporate Legal Personality," *Yale Law Journal* 35, no. 6 (April 1926): 660 (emphasis in original). See also Peter d'Errico, "Corporate Personality and Human Commodification," *Rethinking Marxism* 9, no. 2 (June 1996): 99–113. https://doi.org/10.1080/08935699608685489.

11. *Burwell v. Hobby Lobby,* 573 U.S. 682 (2014).

12. Public Law 95–608, 95 Congress, Session 2, An Act: To Establish Standards for the Placement of Indian Children in Foster or Adoptive Homes, to Prevent the Breakup of Indian Families, and for Other Purposes, *U.S. Statutes at Large* 92, Main Section (1978): 3069–3079.

13. Leonard B. Jimson, "Parent and Child Relationships in Law and in Navajo Custom," in *The Destruction of American Indian Families,* ed. Steven Unger (New York: Association on American Indian Affairs, 1977, 67–78).

14. Wilfred Pelletier. *Childhood in an Indian Village* (Somerville, MA: New England Free Press, undated; originally in *This Magazine Is About Schools,* 1969).

15. Stanley Diamond. *In Search of the Primitive: A Critique of Civilization* (New Brunswick, NJ: Transaction Books; distributed by E. P. Dutton (New York, 1974), 257, 260).

16. A. L. Kroeber, "Nature of the Land-Holding Group," *Ethnohistory,* 2, no. 4 (Autumn 1955), 303, 313–314 (respectively).

17. Morton H. Fried, *The Notion of Tribe.* Cummings Modular Program in Anthropology. Menlo Park, CA: Cummings Pub. Co, 1975, preface.

18. Chapter 119, 49 Congress, Session 2, An Act: To Provide for the Allotment of Lands in Severalty to Indians on the Various Reservations, and to Extend the Protection of the Laws of the United States and the Territories Over the Indians, and for Other Purposes, *U.S. Statutes at Large 24, Main Section* (1887): 388–391.

19. Kristen A. Carpenter, "Real Property and Peoplehood," *Stanford Environmental Law Journal* 27, no. 2 (2008): 313–396.

20. Rose Stremlau, "'To Domesticate and Civilize Wild Indians': Allotment and the Campaign to Reform Indian Families, 1875–1887," *Journal of Family History* 30, no. 3 (July 2005): 265–286. https://doi.org/10.1177/0363199005275793.

21. Theodore Roosevelt, "Message of the President of the United States Communicated to the Two Houses of Congress at the Beginning of the First Session of the Fifty-Seventh Congress," December 3, 1901. Washington, DC, U.S. Government Publishing Office.

22. Public Law 73–383 / Chapter 576, 73 Congress, Session 2, An Act: To Conserve and Develop Indian Lands and Resources; to Extend to Indians the Right to Form Business and Other Organizations; to Establish a Credit System for Indians; to Grant Certain Rights of Home Rule to Indians; to Provide for Vocational Education for Indians; and for Other Purposes," *U.S. Statutes at Large* 48 (1934): 984–988.

23. EagleWoman, "Tribal Nation Economics, 399.

24. House Concurrent Resolution 108, *U.S. Statutes at Large* 67 (1953): B132.

25. Richard Nixon, "Special Message to the Congress on Indian Affairs—July 8, 1970," *Public Papers of the Presidents of the United States* 1970 (1970): 564–576

26. Public Law 93–638, 93 Congress, Session 2, An Act: To Provide Maximum Indian Participation in the Government and Education of the Indian People; to Provide for the Full Participation of Indian Tribes in Programs and Services Conducted by the Federal Government for Indians and to Encourage

the Development of Human Resources of the Indian People; to Establish a Program of Assistance to Upgrade Indian Education; to Support the Right of Indian Citizens to Control Their Own Educational Activities; and for Other Purposes," *U.S. Statutes at Large* 88, Main Section (1975): 2203–2217.

27. Vine Deloria, Jr., and Clifford M. Lytle, *American Indians, American Justice* (Austin: University of Texas Press, 1983), 24.

28. Glenn Thrush and Michael Crowley, "Obama Warns That Dropped Charges Against Flynn Put 'Rule of Law' at Risk." *New York Times*, May 9, 2020, sec. U.S. https://www.nytimes.com/2020/05/09/us/politics/obama-flynn-coronavirus -trump.html (accessed July 7, 2021)

29. Ed Pilkington, "Riots Helped Elect Nixon in 1968. Can Trump Benefit from Fear and Loathing Too?" *The Guardian,* June 16, 2020. http://www.theguardian .com/us-news/2020/jun/16/trump-nixon-1968-law-and-order-america (accessed January 31, 2021).

30. Vine Deloria, Jr., *God Is Red: A Native View of Religion* (New York: Dell, 1973).

31. Colin M. Turnbull, *The Lonely African* (New York: Simon and Schuster, 1962), 250.

32. EagleWoman, "Tribal Nation Economics," 402.

33. Turnbull, *Lonely African*, 246.

34. James Axtell, *The Invasion Within: The Contest of Cultures in Colonial North America,* The Cultural Origins of North America 1 (New York: Oxford University Press, 1985, 327).

35. Sebastian Junger, *Tribe: On Homecoming and Belonging* (New York: Twelve, 2016), 2–3.

36. Peter d'Errico, "Jeffrey Amherst and Smallpox Blankets" https://people .umass.edu/derrico/amherst/lord_jeff.html (accessed January 31, 2021).

37. Junger, *Tribe*, 9–10.

38. Junger, *Tribe*, 125.

39. Friedrich Wilhelm Nietzsche, "On the New Idol," *Thus Spoke Zarathustra,* in *The Portable Nietzsche,* trans. Walter Kaufmann (New York: Viking Press, 1954), 160.

40. Unconscionable Contract or Clause, Uniform Commercial Code § 2–302.

41. American Bar Association, "Professionalism & Ethics in Lawyer Advertising" (July 20, 2020). https://www.americanbar.org/groups/professional_responsibility /resources/professionalism/professionalism_ethics_in_lawyer_advertising/ (accessed March 21, 2021).

42. *Williams v. Lee,* 358 U.S. 217 (1959).

43. *Dolgencorp, Inc. v. Mississippi Band of Choctaw Indians,* 746 F.3d 167, 174 (5th Cir. 2014); affirmed, *Dollar Gen. Corp. v. Mississippi Band of Choctaw Indians,* 136 S. Ct. 2159 (2016). (Note that after the death of Justice Antonin Scalia, that left only eight justices on the Court at that time. Thus, the decision was 4–4, which kept the lower court's decision standing as final for the case. This is not the same as a decision upholding the lower court because an equally divided

ruling is not based on the merits of the case. Rather, it is a statement of inability to come to a decision.)

44. New Mexico Advisory Committee to the United States Commission on Civil Rights, *The Farmington Report: A Conflict of Cultures* (Washington, DC: U.S. Commission on Civil Rights, 1975). https://www.usccr.gov/pubs/docs/122705 _FarmingtonReport.pdf (accessed July 7, 2021).

## Chapter 2: "Indians"

1. Vizenor, *Manifest Manners*, vii.

2. Vizenor, *Manifest Manners*, 10–11.

3. Gerald Robert Vizenor, *Fugitive Poses: Native American Indian Scenes of Absence and Presence*. Abraham Lincoln Lecture Series (Lincoln: University of Nebraska Press, 1998), 22 (emphasis in original).

4. Vizenor, *Manifest Manners*, 5–6.

5. *Reel Injun,* Rezolution Pictures Inc., Film Board of Canada National, Newsworld CBC, and Films (Firm) Lorber. Videorecording. Edited by Neil Diamond, Catherine Bainbridge, Jeremiah Hayes, et al. Letterboxed. New York: Lorber Films, 2010.

6. Vizenor, *Manifest Manners*, 14.

7. Gerald Vizenor, "Aesthetics of Survivance, Literary Theory and Practice," in Gerald Robert Vizenor, ed., *Survivance: Narratives of Native Presence* (Lincoln: University of Nebraska Press, 2008), 1.

8. Jonas Bens, *The Indigenous Paradox: Rights, Sovereignty, and Culture in the Americas* (Philadelphia: University of Pennsylvania Press, 2020), 7, 49.

9. University of South Carolina, "New Evidence Puts Man in North America 50,000 Years Ago." *ScienceDaily*, November 18, 2004, www.sciencedaily.com /releases/2004/11/041118104010.htm. See also Derek T. Anderson, "Topper Site," Mississippi State University, http://stoneandbone.cobb.msstate.edu/topper .html (accessed March 1, 2021).

10. Vine Deloria, Jr. *Red Earth, White Lies: Native Americans and the Myth of Scientific Fact* (New York: Scribner, 1995).

11. David Coventry Smith, "Defending Indian Lands After Carcieri," *Emerging Issues in Tribal-State Relations,* (Eagan, MN: Thomson Reuters/Aspatore, 2014), WL 2326354, 1.

12. *Cobell v. Norton*, 229 F.R.D. 5, 7 (2005), *vacated sub nom. Cobell v. Kempthorne*, 455 F.3d 317 (2006), *cert. denied,* 549 U.S. 1317 (2007).

13. Strickland, "Genocide-at-Law": 719.

14. Carroll P. Kakel, *The American West and the Nazi East: A Comparative and Interpretive Perspective* (Houndmills, UK, and New York: Palgrave Macmillan, 2011), 3.

15. David E. Stannard, *American Holocaust: Columbus and the Conquest of the New World* (New York: Oxford University Press, 1992), 124.

16. Ernest L. Wilkinson, Esq., representing various Indian tribes. Testimony on Creation of Indian Claims Commission, Hearings Before the House

Committee on Indian Affairs (HRG-1945-INH-0002; 79th Cong., 1st Sess., June 11, 1945), 108.

17. Lia Mandelbaum, "Honoring Native American Voices: Recognizing Tragic History and Praising Brave Spirits," *Jewish Journal,* February 25, 2016, https://jewishjournal.com/culture/food/182867/honoring-native-american-voices-recognizing-tragic-history-and-praising-brave-spirits/ (accessed February 13, 2020).

18. Edward John, United Nations Permanent Forum on Indigenous Issues Secretariat, *Study on the Impacts of the Doctrine of Discovery on Indigenous Peoples, Including Mechanisms, Processes and Instruments of Redress.* United Nations Economic and Social Council, Document E/C.19/2014/3; February 20, 2013, Section I.3, https://digitallibrary.un.org/record/767270 (accessed July 7, 2021).

19. *Carpenter v. Murphy,* 139 S. Ct. 398 (2018), "Brief for the United States as Amicus Curiae Supporting the Petitioner," 2018 WL 3642789 (July 30, 2018), https://www.supremecourt.gov/DocketPDF/17/17-1107/55946/20180730184937862_17-1107tsacUnitedStates.pdf.

20. Raphael Lemkin, *Les actes constituant un danger general (interétatique) consideres comme delites des droit des gens* (Paris: A. Pedone, 1933); James T. Fussell, translator, *Acts Constituting a General (Transnational) Danger Considered as Offences Against the Law of Nations* (Washington, DC: Prevent Genocide International, undated). http://www.preventgenocide.org/lemkin/madrid1933-english.htm (accessed May 10, 2022).

21. Raphael Lemkin, *Axis Rule in Occupied Europe: Laws of Occupation—Analysis of Government—Proposals for Redress* (Washington, DC: Carnegie Endowment for International Peace, 1944), 79–95, http://www.preventgenocide.org/lemkin/AxisRule1944-1.htm.

22. *Carpenter v. Murphy,* "Brief for the United States," 17, https://www.supremecourt.gov/DocketPDF/17/17-1107/55946/20180730184937862_17-1107tsacUnitedStates.pdf.

23. *Carpenter v. Murphy,* "Brief for the United States," 19, https://www.supremecourt.gov/DocketPDF/17/17-1107/55946/20180730184937862_17-1107tsacUnitedStates.pdf.

24. *Carpenter v. Murphy,* "Brief for the United States, 12), https://www.supremecourt.gov/DocketPDF/17/17-1107/55946/20180730184937862_17-1107tsacUnitedStates.pdf.

25. *Carpenter v. Murphy,* "Brief for the United States," 13, quoting 31 Cong. Rec. 5593 (1898) (Sen. Bate).

26. Mr. Bate, Congressional Record—Senate 31 (June 7, 1898): 5580–5624.

27. *Carpenter v. Murphy,* "Brief for Amicus Curiae Muscogee (Creek) Nation in Support of Respondent," 2018 WL 5429227 (September 2018), 14, https://www.supremecourt.gov/DocketPDF/17/17-1107/64965/20180926161001792_17-1107%20Amicus%20Brief%20of%20Muscogee%20Creek%20Nation.pdf.

28. *Carpenter v. Murphy,* "Brief for Amicus Curiae Muscogee (Creek) Nation," 10, 12.

29. *Carpenter v. Murphy,* "Brief for Amicus Curiae Muscogee (Creek) Nation," 25.

30. *Sharp v. Murphy,* https://www.supremecourt.gov/search.aspx?filename=/docket/docketfiles/html/public/17-1107.html (accessed March 2, 2020); See the order for supplemental briefs at *Carpenter v. Murphy,* 139 S. Ct. 626 (2018).

31. *McGirt v. Oklahoma,* 140 S.Ct. 2452 (2020).

32. *McGirt v. Oklahoma,* 140 S.Ct. 2452 (2020).

33. *Lone Wolf v. Hitchcock,* 187 U.S. 553, 555–566 (1903).

34. Emory Washburn, *A Treatise on the American Law of Real Property* (Boston: Little, Brown, 1864), Book III, Ch. III, Title by Grant, § 1 Public Grant.

35. *McGirt v. Oklahoma,* at 2482.

36. Hans Christian Andersen, "The Emperor's New Clothes," in *Fairy Tales Told for Children, First Collection, Third Booklet* (Copenhagen: C. A. Reitzel, 1837).

37. Ronald Mann, "Justices Call for Reargument in Dispute about Oklahoma Prosecutions of Native Americans," SCOTUSblog, July 2, 2019, https://www.scotusblog.com/2019/07/justices-call-for-reargument-in-dispute-about-oklahoma-prosecutions-of-native-americans/ (accessed March 2, 2020).

38. Williams, "The Algebra of Federal Indian Law," 242, 298.

39. Gary Clayton Anderson, *Ethnic Cleansing and the Indian: The Crime That Should Haunt America* (Norman: University of Oklahoma Press, 2014), 21.

40. Anderson, *Ethnic Cleansing,* 4.

41. Anderson, *Ethnic Cleansing,* 10.

42. Anderson, *Ethnic Cleansing,* 341n17.

43. "Holocaust Deniers and Public Misinformation," *Holocaust Encyclopedia* (Washington, DC: U.S. Holocaust Memorial Museum), https://encyclopedia.ushmm.org/content/en/article/holocaust-deniers-and-public-misinformation (accessed July 7, 2021).

44. Anderson, *Ethnic Cleansing,* 11.

45. "Introduction to the Holocaust," *Holocaust Encyclopedia* (Washington, DC: U.S. Holocaust Memorial Museum), https://encyclopedia.ushmm.org/content/en/article/introduction-to-the-holocaust (accessed July 7, 2021).

46. Anderson, *Ethnic Cleansing,* 341n17.

47. "Frequently Asked Questions about the Holocaust for Educators," *Fundamentals of Teaching the Holocaust,* United States Holocaust Memorial Museum. Washington, DC. https://www.ushmm.org/teach/fundamentals/holocaust-questions (accessed May 4, 2022).

48. Adolf Hitler, *Mein Kampf* (New York: Reynal and Hitchcock, 1939), 220.

49. Peter d'Errico, "Jeffrey Amherst and Smallpox Blankets," http://people.umass.edu/derrico/amherst/lord_jeff.html.

50. Ian Kershaw, "Improvised Genocide? The Emergence of the 'Final Solution' in the 'Warthegau,'" *Transactions of the Royal Historical Society* 2 (1992): 51–78, doi:10.2307/3679099 (accessed July 7, 2021).

51. Kershaw, "Improvised Genocide" 61–62.

52. Anderson, *Ethnic Cleansing,* 8.

53. United Nations General Assembly, *Convention on the Prevention and Punishment of the Crime of Genocide,* 78 U.N.T.S. 277 (G.A. Resolution 260 A(III) of

December 9, 1948; entry into force on January 12, 1951, in accordance with Article XIII), Article II.

54. Public Law 95–608, 95 Congress, Session 2, An Act: To Establish Standards for the Placement of Indian Children in Foster or Adoptive Homes, to Prevent the Breakup of Indian Families, and for Other Purposes *U.S. Statutes at Large* 92, Main Section (1978): 3069–3079.

55. Kristina Bross, "'Come Over and Help Us': Reading Missing Literature," *Early American Literature* 38, no. 3 (2003): 395–400, doi:10.1353/eal.2003.0034, 398.

56. *Proceedings of the Twentieth Annual Meeting of the Lake Mohonk Conference of Friends of the Indian, 1902,* reported and edited by Isabel C. Barrows (New York: Lake Mohonk Conference, 1903), Fourth Session (Thursday Night, October 23, 1902), "Address by Col. R.H. Pratt," 134.

57. Captain Richard H. Pratt, "The Advantages of Mingling with Whites." *Proceedings of the Nineteenth Annual National Conference of Charities and Correction* (June 23–29, 1892), reported and edited by Isabel C. Barrows (Boston: George H. Ellis, 1892), 45–59.

58. Roosevelt, "Message of the President of the United States Communicated to the Two Houses of Congress at the Beginning of the First Session of the Fifty-Seventh Congress."

59. Gilbert King, "Geronimo's Appeal to Theodore Roosevelt," Smithsonian .com (November 9, 2012), https://www.smithsonianmag.com/history/geronimos -appeal-to-theodore-roosevelt-117859516/ (accessed May 28, 2019).

60. *Proceedings of the Twentieth Annual Meeting of the Lake Mohonk Conference of Friends of the Indian, 1902,* 134.

61. Naomi Schaefer Riley, *The New Trail of Tears: How Washington Is Destroying American Indians* (New York: London: Encounter Books, 2016).

62. "CERA—Citizens Equal Rights Alliance/CERF—Citizens Equal Rights Foundation," https://citizensalliance.org/ (accessed December 2, 2020).

63. See, for example, Graham Hughes, "Reparations for Blacks," *New York University Law Review* 43, no. 6 (December 1968): 1064.

64. Lewis Meriam, *The Problem of Indian Administration: Report of a Survey Made at the Request of Honorable Hubert Work, Secretary of the Interior, and Submitted to Him,* February 21, 1928 (Baltimore: Johns Hopkins University Press, 1928), viii.

65. Public Law 79–726 / Chapter 959, 79 Congress, Session 2, An Act: To Create an Indian Claims Commission, to Provide for the Powers, Duties and Functions Thereof, and for Other Purposes, *U.S. Statutes at Large* 60, Main Section (1946): 1049–1056.

66. Lynn Adams, Esq., special attorney for the Chickasaw Indians, Testimony on Creation of Indian Claims Commission, Hearings Before the House Committee on Indian Affairs (HRG-1945-INH-0002; 79th Cong., 1st Sess. 79, March 2, 1945. 8.

67. William Stigler, Congressman from Oklahoma, Testimony on Indian Claims Commission Act, Hearing before the Committee on Indian Affairs,

United States Senate. (HRG-1946-IAS-0001; 79th Congress, 2d Sess., June 1, 1946), 7.

68. *Pawnee Indian Tribe of Oklahoma v. United States,* 109 F. Supp. 860, 869 (Ct. Cl. 1953).

69. Harvey D. Rosenthal, *Their Day in Court: A History of the Indian Claims Commission,* Distinguished Studies in American Legal and Constitutional History (New York: Garland Pub, 1990), 168.

70. Richard W. Yarborough, Chairman; Jerome K. Kuykendall, Chairman; John T. Vance, Chairman; Brantley Blue, Chairman; Margaret H. Pierce, Chairman, House Documents, Vol. 21, *U.S. Indian Claims Commission, Final Report* (H. Doc. 96–383; 96th Congress, 2d Sess.) (Washington, DC: Government Printing Office, April 15, 1980).

71. Meriam, *The Problem of Indian Administration,* 19.

72. Henry Martin Jackson, Democratic Party representative from Washington, *Creating an Indian Claims Commission,* Committee of the Whole House, House Committee on Indian Affairs, House (10936 H.rp.1466), 79th Congress, 1st Sess. (December 20, 1945). 10, 3.

73. "Statement by the President Upon Signing Bill Creating the Indian Claims Commission," August 13, 1946, *Public Papers,* Truman, 1946, 414. Quoted in David E. Wilkins, "Native Peoples and American Indian Affairs During the Truman Presidency," in *Native Americans and the Legacy of Harry S. Truman,* Brian Hosmer, ed. (Kirksville, MO: Truman State University Press, 2010), 71.

74. "Veto of Bill Establishing a Program in Aid of the Navajo and Hopi Indians," October 17, 1949, in *Public Papers,* Truman, 1949, 516. Quoted in David E. Wilkins, "Native Peoples and American Indian Affairs During the Truman Presidency," in *Native Americans and the Legacy of Harry S. Truman,* Brian Hosmer, ed., (Kirksville, MO: Truman State University Press, 2010), 70.

75. *Navajo Tribe of Indians v. State of N.M.,* 809 F.2d 1455, 1461 (10th Cir. 1987).

76. *Western Shoshone Legal Defense & Education Association v. United States,* 531 F.2d 495 (Ct. Cl. 1976).

77. Elmer R. Rusco, "Historic Change in Western Shoshone Country: The Establishment of the Western Shoshone National Council and Traditionalist Land Claims," *American Indian Quarterly* 16, no. 3 (1992): 345–347, et seq. doi:10.2307/1185796.

78. Public Law 108–270, 108 Congress Session 1, Western Shoshone Claims Distribution Act, *United States Statutes at Large* 118, Main Section (2004): 805–811.

79. Rosenthal, *Their Day,* 94.

80. David E. Wilkins, "Native Peoples and American Indian Affairs During the Truman Presidency," in Brian Hosner, ed., *Native Americans and the Legacy of Harry S. Truman* (Kirksville, MO: Truman State University Press, 2010), 71.

81. House Concurrent Resolution 108, *U.S. Statutes at Large* 67 (1953): B132.

82. Public Law 83–280 / Chapter 505, 83 Congress, Session 1, An Act: To Confer Jurisdiction on the States of California, Minnesota, Nebraska, Oregon, and Wisconsin, with Respect to Criminal Offenses and Civil Causes of Action

Committed or Arising on Indian Reservations within such States, and for Other Purposes," *U.S. Statutes at Large* 67 (1953): 588–590.

83. Public Law 84–959 / Chapter 930, 84 Congress, Session 2, An Act: Relative to Employment for Certain Adult Indians on or near Indian Reservations, *U.S. Statutes at Large* 70, Main Section (1956): 986–987.

84. David E. Wilkins, *American Indian Sovereignty and the U.S. Supreme Court: The Masking of Justice* (Austin: University of Texas Press, 1997), 167.

## Chapter 3: Federal Anti-Indian Law

1. Robert M. Cover, "Violence and the Word," *Yale Law Journal* 95, no. 8 (July 1986): 1601–1630., 1601, 1607n16.

2. *Warren Trading Post Co. v. Arizona State Tax Commission*, 380 U.S. 685, 686 (1965).

3. *Warren Trading Post,* at 690.

4. *Warren Trading Post,* at 691.

5. *Warren Trading Post,* at 691.

6. *Warren Trading Post,* at 686, 688 (respectively).

7. *Menominee Tribe of Indians v. United States*, 391 U.S. 404 (1968).

8. The Menominee Termination Act was repealed in 1973. Public Law 93–197, 93 Congress, Session 1, An Act: To Repeal the Act Terminating Federal Supervision over the Property and Members of the Menominee Indian Tribe of Wisconsin; to Reinstitute the Menominee Indian Tribe of Wisconsin as a Federally Recognized Sovereign Indian Tribe; and to Restore to the Menominee Tribe of Wisconsin Those Federal Services Furnished to American Indians Because of Their Status as American Indians; and for Other Purposes, *U.S. Statutes at Large* 87, Main Section (1973): 770–774.

9. *Menominee Tribe of Indians v. United States,* at 413 (citing 100 Congressional Record 8538).

10. "Menomonees: Treaty with the Menomonees," *U.S. Statutes at Large* 10, Main Section (1854): 1064–1069.

11. Senator Arthur Watkins. "On the Signing of the Menominee Indian Bill," Congressional Record 100 (1954): 8537, 8538.

12. *Menominee Tribe of Indians v. United States,* at 411.

13. Felix S. Cohen, *Handbook of Federal Indian Law: With Reference Tables and Index.* (Washington, DC: U.S. Government Printing Office, 1942).

14. Nathan R. Margold, "Introduction." in Felix S. Cohen, *Handbook of Federal Indian Law: With Reference Tables and Index* (Washington, DC: U.S. Government Printing Office, 1942), VIII.

15. Robert A. Heinlein, *Stranger in a Strange Land* (New York: Putnam, 1961), 40–41 (emphasis in original).

16. National Humanities Center. Council of Castile (Spain), *Requerimiento,* 1510. http://nationalhumanitiescenter.org/pds/amerbegin/contact/text7/requirement.pdf (accessed February 14, 2016).

17. *City of Sherrill v. Oneida Indian Nation,* 544 U.S. 197, 204n1 (2005).

18. *Tee-Hit-Ton Indians v. United States.*

19. Nomaan Merchant and John L. Mone, "Biden Is Facing High Hopes, Tough Choices on Border Wall," Associated Press (December 3, 2020), https://apnews.com/article/joe-biden-donald-trump-us-news-coronavirus-pandemic-texas-7247dce15860a07bf704aaa59aed1acc (accessed July 20, 2021).

20. G. L. Ulmen, "Translator's Introduction," in Carl Schmitt and G. L. Ulmen, *The Nomos of the Earth in the International Law of the Jus Publicum Europaeum* (New York: Telos Press, 2003), 13. (Quoting Carl Schmitt, "Das Rheinland als Objekt interationaler Politik" (1925), in Carl Schmitt, *Positionen und Begriffe im Kampf mit Weimar-Genf-Versailles, 1923–1939* (1940), 2nd ed. (Berlin: Duncker & Humblot, 1988), 27.)

21. Anna Jurkevics, "Hannah Arendt Reads Carl Schmitt's The Nomos of the Earth: A Dialogue on Law and Geopolitics from the Margins." *European Journal of Political Theory* 16, no. 3 (July 2017): 345–366, 354.

22. *Johnson v. McIntosh.*

23. Lindsay Gordon Robertson, *Conquest by Law: How the Discovery of America Dispossessed Indigenous Peoples of Their Lands* (Oxford and New York: Oxford University Press, 2005), xi.

24. *Johnson v. McIntosh,* at 543–545.

25. *Johnson v. McIntosh,* at 563.

26. *Johnson v. McIntosh,* at 551.

27. *Johnson v. McIntosh,* at 567.

28. *Johnson v. McIntosh,* at 568.

29. *Johnson v. McIntosh,* at 572.

30. *Johnson v. McIntosh,* at 567.

31. *Johnson v. McIntosh,* at 543.

32. *Johnson v. McIntosh,* at 573.

33. *Johnson v. McIntosh,* at 573.

34. John Cotton, *Gods Promise to His Plantations as it was Delivered in a Sermon, by John Cotton, B.D. and Preacher of Gods Word in Boston.* London, Printed by William Jones for John Bellamy, and are to be sold at the three Golden Lyons by the Royall Exchange, 1634.

35. "Twenty-First Congress—First Session—Debates in the Senate," *Register of Debates in Congress* 6 (1830): 333.

36. *Johnson v. McIntosh,* at 576–577 (emphasis in original).

37. *Johnson v. McIntosh,* at 576–577.

38. *Johnson v. McIntosh,* at 588.

39. *Johnson v. McIntosh,* at 591–592.

40. William Blackstone, *The Oxford Edition of Blackstone's: Commentaries on the Laws of England: Book II: Of the Rights of Things,* edited by Simon Stern (Oxford: Oxford University Press, 2016), Chapter the Thirteenth, "Of the Title to Things Real, in General," 196.

41. Kent McNeil, *Common Law Aboriginal Title* (Oxford, UK: Clarendon Press, 1989), 218.

42. *Ricard v. Williams*, 20 U.S. 59, 105 (1822).

43. *Willcox v. Stroup*, 467 F.3d 409, 412 (2006).

44. Ken MacMillan, *Sovereignty and Possession in the English New World: The Legal Foundations of Empire, 1576–1640* (Cambridge: Cambridge University Press, 2006), 48.

45. *Johnson v. McIntosh*, at 587–588.

46. McNeil, *Common Law*, 92.

47. McNeil, *Common Law*, 220.

48. McNeil, *Common Law*, 238.

49. McNeil, *Common Law*, 301.

50. McNeil, *Common Law*, 217.

51. *Johnson v. McIntosh*, at 603.

52. Bens, *The Indigenous Paradox*, 24.

53. *Johnson v. McIntosh*, at 574.

54. Bens, *The Indigenous Paradox*, 15–16.

55. Steven Paul McSloy, "Back to the Future: Native American Sovereignty In the 21st Century," *New York University Review of Law & Social Change* 20, no. 2 (1992–1993): 254.

56. Robertson, *Conquest by Law*, xiii, 4.

57. Robertson, *Conquest by Law*, xiii.

58. Jean Edward Smith, *John Marshall: Definer of a Nation* (New York: H. Holt & Co, 1996).

59. Eric Cheyfitz, "Savage Law: The Plot against American Indians in *Johnson and Graham's Lessee v. M'Intosh* and *The Pioneers*," in Amy Kaplan and Donald E. Pease, eds., *Cultures of United States Imperialism* (Durham, NC: Duke University Press, 1993), 117–118.

60. *Lone Wolf v. Hitchcock*, at 564–566.

61. *Sioux Nation of Indians v. United States*, 601 F.2d 1157, 1173 (Ct. Cl. 1979), *aff'd*, 448 U.S. 371 (1980) (Nichols, concurring).

62. *Oliphant v. Suquamish Indian Tribe*, 435 U.S. 191, 206 (1978).

63. Mark Savage, "Native Americans and the Constitution: The Original Understanding," 16 *American Indian Law Review* 57 (1991), 116.

64. Robertson, *Conquest by Law*, xiii, xi.

65. *Johnson v. McIntosh*, at 586.

66. Smith, *John Marshall*, 75n.

67. Walter R. Echo-Hawk, *In the Courts of the Conqueror: The 10 Worst Indian Law Cases Ever Decided* (Golden, CO: Fulcrum Publishing, 2010, 70).

68. Echo-Hawk, *In the Courts of the Conqueror*, 61–62.

69. *Fletcher v. Peck*, 10 U.S. 87 (1810).

70. Echo-Hawk, *In the Courts of the Conqueror*, 59.

71. Francis Newton Thorpe, "The First Charter of Virginia; April 10, 1606," in *The Federal and State Constitutions Colonial Charters, and Other Organic Laws of the States, Territories, and Colonies Now or Heretofore Forming the United States of America*, Vol. 7, 3783 (Washington, DC: Government Printing Office, 1909. https://

avalon.law.yale.edu/17th_century/va01.asp (accessed May 10, 2022) (emphasis in original).

72. McNeil, *Common Law*, 239 (quoting *Pen v. Lord Baltimore*, 27 E.R. 847 (1745) Ridgeway Temp. Hardwicke 332).

73. Swindler, "First and Second Charters," 2.

74. *Johnson v. McIntosh*, at 586.

75. Colin G. Calloway, *The Victory with No Name: The Native American Defeat of the First American Army* (Oxford: Oxford University Press, 2014), 24–25, 26 (respectively).

76. Joel R. Paul, *Without Precedent: John Marshall and His Times* (New York: Riverhead Books, 2018), 474n27.

77. Emer de Vattel, *The Law of Nations; or Principles of the Law of Nature: Applied to the Conduct and Affairs of Nations and Sovereigns* (London: J. Newbery, J. Richardson, S. Crowder, T. Caslon, T. Longman, B. Law, J. Fuller, J. Coote, and G. Kearsly, 1759), Book III, Chapter III (Of the just causes of war), § 41.

78. *Cherokee Nation v. Georgia*, 30 U.S. 1 (1831).

79. *Cherokee Nation v. Georgia*, at 17.

80. Georgia General Assembly, "AN ACT to add the Territory lying within the limits of this State, and occupied by the Cherokee Indians, to the counties of Carroll, DeKalb, Gwinnett, Hall and Habersham; and to extend the laws of this State over the same, and for other purposes" (December 20, 1828), *Acts of the General Assembly of the state of Georgia, passed in Milledgeville at an annual session in November and December, 1828 [volume 1], 1828.* https://dlg.usg.edu/record/dlg_zlgl_8970609#text.

81. Georgia General Assembly, "AN ACT to add the Territory lying within the chartered limits of Georgia, and now in the occupancy of the Cherokee Indians, to the counties of Carroll, DeKalb, Gwinnett, Hall and Habersham, and to extend the laws of this State over the same, and to annual all laws and ordinances made by the Cherokee nation of Indians, and to provide for the compensation of officers serving legal process in said Territory, and to regulate the testimony of Indians, and to repeal the ninth section of the act of eighteen hundred and twenty-eight, upon this subject (December 19, 1829), *Acts of the General Assembly of the state of Georgia, passed in Milledgeville at an annual session in November and December, 1829 [volume 1]. 1829/1831.* https://dlg.usg.edu/record/dlg_zlgl_9655783#text.

82. "Georgia Cession (7-1)," 1 *American State Papers: Public Lands* 28 (1801), 113–114.

83. Bens, *The Indigenous Paradox*, 54.

84. Bens, *The Indigenous Paradox*, 57.

85. Bens, *The Indigenous Paradox*, 54.

86. Glen Coulthard, "From Wards of the State to Subjects of Recognition? Marx, Indigenous Peoples, and the Politics of Dispossession in Denendeh," in Audra Simpson and Andrea Smith, eds., *Theorizing Native Studies* (Durham, NC, and London: Duke University Press, 2014), 74.

87. *Cherokee Nation v. Georgia*, at 3.

88. Richard Peters, *The case of the Cherokee Nation against the State of Georgia: argued and determined at the Supreme Court of the United States, January Term, 1831: with an appendix* (Philadelphia: Grigg, 1831), 4, 5, 110.

89. *Cherokee Nation v. Georgia*, at 15.

90. *Cherokee Nation v. Georgia*, at 16.

91. *Cherokee Nation v. Georgia*, at 16.

92. *Cherokee Nation v. Georgia*, at 17.

93. *Cherokee Nation v. Georgia*, at 20.

94. *Cherokee Nation v. Georgia*, at 2.

95. *Johnson v. McIntosh*, at 592.

96. *Cherokee Nation v. Georgia*, at 17.

97. Peters, *The case of the Cherokee Nation,* 39–40.

98. Stephen Breyer, "The Cherokee Indians and the Supreme Court," *"From the Society." Georgia Historical Quarterly* 87, no. 3/4 (2003): 416.

99. Charles Alan Wright, *The Law of Federal Courts* 60 (5th ed. 1994), quoted in *Black's law Dictionary* (7th ed., 1999), "case-or-controversy requirement," 207.

100. James E. Pfander, "Rethinking the Supreme Court's Original Jurisdiction in State-Party Cases," *California Law Review* 82, no. 3 (May 1994): 560.

101. Pfander, "Rethinking": 605.

102. C. Wright, A. Miller, and E. Cooper, *Federal Practice & Procedure: Jurisdiction 2d,* §§ 4043, 4049 (1988), quoted in Vicki C. Jackson, "The Supreme Court, the Eleventh Amendment, and State Sovereign Immunity," *Yale Law Journal* 98, no. 1 (November 1988): 123n493.

103. *Cohens v. State of Virginia,* 19 U.S. 264, 393 (1821).

104. *Cohens v. State of Virginia*.

105. *Cohens v. State of Virginia,* at 395.

106. *Cohens v. State of Virginia,* at 386.

107. *Cohens v. State of Virginia,* at 391.

108. *Cherokee Nation v. Georgia*, at 5, 20 (respectively).

109. *Cohens v. State of Virginia,* at 404.

110. Pfander, "Rethinking": 644, quoting David P. Currie, "The Constitution in the Supreme Court: The Powers of the Federal Courts, 1801–1835," *University of Chicago Law Review* 49, no. 3 (Summer 1982): 646–724.

111. Mark Rifkin, *Manifesting America: The Imperial Construction of U.S. National Space* (New York: Oxford University Press, 2009), 51.

112. Pfander, "Rethinking": 562.

113. Bens, *Indigenous Paradox*, 64.

114. Bens, *Indigenous Paradox*, 68.

115. Vattel, *The Law of Nations*.

116. Vattel, *The Law of Nations*, Book I, Chapter I, § 6.

117. Vattel, *The Law of Nations*, Book I, Chapter I, § 4.

118. *Cherokee Nation v. Georgia*, at 53.

119. *Cherokee Nation v. Georgia*, at 53–54.

120. *Cherokee Nation v. Georgia*, at 54.

121. Vattel, *The Law of Nations*, Book II, Chapter I, § 7.

122. *Cherokee Nation v. Georgia*, at 70.

123. *Worcester v. Georgia*, 31 U.S. 515 (1832).

124. Craig Joyce, "The Rise of the Supreme Court Reporter: An Institutional Perspective on Marshall Court Ascendancy," *Michigan Law Review* 83, no. 5 (March 1985): 1292.

125. *Worcester v. Georgia*, at 538.

126. *Worcester v. Georgia*, at 536.

127. *Worcester v. Georgia*, at 541.

128. *Worcester v. Georgia*, at 542–543.

129. See, for example, Cathal J. Nolan, *The Age of Wars of Religion, 1000–1650: An Encyclopedia of Global Warfare and Civilization*, Greenwood Encyclopedias of Modern World Wars (Westport, CT: Greenwood Press, 2006. 2 vols.).

130. See Charles R. Young, *The Royal Forests of Medieval England. The Middle Ages*. Philadelphia: University of Pennsylvania Press, 1979.

131. MacMillan, *Sovereignty and Possession*, 116–117.

132. *Worcester v. Georgia*, at 543.

133. *Worcester v. Georgia*, at 543.

134. *Johnson v. McIntosh*, at 591 (emphasis added).

135. *Worcester v. Georgia*, at 573.

136. *Cherokee Nation v. Georgia*, at 573.

137. Robertson, *Conquest by Law*, 133.

138. *Johnson v. McIntosh*, at 603 (emphasis added).

139. Paul Finkelman, *Supreme Injustice: Slavery in the Nation's Highest Court*, The Nathan I. Huggins Lectures (Cambridge, MA: Harvard University Press, 2018), 109.

140. Rifkin, *Manifesting America*, 51.

141. *Clark v. Smith*, 38 US 195, 201 (1839).

142. *Johnson v. McIntosh*, at 586.

143. Eric Kades, "History and Interpretation of the Great Case of Johnson v. M'Intosh," *Law and History Review* 19, no. 1 (Spring 2001): 69.

144. Chapter 130, 37 Congress, Session 2, An Act: Donating Public Lands to the Several States and Territories Which May Provide Colleges for the Benefit of Agriculture and the Mechanic Arts, *U.S. Statutes at Large* 12, Main Section (1862): 503–505.

145. "An Audacious Act: How a High School Dropout Helped Educate America," New England Public Radio. Amherst, MA. November 1, 2013. https://web .archive.org/web/20131101085754/http://nepr.net/morrill/. (accessed July 8, 2021).

146. Robert Lee and Tristan Ahtone. "Land-Grab Universities," *High Country News*. March 30, 2020, https://www.hcn.org/issues/52.4/indigenous-affairs -education-land-grab-universities (accessed 8 July 2021).

147. Kades, "History and Interpretation of the Great Case of Johnson v. M'Intosh": 69.

148. James Warren Springer, "American Indians and the Law of Real Property in Colonial New England," *American Journal of Legal History* 30, no. 1 (January 1986): 35.

149. Stuart Banner, "Conquest by Contract: Wealth Transfer and Land Market Structure in Colonial New Zealand," *Law & Society Review* 34, no. 1 (2000): 58.

150. Banner, "Conquest by Contract": 60–61.

151. *Worcester v. Georgia*, at 561.

152. Carole E. Goldberg and Kevin K. Washburn, "The Indian Law Canon as Narrative: Stories of Legal Strategy and Native Persistence," in Carole E. Goldberg, Kevin Washburn, and Philip P. Frickey, eds., *Indian Law Stories* (New York: Foundation Press/Thomson Reuters, 2011), 15.

153. *Lone Wolf v. Hitchcock,* at 565.

154. Barry Popik, "The Large Print Giveth and the Small Print Taketh Away" (March 30, 2011), https://www.barrypopik.com/index.php/new_york_city /entry/the_large_print_giveth_and_the_small_print_taketh_away (accessed June 1, 2021).

155. *Streich v. General Motors Corp.*, 5 Ill. App. 2d 485, 500 (Ill. App. Ct. 1955).

156. Stroud Francis Charles Milsom, *A Natural History of the Common Law,* James S. Carpentier Lectures (New York: Columbia University Press, 2003), xxi.

157. Claudio Saunt, *Unworthy Republic: The Dispossession of Native Americans and the Road to Indian Territory* (New York: W. W. Norton & Company, 2020), 163.

158. *Worcester v. Georgia*, at 580, 581.

159. C. P. Nettles, *The Emergence of a National Economy 1775–1815* (New York: Holt, Reinhart and Winston), 1962, quoted in Jack P. Greene and J. R. Pole, eds., *The Blackwell Encyclopedia of the American Revolution* (Cambridge, MA: Blackwell Reference, 1991), 370.

160. Robertson, *Conquest by Law*, 92.

161. Robertson, *Conquest by Law*, 86.

162. Henry J. Abraham, *Justices and Presidents: A Political History of Appointments to the Supreme Court.* 3rd ed. (New York: Oxford University Press, 1992), 81, 412–414.

163. *Fletcher v. Peck*, 10 U.S. 87, 142–43 (1810).

164. *Worcester v. Georgia*, at 557.

165. *American State Papers,* House of Representatives, 17th Congress, 1st Session. Indians Affairs: Volume 2, Page 259, No. 177. *Extinguishment of the Indian title of land in Georgia* (1822), https://memory.loc.gov/cgi-bin/ampage?collId=llsp&fileName=008 /llsp008.db&recNum=266 (accessed July 8, 2021).

166. *American State Papers, Extinguishment of the Indian title of land in Georgia,* 260.

167. *American State Papers*, House of Representatives, 18th Congress, 1st Session. Indians Affairs: Volume 2, Page 491, No. 205. *Extinguishment of Indian title to lands in Georgia* (1823), https://memory.loc.gov/cgi-bin/ampage?collId=llsp&fileName=008 /llsp008.db&recNum=498 (accessed July 8, 2021).

168. Edwin A. Miles, "After John Marshall's Decision: *Worcester v. Georgia* and the Nullification Crisis." *Journal of Southern History* 39 (4) (1973): 519–544, doi:10.2307/2205966.

169. Chapter 85, 15 Congress, Session 2, An Act: Making Provision for the Civilization of the Indian Tribes Adjoining the Frontier Settlements, *U.S. Statutes at Large* 3, Main Section (1819): 516–517.

170. *Worcester v. Georgia*, at 557.

171. *Worcester v. Georgia*, at 520–521.

172. Chapter 148, 21 Congress, Session 1, An Act: To Provide for an Exchange of Lands with the Indians Residing in Any of the States or Territories, and for Their Removal West of the River Mississippi, *U.S. Statutes at Large* 4, Main Section (1830): 411–413.

173. MacMillan, *Sovereignty and Possession,* 6 (emphasis in original).

174. *Nevada v. Hicks*, 533 U.S. 353 (2001).

175. *Nevada v. Hicks*, at 361–362.

176. *Nevada v. Hicks*, at 359.

## Chapter 4: The Domination Matrix

1. B. A. Hinsdale, *The Right of Discovery* (Columbus, OH: Hann & Adair, printers, 1888), 27.

2. Carl Schmitt and G. L. Ulmen, *The Nomos of the Earth in the International Law of the Jus Publicum Europaeum* (New York: Telos Press, 2003), 45.

3. William C. Canby, *American Indian Law in a Nutshell,* 2nd ed., Nutshell Series (St. Paul, MN: West Publishing, 1988); quoted in *United States v. Lara*, 541 U.S. 193, 200 (2004).

4. David H. Getches, "Book Survey: The Unsettling of the West: How Indians Got the Best Water Rights," *Michigan Law Review* 99, no. 6 (May 2001): 1486.

5. Jessica A. Shoemaker, "Complexity's Shadow: American Indian Property, Sovereignty, and the Future," *Michigan Law Review* 115, no. 4 (February 2017): 503–504.

6. *Native Village of Venetie I.R.A. Council v. State of Alaska,* 944 F.2d 548, 553 (9th Cir. 1991).

7. *United States v. Kagama,* 118 U.S. 375, 381 (1886).

8. Frank Pommersheim, *Braid of Feathers: American Indian Law and Contemporary Tribal Life* (Berkeley: University of California Press, 1995), 49.

9. Philip P. Frickey, "(Native) American Exceptionalism in Federal Public Law," *Harvard Law Review* 119, no. 2 (December 2005): 435.

10. Frickey, "(Native) American Exceptionalism": 433, 434.

11. Carl Schmitt, *Political Theology: Four Chapters on the Concept of Sovereignty* (Chicago: University of Chicago Press, 2005), 5.

12. Schmitt, *Political Theology,* 12.

13. *Johnson v. McIntosh*, at 591, 592.

14. Thomas Hofweber, "Logic and Ontology," in *Stanford Encyclopedia of Philosophy* (spring 2021 ed.), Edward N. Zalta (ed.), https://plato.stanford.edu/archives/spr2021/entries/logic-ontology/.

15. Vizenor, *Manifest Manners*, 10–11.

16. Thomas R. Gruber, "Ontology," in Ling Liu and M. Tamer Özsu, eds., *Encyclopedia of Database Systems* Springer Reference (New York: Springer, 2009); see https://tomgruber.org/writing/ontology-definition-2007.htm (accessed March 31, 2021).

17. Thomas R. Gruber, "A Translation Approach to Portable Ontology Specifications," *Knowledge Acquisition* 5, no. 2 (1993), 199 (emphasis added); https://www.sciencedirect.com/science/article/pii/S1042814383710083.

18. Gruber, "A Translation Approach": 199.

19. *Cherokee Nation v. Georgia*, at 16.

20. Frickey, "(Native) American Exceptionalism": 437.

21. Frickey, "(Native) American Exceptionalism": 437–438.

22. Gruber, "A Translation Approach": 199 (emphasis on "presumed to exist" added).

23. Bethany R. Berger, "In the Name of the Child: Race, Gender, and Economics in Adoptive Couple v. Baby Girl," *Florida Law Review* 67, no. 1 (January 2015): 359.

24. Joseph William Singer, "Sovereignty and Property," *Northwestern University Law Review* 86, no. 1 (1991–1992): 42.

25. Singer, "Sovereignty and Property": 42.

26. Ball, "Constitution, Court, Indian Tribes": 61.

27. Frickey, "(Native) American Exceptionalism," 487.

28. Roberto Farneti, "Paradoxes of Normativity: On Carl Schmitt's Normative Scepticism," *History of Political Thought* 34, no. 1 (2013): 119, http://www.jstor.org/stable/26225867.

29. *Johnson v. McIntosh*, at 591, 592.

30. Schmitt, *Political Theology*, 12.

31. Schmitt, *Political Theology*, 13.

32. Mark Rifkin, "Indigenizing Agamben: Rethinking Sovereignty in Light of the 'Peculiar' Status of Native Peoples." *Cultural Critique*, no. 73 (September 2009): 90.

33. Daniel Philpott, "Sovereignty," *Stanford Encyclopedia of Philosophy* (fall 2020 ed.), Edward N. Zalta (ed.), https://plato.stanford.edu/archives/fall2020/entries/sovereignty/.

34. Joan Cocks, *On Sovereignty and Other Political Delusions: Theory for a Global Age* (London: Bloomsbury, 2014), 3.

35. Luke Sunderland, *Rebel Barons: Resisting Royal Power in Medieval Culture* (Oxford: Oxford University Press, 2017), 21. 91.

36. Bens, *The Indigenous Paradox,* 7.

37. Bens, *The Indigenous Paradox*, 2.

38. Sarah Jane Gillett and Casey Ross-Petherick, "Effectively Representing Indian Tribes in Tribal-State Law Matters," in *Emerging Issues in Tribal-State Relations* (Eagan, MN: Thomson Reuters/Aspatore. 2013), WL 2136510, at 1.

39. Schmitt, *Political Theology*, 12.

40. *United States v. Blackfeet Tribe*, 364 F. Supp. 192, 194 (1973), adhered to on rehearing, 369 F. Supp. 562 (1973).

41. *United States v. Blackfeet Tribe*, at 195.

42. *United States v. Blackfeet Tribe*, at 195.

43. *United States v. Blackfeet Tribe of Blackfeet Indian Reservation*, 369 F. Supp. 562, 564–565 (1973).

44. N. Bruce Duthu, "Holding a Great Vision: Engaging the Jurisprudential Voice of Tribal Courts" [book review of *Braid of Feathers: American Indian Law and Contemporary Tribal Life*, by Frank Pommersheim (Berkeley and Los Angeles: University of California Press], *North Dakota Law Review* 71, no. 4 (1995): 1129, 1144.

45. Peters, *The case of the Cherokee Nation*, 57.

46. Schmitt, *Political Theology*, 6.

47. *Conners v. United States*, 33 Ct. Cl. 317, 318, 321 (1898), *aff'd*, 180 U.S. 271 (1901).

48. *Conners v. United States*, at 323.

49. *Conners v. United States*, at 320.

50. *Conners v. United States*, at 323–324.

51. *Conners v. United States*, at 324.

52. Schmitt, *Political Theology*, 6.

53. Giorgio Agamben, *Sovereign Power and Bare Life* (Stanford, CA: Stanford University Press, 1998), 17.

54. Frickey, "(Native) American Exceptionalism," 434.

55. Gruber, "A Translation Approach": 199.

56. Agamben, *Sovereign Power*, 17.

57. Agamben, *Sovereign Power*, 27.

58. Giorgio Agamben, *The Omnibus Homo Sacer*, Meridian, Crossing Aesthetics (Stanford, CA: Stanford University Press, 2017), 11.

59. Rifkin, "Indigenizing Agamben," 95.

60. Rifkin, "Indigenizing Agamben," 91.

61. Schmitt, *Political Theology*, 15.

62. Agamben, *Sovereign Power*, 16.

63. *United States v. Johnson*, 637 F.2d 1224, 1244 (9th Cir. 1980).

64. *United States v. Kagama*, 118 U.S. 375, 379–380 (1886).

65. *Blatchford v. Native Village of Noatak & Circle Village*, 501 U.S. 775, 782 (1991).

66. *Idaho v. Coeur d'Alene Tribe*, 521 U.S. 261 (1997).

67. *Idaho v. Coeur d'Alene Tribe*, at 268–269 (emphasis added).

68. Schmitt, *Political Theology*, 15.

69. *United States v. Alcea Band of Tillamooks*, 329 U.S. 40, 54 (1946).

70. *Delaware Tribal Business Committee v. Weeks*, 430 U.S. 73, 84 (1977).

71. *Tee-Hit-Ton Indians v. United States*, 348 U.S. 272, 282 (1955).

72. *Delaware Tribal Business Committee v. Weeks*, at 84.

73. Robert J. Miller, "The Doctrine of Discovery in American Indian Law," *Idaho Law Review* 42, no. 1 (2005): 105.

74. "Sioux Indians: Treaty between the United States of America and different tribes of Sioux Indians," *U.S. Statutes at Large* 15, no. Main Section (1868): 635–649.

75. *United States v. 2,005.32 Acres of Land, More or Less, Situate in Corson County, South Dakota; and Sioux Indians of Standing Rock Reservation, et al., and Unknown Owners*, 160 F. Supp. 193 (1958), vacated and remanded *sub nom. United States of America v. Sioux Indians of Standing Rock Reservation*, 259 F.2d 271 (8th Cir. 1958).

76. *United States v. 2,005.32 Acres of Land*, at 195–196.

77. *United States v. 2,005.32 Acres of Land*, at 195–196.

78. *United States v. 2,005.32 Acres of Land*, at 195–196.

79. *United States v. 2,005.32 Acres of Land*, at 195–196.

80. *Alice in Wonderland* (film), adaptation of Lewis Carrol's *The Adventures of Alice in Wonderland* and *Through the Looking Glass* (Walt Disney Animation Studios and Walt Disney Productions,1951). See "Disney Movie Script," Alice-in-Wonderland.net (blog), https://www.alice-in-wonderland.net/resources/chapters-script/disney-movie-script/ (accessed July 8, 2021).

81. Schmitt, *Political Theology*, 15.

82. *United States v. 2,005.32 Acres*, at 199.

83. *United States v. 2,005.32 Acres*, at 199.

84. Public Law 85–915, 85 Congress, Session 2, An Act: To Provide for the Acquisition of Lands by the United States Required for the Reservoir Created by the Construction of Oahe Dam on the Missouri River and for Rehabilitation of the Indians of the Standing Rock Sioux Reservation in South Dakota and North Dakota, and for Other Purposes, *U.S. Statutes at Large* 72, Main Section (1958): 1762–1766.

85. *United States of America v. Sioux Indians of Standing Rock Reservation*, 259 F.2d 271 (8th Cir. 1958).

86. *Oahe Dam Act*, section 5.

87. Wilkins, *American Indian Sovereignty and the U.S. Supreme Court*, 2.

88. Schmitt, *Political Theology*, 12.

89. Eric Cheyfitz and Shari M. Huhndorf, "Genocide by Other Means: U.S. Federal Indian Law and Violence against Native Women in Louise Erdrich's The Round House," in Elizabeth S. Anker and Bernadette Meyler (eds.), *New Directions in Law and Literature* (New York: Oxford University Press, 2017), 267.

90. Matthew L.M. Fletcher, "Supreme Court and the Rule of Law: Case Studies in Indian Law," *Federal Lawyer* 55, no. 3 (March–April 2008): 26–33.

91. Fletcher, "Supreme Court": 31.

92. Fletcher, "Supreme Court": 27.

93. Fletcher, "Supreme Court": 27.

94. Fletcher, "Supreme Court": 28.

95. Fletcher, "Supreme Court": 30.

96. Fletcher, "Supreme Court": 27.

97. Fletcher, "Supreme Court": 32.

98. Ball, "Constitution, Court": 61.

99. Agamben, *The Omnibus Homo Sacer*, 20.

100. *U.S. Constitution*, Article VI, cl. 2.

101. Agamben, *The Omnibus Homo Sacer*, 20.

102. Schmitt, *Nomos*, 45, 48.

103. Joseph Story, *Commentaries on the Constitution of the United States: With a Preliminary Review of the Constitutional History of the Colonies and States, Before the Adoption of the Constitution* (Boston: Charles C. Little and James Brown, 1851), Volume I, Book I, "History of the Colonies," Chapter I, "Origin of the Title to Territory of the Colonies," §§1–812, pp. 3–4.

104. Story, *Commentaries on the Constitution of the United States*, Volume I, Book I, Chapter I, §§ 2–3, p. 5.

105. Story, *Commentaries on the Constitution of the United States*, Volume I, Book I, Chapter I, § 5, p. 6.

106. Story, *Commentaries on the Constitution of the United States*, Volume I, Book I, Chapter XVI, "General Review of the Colonies," § 152, p. 101.

107. Story, *Commentaries on the Constitution of the United States*, Volume I, Book I, Chapter I, § 8, p. 7.

108. Papal Encyclicals, *Inter Caetera,* May 4, 1493, https://www.papalencyclicals.net/alex06/alex06inter.htm (accessed December 13, 2019).

109. Story, *Commentaries on the Constitution of the United States*, Volume I, Book I, § 5, pp. 5–6.

110. Story, *Commentaries on the Constitution of the United States*, Volume I, Book I, Chapter XVI, "General Review of the Colonies," § 153, 101–102.

111. MacMillan, *Sovereignty and Possession*, 63.

112. Hinsdale, *The Right of Discovery*, 27.

112. Hinsdale, *The Right of Discovery*, 28.

113. Schmitt, *Nomos*, 105.

114. Story, *Commentaries*, Volume I, Book I, *History of the Colonies,* Chapter XVI, "General Review of the Colonies," §153, 102.

115. Steven Newcomb, *Pagans in the Promised Land: Decoding the Doctrine of Christian Discovery* (Golden, CO: Chicago Review Press, 2008), 1.

116. Reid Peyton Chambers, "Judicial Enforcement of the Federal Trust Responsibility to Indians," *Stanford Law Review* 27, no. 5 (May 1975): 1213.

117. "Rethinking the Trust Doctrine in Federal Indian Law," *Harvard Law Review* 98, no. 2 (December 1984): 423.

118. Senator Daniel K. Inouye (D–HI), Indian Self-Determination and Education Assistance Act Amendments of 1987, Senate Select Committee on Indian Affairs (S. Rpt. 100–274). 100th Congress, 1sr Sess. (December 22, 1987), 3.

119. Felix S. Cohen, Rennard Strickland, and Charles F. Wilkinson, *Felix S. Cohen's Handbook of Federal Indian Law* (Charlottesville, VA: Michie, 1982), 221.

120. *Cherokee Nation v. Georgia*, at 17.

121. Ball, "Constitution, Court": 63.

122. Ball, "Constitution, Court": 62.

123. Ball, "Constitution, Court": 61.

124. *United States v. Jicarilla Apache Nation,* 564 U.S. 162, 170–173 (2011).

125. *United States v. Jicarilla Apache Nation*, at 174.

126. *United States v. Jicarilla Apache Nation*, at 174.

127. *Meinhard v. Salmon*, 249 N.Y. 458, 464, 164 N.E. 545, 546 (1928).

128. *United States v. Jicarilla Apache Nation*, at 175.

129. *United States v. Jicarilla Apache Nation*, at 175–176.

130. *United States v. Jicarilla Apache Nation*, at 180.

131. *United States v. Jicarilla Apache Nation*, at 180.

132. *United States v. Jicarilla Apache Nation*, at 180.

133. *United States v. Jicarilla Apache Nation*, at 196.

134. Schmitt, *Political Theology*, 12.

135. *United States v. Mitchell*, 445 U.S. 535, 542 (1980).

136. *United States v. Navajo Nation*, 556 U.S. 287 (2009).

137. *Navajo Nation v. United States*, 46 Fed. Cl. 217, 227 (2000), *rev'd*, 263 F.3d 1325 (Fed. Cir. 2001), *rev'd*, 537 U.S. 488 (2003).

138. *United States v. Dann*, 572 F.2d 222, 226 (9th Cir. 1978).

139. *United States v. Dann*.

140. *United States v. Dann*, 706 F.2d 919, 925 (9th Cir. 1983), *reversed*, 470 U.S. 39 (1985) (emphasis in original).

141. 470 U.S. 39, 45, 48 (respectively).

142. Ball, "Constitution, Court": 65.

143. *Wendt v. Fischer*, 243 N.Y. 439, 443, 154 N.E. 303, 304 (1926).

144. 470 U.S. 39, 44 (emphasis added).

145. Ball, "Constitution, Court": 65.

146. Judicial Branch of California, *Federal Indian Law*, http://www.courts.ca.gov/27002.htm (accessed January 10, 2017).

147. Margold, "Introduction," VIII.

148. Felix Frankfurter, "Foreword," *Rutgers Law Review* 9, no. 2 (Winter 1954): 356.

149. Frank Pommersheim, "Lara: A Constitutional Crisis in Indian Law," *American Indian Law Review* 28, no. 2 (2004): 305.

150. *United States v. Lara*, 541 U.S. 193, 214–215 (Thomas, concurring) (2004).

151. *United States v. Lara*, at 214–215.

152. *United States v. Lara*, at 214–215.

153. *United States v. Lara*, at 219.

154. *United States v. Lara*, at 225.

155. *United States v. Lara*, at 223.

156. *United States v. Bryant*, 579 U.S. 140, 158 (2016), *as revised* (July 7, 2016).

157. Public Law 109–162, 109 Congress Session 1, Violence against Women and Department of Justice Reauthorization Act of 2005, 119 Stat. 2960 (2006); *Domestic Assault by an Habitual Offender*, 18 U.S.C.A. § 117.

158. *United States v. Bryant*.

159. *United States v. Bryant*, at 1967 (Thomas, concurring) (emphasis added).

160. *United States v. Bryant*, at 158–159.

161. *United States v. Bryant*, at 159–160.

162. *United States v. Bryant*, at 160.

163. *United States v. Bryant,* at 160–161.

164. Gillett and Ross-Petherick, "Effectively Representing Indian Tribes" at 9.

165. Vine Deloria, Jr., *Of Utmost Good Faith* (San Francisco: Straight Arrow Books, 1971). 148.

166. Deloria, *God Is Red*, 274.

167. Rifkin, "Indigenizing Agamben," 100, 106–107.

168. Gordley, *The Philosophical Origins*, 8.

169. Gordley, *The Philosophical Origins*, 7.

170. Gordley, *The Philosophical Origins,* 118, quoting David Hume, *A Treatise of Human Nature* (London, 1886), Book 3, Part 2, Section 3 n., at ii. 275, n. I.

171. "Repudiations by Faith Communities," *Doctrine of Discovery,* July 30, 2018, https://doctrineofdiscovery.org/faith-communities/ (accessed January 22, 2021). *See also* Arden Mahlberg, *Beyond Disavowing the Doctrine of Discovery*, https://beyonddisavowing.org/2021/01/13/by-arden-mahlberg-of-christian-colonizer-ancestry/ (accessed January 22, 2021).

172. Newcomb, "The Evidence of Christian Nationalism," 306.

173. Newcomb, *Pagans,* 128.

174. Gordley, *The Philosophical Origins,* 8.

175. *United States v. Cooley,* Docket No. 19-1414, on writ of certiorari to the 9th Circuit, 919 F.3d 1135 (2019).

176. Elizabeth Reese, "Court Struggles with the 'Indefensible Morass' It's Made in Indian Law," *SCOTUSblog* (March 26, 2021, 8:31 PM), https://www.scotusblog.com/2021/03/court-struggles-with-the-indefensible-morass-its-made-in-indian-law/ (accessed March 30, 2021).

177. Lee Epstein, Andrew D. Martin, Kevin M. Quinn, and Jeffrey A. Segal, "Ideological Drift among Supreme Court Justices: Who, When, and How Important?" 101 *Northwestern University Law Review* 1483, 1492 (2007). [Note: the statistical "drift" charts from the article are available at *Papers, Martin-Quinn Scores,* https://mqscores.lsa.umich.edu/press.php]

178. "Oral Argument," *United States v. Joshua James Cooley*, Docket No. 19-1414, https://www.oyez.org/cases/2020/19-1414 [accessed 7 May 2022].

179. "Oral Argument," *United States v. Joshua James Cooley.*

180. "Oral Argument," *United States v. Joshua James Cooley.*

181. Reese, "Court Struggles with the 'Indefensible Morass' It's Made in Indian Law."

182. *United States v. Cooley,* 141 S. Ct. 1638, 1642 (2021).

183. *United States v. Cooley,* at 1643.

184. *United States v. Cooley,* at 1645.

185. *Brackeen v. Haaland,* 994 F.3d 249 (5th Cir. 2021), *cert. granted sub nom. Nation v. Brackeen*, 142 S. Ct. 1204 (2022), and *cert. granted*, 142 S. Ct. 1205 (2022), and *cert. granted sub nom. Texas v. Haaland*, 142 S. Ct. 1205 (2022), and *cert. granted*, 142 S. Ct. 1205 (2022).

186. José R. Martinez Cobo, special rapporteur. U.N. Subcommission on the Prevention of Discrimination and Protection of Minorities, *Study of the Problem of*

*Discrimination against Indigenous Populations. Volume V, Conclusions, Proposals and Recommendations.* Document. E/CN.4/Sub.2/ 1986/7/Add. 4, para. 379 (1987).

187. S. James Anaya, *Indigenous Peoples in International Law.* 2nd ed. (Oxford and New York: Oxford University Press, 2004), 3.

188. Cobo, *Study of the Problem of Discrimination against Indigenous Populations, Volume V, Conclusions, Proposals and Recommendations.*

189. United Nations General Assembly. Declaration on the Rights of Indigenous Peoples. Document A/RES/61/295 (September 13, 2007).

190. John, *Study on the Impacts of the Doctrine of Discovery,* Section I.3.

191. Steven Salaita, *Inter/Nationalism: Decolonizing Native America and Palestine,* Indigenous Americas (Minneapolis: University of Minnesota Press, 2016).

## Chapter 5: Revoking Christian Discovery Doctrine

1. *United States v. Jicarilla Apache Nation,* at 174.

2. Richard B. Collins and Karla D. Miller, "A People without Law," *Indigenous Law Journal* 5 (2006): 85.

3. Collins and Miller, "A People without Law": 84.

4. Echo-Hawk, *In the Courts,* 429.

5. Juan Williams, *Thurgood Marshall: American Revolutionary* (New York: Times Books, 1998), 181.

6. Echo-Hawk, *In the Courts,* 471n6.

7. White House. "Statement by President Joe Biden on Armenian Remembrance Day," April 24, 2021. https://www.whitehouse.gov/briefing-room/statements-releases/2021/04/24/statement-by-president-joe-biden-on-armenian-remembrance-day/; Reuters, "Erdogan Urges Biden to Reverse 'Wrong Step' on Armenian Declaration," April 26, 2021. https://www.reuters.com/world/us/erdogan-calls-biden-reverse-wrong-step-armenian-declaration-2021-04-26/.

8. U.S. Department of State. "Determination of the Secretary of State on Atrocities in Xinjiang." Accessed April 30, 2022. https://2017-2021.state.gov/determination-of-the-secretary-of-state-on-atrocities-in-xinjiang/.

9. Embassy of the People's Republic of China in the United States of America, "The American Genocide of the Indians—Historical Facts and Real Evidence," http://us.china-embassy.gov.cn/eng/zgyw/202203/t20220302_10647120.htm. Accessed April 30, 2022.

10. Emily Prey and Azeem Ibrahim, "The United States Must Reckon With Its Own Genocides." *Foreign Policy* (blog), https://foreignpolicy.com/2021/10/11/us-genocide-china-indigenous-peoples-day-columbus/. Accessed April 30, 2022.

11. See "RED: Continental Comunicaciones—Communications: Medios—Media Abya Yala. "Communique to the Holy See, Vatican State: Dismantling the Doctrine of Discovery," Continental Commission Abya Yala, Valley of Jovel, San Cristobal de Las Casas, Chiapas, Mexico. February 12, 2016. http://redabyayala.blogspot.com/2016/02/declaration-continental-commission-abya.html

(accessed February 13, 2016). See also United Nations Committee on the Elimination of Racial Discrimination, *Concluding observations on the combined sixteenth to twenty-third periodic reports of the Holy See,* advance unedited version, Document CERD/C/VAT/CO/16-23; December 11, 2015, https://tbinternet.ohchr.org /Treaties/CERD/Shared%20Documents/VAT/CERD_C_VAT_CO_16 -23_22502_E.pdf (accessed July 9, 2021)

12. Adrian Jawort, "A Message from the Crow Nation: 'Jesus Christ Is Lord.'" *Indian Country Today,* January 19, 2015. https://indiancountrytoday.com /archive/a-message-from-the-crow-nation-jesus-christ-is-lord (accessed July 9, 2021).

13. *Brown v. Board of Education,* 347 U.S. 483 (1954).

14. Adam Liptak, "Brown v. Board of Education, Second Round," *New York Times,* sec. Week in Review (December 10, 2006).

15. *Tee-Hit-Ton Indians v. United States.*

16. *Pueblo of Jemez v. United States,* 483 F. Supp. 3d 1024 (D.N.M. 2020).

17. Luther A. Huston, "High Court Bans School Segregation; 9-0 Decision Grants Time to Comply," *The New York Times* (May 17, 1954), 1.

18. Brief for the United States as amicus curiae, *Brown v. Board of Education,* December 2, 1952, 1952 WL 82045, at *6.

19. Brief for the United States as amicus curiae, *Brown,* at *1, 2.

20. Nell Jessup Newton, "At the Whim of the Sovereign: Aboriginal Title Reconsidered," *Hastings Law Journal* 31, no. 6 (July 1980): 1241.

21. Wilkins, *American Indian Sovereignty,* 185.

22. Brief for the United States, *Tee-Hit-Ton Indians v. U.S.* (September 21, 1954),1954 WL 72831, 13.

23. Brief for the United States, *Tee-Hit-Ton Indians v. U.S.,* 13.

24. Newton, "At the Whim of the Sovereign": 1215.

25. Brief for the United States as amicus curiae, *Brown,* at 4.

26. Brief for the United States as amicus curiae, *Tee-Hit-Ton Indians v. U.S.* (September 21, 1954),1954 WL 72831, 24, 26.

27. Earl M. Maltz, "Brown and Tee-Hit-Ton," *American Indian Law Review* 29, no. 1 (2004): 99.

28. Vine Deloria, Jr., *Behind the Trail of Broken Treaties: An Indian Declaration of Independence* (New York: Delacorte Press, 1974). 3.

29. Cohen, *Handbook,* V.

30. John Collier, "America's Handling of Its Indigenous Indian Minority," 7 *Indians at Work* 5(January 1940): 11.

31. *Blatchford v. Native Village of Noatak and Circle Village,* 501 U.S. 775, 782.

32. Steven Curry, *Indigenous Sovereignty and the Democratic Project.* Applied Legal Philosophy (Aldershot, UK, and Burlington, VT: Ashgate, 2004), 7.

33. *Dred Scott v. Sandford,* 60 U.S. 393 (1857).

34. *Lone Wolf v. Hitchcock,* 187 U.S. 553 (1903).

35. Stacy L. Leeds, "The More Things Stay the Same: Waiting on Indian Law's Brown v. Board of Education," *Tulsa Law Review* 38, no. 1 (Fall 2002): 74.

36. *Oliphant v. Suquamish Indian Tribe,* 435 U.S. 191 (1978).

37. *Nevada v. Hicks,* 533 U.S. 353 (2001).

38. Leeds, "The More Things Stay the Same," 79.

39. Leeds, "The More Things Stay the Same," 86.

40. *Proceedings of the Twentieth Annual Meeting of the Lake Mohonk Conference of Friends of the Indian, 1902,* 134.

41. Leeds, "The More Things Stay the Same," 75n20.

42. Ralph W. Johnson and E. Susan Crystal, "Indians and Equal Protection," *Washington Law Review* 54, no. 3 (June 1979): 631.

43. William Minor Lile and Nathan Abbott, *Brief Making and the Use of Law Books* (Buffalo, NY.: W. S. Hein Co., 1988), 58.

44. Dena L. Silliman, "Francis Browning Pipestem: A Great and Savage Warrior," *American Indian Law Review* 24 (1999–2000): ix–xiv.

45. National Native American Law Students Association (NALSA), https://www.nationalnalsa.org (accessed July 9, 2021).

46. Native American Rights Fund, https://www.narf.org/ (accessed July 9, 2021).

47. Vine Deloria, Jr,, "This Country Was a Lot Better Off When the Indians Were Running It," *New York Times,* March 8, 1970, Archives, https://www.nytimes.com/1970/03/08/archives/this-country-was-a-lot-better-off-when-the-indians-were-running-it.html. (accessed July 9, 2021); quoted in Strickland, "Genocide-at-Law": 737.

48. Charles F. Wilkinson, *American Indians, Time, and the Law*: Native Societies in a Modern Constitutional Democracy (New Haven, CT: Yale University Press, 1987), 122.

49. Strickland, "The Changing World": 351.

50. Wildenthal, *Native American Sovereignty,* 121.

51. Gale Courey Toensing, "Indian Law Attorneys' Advice to Tribes: 'Stay Out of the Courts!'" *Indian Country Today.* October 28, 2013, https://indiancountrytoday.com/archive/indian-law-attorneys-advice-to-tribes-stay-out-of-the-courts (accessed July 9, 2021).

52. Gale Courey Toensing, "Interview with John Echohawk," *Indian Country Today,* May 6, 2009, https://indiancountrytoday.com/archive/interview-with-john-echohawk (accessed July 9, 2021).

53. Strickland, "Genocide-at-Law": 742.

54. Strickland, "Genocide-at-Law": 742.

55. Smith, "Defending Indian Lands," at *1.

56. *Commonwealth vs. Michael J. Maxim & David S. Greene,* 45 Mass. App. Ct. 49, 429 Mass. 287 (1999).

57. State of Michigan, "Brief for Petitioner," *State of Michigan v. Bay Mills Indian Community,* 572 U.S. 782, Docket No.12-515 (2013).

58. Bay Mills Indian Community, "Brief for Respondent," *State of Michigan v. Bay Mills Indian Community,* 572 U.S. 782, Docket No. 12-515 (2013), 48.

59. *Michigan v. Bay Mills Indian Community,* 572 U.S. 782, 804 (2014).

60. *Dollar General v. Choctaw Indians*, 136 S.Ct. 2159 (2016).

61. Dollar General Corp. and Dolgencorp, LLC. 2015. "Brief for the Petitioners," 17, *Dollar General v. Choctaw Indians*, Docket 13-1496.

62. *Montana v. United States*, 450 U.S. 544, 565–66 (1981).

63. *Dolgencorp, Inc. v. Mississippi Band of Choctaw Indians*, 746 F.3d 167 (5th Cir. 2014).

64. Gregory Ablavsky et al., 2015, "Brief for Amici Curiae Historians and Legal Scholars Gregory Ablavsky, Bethany R. Berger, Ned Blackhawk, Daniel Carpenter, Matthew L. M. Fletcher, Maggie Mckinley, and Joseph William Singer in Support of Respondents," 9, 21, *Dollar General v. Choctaw Indians*, Docket 13-1496., 2015 WL 6445771 (*emphasis in original*).

65. State of Mississippi et al., 2015, "Brief for the States of Mississippi, Colorado, New Mexico, North Dakota, Oregon, and Washington as Amici Curiae in Support of Respondents," *Dollar General v. Choctaw Indians*, Docket 13-1496.

66. *Dollar General v. Choctaw Indians*, Oral Argument, United States Supreme Court, Docket 13-1496 (2015), 40.

67. *Dollar General*, Oral Argument, 63.

68. Ball, "Constitution, Court": 65.

69. Lance Morgan, "The Rise of Tribes and the Fall of Federal Indian Law," *Arizona State Law Journal* 49, no. 1 (Spring 2017): 119.

70. "A Conversation with Phillip Deere."

71. Kristen A. Carpenter and Angela R. Riley, "Privatizing the Reservation," *Stanford Law Review* 71, no. 4 (April 2019): 866.

72. Indian Land Tenure Foundation, *Native Land Law: Can Native American People Find Justice in the U.S. Legal System?*, 2. https://iltf.org/wp-content/uploads/2016/11/native_land_law_2010.pdf (accessed March 19, 2018)

73. Karl N. Llewellyn, *The Bramble Bush: On Our Law and Its Study* (Dobbs Ferry, NY: Oceana Publications, 1960), 38.

74. Federal Rules of Civil Procedure 11(b)(2).

75. Bryan A. Garner and Henry Campbell Black, eds. *Black's Law Dictionary*, 7th ed. (St. Paul, MN: West Group, 1999), 678.

76. Cary Coglianese, "Insuring Rule 11 Sanctions," *Michigan Law Review* 88, no. 2 (November 1989): 382–383.

77. *Plessy v. Ferguson*, 163 U.S. 537 (1896), *overruled by Brown v. Board of Education of Topeka*, 347 U.S. 483 (1954).

78. *Plessy v. Ferguson*, at 550.

79. *Brown v. Board of Education of Topeka*, 347 U.S. 483 (1954).

80. *Smith v. State*, 100 Tenn. 494, 46 S.W. 566, 566–67 (1898).

81. *Smith v. State*, at 570.

82. *Smith v. State*, at 571.

83. *Ohio Val. Ry.'s Receiver v. Lander*, 104 Ky. 431, 47 S.W. 344, 344 (1898).

84. *Ohio Val. Ry.'s Receiver v. Lander*, at 345–346.

85. *Eastway Construction Corporation. v. City of New York*, 637 F. Supp. 558, 574 (E.D.N.Y. 1986), *order modified and remanded*, 821 F.2d 121 (2d Cir. 1987).

86. *Eastway Construction Corporation. v. City of New York*, at 575. The appeals court modified Judge Weinstein's award, increasing it modestly and assessing half of it against the plaintiff's lawyer.

87. *United States v. Mason,* 412 U.S. 391, 399 (1973).

88. *Mason v. United States,* 461 F.2d 1364, 1372 (1972).

89. *United States v. Mason,* at 399.

90. Federal Rules of Civil Procedure 11. Advisory Committee Notes, 1993 Amendment (emphasis added).

91. *Tee-Hit-Ton Indians v. United States*, 348 U.S. 272 (1955).

92. J. A. Krug, Secretary of the Interior. Letter to Joseph W. Martin, Jr., Speaker of the House of Representatives. Tongass National Forest. Hearings Before the Committee on Agriculture, House of Representatives, on H. R. Resolution 205, to Authorize the Secretary of Agriculture to Sell Timber within the Tongass National Forest (HRG-1947-HAG-0025; 80th Congress, 1st Sess., May 26, June 14, July 1, 3, and 9, 1947), 2.

93. Harry S. Truman, "Special Message to the Congress on Alaska—May 21, 1948," *Public Papers of the Presidents of the United States* (1948): 269.

94. Felix S. Cohen, "Alaska's Nuremberg Laws: Congress Sanctions Racial Discrimination," *Commentary* August 1948, at 136, https://www.commentarymagazine.com/ articles/alaskas-nuremberg-lawscongress-sanctions-racial-discrimination/.

95. *Tee-Hit-Ton v. United States*, Brief for the Petitioner on Writ of Certiorari to the Court of Claims, 1954 WL 72830 (U.S.), at *7.

96. *Tee-Hit-Ton v. United States*, Brief for the Petitioner on Writ of Certiorari, at *18.

97. *Tee-Hit-Ton v. United States*, Brief for the United States on Writ of Certiorari, at *46.

98. *Tee-Hit-Ton v. United States*, Brief for the United States on Writ of Certiorari, at * 61.

99. Brief of the State of Utah, Amicus Curiae, *Tee-Hit-Ton,* 1954 WL 72833 (October 8, 1954), 3.

100. Brief of the State of New Mexico, Amicus Curiae, *Tee-Hit-Ton,* 954 WL 72832 (October 8, 1954), 8, 14.

101. *Tee-Hit-Ton v. United States*, at 279.

102. *Tee-Hit-Ton Indians v. United States*, at 291.

103. This quotation and the following excerpts from Justice Stanley Reed's papers are taken from the Special Collections Research Center, University of Kentucky, Stanley Reed collection, *Tee-Hit-Ton v. U.S.,* 348 U.S. 272 (1955), Boxes 186–187. The first quote and the memo that follows are in folder 5. The emphasis in this quote is added.

104. Reed Papers, Box 187, folder 1.

105. Reed Papers, Box 187, folder 2.

106. *Tee-Hit-Ton Indians v. United States*, at 291.

107. *Tee-Hit-Ton Indians v. United States*, at 291.

108. Stephen Haycox, "Tee-Hit Ton and Alaska Native Rights," in John McLaren, Hamar Foster, Chet Orloff, eds., *Law for the Elephant, Law for the Beaver: Essays in the Legal History of the North American West* (Regina, Saskatchewan, Canada: University of Regina, Canadian Plains Research Center; and Pasadena, CA: Ninth Judicial Circuit Historical Society, 1992), 130.

109. Dave Kiffer, "William Paul Was the 'Father of Native Land Claims' and a Pretty Fair College Football Player, Too," *SitNews: Stories in the News* (Ketchikan, AK: February 16, 2009), http://www.sitnews.us/Kiffer/WilliamLewisPaul /021609_william_paul.html (accessed February 22, 2021).

110. Environment and Natural Resources Division, General Functions, 28 *Code of Federal Regulations* 0.65. Created in 1909 as the Public Lands Division, renamed the Lands Division in 1933, then the Land and Natural Resources Division in 1965, and finally the Environment and Natural Resources Division in 1990, it has included land and "Indian" issues from the beginning.

111. John J. Rooney, Representative (NY) and Chair, introducing Witnesses William A. Underhill, Assistant Attorney General, and C. G. Tadlock, Administrative Assistant, to present Department of Justice Lands Division appropriation request to the Subcommittee on Departments of State, Justice, Commerce, and the Judiciary, of the Committee on Appropriations, House of Representatives, Eighty-Second Congress, Second Session, Hearings, Departments of State, Justice, Commerce, and the Judiciary Appropriations for 1953; Department of Justice (HRG-1952-HAP-0019), January 22, 1952. 98.

112. *Red Lake Band of Chippewa Indians v. Swimmer*, 740 F.Supp. 9 (1990).

113. "Public Law 100–497, 100 Congress, Session 2, An Act: To regulate gaming on Indian lands.," *U.S. Statutes at Large* 102, Main Section (1988): 2467– 2489. 25 *U.S.C.A.* Ch. 29,

114. "Indian Gaming Regulation," 25 *U.S.C.A.* Ch. 29, s. 2701(5), October 17, 1988.

115. *California v. Cabazon Band of Mission Indians*, 480 U.S. 202, 207 (1987).

116. *California v. Cabazon Band of Mission Indians*, at 222.

117. *California v. Cabazon Band of Mission Indians*, at 207.

118. *California v. Cabazon Band of Mission Indians*, at 215.

119. "Indian Gaming Regulation," 25 *U.S.C.A.* Ch. 29, s. 2701(1).

120. *Gaming Corporation of America v. Dorsey & Whitney*, 88 F.3d 536, 546 (8th Cir. 1996).

121. *Red Lake Band of Chippewa Indians v. Swimmer*, at 10.

122. *Red Lake Band of Chippewa Indians v. Swimmer*, at 11.

123. *Red Lake Band of Chippewa Indians v. Swimmer*, at 11 (quoting *United States v. Wheeler*, 435 U.S. 313 (1978) and *Native Village of Venetie v. State of Alaska*, 687 F.Supp. 1380, 1392 (D.Alaska 1988)).

124. *Red Lake Band of Chippewa Indians v. Swimmer*, at 11–12 (quoting *Native Village of Venetie v. State of Alaska*, 687 F.Supp. 1380, 1389 (D.Alaska 1988)).

125. *Red Lake Band of Chippewa Indians v. Swimmer*, at 12 (quoting Ann Laquer Estin, "Federal Plenary Power in Indian Affairs after Weeks and Sioux Nation,"

*University of Pennsylvania Law Review* 131, no. 1 (1982–1983): 235–270; and Nell Jessup Newton, "Federal Power over Indians: Its Sources, Scope, and Limitations," *University of Pennsylvania Law Review* 132, no. 2 (January 1984): 195–288).

126. *Red Lake Band of Chippewa Indians v. Swimmer* (quoting *Sioux Nation of Indians v. United States*, 601 F.2d 1157, 1173, 220 Ct.Cl. 442 (1979)).

127. *Red Lake Band of Chippewa Indians v. Swimmer*

128. *Red Lake Band of Chippewa Indians v. Swimmer*, at 13.

129. *Red Lake Band of Chippewa Indians v. Swimmer*, at 13.

130. *Nevada v. Hicks*, 533 U.S. 353 (2001).

131. "Brief for Respondent Floyd Hicks," *Nevada v. Hicks*, No. 99–1994, 2001 WL 57509 (2001), 8.

132. "Brief for Respondent," *Nevada v. Hicks*, at 8, 10.

133. "Brief for Respondent," *Nevada v. Hicks*, at 32, 34.

134. "Brief for Respondent," *Nevada v. Hicks*, at 34.

135. "Brief for Respondent," *Nevada v. Hicks*, at 35.

136. "Brief for Respondent," *Nevada v. Hicks*, at 50.

137. *Nevada v. Hicks*, at 361–362.

138. *United States v. Dann*, 470 U.S. 39 (1985).

139. *United States v. Nye County, Nevada*, United States District Court, District of Nevada, CASE NO.: CV-S-95-00232-LDG (RJJ).

140. *United States v. Nye County*, CV-S-95-232-LDG (RJJ) (U.S.D.C., Nev,), ORDER, July 25, 1995.

141. Appellants Brief, *United States, v. Nye County, Defendant Western Shoshone National Council by its Chief, Raymond D. Yowell, and Chief Raymond D. Yowell as Representative of the Class of Shoshone Persons, Defendants-Appellants.* 1995 WL 17064888 (November 28, 1995), 5.

142. *United States v. Nye County, Nevada*, 133 F.3d 930 (9th Cir. 1997). The Western Shoshone appeal brief can be found online at Westlaw, 1995_WL _17064888. The U.S. brief in opposition is at 1996_WL_33489847.

143. Inter-American Commission on Human Rights. *Mary and Carrie Dann v. United States*, Report No. 75/02, Case 11.140; December 27, 2002, par. 139, http://cidh.oas.org/annualrep/2002eng/USA.11140.htm (accessed February 11, 2021).

144. Inter-American Commission on Human Rights. *Mary and Carrie Dann v. United States*, par. 173.1.

145. United Nations Committee on the Elimination of Racial Discrimination, *Western Shoshone National Council Request for Early Warning Measures and Urgent Procedures, in Relation to the United States of America*, July 25, 2005, https://law.arizona.edu/sites/default/files/Request%20for%20Early%20Warning%20Measures%20and%20Urgent%20Procedures%20to%20CERD.pdf (accessed July 10, 2021).

146. Committee for the Elimination of Racial Discrimination, *Early Warning and Urgent Action Procedure, Decision 1(68)*. Sixty-eighth session, Geneva, February 20–March 10 2006, https://docstore.ohchr.org/SelfServices/FilesHandler.ashx?enc=6QkG1d%2fPPRiCAqhKb7yhspzOl9YwTXeABruAM8pBAK2Noyeqc

MbmxNgOOeCrloILT6ALuItFZLrmUsh7ZwCERBkWbTA8OcfJkc5cIvbu
B0RkaXAS9J6za8eSQJb7rzMU (accessed February 11, 2021).

147. United Nations Committee on the Elimination of Racial Discrimination, *Concluding Observations of the Committee on the Elimination of Racial Discrimination: United States of America,* Document A/56/18,paras.380–407; August 14, 2001, https://law.arizona.edu/western-shoshone (accessed February 25, 2019).

148. *Washington State Department of Licensing v. Cougar Den, Inc.,* 139 S. Ct. 1000 (2019).

149. Reply Brief for the Petitioner, *Washington State Department of Licensing v. Cougar Den, Inc.,* 139 S. Ct. 1000, 2018 WL 5194641, at *2.

150. Brief of Amicus Curiae, Confederated Tribes and Bands of the Yakama Nation in Support of Respondent, *Washington State Department of Licensing v. Cougar Den, Inc.,* 139 S. Ct. 1000, 2018 WL 4739661, at *5–6.

151. Brief of Amicus Curiae, 12–13.

152. *Cougar Den,* at 1026.

153. *Cougar Den,* at 1029.

154. United Nations General Assembly, Declaration on the Rights of Indigenous Peoples. Document A/RES/61/295 (September 13, 2007).

155. United Nations General Assembly, Declaration on the Rights of Indigenous Peoples, Article 26.

156. R. B. J. Walker, *Inside/Outside: International Relations as Political Theory,* Cambridge Studies in International Relations 24 (Cambridge, UK, and New York: Cambridge University Press, 1993), 21.

157. Charmaine White Face, *Indigenous Nations' Rights in the Balance: An Analysis of the Declaration on the Rights of Indigenous Peoples* (St. Paul, MN: Living Justice Press, 2013), 4.

158. White Face, *Indigenous Nations' Rights in the Balance,* 92–93.

159. Department of Economic and Social Affairs, Division for Social Policy and Development, Secretariat of the Permanent Forum on Indigenous Issues, *The Concept of Indigenous Peoples,* Document PFII/2004/WS.⅓; New York, 19–21 January 2004. Para. 1, http://www.un.org/esa/socdev/unpfii/documents/workshop_data_background.doc. (accessed January 23, 2021)

160. Martinez Cobo, *Study on the Problem of Discrimination against Indigenous Populations.*

161. United Nations General Assembly, *Declaration,* Preamble.

162. U.S. Department of State, "Announcement of U.S. Support for the United Nations Declaration on the Rights of Indigenous Peoples," January 12, 2011, https://2009-2017.state.gov/documents/organization/154782.pdf. See also https://2009-2017.state.gov/s/srgia/154553.htm; and the White House, "Remarks by the President at the White House Tribal Nations Conference," December 16, 2010, https://obamawhitehouse.archives.gov/the-press-office/2010/12/16/remarks-president-white-house-tribal-nations-conference.

163. U.S. Department of State, "Announcement of U.S. Support for the United Nations Declaration on the Rights of Indigenous Peoples."

164. U.S. Department of State, "Announcement of U.S. Support for the United Nations Declaration on the Rights of Indigenous Peoples."

165. U.S. Department of State, "Announcement of U.S. Support for the United Nations Declaration on the Rights of Indigenous Peoples."

166. Rifkin, "Indigenizing Agamben": 90, 106, 97 (respectively).

167. Sharon H. Venne, "The Road to the United Nations and Rights of Indigenous Peoples," 20 *Griffith Law Review* 557 (2011): 557.

168. Charter of the United Nations, Chapter I, Article 1, section 2 (1945).

169. Rifkin, "Indigenizing Agamben," 105.

170. Permanent Forum on Indigenous Issues. United Nations Economic and Social Council. Report on the Thirteenth Session (May 12–23, 2014), Official Records, 2014, Supplement No. 23, Document E/2014/43-E/C.19/2014/11; June 6, 2014. "Draft Decision IV," https://core.ac.uk/reader/44288720 (accessed July 10, 2021)

171. John, *Study on the Impacts of the Doctrine of Discovery on Indigenous Peoples.*

172. United Nations General Assembly. *Outcome Document of the High-Level Plenary Meeting of the General Assembly Known as the World Conference on Indigenous Peoples,* Document A/RES/69/2; September 22, 2014, https://undocs.org /en/A/RES/69/2 (accessed July 10, 2021)

173. EagleWoman, "The 15th-Century Doctrine" at *6.

174. For an overview, see David C. Gray, "Why Justice Scalia Should Be a Constitutional Comparativist . . . Sometimes," *Stanford Law Review* 59, no. 5 (March 2007): 1249–1280.

175. Donald Earl Childress II, "Using Comparative Constitutional Law to Resolve Domestic Federal Questions," *Duke Law Journal* 53, no. 1 (October 2003): 194.

176. Federal News Service, *Full Written Transcript of Scalia-Breyer Debate on Foreign Law.* U.S. Association of Constitutional Law Discussion, Subject: Constitutional Relevance of Foreign Court Decisions, American University, Washington College of Law, Washington, DC, 4:10 P.M. EST, Thursday, January 13, 2005, https://freerepublic.com/focus/f-news/1352357/posts (accessed July 10, 2021)

## Chapter 6: Federal Anti-Indian Law in the Classroom

1. Strickland and Valencia-Weber, "Observations," 162, 163, 164.

2. Strickland, "The Changing World": 351.

3. Strickland, "Genocide-at-Law": 755.

4. Joseph Story, *The Miscellaneous Writings: Literary, Critical, Juridical, and Political of Joseph Story, Now First Collected* (Boston: J. Munroe and Company, 1835), 456.

5. Story, *The Miscellaneous Writings*, 456.

6. "Abraham Lincoln's Advice to Lawyers." Letter to William H. Grigsby, August 3, 1858. http://www.abrahamlincolnonline.org/lincoln/speeches/law .htm (accessed July 10, 2021) (emphasis in original).

7. Llewellyn. *The Bramble Bush*, 68–70.

8. Llewellyn. *The Bramble Bush*, 68–70.

9. John Borrows, *Law's Indigenous Ethics* (Toronto: University of Toronto Press, 2019), 324n4.

10. Karl Nickerson Llewellyn and Edward Adamson Hoebel, *The Cheyenne Way: Conflict and Case Law in Primitive Jurisprudence* (University of Oklahoma Press, 1941).

11. "The Path of the Law," An Address delivered by Mr. Justice Holmes, of the Supreme Judicial Court of Massachusetts, at the dedication of the new hall of the Boston University School of Law, on January 8, 1897. *Harvard Law Review* 10, no. 8 (1896–1897): 460–461.

12. Oliver Wendell Holmes, "Natural Law," *Harvard Law Review* 32, no. 1 (1918–1919): 42.

13. See Robert M. Cover, "Foreword: Nomos and Narrative," *Harvard Law Review* 97, no. Issue1 (November 1983): 56, discussing "the authoritarian application of violence . . . the hermeneutic of jurisdiction." See also Cover, "Violence and the Word"; and Stephen L. Carter, "Must Liberalism Be Violent—A Reflection on the Work of Stanley Hauerwas," *Law and Contemporary Problems* 75, no. 4 (2012): 214: "The state must enforce its laws, and violently, which is precisely why liberal theory exists: to cabin the range of possible laws the state can permissibly enact."

14. Rodger D. Citron, "The Nuremberg Trials and American Jurisprudence: The Decline of Legal Realism, the Revival of Natural Law, and the Development of Legal Process Theory," *Michigan State Law Review* 2006, no. 2 (Summer 2006): 385–410.

15. Patrick Devlin, *The Judge* (Oxford, UK: Oxford University Press, 1979), 61.

16. Lile and Abbott, *Brief Making*, 2.

17. Monroe E. Price, *Law and the American Indian: Readings, Notes, and Cases* (Indianapolis: Bobbs-Merrill, 1973).

18. Carole E. Goldberg, Rebecca Tsosie, Robert N. Clinton, and Angela R. Riley, *American Indian Law: Native Nations and the Federal System: Cases and Materials* (LexisNexis, 2015). xiv.

19. Strickland and Valencia-Weber, "Observations," 158.

20. Drew L. Kershen, "Law and the American Indian: Readings, Notes and Cases, Monroe E. Price," Book Review. *American Indian Law Review* 1 (1973): 94–95.

21. *Apache Stronghold v. United States*, No. CV-21-00050-PHX-SPL, 2021 WL 535525 (D. Ariz. Feb. 12, 2021).

22. Kershen, "Law and the American Indian: Readings, Notes and Cases, Monroe E. Price": 96.

23. Cohen, *Handbook of Federal Indian Law*, V.

24. Price, *Law and the American Indian*, vii.

25. Goldberg et al., *American Indian Law*, xiv.

26. David H. Getches, Daniel M. Rosenfelt, and Charles F. Wilkinson, *Cases and Materials on Federal Indian Law,* American Casebook Series (St. Paul, MN: West Publishing Company, 1979), XIII.

27. David H. Getches, Charles F. Wilkinson, and Robert A. Williams, *Cases and Materials on Federal Indian Law,* 3rd ed., American Casebook Series (St. Paul, MN: West Publishing Company, 1993), v.

28. Felix S. Cohen and Nell Jessup Newton, *Cohen's Handbook of Federal Indian Law* (New Providence, NJ: LexisNexis, 2012), viii.

29. *Native Village of Venetie v. State of Alaska,* 687 F. Supp. 1380, 1390 (1988). Joseph D. Matal discusses Kleinfeld's remark and criticizes versions of the *Handbook* in "A Revisionist History of Indian Country," *Alaska Law Review* 14, no. 2 (December 1997): 283–352.

30. Robert N. Clinton, "There Is No Federal Supremacy Clause for Indian Tribes," *Arizona State Law Journal* 34, no. 1 (Spring 2002): 232.

31. Public Law 90–284, 90 Congress, Session 2, An Act: To Prescribe Penalties for Certain Acts of Violence or Intimidation, and for Other Purposes, *U.S. Statutes at Large* 82, Main Section (1968): 73–92. Title VII—MATERIALS RELATING TO CONSTITUTIONAL RIGHTS OF INDIANS—SECRETARY OF INTERIOR TO PREPARE, section 701(2). The act is better known as the Indian Civil Rights Act of 1968, from Title II—Rights of Indians.

32. Felix S. Cohen and Rennard Strickland, *Felix S. Cohen's Handbook of Federal Indian Law, 1982 edition* (Charlottesville, VA: Michie: Bobbs-Merrill, 1982). Meanwhile, in 1971, the American Indian Law Center and the University of New Mexico Press published a facsimile reprint of the 1942 *Handbook,* listed as entry 1526 in *American Indian Legal Materials: A Union List* (Stanfordville, NY: E. M. Coleman, 1980). See also Joseph F. Rarick, "Book Review of Felix S. Cohen's Handbook of Federal Indian Law," *American Indian Law Review* 11, no. 1 (1983): 85–88.

33. Russel Lawrence Barsh, "Felix S. Cohen's Handbook of Federal Indian Law, 1982 Edition," *Washington Law Review* 57, no. 4 (November 1982): 799.

34. Cohen and Newton, *Cohen's Handbook,* vii.

35. Cohen and Newton, *Cohen's Handbook,* 2.

36. Cohen and Newton, *Cohen's Handbook,* 2.

37. *United States v. Blackfeet Tribe,* at 194.

38. Cohen and Newton, *Cohen's Handbook,* 2.

39. Cohen and Newton, *Cohen's Handbook,* 2.

40. Cohen and Newton, *Cohen's Handbook,* 2.

41. Getches, et al., *Cases and Materials,* vii, viii.

42. Llewellyn, *The Bramble Bush,* 73–76.

43. Oliver Wendell Holmes, *The Common Law* (Boston: Little, Brown, and Company, 1881), 1.

44. Margold, "Introduction," XII.

45. Margold, "Introduction," XI.

46. Cohen and Newton, *Cohen's Handbook,* 1.

47. Cohen and Newton, *Cohen's Handbook*, 1.

48. Cohen and Newton, *Cohen's Handbook*, § 5.01[2] n17.

49. Cohen and Newton, *Cohen's Handbook*, § 6.01[1] n4.

50. Cohen and Newton, *Cohen's Handbook*, § 1.02[1].

51. Cohen and Newton, *Cohen's Handbook*, § 5.02[4].

52. Cohen and Newton, *Cohen's Handbook*, § 5.04[3][a].

53. Cohen and Newton, *Cohen's Handbook*, § 5.04[3][b].

54. *Northwestern Bands of Shoshone Indians v. United States*, 324 U.S. 335 (1945), 355.

55. *Tee-Hit-Ton Indians v. United States*, at 281.

56. *United States v. Jicarilla Apache Nation*, at 179.

57. Cohen and Newton, *Cohen's Handbook*, § 15.04[2].

58. *Johnson v. McIntosh*, 21 U.S. 543, 591 (1823), at 592.

59. *Northwestern Bands of Shoshone Indians v. United States*, 339.

60. *Tee-Hit-Ton Indians v. United States*, at 279 (emphasis added).

61. *City of Sherrill v. Oneida Indian Nation*, 544 U.S. 197, 204 (2005).

62. Cohen and Newton, *Cohen's Handbook*, § 15.06[1].

63. *Johnson v. McIntosh*, at 586.

64. *Clark v. Smith*, 38 US 195, 201 (1839).

65. Cohen and Newton, *Cohen's Handbook*, § 15.06[1].

66. Barsh, "Felix S. Cohen's Handbook," 809.

67. Goldberg et al., *American Indian Law*, 46.

68. Peter Nabokov, ed., *Native American Testimony: A Chronicle of Indian-White Relations from Prophecy to the Present, 1492–1992* (New York: Viking, 1991), 122.

69. Goldberg et al., *American Indian Law*, 51.

70. Francis Jennings, *The Invasion of America: Indians, Colonialism, and the Cant of Conquest* (Chapel Hill: University of North Carolina Press, 1975), 6 (emphasis added).

71. Story, *Commentaries*, §§ 5, 8, 152.

72. Story, *Commentaries*, Volume I, Book I, Chapter XVI, "General Review of the Colonies," § 152, 101 (emphasis added).

73. Cohen and Newton, *Cohen's Handbook*, § 5.07[1].

74. Schmitt and Ulmen, *The Nomos of the Earth*, 49, 137–138.

75. Schmitt and Ulmen, *The Nomos of the Earth*, 56.

76. Thomas Joseph Lawrence, *The Principles of International Law* (New York: D. C. Heath & Company, 1895), Chapter IV, "The Subjects of Interntional Law," 59, 68.

77. *Johnson v. McIntosh*, at 572–573.

78. *Cherokee Nation v. Georgia*, at 21.

79. *Cherokee Nation v. Georgia*, at 27.

80. Cohen and Newton, *Cohen's Handbook*, § 5.07[1].

81. United Nations General Assembly, Declaration on the Rights of Indigenous Peoples. Document A/RES/61/295 (September 13, 2007).

82. Tonya Gonnella Frichner and United Nations Permanent Forum on Indigenous Issues, *Preliminary Study of the Impact on Indigenous Peoples of the*

*International Legal Construct Known as the Doctrine of Discovery*. United Nations Economic and Social Council, Document E/C.19/2010/13; February 4, 2010, http://www.un.org/esa/socdev/unpfii/documents/E.C.19.2010.13%20EN.pdf (accessed July 11, 2021).

83. John, *Study on the Impacts of the Doctrine of Discovery on Indigenous Peoples.*

84. Goldberg et al., *American Indian Law,* 1447.

85. James Baldwin, "The White Man's Guilt," *Ebony,* 20, no. 10 (August 1965): 47.

86. William Faulkner, *Requiem for a Nun* (New York: Random House, 1951), 73.

87. Smith, "Defending Indian Lands," at * 1.

88. Frederic William Maitland, A. H. Chaytor, and W. J. Whittaker, *Equity, Also, the Forms of Action at Common Law: Two Courses of Lectures* (Cambridge: Cambridge University Press, 1909), 296.

89. Goldberg et al., *American Indian Law,* xiv–xv.

90. Goldberg et al., *American Indian Law,* 110.

91. *Flores v. S. Peru Copper Corp.,* 414 F.3d 233, 248 (2d Cir. 2003).

92. Lile, *Brief Making.* 58.

## Chapter 7: Call to Consciousness

1. Blake A. Watson, "The Impact of the American Doctrine of Discovery on Native Land Rights in Australia, Canada, and New Zealand," *Seattle University Law Review* 34, no. 2 (Winter 2011): 507, 508–509 (respectively).

2. Yale D. Belanger, "The Six Nations of Grand River Territory's Attempts at Renewing International Political Relationships, 1921–1924." *Canadian Foreign Policy* 13, no. 3 (2007): 30.

3. Belanger, "The Six Nations": 30n2.

4. *Akwesasne Notes,* ed., *A Basic Call to Consciousness* (Summertown, TN: Book Publishing Company, 1995), 25.

5. *Akwesasne Notes, A Basic Call to Consciousness,* 6.

6. *Akwesasne Notes, A Basic Call to Consciousness,* 65, 76.

7. *Akwesasne Notes, A Basic Call to Consciousness,* 76–77.

8. *Akwesasne Notes, A Basic Call to Consciousness,* 74.

9. George Manuel and Michael Posluns, *The Fourth World: An Indian Reality* (Minneapolis and London: University of Minnesota Press, 2019), 264. As Glen Coultard explains in his introduction to the 2019 reissuance of the book, "Posluns wrote the manuscript based on forty hours of taped, in-depth interviews with Manuel."

10. Gen. 12:1, 6–7 (New International Version).

11. Gen. 15:18–21 (NIV).

12. Num. 32:10–11, 13 (NIV).

13. Judg. 2: 1–3 (NIV).

14. Gen. 1:28 (NIV).

15. Reverend William Symonds, *"To goe likewise abroad"; an excerpt from Virginea Britannia. A Sermon Preached At White Chappel, In The presence of many the Adventurers, and Planters for Virginia by Reverend William Symonds* (1609). In *Encyclopedia Virginia* (December 7, 2020), https://encyclopediavirginia.org/entries/to-goe-likewise-abroad-an-excerpt-from-virginea-britannia-a-sermon-preached-at-white-chappel-in-the-presence-of-many-the-adventurers-and-planters-for-virginia-by-reverend-william-symonds-1609 (accessed March 13, 2021).

16. Rebecca Anne Goetz, *The Baptism of Early Virginia: How Christianity Created Race. Early America: History, Context, Culture* (Baltimore: Johns Hopkins University Press, 2012), 46.

17. 6 *Register of Debates* 333, Senate, 21st Congress (Record ID RD-1830-0415; April 15, 1830).

18. *Tee-Hit-Ton v. United States,* Brief for the United States on Writ of Certiorari to the Court of Claims, 1954 WL 72831 (1954), at 16.

19. *Tee-Hit-Ton v. United States*, at 279. See Chapter 5 for a detailed look at the Court's handing of the U.S. Brief.

20. Chris Mato Nunpa, *The Great Evil (Wosice Tanka Kin): Christianity, the Bible, and the Native American Genocide* (Tucson, AZ: See Sharp Press, 2020), 177.

21. Matt. 28:18–20 (NIV).

22. John Neville Figgis, *Studies of Political Thought from Gerson to Grotius: 1414–1625* (Cambridge: Cambridge University Press, 1907), 77.

23. R. A. Fletcher, *The Barbarian Conversion: From Paganism to Christianity* (New York: Henry Holt and Co., 1997), 15, 16.

24. Fletcher, *The Barbarian Conversion*, 34.

25. *Akwesasne Notes, A Basic Call to Consciousness,* 74.

26. Fletcher, *Barbarian Conversion*, 195.

27. Fletcher, *Barbarian Conversion*, 216.

28. National Humanities Center, *Requerimiento.*

29. National Humanities Center, *Requerimiento,* 1.

30. National Humanities Center, *Requerimiento,* 2.

31. Bartolomé de las Casas, *History of the Indies* (New York: Harper & Row, 1971), 196.

32. Morris Berman, *Coming to Our Senses: Body and Spirit in the Hidden History of the West* (New York: Simon and Schuster, 1989), 191.

33. Berman, *Coming to Our Senses*, 193–194.

34. Harold Joseph Berman, *Law and Revolution: The Formation of the Western Legal Tradition* (Cambridge, MA: Harvard University Press, 1983), 65.

35. Berman, *Law and Revolution*, 23.

36. Berman, *Law and Revolution*, 558.

37. Deloria, *God Is Red*, 66–67.

38. Berman, *Coming to Our Senses*, 204.

39. Schmitt, *Nomos*, 56.

40. Schmitt, *Nomos,* 69.

41. Schmitt, *Nomos*, 49, 58.

42. R. B. J. Walker, "Space/Time/Sovereignty," in Mark E. Denham and Mark Owen Lombardi, eds. *Perspectives on Third-World Sovereignty: The Postmodern Paradox*, International Political Economy Series (New York: St. Martin's Press, 1996), 22.

43. Paul Avis, "Polity and Polemics: The Function of Ecclesiastical Polity in Theology and Practice," *Ecclesiastical Law Journal* 18, no. 1 (January 2016): 2–13.

44. Pier Giuseppe Monateri, "Political Theology from Satan to Legitimacy," *Pólemos* 16, no. 1 (2022): 9–23, 13, 14, 16 (respectively).

45. Carla Spivack, "From Hillary Clinton to Lady Macbeth: Or, Historicizing Gender, Law, and Power through Shakespeare's Scottish Play," *William and Mary Journal of Women and the Law* (2008) 15, no. 1: 51, 69.

46. Richard J. Ross, "The Commoning of the Common Law: The Renaissance Debate over Printing English Law," 1520–1640, 146 *University of Pennsylvania Law Review* (1998) 323, 428 (respectively).

47. Monateri, "Political Theology," 17, quoting James I, "Speech of the Star Chamber" (1616), in Charles Howard McIlwain, editor, *The Political Works of James I* (Cambridge: Harvard University Press, 1918), 333–334.

48. Earthjustice, "FAQ: Standing Rock Litigation," May 21, 2021, https://earthjustice.org/features/faq-standing-rock-litigation.(accessed July 5, 2021).

49. Peter d'Errico, "Memo to Briefcase Warriors: Be Bold!" *Indian Country Today,* September 19, 2016, https://indiancountrytoday.com/archive/memo-to-briefcase-warriors-be-bold (accessed June 29, 2021).

50. Peter d'Errico, "The Cerebral Battle of DAPL: What If Standing Rock Retained TigerSwan?" *Indian Country Today,* June 5, 2017, https://indiancountrytoday.com/archive/cerebral-battle-dapl-standing-rock-retained-tigerswan (accessed June 29, 2021).

51. d'Errico, "The Cerebral Battle of DAPL."

52. TigerSwan Video, "Dan Rather Interviews James Reese," YouTube (June 25, 2013), https://www.youtube.com/watch?v=id9mN1Cv-14, at 2:18.

53. "Southeast Arizona Land Exchange and Conservation," 16 U.S.C.A. § 539p (Pub.L. 113–291, Div. B, Title XXX, § 3003, December 19, 2014, 128 Stat. 3732), https://www.congress.gov/113/plaws/publ291/PLAW-113publ291.pdf (accessed July 11, 2021).

54. Southeast Arizona Land Exchange and Conservation, §§ (c)(2)(A), (B), and (10).

55. *Apache Stronghold v. United States*, No. 21–15295 (9th Circuit, 2021).

56. Raul M. Grijalva, "H.R.1884—117th Congress (2021–2022): Save Oak Flat Act," Legislation, April 28, 2021, 2021/2022, https://www.congress.gov/bill/117th-congress/house-bill/1884 (accessed June 29, 2021).

57. Flossie Baker, "Alberta's Oil Sands Bring Jobs, Services and Despair," Inter Press Service (August 5, 2013), http://www.ipsnews.net/2013/08/albertas-oil-sands-bring-jobs-services-and-despair/ (accessed July 5, 2021).

58. Harrison Talgo, former chairman, San Carlos Apache Tribe of the San Carlos Reservation, Arizona, testimony on H.R. 1904, the Southeast Arizona Land Exchange and Conservation Act of 2011, Subcommittee on National Parks,

Forests and Public Lands, House Committee on Natural Resources (HRG-2011-HNR-0047; 112th Congress, 1st Sess., June 14, 2011), 68.

59. Shan Lewis, vice chairman, Fort Mojave Indian Tribe, president of the Inter-Tribal Association of Arizona, testimony on H.R. 1884, the Save Oak Flat Act, Subcommittee on Indigenous Peoples of the United States, House Committee on Natural Resources (H58-20210428-213489; 117th Congress, 1st Sess., April 28, 2021), https://www.congress.gov/event/117th-congress/house-event/111424 (accessed June 29, 2021).

60. United Nations, "Secretary-General's Message on the International Day of the World's Indigenous Peoples," August 9, 2013. https://www.un.org/sg/en/content/sg/statement/2013-08-09/secretary-generals-message-international-day-worlds-indigenous.

61. UN Global Compact, *Business Reference Guide to the UN Declaration on the Rights of Indigenous Peoples* (New York: UN Global Compact, 2013), cover statement, 4, 7, http://www.unglobalcompact.org/docs/issues_doc/human_rights/IndigenousPeoples/BusinessGuide.pdf (accessed March 3, 2021).

62. United Nations, "Secretary-General's Message on the International Day of the World's Indigenous Peoples."

63. William E. Connolly, "The Complexities of Sovereignty," in *Giorgio Agamben: Sovereignty and Life,* Matthew Calarco and Steven DeCaroli, eds. (Stanford, CA: Stanford University Press, 2007), 38, 41.

64. Connolly, "The Complexities of Sovereignty," 40.

65. Connolly, "The Complexities of Sovereignty," 40.

66. Rifkin, "Indigenizing Agamben," 94–95 (emphasis added).

67. Wenona T. Singel, "Cultural Sovereignty and Transplanted Law: Tensions in Indigenous Self-Rule," *Kansas Journal of Law & Public Policy* 15, no. 2 (Winter 2006): 359, 362 (respectively).

68. Singel, "Cultural Sovereignty and Transplanted Law": 367.

69. United Nations, "Secretary-General's message on the International Day of the World's Indigenous Peoples."

70. EagleWoman, "Tribal Nation Economics," 384.

71. EagleWoman, "Tribal Nation Economics," 383.

72. EagleWoman, "Tribal Nation Economics," 387.

73. EagleWoman, "Tribal Nation Economics," 385.

74. EagleWoman, "Tribal Nation Economics," 384.

75. EagleWoman, "Tribal Nation Economics," 396.

76. EagleWoman, "Tribal Nation Economics," 387.

77. EagleWoman, "Tribal Nation Economics," 396–397.

78. Waziyatawin and Michael Yellow Bird, *For Indigenous Minds Only: A Decolonization Handbook* (Santa Fe, NM: School of American Research Press, 2012), 5.

79. Robert A. Williams, Jr., *The American Indian in Western Legal Thought* (Oxford University Press, 1990), 327–328.

80. "A Conversation with Phillip Deere."

81. EagleWoman, "Tribal Nation Economics," 422.

82. Manuel, *The Fourth World*, 219, 224, 229 (respectively).

83. Audra Simpson, *Mohawk Interruptus: Political Life across the Borders of Settler States* (Durham, NC: Duke University Press, 2014), 12.

84. Audra Simpson, "On Ethnographic Refusal: Indigeneity, 'Voice' and Colonial Citizenship," *Junctures: The Journal for Thematic Dialogue*, no. 9 (December 2007), 73.

85. Independent Lakota Nation, Declaration on Lakota Nationhood and the Dakota Access Pipeline Conflict to the United Nations and the International Community (November 4, 2016), https://cantetenza.wordpress.com/2016/11/04 /declaration-on-lakota-nationhood-and-the-dakota-access-pipeline-conflict-to -the-united-nations-and-the-international-community/ (accessed June 29, 2021).

86. Simpson, *Mohawk Interruptus,* 158–159.

87. Rifkin, "Indigenizing Agamben," 95.

88. Ernesto Laclau, "Bare Life or Social Indeterminacy," in *Giorgio Agamben: Sovereignty and Life,* Matthew Calarco and Steven DeCaroli, eds. (Stanford, CA: Stanford University Press, 2007), 14.

89. Eric Cheyfitz and Shari M Huhndorf, "Genocide by Other Means: U.S. Federal Indian Law and Violence against Native Women in Louise Erdrich's *The Round House,*" in *New Directions in Law and Literature*, Elizabeth S. Anker and Bernadette Meyler, eds. (Oxford University Press, 2017), 264–265.

90. Robert M. Cover, "Foreword: Nomos and Narrative," 97 *Harvard Law Review* 4 (November 1983), 4, 5.

91. Cover, "Violence and the Word": 1601.

92. Vizenor, *Manifest Manners*, vii.

93. James W. Zion, "Monster Slayer and Born for Water: The Intersection of Restorative and Indigenous Justice," *Contemporary Justice Review*, 2, no. 4 (December 1999), 377.

94. Schmitt, *Nomos*, 354, 355.

95. G. L. Ulmen, "The Concept of Nomos: Introduction to Schmitt's 'Appropriation/Distribution/Production,'" *Télos* no. 95 (1993): 49–50.

96. Steven DeCaroli, "Boundary Stones: Giorgio Agamben and the Field of Sovereignty," in *Giorgio Agamben: Sovereignty and Life,* Matthew Calarco and Steven DeCaroli, eds. (Stanford, CA: Stanford University Press, 2007), 44.

97. Tony Hillerman, "Who Has Sovereignty over Mother Earth?" *New York Times,* September 18, 1997, sec. Opinion, https://www.nytimes.com/1997/09/18 /opinion/who-has-sovereignty-over-mother-earth.html (accessed July 11, 2021).

98. Gerald R. Alfred, *Peace, Power, Righteousness: An Indigenous Manifesto* (Don Mills, Ontario, Canada: Oxford University Press, 1999), 25.

99. Jose Barreiro, "A Generation Passes." *Native Americas* XIV, no. 2 (Jun 30, 1997): 2.

100. Jens Bartelson, *A Genealogy of Sovereignty,* Cambridge Studies in International Relations 39 (Cambridge and New York: Cambridge University Press, 1995), 108.

101. Berman, *Coming to Our Senses*, 204.

102. Michael Dorris, "Twentieth Century Indians: The Return of the Natives." in *Ethnic Autonomy: Comparative Dynamics, the Americas, Europe, and the Developing World,* Raymond L. Hall, ed., Pergamon Policy Studies on Ethnic Issues (New York: Pergamon Press, 1979), 75–76.

103. Manuel, *The Fourth World,* 264–265.

104. Felix S. Cohen, "The Erosion of Indian Rights, 1950–1953: A Case Study in Bureaucracy," *Yale Law Journal* 62, no. 3 (February 1953): 390.

105. Finis Dunaway, "The 'Crying Indian' Ad That Fooled the Environmental Movement | Essay," *Zócalo Public Square,* November 9, 2017, https://www.zocalopublicsquare.org/2017/11/09/crying-indian-ad-fooled-environmental-movement/ideas/essay/ (accessed February 27, 2021).

106. *Johnson v. McIntosh*, at 573.

107. Jean-Jacques Rousseau, *A Discourse on Inequality* (Open Road Integrated Media, Inc., 2010), 36: "It is iron and corn, which have civilized men, and ruined mankind. Accordingly both one and the other were unknown to the savages of America, who for that very reason have always continued savages." See also Thomas Hobbes, *Leviathan* (Minneapolis: Lerner Publishing Group, 2018), 115, 116: "During the time men live without a common Power to keep them all in awe, . . . the life of man [is] solitary, poore, nasty, brutish, and short. . . . The savage people in many places of America, except the government of small Families, the concord whereof dependeth on naturall lust, have no government at all; and live at this day in that brutish manner."

108. David Graeber and David Wengrow, *The Dawn of Everything: A New History of Humanity* (NewYork: Farrar, Strauss, and Giroux, 2021), 9.

109. Patrice Lumumba, *Lumumba Speaks: The Speeches and Writings of Patrice Lumumba, 1958–1961,* Jean van Lierde, ed., Helen R. Lane, trans. (Boston: Little and Brown, 1972), 349.

110. John Mohawk, "Traditionalism: The Wave of the Future," *Akwesasne Notes* (Late Spring, 1982), 4–6, in José Barreiro, ed., *Thinking in Indian: A John Mohawk Reader* (Golden, CO: Fulcrum Publishing, 2010), 199, 202.

111. Idle No More, "About the Movement," https://idlenomore.ca/about-the-movement/ (accessed January 8, 2022).

112. *Manoomin v. Minnesota Department of Natural Resources*, Case No. GC21-0428, Complaint for Declaratory and Injunctive Relief (August 4, 2021 Draft), 11, https://whiteearth.com/assets/files/programs/judicial/cases/Manoomin%20et%20al%20v%20DNR%20Complaint%20w%20Exhibits%208-4-21.pdf (accessed January 8, 2022).

113. *Manoomin v. Minnesota Department of Natural Resources*, White Earth Band of Ojibwe Court of Appeals, Case No. AP21-0516 (March 10, 2022) (Opinion). https://whiteearth.com/assets/files/programs/judicial/cases/Manoomin%20opinion%20AP21-0516.pdf (accessed April 30, 2022).

114. *Manoomin*, Motion for Reconsideration (March 25, 2022), https://whiteearth.com/assets/files/programs/judicial/cases/Rights%20of%20Manoomin%20Motion%20for%20Reconsideration%20with%20Exhibits%203-25-2022.pdf; and *Manoomin*, Supplemental Brief (April 6, 2022), https://whiteearth.com/assets/files/programs/judicial/cases/White%20Earth%20Manoomin%20Supplemental%20Brief%204-6-2022.pdf (respectively) (both accessed April 30, 2022).

# Index

Note: Page numbers in *italics* denote figures.

Manuel, George, 166, 170, 180, 183

Maori lands (New Zealand), 64, 164

Margold, Nathan, 37, 93, 96, 98, 154–155

Marshall, John, xxi–xxii, 38–69, 184; Christian discovery doctrine and, 38, 40–49, 54, 61–62, 73; *Cohens v. State of Virginia* decision, 54–58; conflict of interest, 47–48; critiques of decisions, xxii, 49, 57; dicta of, 57–58; exception to law created by decisions, 36, 44–45, 59; federalism of, 46; Indigenous history summarized by, 60–61; mendacity of, 55–56; normative dilemma and, 74–75; organizing principle of, 59; property speculation by, 47–48

Marshall trilogy (of cases), xxi–xxii, 38–69, 154; critiques of, 85–86; international law references in, 160; *Johnson v. McIntosh* (1823), v, xxi–xxii, 40–49, 154; *Cherokee Nation v. Georgia* (1831), xxii, 49–59, 154; *Worcester v. Georgia* (1832), xxii, 59–69, 154. *See also specific cases*

Marshall, Thurgood, 93, 107, 121

Martinez Cobo, Jose R., 138

Mashpee Wampanoag, xvii, 116; Mashpee Nine, xv–xvi

Massachusetts Bay Colony seal, 27, *28*

Maxim, Michael, 116

*McGirt v. Oklahoma* (2020), xxii, xxiii, 22–24; citations traced to *Johnson v. McIntosh*, 23; Gorsuch on, xxiii, 22–24

McNeil, Kent, xxiii, 45, 48

Menominee Tribe, 36–37; fishing rights case, 36–37; Menominee Indian Termination Act of 1954, 36; *Menominee Tribe of Indians v. United States* (1968), 36–37; Treaty of Wolf River (1854), 37; treaty rights, 36–37

Meriam, Lewis, 30

*Meriam Report*, 30–31, 32

Mickelson, George, 83–84, 87

Miller, Karla D., 106

Miller, Robert, 82

Miller, Samuel Freeman, 79–80

Milsom, S. F. C., 65

Mineral and resource extraction, 148, 174–176, 179

Mining, 175–176, 179; miner's canary, 183

Minority terminology, 112–113

Missionaries, Christian, 59–60, 172

Mitchell, Ted, xv

Mohawk, John, 196

Mohawk peoples, 165–166, 180, 182

Monateri, Pier Giuseppe, 173

Monopsony, 63–64, 157

Monroe, James, xxii

*Montana v. United States* (1981), 117

Morality, 90–91, 156; moral deserts, 127, 156

Morgan, Lance G., 120

Morrill Act, 63–64

Multiculturalism, 180

Muscogee Creek nation, 120; *Carpenter v. Murphy* (2018), 18, 19–22; extinguishment intent of U.S. Congress, 19–20; extinguishment not completed (but still possible), 22–24; *McGirt v. Oklahoma* (2020), 22–24; resistance to disestablishment, 20–21

National Native American Law Students Association (NNALSA), 115

Native American Graves Protection and Repatriation Act (1990), xvi

Native American Rights Fund (NARF), 115

*Native American Sovereignty on Trial* (Wildenthal), xxiv

Native Americans: about (introduction to issues), 1–34; existence in

## About the Author

**Peter P. d'Errico, JD (LL.B.),** Yale Law School, BA, Bates College (Philosophy), is professor emeritus of legal studies at the University of Massachusetts at Amherst, where he taught for more than thirty years. He is a member of the New Mexico Bar and was staff attorney at Dinébe'iiná Náhiiłna be Agha'diit'ahii (Navajo Legal Services). He has litigated Indigenous land and fishing rights and Native spiritual freedom rights in prisons, and consulted of-counsel in other Native cases. He is a regular presenter of online seminars about Indigenous peoples' legal issues at Redthought.org and elsewhere, including National Endowment for the Humanities Summer Institutes for Teachers on "Teaching Native American Histories." He has been a columnist for the Indian Country Today Media Network and is the coauthor (with Professor Deng Zibin) of *In Front of the Door of Law* (2012), which was listed in 2015 by the China Lawyers' Reading Salon among its "100 Best Books."

www.ingramcontent.com/pod-product-compliance
Lightning Source LLC
Chambersburg PA
CBHW050410280326
41932CB00013BA/1801